American Public Policy

American Public Policy
Promise and Performance
FOURTH EDITION

B. Guy Peters
Maurice Falk Professor of American Government
University of Pittsburgh

Chatham House Publishers, Inc.
Chatham, New Jersey

American Public Policy: Promise and Performance
Fourth Edition

Chatham House Publishers, Inc.
Post Office Box One
Chatham, New Jersey 07928

Copyright © 1982, 1986, 1993, and 1996 by B. Guy Peters

All rights reserved. No part of this publication may be reproduced, stored in a retrieval system, or transmitted in any form or by any means, electronic, mechanical, photocopying, recording, or otherwise, without the prior permission of the publisher.

Publisher: Edward Artinian
Managing editor: Katharine Miller
Production editor: Chris Kelaher
Cover design: Lawrence Ratzkin
Composition: Bang, Motley, Olufsen
Printing and binding: R.R. Donnelley and Sons Company

Library of Congress Cataloging-in-Publication Data

Peters, B. Guy.
    American public policy: promise and performance / B. Guy Peters.
—4th ed.
        p.   cm.
    Includes bibliographical references and index.
    ISBN 1-56643-024-0
    1. United States—Politics and government—1945–1989.
2. United States—Politics and government—1989–1993. 3. Political
planning—United States. 4. Policy sciences. I. Title.
JK271.P43   1996
320′.6′0973—dc20   95-13597
                                                            CIP

Manufactured in the United States of America
10 9 8 7 6 5 4 3 2 1

Contents

Tables

Figures

Preface to the Fourth Edition

The preface to the third edition of *American Public Policy* commented on the immense changes that had occurred following the publication of the second edition. Changes since the publication of the third edition have been at least as great, although they have been somewhat different in nature. Whereas prior to the third edition the principal changes were in the international environment of policy—the end of the Cold War particularly—the major changes just prior to the fourth edition more clearly reflect changes in American social and political life. To the chapter on defense policy, therefore, I have added criminal justice policy—because major issues of security are becoming defined as much internally as externally.

The politics of public policy has also changed dramatically since the third edition was published. We now have a Democratic president and a Republican Congress, a reverse of the earlier situation. Further, the politics of policy, reflecting contemporary political culture generally, appears to have become increasingly skeptical about the capacity of government, and especially of the federal government, to solve major social and economic problems. Rather than asking what can government do about a problem, the more common reaction in the mid-1990s is to assume that government *is* the problem. This skepticism is being driven by continuing financial problems for government, and many Americans openly express hostility to the federal government and its programs.

Although much has changed since the previous edition, a great deal has remained constant. One constant factor is the extreme complexity of policymaking in the United States. The policymaking process is a blend of political, economic, and social considerations. This is true anywhere, but is especially so within the United States because of the separation of powers at the constitutional level, the division of the Congress and the public bureaucracy into a number of subgovernments, and the role of subnational governments in a federal political system. Further, because so many Americans hold negative views toward their governments, those governments have had to devise indirect means of influencing the economy and society. These means further increase the complexity of the policymaking system and, to some extent, reduce the accountability of government for its actions. Attempting to make this system comprehensible for the reader remains a formidable task.

In addition to understanding the process by which policies are made, anyone who wishes to understand the outcomes of the policymaking process must grapple with the content of the policies themselves. This is no easy task, given that each policy area has a language and jargon of its own and therefore requires the student to grasp something about its technical content. Even in areas about which most citizens have opinions, such as education, the substantive issues and the wealth of available information constitute a formidable barrier to effective involvement. The chapters in part three of this volume will not make readers instant policy experts, but those chapters do introduce the basic issues and assumptions that guide policymakers.

In addition to the policy process and the substantive policy issues, a student of public policy should understand the means of evaluating and analyzing policies. This presents further challenges. First, it is difficult to predict just what results a policy will produce. Government always operates with great uncertainty about the effects of new policies, and that uncertainty must be taken into account when devising strategies. Then, even when we observe the outcomes of a policy, it is not entirely clear how to evaluate them. Most analytic schemes depend upon a utilitarian logic and economic valuation, but other values can and should be applied to the evaluation of programs. Alternative forms of valuation will produce different assessments of the desirability of programs and, therefore, provide another dimension to the fundamental political process of policy selection.

This edition represents no radical departure from the previous editions. The material has been updated, although in many areas there is substantial uncertainty about the desire and capacity of American government to make new policy interventions. Further, it is not clear what those interventions might be. This uncertainty makes some of the policy discussion speculative, but understanding the options is all the more important if we are to participate in the public-policy debate as well-informed citizens.

As in previous editions, there are a number of people to be thanked. Several graduate students provided research assistance, responding efficiently to numerous requests for obscure pieces of information. Edward Artinian, Chris Kelaher, and Katharine Miller at Chatham House provided excellent editorial advice, as well as subtle and not-so-subtle hints about completing the manuscript. My family had to bear the usual mania involved in finishing a project. Finally, the telecommunications revolution made completing the book in a timely fashion easier for all of us.

PART ONE

The Nature of Public Policy

1. What Is Public Policy?

Government in the United States has grown from a small, simple "night-watchman state" providing defense, police protection, tax collection, and some education into an immense network of organizations and institutions affecting the daily lives of all citizens in countless ways. The size and complexity of modern government make it necessary to understand what public policies are, how those policies are made and changed, and how to evaluate the effectiveness and morality of policies.

Government in the United States is large. Today its revenues account for one dollar in three of total national production. This money is rarely wasted; most of the money returns to citizens through a variety of cash-benefit programs or in the form of public services. Likewise, one working person in six is employed by government. But the range of activities of modern government in the United States is not confined to such simple measures as spending money or hiring workers. Governments also influence the economy and society in many less obvious ways, such as regulation, insurance, and loan guarantees.

Government in the United States also is complex and is becoming more complex every day. The institutions of government are becoming more complicated and numerous. More public business is conducted through public corporations and quasi-autonomous public bodies, and over 86,700 separate governments now exist in the United States.[1] There are also a number of increasingly complex relationships between the public and private sectors for the delivery of services. And the subject matter of government policy is more complex and technical now than it was years ago. Governments must make decisions about the risks of nuclear weapons, the reliability of technologically sophisticated weapons systems, and the management of a huge economic system. Attempting to influence socioeconomic problems—poverty, homelessness, education—may be even more difficult than addressing problems arising in the physical and scientific world. Even when the subject matter of policy is less complex, increasing requirements for participation and accountability make managing a public program a difficult undertaking—often more difficult than managing in the private sector.

This book is intended to help the reader understand the fundamental processes and content of public policy that underlie the size and complexity of government. It is meant to increase knowledge about how public policies are made, what the policies of the United States are in certain areas, and what standards of evaluation should be applied to those policies. I begin with a discussion of the policy process in the United States—concentrating at the federal level—and the impact that the structures and procedures of that government have on the content of policies. I then discuss the means that professionals and citizens alike can use to evaluate the effects of public policies and the methods that will enable them to decide what they want and can expect to receive from government.

Defining Public Policy

Mark Twain once commented that patriotism was the last refuge of fools and scoundrels. To some degree, "public policy" has become just such a refuge for some academic disciplines. As public policy studies are now popular, everything government does is labeled "policy." I adopt a somewhat more restrictive definition of public policy.

Stated most simply, public policy is the sum of government activities, whether acting directly or through agents, as those actions have an influence on the lives of citizens. Operating within that definition, we can distinguish three separate levels of policy, defined by the degree to which they make real differences in the lives of citizens. At the first level, we have policy choices—decisions made by politicians, civil servants, and others granted authority and directed toward using public power to affect the lives of citizens. Congressmen, presidents, governors, administrators, and pressure groups, among others, make such policy choices. What emerges from all those choices is a policy that can be put into action.

At the second level, we can speak of policy outputs—policy choices being put into action. Here the government is doing things: spending money, hiring people, or promulgating regulations designed to affect the economy and society. Outputs may be virtually synonymous with the term "program" commonly used in government circles.[2]

Finally, at the third level, we have policy impacts—the effects that policy choices and policy outputs have on citizens. These impacts may be influenced in part by other factors in the society—wealth, education, and the like—but they also reflect to some degree the success or failure of public policy. And these policy outputs may reflect the interaction of a number of different programs. The successful alleviation of poverty, for example, may depend on a number of social programs, economic programs, and the tax system.

Several aspects of public policy require some explanation. First, although we are focusing on the federal level, we must remember that the United States is a federal system of government in which a large number of subnational governments also make decisions. Even when they attempt to cooperate, those governments often experience conflicts over policy. For example, even within the federal government, the actions of one agency may conflict with those of another. The U.S. Department of Agriculture, for example, subsidizes the growing of tobacco, while the U.S. Office of the Surgeon General encourages citizens not to smoke.

Second, not all government policies are implemented by government employees. Many are actually implemented by private organizations or individual citizens. We must understand this if we are to avoid an excessively narrow definition of public policy as concerning only those programs directly administered by a public agency. A number of agricultural, social, and health policies involve the use of private agencies operating with the sanction of, and in the name of, government. Even the cabin attendant on an airplane making an announcement to buckle seat belts and not to smoke is implementing a public policy. The federal government also depends on state and local governments to implement a large number of its programs, including major social programs such as Medicaid and Aid to Families with Dependent Children. As government has begun to use an increasing number of mechanisms such as contracts for implementation, these private actors become even more important.

Third, and most important, we are concentrating on the effects of government choices on the lives of individuals within the society. The word *policy* is commonly used in a number of ways. In one usage it denotes a stated intent of government, as expressed in a piece of legislation or a presidential speech. Unfortunately, any number of steps are required to turn a piece of legislation into an operating program, and all too frequently significant changes in the intended effects of the program result from difficulties in translating ideas and intentions into actions. In this analysis we evaluate policies on the basis of their effects rather than their intentions. We must also have some degree of concern for the legislative process, which produces the good intentions that may or may not come to fruition.

Our definition recognizes the complexity and interorganizational nature of public policy. Few policy choices are decided and executed by a single organization or even a single level of government. Instead, policies, in terms of their effects on the public, emerge from a large number of programs, legislative intentions, and organizational interactions to affect the daily lives of citizens. This conception of policy also points to the frequent failure of governments to coordinate programs, with the consequence that programs cancel out one another or have costly duplication of effort.[3] The question about government posed many years ago by Harold Lasswell, "Who gets what?" is still central in understanding public policy.

The Instruments of Public Policy

Governments have a number of instruments through which they can influence society and the economy and can produce changes in the lives of citizens. The choice of which instrument to employ in any particular instance may depend on the probable effectiveness of the instrument, its political palatability, the experiences of the policy designers, and national or organizational tradition. Further, some policy instruments may be effective in some circumstances but not in others. Unfortunately, governments do not yet have sufficient knowledge about the effects of their "tools," or the relationship of particular tools to particular policy instruments, to be able to make effective matches.[4] It appears that most choices are now made out of habit and familiarity, not out of certain knowledge of effectiveness.

Law

Law is a unique resource of government. It is not available to private actors who have access to the other instruments of policy we plan to discuss.[5] Governments have the right to make authoritative decrees and back up those decrees with the legitimate power of the state. In most instances, simply issuing a law is sufficient to produce compliance, but monitoring and enforcement are still crucial to the effectiveness of the instrument. Citizens may obey speeding laws most of the time, but the prospect of a policeman hiding with a radar set makes compliance more probable. Citizens daily obey many laws without thinking about them, but police, tax collectors, and agencies that monitor environmental damage, occupational safety, and product safety (to name only a few) are also busy trying to ensure enforcement and compliance.

We should make several other points about the use of law as an instrument of public policy. First, laws are used as the means of producing the most important outputs of government: rights. Such laws are usually of a fundamental or constitutional nature and are central in defining the position of citizens in society. In the United States the fundamental rights of citizens are defined in the Constitution and its amendments, but rights have been extended in a variety of other legislation. This extension has been most significant for the rights of nonwhites and women, as reflected in the passage of the Voting Rights Act of 1965, the Equal Employment Opportunity Act of 1972, and the Civil Rights Act of 1991.

Second, the United States uses laws to regulate economic and social conditions to a greater extent than most countries do. The United States is frequently cited as having a small public sector in comparison with other industrialized countries because of lower levels of taxing and spending. If, however, the effects of regulations are included, government in the United States approaches being as pervasive as European governments.[6] The costs of government's interventions in the United States tend to appear in the price of products, however, as much as in citizens' tax bills.[7]

Third, law can be used to create burdens as well as benefits. This is certainly true for tax laws and is also true for legislation that mandates citizens to recycle metal or glass. Often a law that creates benefits for one group of citizens is perceived by others to be creating a burden; environmental laws benefit conservationists but often impose costs on businesses. Any action of government requires some legal peg on which to hang, but the ability of a simple piece of paper to create both rights and obligations is one of the essential features of American public policy.

Services

Governments also provide a number of services directly to citizens, ranging from defense to education to recreation. In terms of employment, education is by far the largest directly provided public service, employing nearly 7 million people. Defense employs another 3 million, both military and civilian. Government tends to provide services when there is a need to ensure that the service is provided in a certain way (education) or where the authority of the state (policing) is involved.

The direct provision of public services raises several questions, especially as there are pressures for government to control expenditures and to "privatize."[8] An obvious question is whether the direct provision of services is the most efficient means of ensuring that a service is delivered to citizens. Could it be contracted out instead? A number of public services have been contracted out to private corporations; these include traditional government services such as firefighting, tax collection, and prisons.[9] Contracting out removes the problem of personnel management from government, a problem made greater by the tenure rights and pension costs of public employees under merit systems. Also, government tends to build a capacity to meet maximum demands for services such as fire protection and emergency medical care, resulting in an underutilization of expensive personnel and equipment. This capacity problem can be corrected in part by contracting out.

Another interesting development in the direct provision of services is the use of quasi-governmental organizations to provide services.[10] Frequently, there are services that government does not want to undertake entirely but that require public involvement for financial or other reasons. The best example here is Amtrak, a means of providing passenger train service with public subsidies in the face of declining rail service in the United States.

7

Government may also choose quasi-government organizations for programs that require a great deal of coordination with private-sector providers of the same service or when the service is in essence a marketable service.

Money

Governments also provide citizens, organizations, and other governments with money. Approximately 51 percent of all money collected in taxes by the federal government is returned to the economy as transfer payments to citizens. Transfers to citizens range from Social Security and unemployment benefits to payments to farmers to support commodity prices. Interest on the public debt is also a form of transfer payment. Another 12 percent of tax receipts is transferred to other levels of government to support their activities.

The use of money transfers to attempt to promote certain behaviors is in many ways an inefficient means for reaching policy goals. The money paid out in Social Security benefits, for example, is intended to provide the basics of life for the recipients, but nothing prevents them from buying food for their pets rather than food for themselves. The claims about how Aid to Families with Dependent Children payments are used and abused are legion, if often inaccurate. Thus, while the direct provision of services is costly and requires hiring personnel and erecting buildings, many less expensive transfer programs are much less certain of reaching the individuals and achieving the goals for which they were intended.

The use of money dispersed to other levels of government can be restricted or unrestricted. Of the $195 billion given in 1993 to state and local governments, most was given as categorical grants and the rest was given as block grants. Categorical grants channel resources more directly to the problems identified by the federal government as needing attention, but they also tend to centralize decision making about public policy in Washington.[11] Categorical grants often also encourage state and local spending through matching provisions, and to create clienteles that governments may not be able to eliminate after the federal support has been exhausted. The federal government has less control over the impact of block grants than over the effects of categorical grants.[12] Block grants allow greater latitude for state and local governments to determine their own priorities, but still have some strings attached. Also, giving block grants to the states tends to concentrate power in state governments, rather than allow local (especially city) governments to deal with Washington directly. Given that state governments are, on average, more conservative than local governments—especially the large city governments that need federal grant money the most—block grants have been a useful tool for Republican administrations.[13]

Taxes

The government giveth and the government taketh away. But the way in which it chooses to take away may be important in changing the distribution of burdens and benefits in society. In the United States we are familiar with tax loopholes, or more properly tax expenditures.[14] The latter term is derived from the theory that granting tax relief for an activity is the same as subsidizing that activity directly through an expenditure program.[15] For example, in 1994 the federal government did not collect over $51.8 billion in income tax payments because of mortgage interest payments, and another $13.8 billion because state and local property taxes were deductible. This is in many ways exactly the same as government subsidizing private housing in the same amounts, a sum far greater than the amount spent on public housing by all levels of government. The use of the tax system as a policy instrument as well as for revenue collection is perhaps even less certain in its effects than transfer payments, for the system is essentially providing incentives instead of mandating activities. Citizens have a strong incentive to buy a house, but there is no program to build houses directly. These instruments are, however, very cheap to administer, given that citizens make all the decisions and then file their own tax returns.

Taxes may also be used more directly to implement policy decisions. For example, there are proposals to substitute taxes on pollution for direct prohibitions and regulation of emissions. The logic is that such an action would establish a "market" in pollution: those willing to pay the price of polluting would be able to pollute, while those less willing (or more important, able) because of inefficient production means would have to alter their modes of production or go out of business. The use of market mechanisms is assumed to direct resources toward their most productive use; regulations at times may inhibit production and economic growth. Critics argue that what is being created is a "market in death" with the only real solution to the problem being the prohibition or severe restriction of pollution.

Tax incentives are a subset of all incentives available to government to encourage or discourage activities. The argument for their use, as well expressed by Charles Schultze, is that private interests (e.g., avarice) can be used for public purposes.[16] If a system of incentives can be structured effectively, then demands on the public sector can be satisfied in a more efficient and inexpensive manner than through direct regulation. Clearly, this form of policy instrument is applicable to a rather narrow range of policies, mostly those now handled through regulation, but even in that limited range the savings in costs of government and in costs imposed on society may be significant. It would also conform to traditional American ideas about limited government and the supremacy of individual choice.

Other Economic Instruments

Government has a number of other economic weapons at its disposal.[17] Governments supply credit for activities such as a farmer's purchase of land and supplies. When it does not directly lend money, government may guarantee loans, thus making credit available (e.g., for student loans or FHA mortgages) when it might not otherwise be. Governments can also insure certain activities and property. For example, federal flood insurance made possible the development of some lands along the coasts of the United States. Almost all money in banks and thrift institutions is now insured by one of several insurance corporations within the federal government.

These instruments share the attribute that although they may be important to their beneficiaries and may influence the spending of large sums of money, they do not appear as large expenditures in most government accounting schemes. Thus, as with regulations and their costs, the true size of government in the United States may be understated by looking simply at expenditure and employment figures. In addition, the ability of these programs to operate "off budget" makes them not only less visible to voters but also more difficult for political leaders and citizens to control. Only when there are major problems, as in the savings-and-loan industry in the early 1990s, do government insurance or guarantee schemes make the news.

Suasion

When all other instruments of policy fail, governments can use moral suasion to attempt to influence society. Government as a whole or particular political officials are often in good positions to use such suasion. They have the ability to speak in the name of the public interest and to make those who oppose them appear unpatriotic and selfish. As Theodore Roosevelt said, the presidency is a "bully pulpit." Suasion, however, is often the velvet glove disguising the mailed fist, for governments have formal and informal means of ensuring that their wishes are fulfilled. So when Lyndon Johnson "jawboned" steel industry officials to roll back a price increase, the patriotism of the steel officials was equaled by their fear of lost government contracts and Internal Revenue Service investigations of their corporate and personal accounts.

Suasion is an effective instrument as long as the people regard the government as a legitimate expression of their interests. There is evidence that the faith and trust of American citizens in government is declining (see table 1.1). This decline is in response to the excesses of Vietnam, Watergate, the savings-and-loan crisis, Whitewater, and so forth. It is also in response to the continuing economic problems experienced in the United States, especially declining wages. As governments lose some of their legitimacy, their ability to use suasion naturally declines. One exception may be in times of war,

TABLE 1.1

PERCEPTION OF HONESTY AND ETHICS

(PERCENTAGE "VERY HIGH" AND "HIGH" COMBINED)

	1976	1981	1985	1988	1990	1992
Pharmacists	n.a.	59	65	66	62	66
Clergy	n.a.	63	67	60	57	54
Medical doctors	56	51	50	53	52	52
College teachers	49	45	53	54	51	50
Engineers	49	48	53	48	50	48
Policemen	n.a.	44	47	47	49	42
Journalists	33	32	31	23	30	27
Bankers	n.a.	39	38	32	32	27
Lawyers	25	25	27	22	22	18
Business executives	20	19	23	16	25	18
Local officeholders	n.a.	14	18	14	21	15
Real estate agents	n.a.	14	15	13	16	14
Labor union leaders	12	14	13	14	15	14
U.S. senators	19	20	23	19	24	13
State officeholders	n.a.	12	15	11	17	11
Congressmen	14	15	20	16	20	11
Car salesmen	n.a.	6	5	6	6	5

SOURCE: *Gallup Monthly,* July 1992, 3.

as President Bush showed during the Persian Gulf war. In the event of declining ability to use suasion, government will have to use more direct tools of intervention. This may mean an increasing size of government taxation and employment and perhaps an increased downward spiral of authority in government.

The Effects of Tools

Governments have a number of instruments with which they attempt to influence the economy and society. Using these various instruments, governments distribute what burdens and benefits they have at their disposal. The most fundamental things governments have are rights. These are largely legal and participatory, but with the growth of large entitlement spending programs that distribute benefits to citizens, rights may now be said to include cash-benefit programs as well.

Governments also distribute goods and services. They do this directly by giving money to people who fall into certain categories (e.g., the unemployed) or by directly providing public services such as education. They do this less directly by structuring incentives for individuals to behave in certain ways and to make one economic decision rather than another. Governments also distribute goods and services through private organizations and through other governments in order to reach their policy goals. A huge amount of money flows through the public sector, where it is shuffled around and given to different people.[18] The net effect is not as great as might be expected, given the number of large expenditure and revenue programs in operation in the United States, but that effect is to make the distribution of income and wealth somewhat more equal than that produced through the market.[19]

Finally, governments distribute burdens as well as benefits. They do this through taxation and through programs such as conscription for military service.[20] Like expenditures, taxes are distributed broadly across the population, with state and local taxes tending to be collected from an especially broad spectrum of the population. Even the poorest citizens will have to pay sales taxes on many things they purchase, and must pay Social Security taxes as soon as they begin to work. In other words, everyone in society benefits from the activities of government, but everyone also pays the price.

The Environment of Public Policy

Several characteristics of the political and socioeconomic environment in the United States influence the nature of policies adopted and the effects of those policies on citizens. Policy is not constructed in a vacuum; it is the result of the interaction of all these background factors with the desires and decisions of those who make policies. Neither individual decision makers nor the nature of "the system" appears capable alone of explaining policy outcomes. Instead, policy emerges from the interaction of a large number of forces, many of which are beyond the control of decision makers.

Conservatism

American politics is relatively conservative in policy terms. The social and economic services usually associated with the mixed-economy welfare state are generally less developed in the United States than those in Europe. This is especially true of government involvement in the management and ownership of economic enterprises such as public utilities and basic industries such as coal and steel. In general this is the result of the continuing American belief in limited government. As Anthony King has said, "the State plays a more limited role in America than elsewhere because Americans, more than other people, want it to play a limited role."[21]

Several points should be brought out in opposition to the description of American government as a welfare state laggard. First, the government of the United States regulates and controls the economy in ways not common in Europe, and in some areas, such as product safety, the United States appears to be ahead of European governments. If the effects of regulation are tabulated along with more direct public interventions into the economy, the government of the United States appears more similar to other industrialized countries. We also have a tendency to forget about the activities of state and local governments, which frequently provide gas, electricity, water, and even banking services to their citizens.

Also, it is easy to underestimate the extent of the changes in public expenditures and the public role in the economy that followed World War II. Let us take 1948 as the starting point. Even in that relatively peaceful year, defense expenditures were 29 percent of total public expenditures and 36 percent of federal expenditures. At the height of the Cold War in 1957, defense expenditures were 62 percent of federal expenditures and 37 percent of total public expenditures. In contrast, in 1988 defense expenditures were 18 percent of total expenditures and 26 percent of federal expenditures. Spending on social services—including education, health, social welfare, and housing—increased from 21 percent of total spending in 1948 to 48 percent in 1988. Even for the federal government, social spending now accounts for 36 percent of total expenditures. American government and its policies may be conservative, but they are less so than commonly believed, and less so in the 1990s than in the 1950s.

It is also easy to overestimate the conservatism of the American public because Americans are often very ambivalent about government.[22] Free and Cantril referred to Americans as "ideological conservatives" and "operational liberals."[23] Americans tend to respond negatively to the idea of a large and active government, but also tend to respond positively to individual public programs (e.g., Social Security). For example, voters leaving the polls in California after voting in favor of Proposition 13 to cut taxes severely in that state had majorities in favor of reducing public expenditures for only one program—social welfare. For most programs mentioned by the researchers, larger percentages of respondents wanted to increase expenditures than reduce them.[24] The huge federal deficit is to some degree a function of this set of mismatched ideas about government; politicians can win votes both by advocating reducing taxes and by advocating spending for almost any program.

Participation

Another attitudinal characteristic that influences public policy in the United States is the citizen's desire to participate in government. A natural part of democratic politics, public participation has a long history in American politics. The cry of "No taxation without representation" was essentially a demand to participate. In a large and decentralized political system that deals with complex issues, effective participation may be difficult to achieve. The low rates of participation in most elections seem to indicate that citizens do not consider the voting process a particularly efficacious means of affecting government. Further, many experts believe that citizens are not sufficiently informed to make decisions about such complex technical issues as nuclear power. Citizens, however, argue that they should and must have a role in those decisions.

Government has increasingly fostered participation. The laws authorizing community action in 1964 were the first to mandate "maximum feasible participation" of the affected communities in renewal decisions. Similar language was then written into a number of other social and urban programs. Also, the regulatory process has requirements for notification and participation that, in addition to their positive effects, have slowed the process considerably.

The desire for effective participation has to some degree colored popular impressions of government. Citizens tend to demand local control of policy and to fear the "federal bulldozer." Although objective evidence may be to the contrary, citizens tend to regard the federal government as less benevolent and less efficient than local governments. The desire to participate and to exercise local control then produces a tendency toward decentralized decision making and a consequent absence of national integration. In many policy areas, such decentralization is benign or actually beneficial. In others, it may produce inequities and inefficiencies. But the ideological and cultural desires for local control may override practical arguments.

Ideas about participation in the United States also have at times had a strong strand of populism, meaning the belief that large institutions—whether in government, business, or even labor—are inimical to the interests of the people. Further, there is the belief that those institutions are structured to prevent effective participation. Those institutions have, however, themselves begun to respond to the demands for effective participation, and "empowerment" has become one of the more commonly used words in government circles.[25]

Pragmatism

The reference to ideological desires seemingly contradicts another cultural characteristic of American policymaking that is usually, and quite rightly, discussed. This characteristic is pragmatism, the belief that one should do whatever works rather than follow a basic ideological or philosophical system. American political parties have tended to be centrist and nonideological, and perhaps the surest way to lose an election in the United States is to discuss philosophies of government. Ronald Reagan to some degree questioned that characteristic of American politics and interjected an ideology of government that was continued at least in part by George Bush. President Clinton's self-description as a "new Democrat" represented a return to greater pragmatism. This pragmatism tends to make American politics a clash of platitudes and narrow programmatic issues, rather than of ideas such as Marxism or fascism—probably mercifully.

One standard definition of what will work in government is "that which is already working," and so policies tend to change slowly and incrementally.[26] The basic centrist pattern of political parties tends to result in agreement on most basic policies, and each successive president tends to jiggle and poke policy but not to produce significant change. A crisis such as the Great Depression or a natural political leader such as Reagan may produce some significant changes, but stability and gradual evolution are the most acceptable patterns of policymaking. Indeed, American government is different after Reagan, but not as different as he had hoped or intended.[27]

The pragmatism of American politics seems to be declining. Several issues, over which there appears to be little room for compromise, have arisen that have split the American public. The obvious example is the abortion issue. Abortion intruded into the debate over national health-care reform, with some members of Congress refusing to support any bill that paid for abortions and another group refusing to support any bill that did not fund abortions.[28] Other issues of a moral or religious or ethnic basis also have taken prominent places in the political debate, with fewer possibilities for compromise or pragmatic resolution of disputes.

Wealth

Another feature of the environment of American public policy is the great wealth of the country. Although it is no longer the richest country in the world in per capita terms, the United States is the largest single economy in the world by a large margin. This wealth still permits great latitude for action by American government, so even the massive deficits of the past decade have not required government to alter its folkways. The federal government can continue funding a huge variety of programs and policy initiatives, despite its efforts to control the size of the budget deficit (see chapter 5).

This great wealth is threatened by two factors. First, the U.S. economy is increasingly dependent on the rest of the world. This is true in financial and monetary policy as the United States becomes the world's largest debtor, but it is true especially in terms of dependence on raw materials from abroad. We are familiar with this nation's dependence on foreign oil, but the economy is also heavily dependent on other countries for a range of commodities necessary to maintain our high standard of living. The American economy historically has been relatively self-sufficient, but the increasing globalization of the 1980s and 1990s has emphasized the relationship to the world economy.

Wealth in the United States is also threatened by the relatively slow rate of productivity growth and capital investment. The average American worker is still productive, but increasingly less productive than workers in many other countries. Also, U.S. factories are increasingly outmoded, so competition on the world market is difficult. These factors, combined with relatively high wages, mean that many U.S. manufacturing jobs have gone overseas, and more are likely to do so. The U.S. government has had to borrow abroad to fund its huge deficits, and we also have chronic balance-of-payments problems because of a relative inability to export. These problems are not often direct domestic concerns of American politicians, other than a few such as Congressman Richard Gephardt, but they do affect the ability of the nation to spend money for the programs that many politicians and citizens want.

Diversity

The American society and economy are also diverse. This at once provides a great deal of richness and strength to the country and presents real policy problems. One of the most fundamental diversities is the uneven distribution of income and wealth in the society. Even with the significant social expenditures mentioned earlier, almost 40 million people in the United States live below the poverty line, and that number has been increasing, especially among children (see p. 297). The persistence of poverty in the midst of plenty remains perhaps the most fundamental policy problem for the United States, if for no other reason than it affects so many other policy areas, including health, housing, education, crime, and race relations.

Diversity of racial and linguistic backgrounds is also a significant factor affecting policy in the United States. The underlying problems of social inequality and racism persist despite many attempts to correct them. The concentration of minority-group members in urban areas, the continuing influx of immigrants, and the continuing economic uncertainty of the 1990s are all combining to exacerbate these underlying problems, as is the widespread availability of drugs. Again, this diversity affects a variety of policy areas, especially education. Race in particular pervades policymaking and politics in the United States and this fundamental fact conditions our understanding of education, poverty, and human rights.[29]

The social and economic characteristics of the country taken as a whole are also diverse. The United States is both urban and rural, both industrial and agricultural, both young and old. It is a highly educated society with several million illiterates; it is a rich country with millions of people living in poverty. American policymakers cannot concentrate on a single economic class or social group but must provide something for everyone if the interests of the society as a whole are to be served. But, in serving that whole range of social interests, the resources that would be required to rectify the worst inequalities of income and opportunity must be spent for other purposes.

World Leadership

Finally, the United States is an economic, political, and military world leader. With the collapse of the Soviet Union, it is the only remaining superpower. If America sneezes, the world still catches cold because the sheer volume of the American economy is so important in influencing world economic conditions. Also, despite the upheaval in global political alignments, the world still expects military leadership for the West to come from the United States. The failure of the world to make a systematic response to the war in former Yugoslavia is due in large part to American diffidence on the subject. The United States also has become a leader in international bargaining and negotiation, as first Camp David and more recently the Middle East peace accords have demonstrated.

The position as world leader imposes burdens on American policymakers. This continues to be true of defense policy even after the end of the Cold War; the role of peacekeeper requires a good deal of military might. It also is true for the need to provide diplomatic and political leadership. The U.S. dollar, despite some battering and significant competition, is still a major reserve currency in the world economy, and this status imposes additional economic demands on the country. The role of being a world leader is an exhilarating one, but it is also one filled with considerable responsibility and economic costs for the United States.

The policies that emerge from all these influences are filtered through a large and extremely complex political system. The characteristics of that government and the effects of those institutional characteristics on policies are the subject of the next chapter. Policy choices must be made, and thousands are made each day in government; the sum of those choices, rather than any one, will decide who gets what as a result of public policies. In the United States more than most countries, there are a number of independent decision makers whose choices must be factored into the final determination of policy.

Conclusion

American public policy is the result of complex interactions among a number of equally complex institutions. It also involves a wide range of values about what the goals of policy should be, and what the best means of reaching those goals are. In addition to the interactions that occur within the public sector there are a number of interactions with an equally complex society and economy. Making policy requires obtaining some form of social and political consensus among all these forces. There does not have to be full agreement on all the values and all the points of policy, but enough common ground must be found to pass and implement legislation.

Notes

1. U.S. Bureau of the Census, *1992 Census of Governments* (Washington, D.C.: Government Printing Office, 1993).

2. Richard Rose, "The Programme Approach to the Growth of Government," *British Journal of Political Science* 15 (1985): 1–28.

3. Brian W. Hogwood and B. Guy Peters, *The Pathology of Public Policy* (Oxford: Oxford University Press, 1985).

4. Helen Ingram and Anne Schneider, "Improving Implementation through Framing Smarter Statutes," *Journal of Public Policy* 10 (1990): 67–88; Stephen H. Linder and B. Guy Peters, "The Study of Policy Instruments," *Policy Currents* 2 (May 1992): 1, 4–7.

5. Private actors do, of course, have recourse to law as a means of influencing policy and forcing government action. This is especially true in the United States where the courts are so important for determining policy. For example, in addition to the enforcement activities of the Federal Trade Commission and the Antitrust Division of the Department of Justice, private individuals bring suit to enforce these laws.

6. B. Guy Peters and Martin O. Heisler, "Thinking about Public Sector Growth," in *Why Governments Grow: Measuring Public Sector Size*, ed. C.L. Taylor (Beverly Hills, Calif.: Sage, 1983).

7. Murray Wiedenbaum, "The High Costs of Government Regulation," *Challenge*, November 1979, 32–39.

8. William T. Gormley, *Privatization and Its Alternatives* (Madison: University of Wisconsin Press, 1991).

9. Penelope Lemov, "Jailhouse, INC," *Governing* 6 (May 1993): 44–48.

10. Donald F. Kettl, *Government by Proxy: (Mis)Managing Federal Programs?* (Washington, D.C.: CQ Press, 1988).

11. Charles H. Levine and Paul L. Posner, "The Centralizing Effects of Fiscal Austerity on the Intergovernmental System," *Political Science Quarterly* 96 (1981): 67–85.

12. James D. Chesney, "Intergovernmental Politics in the Allocation of Block Grant Funds for Substance Abuse in Michigan," *Publius* 24 (1994): 39–46; Doug Peterson, "Block Grant 'Turn-Backs' Revived in Bush Budget," *Nation's Cities Weekly* 15 (3 February 1992): 6.

13. Neal R. Pierce, "Bush 'Turnback' Plan Sounds Nice but It's 'Irrelevant'," *Nation's Cities Weekly* 14 (18 February 1991): 12.

14. Stanley S. Surrey and Paul R. McDaniel, *Tax Expenditures* (Cambridge, Mass.: Harvard University Press, 1985).

15. Aaron Wildavsky, "Keeping Kosher: The Epistemology of Tax Expenditures," *Journal of Public Policy* 5 (1985): 413–31.

16. Charles L. Schultze, *The Public Use of Private Interest* (Washington, D.C.: Brookings Institution, 1977).

17. See, for example, F. Anderson, *Environmental Improvement through Economic Incentives* (Baltimore: Johns Hopkins University Press, 1977); Richard C. Hula, *Market-based Public Policy* (New York: St. Martin's, 1990).

18. Thomas Anton, *Moving Money* (Cambridge, Mass.: Oelgeschlager, Hain and Gunn, 1980).

19. Johan Fritzell, "Income Inequality Trends in the 1980s: A Five-Country Comparison," *Acta Sociologica* 36 (1993): 47–62; Sheldon Danziger and Peter Gottschalk, *Uneven Tides: Rising Inequality in America* (New York: Russell Sage, 1993).

20. On taxation, see B. Guy Peters, *The Politics of Taxation: A Comparative Perspective* (Oxford: Blackwells, 1991).

21. Anthony King, "Ideas, Institutions and Policies of Government: A Comparative Analysis," *British Journal of Political Science* 5 (1975): 418.

22. See Linda M. Bennett and Stephen Earl Bennett, *Living With Leviathan: Americans Coming to Terms with Big Government* (Lawrence: University Press of Kansas, 1990).

23. Lloyd A. Free and Hadley Cantril, *The Political Beliefs of Americans* (New York: Simon and Schuster, 1968).

24. David O. Sears and Jack Citrin, *Tax Revolt: Something for Nothing in California*, rev. ed. (Berkeley: University of California Press, 1991).

25. Peter Bachrach and Aryeh Botwinick, *Power and Empowerment: A Radical Theory of Participatory Democracy* (Philadelphia: Temple University Press, 1992).

26. Michael T. Hayes, *Incrementalism* (New York: Longman, 1992).

27. See, for example, Charles O. Jones, *The Reagan Legacy* (Chatham, N.J.: Chatham House, 1989).

28. Robin Toner, "House Democrats Support Abortion in Health Plans," *New York Times,* 14 July 1994.

29. Andrew Hacker, *Two Nations: Black and White, Separate, Hostile, Unequal* (New York: Scribners, 1992).

2. The Structure of Policymaking in American Government

The structures through which public policy is formulated, legitimated, and implemented in the United States are extremely complex. It could be argued that American government has a number of structures but no real organization, for the fundamental characteristic of these structures is the absence of effective coordination and control. This absence of central control is largely intentional. The framers of the Constitution were concerned about the potential for tyranny of a powerful central executive within the federal government; they also feared the control of the central government over the constituent states. The system of government the framers designed divides power among the three branches of the central government and further between the central government and state and local governments. As the system of government has evolved, it has become divided even further, with individual policy domains able to gain substantial autonomy from central coordination. To understand American policymaking, therefore, we must understand the extent of fragmentation that exists and the few mechanisms devised to control that fragmentation.

The fragmentation of American government does have some advantages. First, having a number of decision makers involved in every decision should reduce errors, as all must agree before a proposal can become law or can be implemented as an operating program. Also, the existence of multiple decision makers should permit greater innovation in both the federal government and state and local governments. And, as the framers intended, power is diffused, reducing the capacity of one central government to run roughshod over the rights of citizens or the interests of socioeconomic groups. For citizens, the numerous points of access permit losers at one level of government or in one institution to become winners at another.

Americans also pay a price for this lack of policy coordination. It is sometimes difficult to accomplish *anything,* and elected politicians with policy ideas find themselves thwarted by the large number of decision points in the policymaking system. The policymaking situation in the United States in the 1980s and 1990s has been described as "gridlock," in which the different institutions block one another from developing and enforcing policies.[1] Likewise, programs may cancel out each other as progressive (if decreasingly so) federal taxes and regressive state and local taxes combine to produce a tax system in which most people pay about the same proportion of their income as tax, or as the Office of the Surgeon General's antismoking policies and the Department of Agriculture's tobacco subsidies attempt to please both pro- and antitobacco advocates.[2] The apparent inability or unwillingness of policymakers to choose among options means that policies will be incoherent and the process seemingly without any closure, and that decisions may cancel one another out. It also means that because every interest in society receives some support from the public sector, taxes and expenditures are higher than they might otherwise be.

I have already mentioned the divisions that exist in American government. I now look at the more important dimensions of that division and the ways in which they act and interact to affect policy decisions and real policy outcomes for citizens. "Divided government" and "gridlock" have become standard descriptions of American government, and the impact of these divisions must be understood to understand the way in which policy emerges from this political system.

Federalism

The most fundamental division in American government traditionally has been federalism, or the constitutional allocation of governmental powers in the United States between the federal government and the state governments. This formal allocation at once reserves all powers not specifically granted to the federal government to the states (Ninth and Tenth amendments) and establishes the supremacy of federal law when there are conflicts with state and local laws (Article 6). Innumerable court cases and, at least in part, one civil war have resulted from this somewhat ambiguous division of powers among levels of government.

By the 1990s American federalism had changed significantly from the federalism described in the Constitution. The original constitutional division of power assumed that certain functions of government would be performed entirely by the central government and that other functions would be carried out by state or local governments. In this "layer cake" federalism, or "separated powers model," the majority of public activities were to be performed by subnational governments with a limited number of functions, such as national defense and minting money, being the responsibility of the federal government.[3]

As the activities of government at all levels expanded, the watertight separation of functions broke down, and federal, state, and local governments became involved in many of the same activities. The layer cake then was transformed into a "marble cake," with the several layers of government still distinct, although no longer vertically separated from one another. This form of federalism, however, still involved intergovernmental contacts through central political officials. The principal actors were governors and mayors, and intergovernmental relations remained on the level of high politics, with the representatives of subnational governments acting almost as ambassadors from sovereign governments and as suppliants for federal aid. Further, in this form of federalism the state government retained its role as intermediary between the federal government and local governments.

Federalism evolved further from a horizontal division of activities into a set of vertical divisions. Whereas functions were once neatly compartmentalized by level of government, the major feature of "picket fence" federalism is the development of subsystems defined by policy rather than level of government.[4] Thus, major decisions about health policy are made by specialized networks involving actors from all levels of government and from the private sector. Those networks, however, may be relatively isolated from other subsystems making decisions about highways, education, or whatever. The principal actors in these subsystems frequently are not political leaders but administrators and substantive policy experts. Local health departments work with state health departments and with the Department of Health and Human Services (HHS) in Washington in making health policy, and these experts are not dependent on the intervention of political leaders to make the process function. This form of federalism is as much administrative as it is political.

In many ways, it makes little sense to discuss federalism in its original meaning; it has been argued that contemporary federalism is as much facade as picket fence. A term such as *intergovernmental relations* more accurately describes the complex crazy quilt of overlapping authority and interdependence among levels of government than does a more formal, constitutional term such as federalism.[5] In addition to being more oriented toward administrative issues than high politics, contemporary intergovernmental relations is more functionally specific and lacks the coordination that might occur if higher political officials had to make the principal decisions. Thus, like much of the rest of American politics, intergovernmental relations often now lacks the mechanisms to generate effective policy control.

Despite the complexity, overlap, and incoherence that exist in intergovernmental relations, one can still argue that centralization of control in the federal system has increased.[6] State and local governments are increasingly dependent on central government financing of their services, given the more buoyant character of federal revenues and the ability of the federal government to borrow more readily. With financing has come increased federal control over local government activities. In some cases that control is absolute, as when the federal government mandates equal access to education for the handicapped or sets water-quality standards for sewerage treatment facilities. In other instances the controls on state and local governments are more conditional, based on the acceptance of a grant; if a government accepts the money, it must accept the controls accompanying that money.

In general, the number and importance of mandates on state and local governments, and the number of conditions attached to those grants, have been increasing. The Department of Health and Human Services has threatened to cut off funding for immunization and other public health programs in states that do not implement restrictions on procedures performed by doctors and dentists with AIDS. Even the existence of many federal grant programs may be indicative of control from the center, inasmuch as it directs the attention and money of local governments in directions they might not have chosen had it not been for the presence of the federal grant programs.

In addition to controls exercised through the grant process, the federal government has increased its controls over subnational governments through intergovernmental regulation and mandating. These regulations require the subnational government to perform a function such as wastewater treatment, whether or not there is federal money available to subsidize the activity. These regulations are certainly intrusive and can be expensive for state and local governments. Even when the mandates are not expensive and are probably effective, such as the requirement that states raise the minimum drinking age to twenty-one or lose 5 percent of their federal highway money, they can still be perceived as "federal blackmail" of the states.[7] Even the Reagan and Bush administrations, dedicated to restoring the balance in favor of the states in federalism, found mandates an almost irresistible means for implementing their policy goals.

One complicating factor for intergovernmental relations in the United States has been the proliferation of local governments. As fiscal restrictions on local governments have caused problems for mayors and county commissioners, a number of new local governments have been created to circumvent those restrictions. States frequently restrict the level of taxation or bonded indebtedness of local governments. When a local government reaches its legal limit, it may create a special authority to undertake some functions formerly performed by the general-purpose local authority. For example, as Cleveland faced severe fiscal problems in 1979 and 1980, it engaged in a "city garage sale" in which it sold its sewer system and transportation system to special-purpose local authorities. The fiscal crisis in New York in the early 1990s prompted the city and even the state to sell off facilities such as roads and prisons to special-purpose authorities.[8] During the

1980s and early 1990s, an average of almost 500 local governments were created every year, primarily special districts to provide services such as transportation, water, sewerage, fire protection, and other traditional local government services.[9]

These new special-purpose governments present that many more problems of coordination and may pose a problem for citizens who want to control the level of taxation but find that every time they limit the power of one government, a new one is created with more fiscal powers. The new local governments also present problems of democratic accountability. The leaders of special-purpose governments often are not elected, and the public can influence their actions only indirectly through the general-purpose local governments (cities and counties) that appoint the boards of the special-purpose ones.[10]

The Reagan and Bush administrations attempted to reverse some of the historic course of centralization in the federal system. One approach was to reduce the amount of money spent for intergovernmental grants, including general revenue sharing as an all-purpose subsidy for subnational governments. Their strategies also involved eliminating a number of categorical (program) grants—including Urban Development Action Grants to cities —and providing more federal grants to subnational governments in the form of large block grants to the states. Block grants are meant to provide for all programs in a broad policy area, such as maternal and child health or community development. These grants at once give state governments power over local (especially city) governments and provide those governments with more capacity to make decisions about how the money will be spent.

The economic circumstances of the late 1980s tended to push power back toward the states, with mounting federal deficits and the then-healthy state treasuries.[11] The recession of the early 1990s ended public surpluses in almost all states and turned eyes in state capitols back toward Washington. Those eyes became even more hopeful and searching with a Democratic administration in Washington. Even during the several periods of changing fiscal relations among the levels of government, however, the federal government has continued to implement numerous new federal mandates, as this was an inexpensive way for it to achieve national policy goals.[12]

Thus, while the United States retains some features of a federal system of government, the balance of power within that system has shifted in the direction of the central government. The grant system has been purchasing a more centralized form of government. The shift in power appears to have resulted less from power-hungry federal bureaucrats and politicians than from the need to standardize many basic public services and the need to promote greater equality for minorities. Further, even if programs are intended to be managed with "no strings attached," there is a natural tendency, especially in Congress, to demand the right to monitor the expenditures of public funds and to ensure that those funds are used to obtain desired goals. In an era in which the accountability of government is an increasingly important issue, such monitoring is likely to grow in intensity.

Separation of Powers

The second division of American government exists within the federal government itself and incidentally within most state and local governments as well. The Constitution distributes the powers of the federal government among three branches, each capable of applying checks and balances to the other two. In addition to providing employment for constitutional lawyers, this division of power has a substantial impact on public policies. In particular, the number of clearance points in the federal government alone makes initiating any policy difficult and makes preventing change relatively easy. It also means, as we mentioned in our discussion of the incoherence of American public policy, that the major task in making public policy is forming a coalition across a number of different institutions and levels of government. Without "legislating together" in such a coalition, either nothing will happen or the intentions of a policymaker will be modified substantially.[13] The United States is not a tightly administered political system in which one actor makes a decision and all other actors must fall neatly into line. This country has an intensely political and highly complex policymaking system in which initiatives must be shepherded through the process step by step if anything positive is to occur.

The president, Congress, and the courts are constitutionally designated institutions that must agree to a policy before it can be fully legitimated. The bureaucracy, however, although it is only alluded to in the Constitution, is now certainly a political force with which elected politicians must contend. Despite its conservative and obstructionist image, the bureaucracy is frequently the institution most active in promoting policy change.[14] The bureaucracy, or more properly the individual agencies of which it is composed, has interests that can be served through legislation. The desired legislation may only expand the budget of the agency, but it usually has a broader public policy purpose as well. Administrative agencies can, if they wish, also impede policy change or perhaps even block it entirely. Almost every elective or appointed politician has experienced delaying tactics of nominal subordinates who disagree with a policy choice and want to wait until the next election or cabinet change to see if someone with more compatible policy priorities will come into office. The permanence of the "bureaucrats," and their command of technical details and the procedural machinery, provides agencies within the public bureaucracy a great deal more power over public policies than one would assume from reading the formal descriptions of government institutions.

The institutional separation in American government has led to a number of critiques based on the concept of "divided government."[15] The argument is that American government is incapable of being the decisive governance system required in the late twentieth century and that some means must be found of generating coherent decisions. This was especially true when the two major institutions were controlled by different political parties, as they were during the Reagan and Bush presidencies and part of Clinton's first term. The Clinton presidency indicated that even when the same party controls both branches, there are still enough differences within parties, and enough institutional rivalry, to make cooperation difficult.[16] Yet David Mayhew, Charles O. Jones, and other scholars have argued that the system is capable of making decisions and even of rapid policy innovation, and that it can govern effectively.[17]

Whether the system is efficient or not, one principal result of the necessity to form coalitions across a number of institutions is the tendency to produce small, incremental changes rather than a major revamping of policies.[18] This might be best described as policymaking by the lowest common denominator. The need to involve and placate all four institutions within the federal government—as well as many component groups of individuals within each—and perhaps state and local governments means only rarely can there be little change in the established commitments to clients and producer groups if the policy change is to be successful.[19] The resulting pattern of incremental change has been both praised and damned. It has been praised as providing stability and limiting the errors that might result from more significant shifts in policy. If only small policy changes are made, and these changes do not stray far from previously established paths, it is unlikely that major mistakes will be made.

The jiggling and poking of policies characteristic of incremental change is perfectly acceptable if the basic patterns of policy are also acceptable, but in some areas of policy, such as health and mass transportation, a majority of Americans have said (at least in polls) that they would like some significant changes from the status quo.[20] The existing system of policymaking appears to have great difficulty in producing the major changes desired. In addition, the reversibility of small policy changes, assumed to be an advantage of incrementalism, is often overstated.[21] Once a program is implemented, a return to the conditions that existed before the policy choice is often difficult. Clients, employees, and organizations are created by any policy choice, and they usually will exert powerful pressures for the continuation of the program.

The division of American government by the constitutional separation-of-powers doctrine represents a major institutional confrontation in the center of the federal government. Conflicts between the president and Congress over such matters as war powers, executive privilege, and the budget represent conflicts over those manifest issues as well as a testing and redefinition of the relative powers of institutions. Is the modern presidency inherently imperial, or is it subject to control by Congress and the courts? Does too much checking by each institution over the others generate gridlock and indecision? Likewise, can the unelected Supreme Court have as legitimate a role as a rulemaking body in the political system as does the elected Congress? Further, do the regulations made by the public bureaucracy really have the same standing as law as the legislation passed by Congress or decrees from the court system? These are the kinds of questions posed by the separation-of-powers doctrine. These questions influence substantive policy as well as relationships among the institutions.

Subgovernments

A third division within American government cuts across institutional lines within the federal government and links the federal government directly to the picket fence of federalism. The results of this division have been described variously as "iron triangles," "cozy little triangles," "whirlpools," and "subgovernments."[22] The underlying phenomenon described by these terms is that the federal government rarely acts as a unified institution making policy choices, but tends instead to endorse the decisions made by portions of the government. Each functional policy area tends to be governed as if it existed in splendid isolation from the remainder of government, and frequently the powers and legitimacy of government are used for the advancement of individual or group interests in society, rather than for a broader public interest.[23]

Three principal actors are involved in the iron triangles so important for explaining policymaking in the United States. The first is the interest group. The interest group wants something from government, usually a favorable policy decision, and must attempt to influence the institutions that can act in its favor. Fortunately for the interest group, it usually need not influence all of Congress or the entire executive branch, but only the relatively small portion concerned with the particular policy area. For example, tobacco growers who want continued or increased crop supports need not influence the entire Department of Agriculture but only those within the Agricultural Stabilization and Commodity Service who are directly concerned with their crop. Likewise, in Congress (although the heightened politicization of the smoking issue may require a somewhat different strategy) they need only influence the Tobacco Subcommittee of the House of Representatives Agriculture Committee, the Senate Subcommittee on Agricultural Production and Stabilization of Prices, and the Rural Development, Agriculture, and Related Agencies Subcommittees of the appropriations committees in the Senate and House. In addition to the usual tools of information and campaign funds, interest groups have an important weapon at their disposal: votes. They represent organizations of interested individuals and can influence, if not deliver, votes for the congressman. Interest groups also have research staffs, technical information, and other support services that, although their outputs must be regarded with some skepticism, may be valuable resources for congressmen or administrative agencies seeking to influence the policy process.

The second component of these triangular relationships is the congressional committee or subcommittee. These bodies are designated to review suggestions for legislation in a policy area and to make recommendations to the whole Senate or House of Representatives. An appropriations subcommittee's task is to review expenditure recommendations from the president, then to make its own recommendations on the appropriate level of expenditures to the entire committee and the whole house of Congress. Several factors combine to give these subcommittees substantial power over legislation. First, subcommittee members develop expertise over time and are regarded as more competent to make decisions concerning a policy than is the whole committee or the whole house.[24] Norms have also been developed that support subcommittee decisions for less rational, and more political, reasons.[25] If the entire committee or the entire house were to scrutinize any one subcommittee's decisions, it would have to scrutinize all such decisions and then each subcommittee would lose its powers. These powers are important to individual congressmen, and each congressman wants to develop his or her own power base. Finally, the time limitations imposed by the huge volume of policy decisions being made by Congress each year mean that accepting a subcommittee decision may be a rational means of reducing the total workload of each individual legislator.

Congressional subcommittees are not unbiased; they tend to favor the very interests they are intended to oversee and control. This is largely because the congressmen on a subcommittee tend to represent constituencies whose interests are affected by the policy in question. As one analyst argued, "... a concerted effort is made to insure that the membership of the subcommittee is supportive of the goals of the subgovernment."[26] For example, in 1990 the Tobacco and Peanut Subcommittee of the House Agriculture Committee included three representatives from North Carolina, two each from Texas and Kentucky, and one each from Georgia, Oklahoma, South Carolina, and Florida—all states that produce these commodities. There was also one representative from Wisconsin. Similarly, the Cotton, Rice and Sugar Subcommittee had representatives from California, Georgia, Louisiana, Oklahoma, Tennessee, Texas, South Carolina, and Washington—all states that produce those commodities. These patterns are not confined to agriculture. The Housing and Community Development Subcommittee of the House Banking, Finance, and Urban Affairs Committee has representatives from all the major urban areas of the United States.

These patterns of committee and subcommittee membership are hardly random; they increase the ability of congressmen to deliver certain kinds of benefits to constituents as well as their familiarity with the substantive issues of concern to constituents. Subcommittee members also develop patterns of interaction with the administrative agencies over which they exercise oversight. The individual members of Congress and agency officials may discuss policy with one another and meet informally. As both parties in these interactions tend to remain in Washington for long periods of time, the same congressmen and officials may interact for twenty years or more. The trust, respect, or simple familiarity this interaction produces further cements the relationships between committee members and agency personnel.

Obviously, the third component of the iron triangle is the administrative agency. The agency, like the pressure group, wants to promote its interests through the policymaking process. The principal interests of an agency are its survival and its budget. The agency need not be, as is often assumed, determined to expand its budget. Agencies frequently do not wish to expand their budget share, but only to retain their "fair share" of the budget pie as it expands.[27] Agencies also have policy ideas that they wish to see translated into operating programs, and they need the action of the congressional committee or subcommittee for that to happen. They also need the support of organized interests.

Each actor in an iron triangle needs the other two in order to reach its goal, and the style that develops is symbiotic. The pressure group needs the agency to deliver services to its members and provide a friendly point of access to government, while the agency needs the pressure group to mobilize political support for its programs among the affected clientele. Letters from constituents to influential congressmen must be mobilized to argue that the agency is doing a good job and could do an even better job, given more money or a certain policy change. The pressure groups needs the congressional committee again as a point of access and as an internal spokesperson in Congress. And the committee needs the pressure group to mobilize votes for its congressmen and explain to group members how and why they are doing a good job in Congress. The pressure group can also be a valuable source of policy ideas and research for busy politicians. Finally, the committee needs the agency as an instrument for producing services to their constituents and developing new policy initiatives. The agency has the research and policy analytic capacity that congressmen often lack, so committees can profit from their association with the agencies. And the agency obviously needs the committee to legitimate its policy initiatives and provide it with funds.

All those involved in a triangle have similar interests. In many ways they all represent the same individuals, variously playing the role of voter, client, and organization member. Much of the domestic policy of the United States can be explained by the existence of functionally specific policy subsystems and by the absence of effective central coordination. This system of policymaking has been likened to feudalism, with the policies being determined not by any central authority but by aggressive subordinates—the bureaucratic agencies and their associated groups and committees.[28] Both the norms concerning policymaking and the time constraints of political leaders tend to make central coordination and policy choice difficult. The president and his staff (especially the Office of Management and Budget, or OMB) are in the best organizational position to exercise this control, but the president must serve political interests, just as the Congress must, and he faces an even more extreme time constraint. Thus, decisions are rarely reversed once they have been made within the iron triangles.

One effect of this subdivision of government into a number of functionally specific subgovernments is the incoherence of public policy I have already mentioned. All societal interests are served through their own agencies, and there is little attempt to make overall policy choices for the nation. Further, these functional subgovernments at the federal level are linked with functional subsystems in intergovernmental relations described earlier. The result is that local governments and citizens alike may frequently receive contradictory directives from government and may become confused and cynical about the apparent inability of their government to make up its mind.

A second effect of the division of American government into a number of subgovernments is the involvement of a large number of official actors in any one policy area. This is in part a recognition of the numerous interactions within the public sector, and between the public and private sectors, in the formulation and implementation of a public policy. For an issue area such as health care, the range of organizations involved cannot be confined to those labeled "health" but must inevitably expand to include consideration of the social welfare, nutrition, housing, education, and environmental policies that may have important implications for citizens' health.[29] But the involvement of an increasing number of agencies in each issue area also reflects the lack of central coordination so that agencies can gain approval from friendly congressional committees for expansion of their range of programs and activities. Periodically, a president will attempt to streamline and rationalize the delivery of services in the executive branch and in the process frequently will encounter massive resistance from agencies with entrenched interests. For example, in creating the cabinet-level Department of Education, President Jimmy Carter sought to move the educational programs of the (then) Veterans Administration into the new department.[30] In this attempt he locked horns with one of the best organized and most powerful iron triangles in Washington—the Veterans Administration, veterans' organizations, and their associated congressional committees. The president lost. Subsequently the veterans' lobby was sufficiently powerful to have the VA made into a cabinet-level department.

As easy as it is to become enamored of the idea of iron triangles in American government—they do help explain many of the apparent inconsistencies in policy when viewed broadly—there is some evidence that the iron in the triangles is becoming rusty.[31] More groups are now involved in making decisions, and it is more difficult to exclude interested parties from decisions; Charles O. Jones describes the current pattern as "big sloppy hexagons," rather than "cozy little triangles."[32] For example, the health-care debate in 1994 did not include just representatives of the medical professions, the hospitals, and health insurers but a range of other interests such as small businessmen, organized religion, and trade unions.

The concepts of *issue networks* and *policy communities,* involving large numbers of interested parties, each with substantial expertise in the policy area, now appear more descriptive of policymaking in the United States, as well as other industrialized democracies.[33] These structures of interest groups surrounding an issue are less unified about policy than were "iron triangles" and may contain competing ideas and interests to be served through public policy—the tobacco subsystem may even be invaded by health advocates. As important as the network idea is to explain changes in federal policymaking, it does not detract from the basic idea that policymaking is very much an activity that occurs within subsystems.

American government, although originally conceptualized as divided vertically by level of government, is now better understood as divided horizontally into a number of expert and functional policy subsystems. These feudal subsystems divide the authority of government and attempt to appropriate the name of the public interest for their own, more private interests. Few if any of the actors making policy, however, have any interest in altering these stable and effective means of governing. The system of policymaking is effective politically because it results in the satisfaction of most interests in society. It also links particular politicians and agencies with the satisfaction of those interests, thereby ensuring their continued political success.

The basic patterns of decision making are logrolling and the pork barrel, through which, instead of conflicting over the allocation of resources, actors minimize conflict by giving each other what they want. For example, instead of conflicting over which river and harbor improvements will be authorized in any year, Congress tends to approve virtually all so that all congressmen can tell their constituents that they produced something for the folks back home. Or congressmen from farming areas may trade positive votes on urban development legislation for support of farm legislation by inner-city congressmen. These patterns of policymaking are very effective as long as there is sufficient wealth and economic growth to pay for the subsidization of large numbers of public programs.[34] Nevertheless, this pattern of policymaking was one (but by no means the sole) reason for massive deficits of the federal government in the 1980s and early 1990s, and it appears that the pattern can no longer be sustained comfortably. Given the divisions within American government, however, it is difficult for the policymaking system as a whole to make the difficult choices among competing goals and competing segments of society that would be necessary to stop the flow of red ink from Washington.

Public and Private

The final qualitative dimension of American government that is important in understanding the manner in which contemporary policy is made is the increasing confusion of public and private interests and organizations. These two sets of actors and actions have now become so intermingled that it is difficult to ascertain where the boundary line between the two sectors lies. The leakage across the boundary between the public and private sectors, as artificial as that boundary may be, has been occurring in both directions. Activities that once were almost entirely private now have a greater public-sector involvement, although frequently through quasi-public organizations that mask the real involvement of government. Also, functions that are nominally public have significantly greater private-sector involvement. The growth of institutions for formal representation and for implementation by interest groups has given those groups perhaps an even more powerful position in policymaking than that described in the discussion of iron triangles. Instead of vying for access, interest groups are accorded access formally and have a claim to their position in government.

The other major component of change in the relationship between public and private has been the push toward privatization of public activities.[35] This trend began to some degree in the 1970s with Presidents Ford and Carter, but was pronounced during the 1980s under President Reagan. The United States traditionally has had an antigovernment ethos; that set of values was articulated strongly, and the positive role of the federal government minimized, during the 1980s.[36] For example, a large amount of federal land was sold by the Department of the Interior, and a number of public services were contracted out to the private sector. At one extreme, security checks for the Department of the Navy were being contracted out to a private security firm. It was not only at the federal level that privatization and contracting was popular. At the state and local levels, a large number of functions—hospitals, garbage collection, janitorial services, and even prisons—were contracted out or sold off as a means of reducing the costs of government.[37]

The blending of public and private is to some degree reflected in employment.[38] Table 2.1 demonstrates public and private employment in twelve policy areas, as well as changes that occurred from 1970 to 1985. By 1980, for example, only education retained more than 80 percent public employees, and that percentage was dropping. Even two presumed public monopolies—defense and police protection—had significant levels of private employment. These two policy areas differ, however, in the form of private employment. Defense employment in the private sector is in the production of goods and services used by the armed forces, whereas in police protection a number of private policemen actually provide the service.

The development of mechanisms for direct involvement of interest groups in public decision making is frequently referred to as *corporatism* or *neocorporatism*.[39] These terms refer to the representation in politics of members of the political community not as residents of a geographical area but as members of functionally defined interests in the society—labor, management, farmers, students, the elderly, and so forth. Associated with this concept of representation is the extensive use of interest groups both as instruments of input to the policy process and as a means of implementing public policies. The United States is a less corporatist political system than most industrialized democracies, but there are still corporatist elements. Most urban programs mandate the participation of community residents and other interested parties in decision making for the program. Crop-allotment programs of the U.S. Department of Agriculture have used local farmers' organizations to monitor and implement the programs for some time. County medical societies are used as Professional Standards Review Organizations for Medicare and Medicaid as a means of checking on quality and costs of services. In addition, in the early 1990s there were approximately 6,000 advisory bodies in the federal government, many containing substantial interest-group representation.[40]

In addition to the utilization of interest groups to perform public functions, a number of other organizations in the society implement public policy. For example, when cabin attendants in an airplane require passengers to fasten their seat belts, they are implementing Federal Aviation Administra-

TABLE 2.1

PERCENTAGES IN PUBLIC EMPLOYMENT, SELECTED POLICY AREAS

1970–85

Policy area	1970	1980	1985
Education	87	85	84
Post office	92[a]	73[a]	74[a]
Highways	74[b]	68[b]	68[b]
Tax administration	90[c,d]	57[c]	57[c]
Police	85[e]	60[e]	58[e]
Defense	63[f]	59[f]	60[f]
Social services	26[g]	35[g]	34[g]
Transportation	33	31	32
Health	26	30	33
Gas/electricity/water	25	27	26
Banking	1	1	1
Telecommunications	[h]	1	1

SOURCES: U.S. Bureau of the Census, *Census of Governments,* 1972 and 1987; U.S. Department of Defense, *Defense Manpower Statistics,* annual; U.S. Employment and Training Administration, *Annual Report.*

a. Private employees are employees of private services, couriers, etc.

b. Contracting firms involved in highway construction.

c. Estimate of tax accountants and staffs, H&R Block employees, including seasonal employees.

d. Rough estimate.

e. Industry estimate of private guards, private policemen, etc.

f. U.S. Department of Labor estimate of employment generated by military purchases.

g. Private social work and philanthropy; large percentage employed only part-time.

h. Less than .5 percent.

tion policies. Also, universities are required to help implement federal drug policies (statements of nonuse by new employees) and federal immigration policies (certification of citizenship or immigration status of new employees). Manufacturers of numerous products implement federal safety and environmental standards (e.g., seat belts and pollution-control devices in automobiles).

The increasing use of quasi-public organizations, changes in the direction of a limited corporatist approach to governance in the United States, and privatization (largely through contracting) raise several questions concerning responsibility and accountability in government. These changes involve the use of public money and, more important, the name "public" by groups and for groups that may not be entirely public. In an era in which the public appears to be attempting to exercise greater control over its governments, the development of these forms of policymaking "at the margins of the state" may be understandable in terms of financial hardships but may only exacerbate the underlying problems of public loss of trust and confidence in government.

The Size and Shape of the Public Sector

We have looked at some qualitative aspects of the contemporary public sector in the United States. What we have yet to do is examine the size of that public sector and the distribution of funds and personnel among the various purposes of government. As was pointed out, drawing any clear distinctions between public and private sectors in the mixed-economy welfare state is difficult, and growing more difficult, but we will concentrate on the expenditures and personnel that are clearly governmental. As these figures are only those that are clearly public, they inevitably understate the size and importance of government in the United States.

Table 2.2 contains information about the increasing size of the public sector in the United States during the post–World War II era and the changing distribution of the total levels of expenditures and employment. Most obvious in this table is that the public sector has indeed grown, with expenditures increasing from less than one-quarter to more than one-third of gross national product. Likewise, public employment has increased from 11 percent of total employment to about 15 percent. The relative size of the public sector, however, has decreased since the mid-1970s, especially in terms of percentage of employment. Although the number of public employees increased by over 3 million from 1975 to 1990, government's share of total employment dropped by 2.5 percentage points.

It is also evident that growth levels of public expenditures are more than twice as large, relative to the rest of the economy, as public employment figures. Also, public expenditures as a share of gross national product have continued to increase slightly. The differences relative to the private sector and the differences in the patterns of change are largely the results of transfer programs, such as Social Security, which involve expenditures of large amounts of money but require relatively few administrators. In addition, purchases of goods and services from the private sector (e.g., the Department of Defense's purchases of weapons from private firms) involve expenditures of large amounts of money with little or no employment generated in the public sector. In 1988, however, those purchases did create

TABLE 2.2

GROWTH OF PUBLIC EMPLOYMENT AND EXPENDITURES, 1950–91

	Public employment, civilian (ooo omitted)			Public expenditures (ooo omitted)		
Year	Federal	State and local	Total	Federal	State and local	Total
1950	2,117	4,285	6,402	$44,800	$25,534	$70,334
1960	2,421	6,387	8,808	97,280	54,008	151,288
1970	2,881	10,147	13,028	208,190	124,795	332,985
1975	2,890	12,083	14,973	341,517	218,612	560,129
1980	2,876	13,315	16,191	576,700	432,328	1,009,028
1990	3,105	14,976	18,081	1,197,200	1,016,200	2,213,400
1991	3,103	15,452	18,555	1,320,519	1,251,109	2,571,628

	As percentage of total employment			As percentage of GNP		
1950	3.6	7.3	10.9	15.7	8.9	24.6
1960	3.7	9.7	13.4	19.2	10.7	29.9
1970	3.7	12.9	16.6	21.2	12.7	33.9
1975	3.4	14.2	17.6	22.5	14.4	36.9
1980	2.9	13.1	16.0	20.0	16.4	36.4
1990	2.6	12.5	15.1	22.0	19.5	41.5
1991	2.3	12.4	14.7	21.8	19.7	41.5

approximately 2.1 million jobs in the private sector, a figure similar to the number of people then in the armed forces. From these data it appears that some portions of "big government" in the United States are more controllable than others, even with eight years of a popular president determined to reduce the size of the public sector.

The distribution of expenditures and employment among levels of government also has been changing. In 1950 the federal government spent 64 percent of all public money and employed 33 percent of all public employees. By 1991, the federal government spent 63 percent of all public money but employed only 18 percent of all civilian public employees.[41] The remarkable shift in employment relative to expenditures is again in part a function of the large federal transfer programs, such as Social Security. It also reflects the expansion of federal grants to state and local governments and the ability of the federal government to borrow money to meet expenditure needs, as contrasted to the need of state and local governments to balance their current expenditure budgets.

In addition, the programs provided by state and local governments —education, social services, police and fire protection—are labor intensive. The major federal program that is labor intensive, defense, had declining civilian and uniformed employment even before the apparent end of the Cold War in the late 1980s. These data appear to conflict somewhat with the characterization of the federal government as increasingly important in American economic and social life. While certainly it is a large institution, employing almost 5 million people when the armed forces are included, it actually has been declining in some respects, with the major growth of government occurring at state and local levels.

Another factor involved in the declining share of employment in the federal government is the shift from defense programs toward social programs. In 1952, national defense accounted for 46 percent of all public expenditures and for 49 percent of all public employment. By 1991, defense expenditures had been reduced to 16 percent of all expenditures (up from 14 percent in 1978) and 6 percent of public employment. By contrast, a panoply of welfare state services (health, education, and social services) accounted for 20 percent of public expenditures in 1952 and 24 percent of public employment. By 1991, these services accounted for 49 percent of expenditures (down from 50 percent in 1980) and 53 percent of all public employment. Within the welfare state services, education was the biggest gainer in employment, with over 5.5 million more employees in 1991 than in 1952. And Social Security programs alone increased their spending by well over $300 billion during that time period. The United States is often described as a "welfare state laggard," but the evidence is that although it is still behind most European nations regarding the range of social services, a marked increase has been occurring in the social component of American public expenditures.

It was argued that the landslide victories of the Republican Party in the presidential elections from 1980 to 1988 were a repudiation of this pattern of change and that we could expect to see little increase, or actual decreases, in the level of public expenditures for social programs. There was a slight relative decrease in social spending from 1980 until 1991—in part a function of increasing expenditures for other purposes, such as interest on the public debt—but sustained decreases have proven difficult to obtain. Most social programs are entitlement programs, and once a citizen has been made a recipient of benefits, or has made the insurance "contributions" for Social Security, future governments will find it difficult to remove those benefits. This is especially true of programs for the retired elderly, as they cannot be expected to return to active employment to make up losses in benefits. Unfortunately for budget cutters, public expenditures are increasingly directed toward the elderly. For example, in the early 1990s, over 42 percent of the federal budget went to programs (Social Security, Medicare, housing programs, and so forth) for the elderly. As the American population continues to grow older, expenditures for this social group can only be expected to increase. What is true in particular for the elderly is true in general for all entitlement programs, and reducing the size of the government social budget will be difficult indeed.

We have been concentrating attention on public employment and public expenditures as measures of the "size" of government, but we should remember that government influences the economy and society through a number of other mechanisms as well. For example, the federal government has a much larger housing program run through the tax system (deductibility of mortgage interest and property taxes) than it does through the Department of Housing and Urban Development. Likewise, government has a major education program of subsidized student loans that shows up only indirectly in public expenditures. The regulatory impact of government on the economy can be counted in the billions of dollars—one estimate was $542 billion in 1992.[42] Government in the United States tends to use these indirect methods of influence somewhat more than other governments do, given the generally antistatist views of many American citizens. This tendency was heightened by the conservative governments of the 1980s and early 1990s. Therefore, we must be very careful in making an assessment about the size, shape, and impact of government in the United States based solely on figures about public expenditures and public employment.

American government in the 1990s is large, complex, and to some degree unorganized. Each individual section of government, be it a local government or an agency of the federal government, tends to know what it wants, but the system as a whole lacks overall coordination and control. Priority setting is not one of the strongest features of American government. An elected official coming to office and attempting to give direction to the system of government will be disappointed by his or her inability to produce desired results, by the barriers to success, and by the relatively few ways in which the probability of success can be increased. These difficulties of control, however, may be compensated for by the flexibility and multiple opportunities for citizen inputs characteristic of American government.

Despite the problems of coordination and control, and the tradition of popular distrust of government, contemporary American government is active. It spends huge amounts of money and employs millions of people to perform a bewildering variety of tasks. These activities are not confined to a single level of government; instead, all three levels of government are involved in making policy, taxing, spending, and delivering services. This activity is why the study of public policy is so important. It is a means of understanding what goes on in the United States, and why government does the things it does. The emphasis on the next portion of the book is on the processes through which policy is made. All governments must do about the same things when they make policy: identify issues, formulate policy responses to problems, evaluate results, and change programs when they are not producing desired results. American governments do all these things, but they do them in a distinctive way and produce distinctive results.

Notes

1. Charles H. Levine, "Human Resource Erosion and the Uncertain Future of the U.S. Civil Service: From Policy Gridlock to Structural Fragmentation," *Governance* 1 (1988): 115–43.

2. Peter H. Stone, "Tobacco's Road," *National Journal,* 1 January 1994, 19–23.

3. See Terry Sanford, *Storm over the States* (New York: McGraw-Hill, 1967), 80.

4. Deil S. Wright, *Understanding Intergovernmental Relations,* 3d ed. (Belmont, Calif.: Brooks/Cole, 1988), 83–86.

5. Ibid.

6. For a somewhat different view, see Jae-Won Yoo and Deil S. Wright, "Public Policy and Intergovernmental Relations: Measuring Perceived Changes in National Influences," *Policy Studies Journal* 21 (1993): 687–99.

7. John Kincaid, "From Cooperative to Coercive Federalism," *The Annals* 509 (1990): 139–52.

8. *New York Times,* 13 October 1991.

9. U.S. Bureau of the Census, *Census of Governments, 1992* (Washington, D.C.: Government Printing Office, 1993).

10. Jerry Mitchell, *Public Authorities and Public Policy: The Business of Government* (New York: Greenwood, 1992).

11. During the mid-1980s the states averaged over 11 percent surpluses in the total budgets. See the Tax Foundation, *Facts and Figures on Government Finance,* 1991 (Baltimore: Johns Hopkins University Press, 1991), table E2.

12. Michael Fix and Daphne A. Kenyon, eds., *Coping with Mandates: What Are the Alternatives?* (Washington, D.C.: Urban Institute Press, 1990).

13. Mark Peterson, *Legislating Together* (Cambridge, Mass.: Harvard University Press, 1992).

14. See, for example, James Q. Wilson, *Bureaucracy* (New York: Basic Books, 1989).

15. Morris P. Fiorina, "An Era of Divided Government," *Political Science Quarterly* 107 (1992): 387–410; James L. Sundquist, *Constitutional Reform and Effective Government,* rev. ed. (Washington, D.C.: Brookings Institution, 1992).

16. For example, other Democrats were active in developing and promoting alternatives to the Clinton health-care reform proposals. See chapter 9. See also

Viveca Novak, "It Still Takes Two," *National Journal,* 25 September 1993, 2301–3.

17. David Mayhew, *Divided We Govern* (New Haven: Yale University Press, 1991); Charles O. Jones, *The Presidency in a Separated System* (Washington, D.C.: Brookings Institution, 1994); Nelson Polsby, *Policy Innovation in America* (New Haven: Yale University Press, 1984); John E. Schwarz, *America's Hidden Success,* rev. ed. (New York: Norton, 1988).

18. Michael T. Hayes, *Incrementalism* (New York: Longman, 1992).

19. Charles E. Lindblom, *The Intelligence of Democracy: Decision Making through Mutual Adjustment* (New York: Free Press, 1965).

20. For example, a poll in late 1993 found that 56 percent of the American population supported a guaranteed health insurance program even if that program were to mean increased taxes. *Gallup Poll Monthly* 338 (November, 1993): 8. In a later poll 77 percent of respondents supported universal coverage for health insurance. *USA Today,* 30 June 1994.

21. Brian W. Hogwood and B. Guy Peters, *Policy Dynamics* (Brighton, England: Wheatsheaf, 1982); Robert E. Goodin, *Political Theory and Public Policy* (Chicago: University of Chicago Press, 1986).

22. The classic statement is J. Leiper Freeman, *The Political Process: Executive Bureau–Legislative Committee Relations* (New York: Random House, 1965).

23. The classic statement of this point is Theodore J. Lowi, *The End of Liberalism,* 2d ed. (New York: Norton, 1979).

24. Peter L. Hall and C. Lawrence Evans, "The Power of Subcommittees," *Journal of Politics* 52 (1990): 335–55.

25. See D. Roderick Kiewiet and Mathew D. McCubbins, *The Logic of Delegation* (Chicago: University of Chicago Press, 1991).

26. D. McCool, "Subgovernments as Determinants of Political Viability," *Political Science Quarterly* 105 (1990): 269–93.

27. Andre Blais and Stephane Dion, *The Budget-Maximizing Bureaucrat* (Pittsburgh: University of Pittsburgh Press, 1992).

28. Peter B. Natchez and Irvin C. Bupp, "Policy and Priority in the Budgetary Process," *American Political Science Review* 67 (1973): 951–63.

29. See Robert H. Salisbury, J.P. Heinz, R.L. Nelson, and Edward O. Laumann, "Triangles, Networks and Hollow Cores: The Complex Geometry of Washington Interest Representation," in *The Politics of Interests,* ed. Mark P. Petracca (Boulder, Colo.: Westview, 1992).

30. Rufus E. Miles, "A Cabinet Department of Education: An Unwise Campaign Promise or a Sound Idea?" *Public Administration Review* 39 (1979): 103–10.

31. See Jack L. Walker, *Mobilizing Interest Groups in America* (Ann Arbor: University of Michigan Press, 1991).

32. Charles O. Jones, *The United States Congress* (Homewood, Ill.: Dorsey, 1982).

33. Some scholars make a great deal over the differences between these concepts, with a community being a more unified and tightly knit set of groups than

a network. See Martin J. Smith, *Pressure, Power and Policy* (Pittsburgh: University of Pittsburgh Press, 1994).

34. See Rose and Peters, *Can Government Go Bankrupt?* (New York: Basic Books, 1978).

35. William T. Gormley, *Privatization and Its Alternatives* (Madison: University of Wisconsin Press, 1991).

36. See Linda M. Bennett and Stephen Earl Bennett, *Living With Leviathan: Americans Come to Terms with Big Government* (Lawrence: University Press of Kansas, 1990).

37. Jonas Prager, "Contracting Out Government Services: Lessons from the Private Sector," *Public Administration Review* 54 (1994): 176–84; Steven Rathgeb Smith and Michael Lipsky, *Nonprofits for Hire: The Welfare State in the Age of Contracting* (Cambridge, Mass.: Harvard University Press, 1993).

38. B. Guy Peters, "Public and Private Provision of Services," in *The Private Provision of Public Services,* ed. Dennis Thompson (Beverly Hills, Calif.: Sage, 1986).

39. This form of organization has not been typical in the United States. See Robert H. Salisbury, "Why No Corporatism in America?" in *Trends Toward Corporatist Intermediation,* ed. Philippe C. Schmitter and Gerhard Lehmbruch (Beverly Hills, Calif.: Sage, 1979); Susan B. Hansen, "Industrial Policy and Corporatism in the American States," *Governance* 2 (1989): 172–97.

40. Donna Batten and Peter D. Dresser, eds., *Encyclopedia of Government Advisory Bodies, 1992–93* (Detroit: Gale Research, 1993).

41. Tax Foundation, *Facts and Figures on Government Finance,* 1993 ed. (Baltimore: Johns Hopkins University Press, 1993).

42. Howard Banks, "The Costs of the Fed's Ketchup and Other Rules," *Forbes* 151 (15 February 1993): 39.

PART TWO

Making Public Policy

3. Agenda Setting and Public Policy

This chapter discusses two aspects of the policymaking process that occur rather early in the sequence of decisions leading to the actual delivery of services to citizens but are nonetheless crucial to the success of the entire process. These two stages of policymaking—agenda setting and policy formulation—are important because they establish the parameters for any additional consideration of the policies. Agenda setting is crucial, for if an issue cannot be placed on the agenda, it cannot be considered, and nothing will happen. Similarly, policy formulation begins to narrow and structure the consideration of the problems placed on the agenda and to prepare a plan of action intended to rectify the problem identified. These two stages are also linked because in many ways it is necessary to have a solution before an issue can be accepted on the agenda. In addition, how an issue is defined as it is brought to the agenda determines the kinds of solutions that will be developed to solve the problem.

Agenda Setting

Before a policy choice can be made by government, a problem in the society must have been accepted as a part of the agenda for the policymaking system—that is, as one member of the set of problems deemed amenable to public action and worthy of the attention of policymakers. Many real problems are not given any consideration by government, largely because the relevant political actors are not convinced that government has any role in attempting to solve those problems. Although problems once accepted as a part of the agenda tend to remain on the agenda for long periods of time, problems do come on and go off the active policy agenda.

One of the best examples of a problem being accepted as part of the agenda after a long period of exclusion is the problem of poverty in the United States. Throughout most of this nation's history, poverty was perceived not as a public problem but as merely the result of the (proper) operation of the free market. The publication of Michael Harrington's *The Other America* and the growing mobilization of poor people brought the problem of poverty to the agenda and indirectly resulted in the launching of a war dedicated to its eradication.[1] Once placed on the agenda, poverty has remained an important public issue, although different administrations definitely have given different amounts of attention to the problem. Also, the relatively poor quality of American elementary and secondary education, especially in science and technology, did not become an issue at the federal level until the Soviet Union launched *Sputnik I*. Although now redefined in terms of economic competitiveness rather than the Cold War, educational quality has remained on the agenda and has gained renewed importance as an issue in the 1990s (see chapter 11). The case of O.J. Simpson may yet place issues of domestic violence in a more prominent position on the agenda of American governments.

The best example of an issue being removed from the policy agenda is perhaps the repeal of Prohibition, when the federal government said that preventing the production and distribution of alcoholic beverages was no longer its concern. Despite the end of Prohibition, all levels of government have retained some regulatory and taxing authority over the production and consumption of alcohol. The movement to privatize some public services also has removed some issues from direct concern by the public sector, although again a regulatory role may continue.

What can cause an issue to be placed on the policy agenda? The most basic cause for placing an issue on the agenda is a perception that something is wrong and that the problem can be ameliorated by public action. This answer produces a second question. What causes the change in perceptions of problems and issues? Why, for example, did Harrington's book have such far-reaching influence when earlier books, such as James Agee's *Let Us Now Praise Famous Men,* had so little impact?[2] Did the timing of the "discovery" of poverty in the United States result from the election of a young, liberal president (Kennedy) who was succeeded by an activist president (Johnson) with considerable sway over Congress? When do problems cease to be invisible and become perceived as real problems for public consideration?

Issues also appear to pass through an "issue attention cycle," in which they are the objects of great public concern for a short period and generate some response from government.[3] The initial enthusiasm for the issue is generally followed by more sober realism about the costs of policy options and the difficulties of making effective policy. This realism is in turn followed by a period of declining public interest as the public seizes on a new issue. The history of environmental policy, drug enforcement, and to some degree the women's movement illustrate this cycle very well. More recently, the "discovery" of sexual harassment as a policy issue during the confirmation hearings of Clarence Thomas for the Supreme Court has been followed relatively quickly with concerns about the possibility of effective enforcement of the laws and the exact definition of the offense. Attention to the issue, and its possible ambiguity, was reinforced by allegations against Senator Robert Packwood.

As well as individual issues going through an issue-attention cycle, the entire political system may also experience cycles of differential activity. One set of scholars has described this pattern as "routine punctuated by orgies."[4] A less colorful description, developed by Jones and Baumgartner, is "punctuated equilibria."[5] Some time periods—because of energetic political leaders, large-scale mobilization of the public, or a host of other possible reasons—are characterized by greater policy activism than are others.

This chapter discusses how to understand, and how to manipulate, the public agenda. How can a problem be converted into an issue and brought to a public institution for formal consideration? In the role of policy analyst, one must understand not only the theoretical issues concerning agenda setting but also the points of leverage within the political system. Much of what happens in the policymaking system is difficult or impossible to control: the ages and health of the participants, their friendships, constitutional structures of institutions and their interactions and external events, to name but a few of the variables. Some scholars have argued that agendas do not change unless there is an almost random confluence of events favoring the new policy initiative.[6] Such random factors may be important in explaining overall policy outcomes, but they are not the only pertinent factors to consider when one confronts the task of bringing about policy changes that one desires. Despite all the imponderables in a policymaking system, there is still room for initiative and for altering the political behavior of important actors in the system.

It is also important to remember that social problems do not come to government fully conceptualized with the labels already attached. Policy problems need to have names attached to them if government is to deal with them, and that is in itself a political process.[7] For example, how do we conceptualize the problem of illegal drugs in the United States? Is it a problem of law enforcement, as it is commonly treated, or is it a public health problem, or a problem of education, or a reflection of poverty and despair? Perhaps the usage of drugs indicates something more about the society in which it occurs than it does about the individual consumers, who usually are branded as criminals. There are a number of possible answers to the definitional questions raised above, but the fundamental point is that the manner in which the problem is conceptualized and defined will determine the remedies proposed, the organizations that will be given responsibility for the problem, and the final outcomes of the public intervention.

Kinds of Agendas

Until now we have been discussing "the agenda" in the singular and with the definite article. There are, however, different agendas for the various institutions of government, as well as a more general agenda for the political system as a whole. The existence of these agendas also is to some degree an abstraction. The agendas do not exist in any concrete form; they exist only in a collective judgment of the nature of public problems or as fragments of written evidence such as legislation introduced, the State of the Union message of the president, or notice of intent to issue regulations appearing in the *Federal Register.*

Cobb and Elder, who have produced some of the principal writing on agendas in American government, distinguish between the systemic and institutional agendas of government. The systemic agenda consists of "all issues that are commonly perceived by members of the political community as meriting public attention and as involving matters within the legitimate jurisdiction of existing governmental authority."[8] This is the broadest agenda of government, being all those issues that might be subject to action or that are already being acted on by government. This definition implies a consensus on the systemic agenda—a consensus that may not exist. Some individuals may consider a problem—abortion, for example—a part of the agenda of the political system (whether to outlaw abortion or to provide public funding for it), while others may regard the issue as entirely one of personal choice. The southern states' reluctance for years to include civil rights as part of the government agenda indicated a disagreement over what fell within the "jurisdiction of existing governmental authority." Setting the systemic agenda is usually not consensual, as it is an important political and policy decision. If a problem can be excluded from consideration, then those who benefit from the status quo are assured of victory.[9] Only when a problem is placed on the agenda and made available for discussion do the forces of change have some opportunity for success.

The second type of agenda that Cobb and Elder discuss is the institutional agenda: "that set of items explicitly up for active and serious consideration of authoritative decision-makers."[10] An institutional agenda is then composed of the issues that those in power within the particular institution actually are considering acting on. These issues may constitute a subset of all problems they will discuss, as the complete set will include "pseudo issues" discussed to placate clientele groups but done without any serious intention to make policy choices.[11] Actors within the institutions do run a risk, however, when they permit pseudo issues to be discussed; once on the docket, something may actually happen about the problem.

A number of institutional agendas exist—as many as there are institutions—and there is little reason to assume any agreement among institutions as to which problems are the most appropriate for consideration. As with the discussion of conflicts over placing issues on the systemic agenda, inter-institutional conflicts will arise about moving problems from one institutional agenda to another. The agendas of bureaucratic agencies are the narrowest, and a great deal of the political activity of those agencies is directed toward placing their issues onto the agendas of other institutions. As an institution broadens in scope, the range of agenda concerns also broadens, and the supporters of any particular issue will have to fight to have it placed on a legislative or executive agenda. This is especially true of *new problems* seeking to be converted into active issues. Some older and more familiar issues will generally find a ready place on institutional agendas. Some older issues are *cyclical issues:* a new budget must be adopted each year, for example, and changes in the debt ceiling must be adopted as frequently (or more frequently in recent years). Other older agenda items may be *recurrent issues,* indicating primarily the failure of previous policy choices to produce the intended or desired impact on society. Even recurrent issues may not be returned easily to institutional agendas, when existing programs are perceived to be "good enough" or when no new solutions are readily available.

Jack Walker classes problems coming on the agenda in four groups.[12] He discusses issues that are dealt with time and time again as either periodically recurring or sporadically recurring issues (similar to our cyclical and recurrent issues). He also discusses the role of crises in having issues placed on the agenda, as well as the difficulties of having new, or "chosen," problems selected for inclusion on agendas. Within each institution, the supporters of an issue must use their political power and skills to gain access to the agenda. The failure to be included on any one institutional agenda may be the end of an issue, at least for the time being.

Who Sets Agendas?

Establishing an agenda for society, or even for one institution, is a manifestly political activity, and control of the agenda gives substantial control over the ultimate policy choices. Therefore, to understand how agendas are determined requires some understanding of the manner in which political power is exercised in the United States. As might be imagined, there are a number of different conceptualizations of the manner in which power is exercised. To enable us to understand the dynamics of agenda setting better, we should discuss three important theoretical approaches to the exercise of political power: pluralist, elitist, and state-centric.

Pluralist Approaches
The dominant, though far from undisputed, approach to policymaking in

the United States is pluralistic.[13] Stated briefly, this approach assumes that policymaking in government is divided into a number of separate arenas and that those who have power in one arena do not necessarily have power in others. The American Medical Association, for example, may have a great deal of influence over health legislation, but has little influence over education or defense policy. Furthermore, interests that are victorious at one time or in one arena will not necessarily win at another time or place. The pluralist approach to policymaking assumes that there is something of a marketplace in policies, with a number of interests competing for power and influence, even within a single arena. These competitors are perceived as interest groups that compete for access to institutions for decision making and for the attention of central actors in the hope of producing their desired outcomes. These groups are assumed, much as in the market model of the economy, to be relatively equal in power, so on any one issue any one of the interests may win. Finally, the actors involved generally agree on the rules of the game, especially the rule that elections are the principal means of determining policy. The principal function of government is to serve as an umpire in this struggle among competing group interests and to enforce the victories through law.

The pluralist approach to agenda setting would lead the observer to expect a relatively open marketplace of ideas for new policies. Any or all interested groups, as a whole or within a particular public institution, should have the opportunity to influence the agenda. These interest groups may not win every time, but neither will they systematically be excluded from decisions, and the agendas will be open to new items as sufficient political mobilization is developed. This style of agenda setting may be particularly appropriate for the United States, given the multiple institutions and multiple points of access inherent in the structure of the system.[14]

Elitist Approaches

The elitist approach to American policymaking seeks to contradict the pluralist approach. It assumes the existence of a "power elite" who dominate public decision making and whose interests are served in the policymaking process. In the elitist analysis, the same interests in society consistently win, and these interests are primarily those of business, the upper and middle classes, and whites.[15] Analysts from an elitist perspective have pointed out that to produce the kind of equality assumed in the pluralist model would require relatively equal levels of organization by all interests in society. They then point out that relatively few interests of working- and lower-class individuals are effectively organized. While all individuals in a democracy certainly have the right to organize, elitist theorists point to the relative lack of resources (e.g., time, money, organizational ability, and communication skills) among members of the working and lower economic classes. Thus, political organization for many poorer people, if it exists at all, may imply only token participation, and their voices will be drowned in the sea of middle-class voices Schattschneider describes.[16]

The implications of the elitist approach are rather obvious. If agenda formulation is crucial to the process of policymaking, then the ability of elites to keep certain issues off the agenda is crucial to their power. Adherents of this approach believe that the agenda in most democratic countries does not represent the competitive struggle of relatively equal groups, as argued by the pluralist model, but that it represents the systematic use of elite power to decide which issues the political system will or will not consider. Jurgen Habermas, for example, argues that the elite uses its power systematically to exclude issues that would be a threat to its interests and that these "suppressed issues" represent a major threat to democracy.[17] If too many significant issues are kept off the agenda, the legitimacy of the political system can be threatened, along with its survival in the most extreme cases.

Bachrach and Baratz's concept of "nondecisions" is important here. They define a nondecision as a decision that results in suppression or thwarting of a latent or manifest challenge to the values or interests of the decision maker.[18] To be more nearly explicit, non-decision-making is a means by which demands for change in the existing allocation of benefits and privileges in the community can be suffocated before they are even voiced; or kept covert; or killed off before they gain access to the relevant decision-making arena; or failing all these things, maimed or destroyed in the decision-implementing stage of the policy process.[19] A decision not to alter the status quo is a decision, whether it is made overtly through the policymaking process or whether it is the result of the application of power to prevent the issue from ever being discussed.

State-Centric Approaches

Both the pluralist and elitist approaches to policymaking and agenda setting assume that the major source of policy ideas is the environment of the policymakers—primarily interest groups or other powerful interests in the society. It is, however, quite possible that the political system itself is responsible for its own agenda.[20] The environment, in a state-centric analysis, is not filled with pressure groups but with "pressured groups."

The state-centered concept of agenda setting conforms quite well to the iron-triangle conception of American government but would place the bureaucratic agency or the congressional committee, not the pressure group, in the center of the process.[21] This approach does emphasize the role of specialized elites within government but, unlike elitist theorists, does not assume that these elites are pursuing policies for their own personal gain. Certainly their organizations may obtain a larger budget and more prestige from the addition of a new program, but the individual administrator has little or no opportunity to appropriate any of that increased budget.

In addition, the state-centric approach places the major locus of competition over agenda setting in government itself, rather than in the constellation of interests in society. Agencies must compete for legislative time and for budgets; committees must compete for attention for their particular legislative concerns; and individual congressmen must compete for consideration of their own bills. These actors within government are most relevant in pushing agenda items, rather than interests in the society.

One interesting question arises about agenda setting in the state-centric approach: what are the relative powers of bureaucratic and legislative actors in setting the agenda? A 1980 study by the Advisory Commission on Intergovernmental Relations argued that the source of the continued expansion of the federal government at that time was within Congress.[22] The authors of this study argued that congressmen, acting out of a desire to be reelected or from a sincere interest in solving certain policy problems, have been the major source of new items on the federal agenda. Other analyses have placed the source of most new policy ideas within the bureaucracy as much or more than in Congress.[23] Given the complexity of the chains of events leading to new policies, it may be difficult to determine exactly where ideas originated, but there is (at least in this model) no shortage of policy advocates.

The agenda resulting from a state-centric process might be more conservative than one resulting from a pluralist process but less conservative than one from the elitist model. Government actors may be constrained in the amount of change they can advocate on their own initiative; they may instead have to wait for a time when their ideas will be more acceptable to the general public. Congressmen can adopt a crusading stance, but this is a choice usually denied to the typical bureaucratic agency. Except in rare instances—the Office of the Surgeon General and the Food and Drug Administration concerning the regulation of cigarette smoking perhaps—a government-sponsored agency may be ahead of public opinion, but only slightly so.

Which approach to policymaking and agenda formation is most descriptive of the process in the United States? The answer is probably all of them, for the proponents of each can muster a great deal of evidence for their position. More important, policymaking for certain kinds of problems and issues can best be described by one approach rather than another. For example, we would expect policies that are very much the concern of government itself (e.g., civil service laws or perhaps even foreign affairs) to be more heavily influenced by state-centric policymaking than would other kinds of issues. Likewise, certain kinds of problems that directly affect powerful economic interests would be best understood through an elite analysis. Energy policy and its relationship to the major oil companies might well fit into that category. Finally, policy areas with a great deal of interest-group activity and relatively high levels of group involvement, both by clients and producers, might be best understood by means of the pluralist approach. Education might be a good example of this last kind of policy. Unfortunately, these are largely speculations, for the kind of detailed analysis required to track issues as they move on and off agendas has only begun to be done.[24]

From Problem to Issue: How to Get Problems on the Agenda

Problems do not move themselves on and off agendas. Nevertheless, their characteristics can have an influence in their being accepted as part of systemic and institutional agendas. A number of the characteristics of problems can affect their chances of becoming part of an active agenda. We should remember, however, that most problems do not come with these characteristics clearly visible to most citizens, or even to most political actors. Agendas must be constructed and the issues must be defined by a social and political process in a manner that will make them most amenable to political action.[25] Further, it usually requires an active policy entrepreneur to construct the necessary political packaging that can make an issue appear on an agenda.[26]

The Effects of the Problem

The first aspect of a problem that can influence its placement on an agenda is whom it affects, and how much it affects them. We can think about the extremity, concentration, range, and visibility of problems as influencing their placement on agendas. First, the more extreme the effects of a problem, the more likely it is to be placed on an agenda. An outbreak of a disease causing mild discomfort, for example, is unlikely to produce public action, but the chance of an epidemic life-threatening disease, such as the AIDS epidemic, usually provokes some kind of public action.

Even if the problem is not life threatening, a concentration of victims in one area may produce public action. The unemployment of an additional 50,000 workers, while certainly deplorable, might not cause major public intervention if the workers are scattered around the country, but may well do so if the workers are concentrated in one geographical area. Most industries in the United States are concentrated geographically (automobiles in Michigan, aerospace in California, oil in Texas and Louisiana), and that makes it easier for advocates of assistance to any troubled industry to get the help they want from government.

The range of persons affected by a problem may also influence the placement of the issue on an agenda. In general, the more people affected or potentially affected by a problem, the greater is the probability that the issue will be placed on the agenda. There are limits, however; a problem may be so general that no single individual believes that he or she has anything to gain by organizing political action about it. Thus an issue that has broad but only minor effects may have less chance of being placed on the agenda than a problem that affects fewer people but affects them more severely.

The intensity of effects, and therefore of policy preferences, is a major problem for those who take the pluralist approach to agenda setting.[27] Many real or potential interests in society are not effectively organized because few individuals believe that they have enough to gain from establishing or joining an organization. For example, although every citizen is a consumer, few effective consumer organizations have been established, whereas producer groups are numerous and are effective politically. The specificity and intensity of producer interests, as contrasted to the diffuseness of consumer interests, creates a serious imbalance in the pattern of interest-group organization that favors producers. An analogous situation would be the relative ineffectiveness of taxpayers' organizations compared to clientele groups, such as defense industries and farmers, which are interested in greater federal spending. The organizational imbalance against consumers and taxpayers was mitigated somewhat during the 1980s, but it still exists.[28]

Finally, the visibility of a problem may affect its placement on an agenda as an active issue. This might be called the "mountain climber problem." Society appears willing to spend almost any amount of money to rescue a single stranded mountain climber but will not spend the same amount of money to save many more lives by, for example, controlling automobile accidents. Statistical lives are not nearly so visible and comprehensible as an identifiable individual stuck on the side of a mountain. Similarly, the issue of the risks of nuclear power plants have been highly dramatized in the media, while less visibly an average of 150 men die each year in mining accidents and many others die from black-lung disease contracted in coal mines. Likewise, the existing environmental effects of burning coal, although certainly recognized, appear to pale in the public mind when compared to the possible effects of a nuclear accident.

Analogous and Spillover Agenda Setting

Another important aspect of a problem that can affect its being placed on an agenda is the presence of an analogy to other public programs. The more a new issue can be made to look like an old issue, the more likely it is to be placed on the agenda. This is especially true in the United States because of the traditional reluctance of American government to expand the public sector, at least by conscious choice. For example, the federal government's intervention into medical-care financing for individuals with Medicare and Medicaid was dangerously close to the (then) feared "socialized medicine."[29] It was made more palatable, at least for Medicare, by making the program appear similar to Social Security, which was already highly legitimate. More recently, the Clinton administration plan for health-care reform was made to appear very much like the existing health maintenance organizations that earlier had been sponsored by federal policy.[30] If a new agenda item can be made to appear as only an incremental departure from existing policies, rather than an entirely new venture, its chances of being accepted are much improved.

Also, the existence of one government program may produce the need for additional programs. This spillover effect is important in bringing new programs onto the agenda and in explaining the expansion of the public sector. Even the best policy analysts in the world cannot anticipate the consequences of all the policy choices made by government. Thus the adoption of one program may soon lead to the adoption of other programs directed at "solving" the problems created by the first program.[31] For example, the Interstate Highway program of the federal government was designed to improve civilian transportation; it was also justified as a means of improving transportation for defense purposes. One effect of building superhighways, however, has been to make it easier for people to live in the suburbs and work in the city. Consequently, these roads assisted in the flight to the suburbs of those who could afford to move. This, in turn, contributed to the decline of central cities. In turn, the federal government has had to pour billions of dollars into urban renewal, Urban Development Action Grants, and a host of other programs for the cities. The cities, of course, probably would have declined without the federal highway program, but the program certainly aided the process.

Policies in modern societies are now tightly interconnected and have so many secondary and tertiary effects on other programs that any new policy intervention is likely to have results that seem to spread like ripples in a clear lake. To some degree the analyst should anticipate those effects and design programs to avoid negative interaction effects, but he can never be perfectly successful in so doing. As a consequence, "policy is its own cause," and one policy choice may beget others.[32]

Relationship to Symbols

The more closely a particular problem can be linked to certain important national symbols, the greater is its probability of being placed on the agenda. Seemingly mundane programs can become involved in rhetoric about freedom, justice, and traditional American values. Phrased differently, a problem will not be placed on the agenda if it is associated with negative values. There are, of course, some exceptions, and although the gay community is not a positive symbol for many Americans, the AIDS issue was placed on the agenda with relative alacrity. This happened even before the possibilities of other sectors of the population becoming infected with the disease became widely known.[33]

There are several interesting examples of the use of positive symbols to market programs and issues that might not otherwise have been accepted on the agenda. The federal government traditionally eschewed most direct involvement with education, but the success of the Soviet Union in launching *Sputnik I* highlighted the weaknesses of American elementary and secondary education. This led to the National *Defense* Education Act, which associated the perceived problem of education with the positive symbol of defense, a long-term federal government concern. More recently, increased federal involvement in education has been associated at least in part with problems of global economic competitiveness. In addition, although the American government has generally been rather slow to adopt social programs, programs associated with children and their families have been more favorably regarded. So, if someone wants to initiate a social welfare program, it is well to associate it with children, or possibly with the elderly. It is perhaps no accident that the basic welfare program in the United States has been Aid to Families with Dependent *Children*. More recently, the 1994 crime bill contained a variety of social programs that might not have even made it to a vote if they were not attached to the symbolic issue of crime control.

Symbol manipulation is an extremely important skill for policy analysts. In addition to being rational calculators of the costs and benefits of their programs, analysts must be capable of relating their programs and program goals to other programs and of justifying the importance of the problem and the program to actors who may be less committed to it and its goals. Placing a problem on the agenda of government means convincing powerful individuals that they should take the time and trouble, and should make the effort necessary, to rectify the problem. The use of symbols may permit this to occur successfully when the problem itself is not likely to gain wide public attention.

The Absence of Private Means

In general, governments avoid accepting new responsibilities, especially in the United States with its laissez-faire tradition and especially in the prevailing climate of budgetary scarcity. There are, however, problems in society that cannot be solved by private market activities alone. Two classic examples of such problems are social problems that involve either "public goods" or "externalities."

Public goods are goods or services that, once produced, are consumed by a relatively large number of individuals, and whose consumption is difficult or impossible to control. This means that it is difficult or impossible for any individual or firm to produce public goods, for they cannot be effectively priced and sold.[34] If national defense were produced by paid mercenaries rather than by government, individual citizens would have little or no incentive to pay that group of fighters; citizens would be protected whether they paid or not. Indeed, citizens would have every incentive to be "free riders" and to enjoy the benefits of the service without paying the cost. In such a situation, government has a remedy for the problem: it can force citizens to pay through its power of taxation.

Externalities are said to exist when the activities of one economic unit affect the well-being of another and no compensation is paid for benefits or costs created externally.[35] Pollution is a classic case of an externality. It is a by-product of the production process, but its social costs are excluded from the selling price of the products made by the manufacturer. Thus, social costs and production costs diverge, and government may have to impose regulations to prevent the private firm from imposing the costs of pollution—such as damage to health, property, and amenities—on the public. Alternatively, government may develop some means of pricing the effects of pollution and then imposing those costs on the polluter. All externalities need not be negative, however, and some activities create public benefits that are not included in the revenues of those producing them. If a dam is built to generate hydroelectric power, the recreational and flood-control benefits cannot be included as part of the revenues of a private utility, although government can include those benefits in their calculations when considering undertaking a project with public money (see chapter 14).

Public goods and externalities are two useful categories for consideration, but they do not exhaust the social and economic problems that have a peculiarly public nature.[36] Of course, the consideration of issues of rights and the application of law is considered peculiarly public. In addition, programs that involve a great deal of risk may require the socialization of that risk through the public sector. Thus, when banks were unwilling to lend money to the Chrysler Corporation, the federal government decided to back the loans to prevent the company from going bankrupt. At a more ordinary level of occurrence, lending to college students who have little credit record is backed by government, as a means of making banks willing to take the risk. These loans are only a few examples of the general principle that the inability of other institutions in society to produce effective and equitable solutions may be sufficient to place an issue on the public agenda.

The Availability of Technology

Finally, problems generally will not be placed on the public agenda unless there is a technology believed to be able to solve the problem. For most of the history of the industrialized nations, it was assumed that economic fluctuations were, like the weather, acts of God. Then the Keynesian revolution in economics produced what seemed to be the answer to these fluctuations, and governments soon placed economic management in a central position on their agendas. In the United States this was reflected in the Employment Act of 1946, pledging the U.S. government to maintain full employment. The promise of "fine tuning" the economy through Keynesian means, which appeared possible in the 1960s, has now become extremely elusive, but the issue of economic management remains on the public agenda.[37] Subsequent governments have provided new technologies (e.g., "supply-side economics" during the Reagan years), but they have not been able to evade responsibility for the economy.

Another way of regarding the role of technology in agenda setting is the "garbage-can model" of decision making, in which solutions find problems, rather than vice versa.[38] Problems may be excluded from the agenda simply because of the lack of an instrument to do the job, and the example of economic management points to the danger of the lack of an available instrument. If government announces that it is undertaking to solve a problem and then fails miserably, public confidence in the effectiveness of government will be shaken. Government must then take the blame for failures along with the credit for successes. The garbage-can model also illustrates the relationship between agenda setting and policy formulation because issues are not accepted as a part of the agenda unless it is known that a policy has been formulated, or is already on the shelf, to solve the problem. Solutions may beg for new problems, like a child with a hammer finding things that need hammering.[39]

As with all portions of the policymaking process, agenda setting is an intensely political activity. It may well be the most political aspect of policymaking because it involves bringing into the public consciousness an acceptance of a vague social problem as something government can, and should, attempt to solve. It may be quite easy for powerful actors who wish to do so to exclude unfamiliar issues from the agenda, and consequently active political mobilization of the less powerful will be required to be successful. Rational policy analysis may play only a small role in setting the agenda for discussion; such analysis will be useful primarily after it is agreed that there is a problem and that the problem is public in nature. In agenda setting, the policy analyst is less a technician and more a politician, understanding the policymaking process and seeking to influence that process toward a desired end. This involves the manipulation of symbols and the definition of often vague social problems. Nevertheless, agenda setting should not be dismissed as simply political maneuvering: it is the crucial first step on the road to resolving any identified problem.

Policy Formulation

After the political system has accepted a problem as part of the agenda for policymaking, the logical question is what should be done about the problem. We call this stage of the policymaking process *policy formulation,* meaning the development of the mechanisms for solving the public problem. At this stage in the process, a policy analyst can begin to apply analytic techniques to attempt to justify one policy choice as superior to others. Economics and decision theory are both useful in assessing the risks of certain outcomes or in predicting likely social costs and benefits of various alternatives. Rational choice, however, need not be dominant; the habits, traditions, and standard operating procedures of government may prevail over rational activity in making the policy choice. But even such seemingly irrational sets of choice factors may be, in their way, quite rational. This is simply because the actors involved have experience with the "formula" to be used, are comfortable with it, and consequently can begin to make it work much more readily than they could a newer instrument in which they may have no confidence, even if that instrument were technically superior.

The federal government has followed several basic formulas in attempting to solve public problems. In economic affairs, for example, the United States has relied on regulation more than on ownership of business, which has been more common in Europe. In social policy, the standard formulas have been social insurance and the use of cash transfer programs rather than direct delivery of services. The major exception to the latter formula has been the reliance on education as a means of rectifying social and economic inequality. And finally there has been a formula that involves the private sector as much as possible in public-sector activity through grants, contracts, and the use of federal money as "leverage" for private money and money from state and local governments. We should not, however, be too quick to criticize the federal government for its lack of innovation in dealing with public problems. Most governments do not use all the "tools" available to them in their tool kit.[40] In addition, there is very little theory to guide government in trying to decide what tools they should use.[41] Thus a great deal of policy formulation is done by inertia or by intuition.

Who Formulates Policy?

Policy formulation is a difficult game to play because any number of people can and do play, and there are few rules. At one time or another, almost every kind of policy actor will be involved in formulating policy proposals. Several actors, however, are especially important in formulating policies. Policy formulation is also very much a political activity, but not always a partisan activity. Political parties and candidates, in fact, are not as good at promulgating solutions to problems as they are in identifying problems and presenting lofty ambitions for society to solve the problems. Expertise begins to play a large role here, given that the success or failure of a policy instrument will depend to some degree on its technical characteristics, as well as its political acceptability.

THE PUBLIC BUREAUCRACY

The public bureaucracy is the institution most involved in taking the lofty aspirations of political leaders and translating them into more concrete proposals. Whether one accepts the state-centric model of agenda setting or not, one must realize that government bureaucracies are central to policy formulation. Even if programs are formally presented by congressmen or the president, it is quite possible that their original formulation and justification came from a friendly bureau.

Bureaucracies presumably are the masters of routine and procedure. This is at once their strength and their weakness. They know how to use procedures and how to develop programs and procedures to reach desired goals. Yet agencies that know how to do these things too well may develop an excessively narrow vision of how to formulate answers for a particular set of problems. As noted earlier, certain formulas have been developed at the governmental level for responding to problems, and much the same is true of individual organizations that have standard operating procedures and rulebooks.

Certainly familiarity with an established mechanism can explain some of the conservatism of organizations in the choice of instruments to achieve ends, and faith in the efficacy of the instrument also helps explain reliance on a limited range of policy tools. One important component of the restrictiveness of choice, however, appears to be self-protection. That is, neither administrators nor their agencies can go very wrong by selecting a solution that is only an incremental departure from an existing program. This is true for two reasons: (1) such a choice will not have as high a probability of going wrong as a more innovative program; and (2) such an incremental choice will almost certainly keep the program in the hands of the existing agency. Hence, reliance on bureaucracy to formulate solutions may be a guarantee of stability, but is unlikely to produce many successful policy innovations.

Also, agencies will usually choose to do *something* when given the opportunity, or the challenge. Making policy choices is their business, and it is certainly in their organizational self-interest to make a response to a problem. The agency personnel know that if they do not respond, some other agency soon will, and their agency will lose an opportunity to increase its budget, personnel, and clout. Agencies do not always act in the self-aggrandizing manner ascribed to them,[42] but when confronted directly with a problem already declared to need solving, they will usually respond with a solution—one that involves their own participation.

There is one final consideration about bureaucratic responses to policy problems: agencies often represent a concentration of a certain type of expertise. Increasingly this expertise is professional, and an increasing proportion of the employees of the federal government have professional qualifications.[43] In addition to assisting an agency to formulate better solutions to policy problems, expertise narrows the vision of the agency and the range of solutions that may be considered. Professional training tends to be narrowing rather than broadening, and it tends to teach that the profession possesses *the* solution to a range of problems. Thus, with a concentration of professionals of a certain type in an agency, it will tend to produce only incremental departures from existing policies. In addition, the occupation of public manager itself is becoming more professionalized, so the major reference group for public managers will be other public managers, a factor that may further narrow the range of bureaucratic responses to policy problems.

THINK TANKS AND SHADOW CABINETS

Other sources of policy formulation are the "think tanks" that encircle Washington and the state capitals around the country. These are organizations of professional analysts and policy formulators who usually work on contract for a client in government—often an agency in the bureaucracy. We would expect much greater creativity and innovation from these organizations than from the public bureaucracy, but other problems arise in the policy options they may propose. First, an agency may be able virtually to guarantee the kind of answer it will receive by choosing a certain think tank. Some organizations are more conservative and will usually formulate solutions relying more on incentives and the private sector, while other consultants may recommend more direct government intervention. These reports are likely to have substantial impact, not only because they have been labeled as expert, but also because they have been paid for and therefore should be used.

Another problem that arises is more of a problem for the consultants in think tanks than for the agencies, but it certainly affects the quality of the policies recommended. If the think tank is to get additional business from an agency, the consultants believe—perhaps rightly—that they have to tell the agency what it wants to hear. In other words, a consulting firm that says that the favorite approach of an agency is entirely wrong and needs to be completely revamped may be technically correct and politically bankrupt all at once. Hence, a problem of ethical judgment arises for the consulting firm, as it might for individual analysts working for an organization: what are the boundaries of loyalty to truth and loyalty to the organization?

Three think tanks have been of special importance in U.S. policy formulation. Traditionally, the two dominant organizations were the Brookings Institution and the American Enterprise Institute. During the Nixon, Ford, and Reagan administrations, the Brookings Institution was described as "the Democratic party in exile." The Carter and Clinton administrations did indeed tap a number of the then present Brookings staff members for appointments. For Clinton these have included Alice Rivlin (more recently at the Congressional Budget Office, now at OMB). On the other side of the fence the American Enterprise Institute (AEI) has housed a number of Nixon and Ford administration personnel, although relatively few were tapped by the more conservative Reagan administration. Both of these think tanks have had wide-reaching publication programs to attempt to influence elite public opinion, in addition to their direct involvement in government. The third major think tank is the Heritage Foundation. It came to prominence during the Reagan years as an advocate of a number of neoconservative policy positions, especially privatization and deregulation.[44] It was less prominent in the Bush administration than it was during the Reagan administration, when its proposals were central to policy formulation in some fields.[45]

Universities also serve as think tanks for government. This is true especially for the growing number of public policy schools and programs across the country. As well as training future practitioners of the art of government, these programs provide a place where scholars and former practitioners can formulate new solutions to problems. Robert Reich, for example, formulated some of the ideas he attempts to implement as Secretary of Labor while at the Kennedy School of Government at Harvard.[46] In addition to the policy programs, specialized institutes such as the Institute for Research on Poverty at the University of Wisconsin and the Joint Center on Urban Studies at Harvard and MIT develop policy ideas concerning their specific policy areas.

INTEREST GROUPS

Interest groups are also important sources of policy formulation. In addition to identifying problems and applying pressure to have them placed on the agenda, successful interest groups have to supply possible remedies for those problems. Those cures will almost certainly be directed at serving the interests of the members of the groups, but that is only to be expected. It is then the task of the authoritative decision makers to take those ideas about policy choices with as many grains of salt as necessary and develop workable plans for solving the problem. Given the existence of iron-triangle relationships, a close connection is likely to exist between the policy formulation ideas of an agency and those of the pressure group. The policy choices advocated by established pressure groups will again be rather conservative, incremental, and rarely produce sweeping changes from the status quo in which they and their associated agency have a decided interest.

Some interest groups contradict the traditional model of policy formulation by interest groups. These are the public-interest groups, such as Common Cause, the Center for the Public Interest, and a variety of consumer and taxpayer organizations. Perhaps the major task of these groups is to break the stranglehold that the iron triangles have on policy and to attempt to broaden the range of interests represented in the policymaking process. These groups are oriented toward reform of policy and policymaking. Some of the issues they have taken up are substantive, such as the reform of safety requirements for a variety of products sold in the marketplace. Other issues are procedural, such as opening the regulatory process to greater public input and campaign reform. In general, however, no matter what issue these groups decide to interest themselves in, they will advocate sweeping reforms as opposed to incremental changes, and these groups are important in providing balance to the policy process and in providing a strong voice for reform and change.

CONGRESSMEN

Finally, individual congressmen are a source of policy formulation. We have previously tended to denigrate the role of politicians in formulating policy, but a number of congressmen do involve themselves in serious formulation activities instead of just accepting advice from friendly sources in the bureaucracy. Like the public-interest groups, these congressmen are generally interested in reform, for if they were primarily interested only in incremental change, there might be little need for their involvement. Some congressmen are also interested in using formulation and advocacy as means of furthering their careers, adopting roles as national policymakers as opposed to the more common pattern of congressmen emphasizing constituency service.

Congress in the 1990s is much better equipped to formulate policy than it has ever been, even given the nature of policy challenges it faces. There has been a continuing growth in the size of congressional staffs, both personal staffs of congressmen and the staffs of committees and subcommittees.[47] For example, in 1965 Congress employed just over 9,000 people; by 1990, the number of employees had increased to over 21,000. These employees are on the public payroll at least in part to assist Congress in doing the research and drafting necessary to be more active in policy formulation

and are quite important in rectifying what some consider a serious imbalance between the power of Congress and that of the executive branch.

How to Formulate Policy

The task of formulating policy involves substantial sensitivity to the nuances of policy (and politics) and a potential for the creative application of the tools of policy analysis. In fact, many of the problems faced by government require substantial creativity because little is known about the problem areas. Nevertheless, governments may have to react to a problem whether or not they are sure of the best, or even a good, course of action. In many instances, the routine responses of an agency to its environment will be sufficient to meet most problems that arise, but if the routine response is unsuccessful, the agency will have to search for a more innovative response and involve more actors in policy formulation. Phrased somewhat more abstractly, a routine or incremental response may be sufficient for most problems, but if it is not, the policymaking system must initiate some form of conscious search behavior. Making policy choices that depart radically from incremental responses will require methods of identifying and choosing among alternatives.

Two major barriers may block government's ability to understand the problems with which it is confronted. One is the lack of some basic factual information. A number of situations can arise in which government lacks information about the basic policy questions at hand. Most obviously, in defense policy governments often lack information about the capabilities and intentions of the opposing side. Similarly, in making risk assessments about dangers from various toxic substances or nuclear power plants, there may not be sufficient empirical evidence to determine the probabilities of undesirable events or the probable consequences of those events.[48] Perhaps even more difficult for government is that frequently there are no agreed upon indicators of the nature of social conditions, and that even widely accepted indicators for economic variables, such as gross national product and unemployment rates, are somewhat suspect.[49]

Perhaps more important, government decision makers often lack adequate information about the underlying processes that have created the problems they are attempting to solve. For example, to decide how to solve the poverty problem one should understand how poverty comes about and how it is perpetuated. But despite the masses of data and information generated, there is no accepted model of causation for poverty. This dearth of a causal model may be contrasted with decisions about epidemic diseases made by public health agencies using well-developed and accepted theories about how diseases occur and spread. Clearly decision making to attempt to solve these two kinds of problems should be different.

Figure 3.1 demonstrates possible combinations of the knowledge of causation and basic factual information about policy problems. The simplest type of policy to make is a *routine policy,* such as Social Security. Making policy in such areas, with adequate information and an accepted theory of causation, requires primarily routine adjustment of existing policies, and for the most part the policies made will be incremental.[50] This relative simplicity could change if the basic theories about creating a desirable retirement situation, or if the mechanism for financing such a system, were altered.

Information	Knowledge of causation	
	High	*Low*
High	Routine	Conditional
Low	Craftsman	Creative

FIGURE 3.1

KINDS OF POLICY FORMULATION

Creative policy formulation lies at the other extreme of information and knowledge held by decision makers. In this instance, they have neither an adequate information base nor an adequate theory of causation. Research and development operations, such as in the National Institutes of Health or in numerous agencies within the Department of Defense, provide important examples of policy formulation of this type in government.[51] Another example may be the formulation of policies for personal social services, such as counseling. In these instances, a great deal of creativity and care must be exercised in matching the particular needs of the individual with the needs of the agency for efficient management and accountability. Such policies require building in reversibility of policy choices so that creative formulations that may be unworkable can be corrected.

In some situations there may be sufficient information but an inadequate understanding of the underlying processes of causation. These policy-making situations require the formulation of *conditional policies,* in which changes in certain indicators would trigger a policy response of some sort, even if that response is only the reconsideration of the existing policy. It may well be that government can know that certain policies will produce desired results, even if the underlying processes are not fully understood. With the declining faith in Keynesian theories of economic management, it may be that macroeconomic policy is made in this manner. There are several agreed indicators of the state of the economy—unemployment, inflation, and economic growth rates, for example—and changes in these indicators may trigger relatively standard reactions, even if the policymakers cannot always specify, or agree on, the underlying logic behind those policy responses.[52] Also, it generally is advantageous to build a certain amount of automaticity into the policy response, or at least to provide some insulation against political delay or interference. In economic management, for example, countries with relatively independent central banks have been more successful than those with more politicized central banks.[53]

Finally, in some policy areas governments may have a model of causation for the problem, but may lack sufficient information to have confidence in any policy response they may formulate. Defense policies may fit this category of *craftsman policies*. Governments appear to understand quite well how to respond to threats and how to go to war, but frequently have only limited and possibly distorted information about the capabilities and intentions of their adversaries. Building policies of this type depends on developing a number of contingencies and possible forms of response, as well as finding means of assessing the risks of certain possible occurrences. The complex policy deliberations of the American government surrounding the possible nuclear capability of North Korea illustrates the "craftsman" nature of defense policy. In other words, formulating such policies may involve building a statistical basis for response instead of relying on the certainty that might be taken for granted in some other policy areas.

Aids for Policy Formulation

Given the difficulties of formulating effective policy responses to many problems, it is fortunate that some techniques have been developed to assist in that formulation. In general, these techniques attempt to make the consequences of certain courses of action more apparent to decision makers and to provide a summation of the probable effects of policy along a single scale of measurement, usually money, so that different policy alternatives can be more effectively compared with one another. I discuss two of these techniques only briefly here, reserving a more detailed exposition and discussion of cost-benefit analysis for chapter 14. It is important, however, to understand at this point the considerations that one might take into account when selecting a policy alternative.

Cost-Benefit Analysis

The most frequently applied tool for policy analysis is cost-benefit analysis (see chapter 14). The utilitarian methodology underlying this technique is to reduce all the costs and benefits of a proposed government program to a quantifiable economic dimension and then to compare available alternative policies. In this process the economic considerations are almost always paramount. As the methodology has been developed there are attempts to place economic values on factors that might be primarily noneconomic, but the principal means of evaluating programs remains utilitarian.

Cost-benefit analysis is in some ways deceptively simple. The total benefits created by the project are enumerated, including those that would be regarded as externalities in the private market (amenity values, recreation, etc.). The costs of the program are also enumerated, again including social costs (e.g., pollution). Long-term costs and benefits are also taken into account, although they are discounted or adjusted because they do occur in the future. Projects whose total benefits exceed their total costs are deemed acceptable and then choices can be made among the acceptable projects, generally by adopting the project with the greatest net total benefit (total benefits minus total costs), and then all others that fit within the total available budget.

Some of the more technical problems of cost-benefit analysis are discussed later, but it is important to talk about some of the ethical underpinnings of the technique here, as they have a pronounced effect on the formulation of policy alternatives. The fundamental ethical difficulties arise from the assumptions that all values are reducible to monetary values and that economic criteria are the most important ones for government to consider when making policy. There may well be other values, such as civil liberties or human life, that many citizens would not want reduced to dollars and cents.[54] Even if such a reduction were possible, it is questionable whether the primary goal of government should be maximizing economic welfare in the society.

Decision Analysis

Cost-benefit analysis assumes that certain events will occur. A dam will be built; it will produce X kilowatts of electricity; Y people from a nearby city will spend Z hours boating and water-skiing on the newly created lake; farmers will save Q dollars in flood protection and irrigation but lose N acres of land for farming. Decision analysis, in contrast, is geared more toward making policy choices under conditions of less certainty.[55] This method assumes that in many or most instances government, with inadequate information, is making probabilistic choices about what to do. In fact, many times, government may be almost playing a game, with nature or other human beings as the opponent. As pointed out, governments often do not have a very good conception of the policy instruments they choose, and that lack of knowledge, combined with inadequate knowledge about patterns of causation within the policy area, is a recipe for disaster. If we have some idea about the probabilities of certain outcomes (even without a model of causation), however, there is a better chance of making better decisions.

Take, for example, a situation in which a hurricane appears to be bearing down on a major coastal city. On the one hand, the mayor of that city can order an evacuation and cause a great deal of lost production, as well as a predictable number of deaths during the rush to escape the city. On the other hand, if he or she does not order the evacuation and the hurricane actually does strike the city, a far larger loss of life will occur. Of course, the hurricane is only forecast to be heading in the general direction of the city, and it may yet veer off. What should the mayor do?[56]

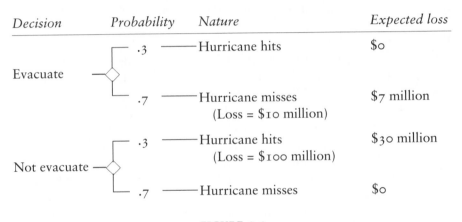

Decision	Probability	Nature	Expected loss
	.3	Hurricane hits	$0
Evacuate			
	.7	Hurricane misses (Loss = $10 million)	$7 million
	.3	Hurricane hits (Loss = $100 million)	$30 million
Not evacuate			
	.7	Hurricane misses	$0

FIGURE 3.2

A DECISION TREE ON EVACUATION

This decision-making problem can be organized as a "decision tree" in which the mayor is essentially playing a game against nature (see figure 3.2). The mayor has two possible policy choices: evacuate or not evacuate. We can assign a probability of the two occurrences in nature—hit or miss the city—based on the best information available from the Weather Bureau, and we have estimates of the losses that would occur as a result of each outcome. In this analysis we assume that if the hurricane does strike, the loss of property will be approximately the same whether or not the city is evacuated. As the problem is set up, the mayor makes the smallest possible error by choosing to evacuate the city. By so doing, he or she might cause an expected unnecessary loss of $7 million ($10 million multiplied by the probability of the event of .70) if the hurricane does not hit, but would cause an expected unnecessary loss of $30 million if the evacuation is not ordered and the hurricane strikes.

In a simple decision such as this, the decision is easy to make if there is sufficient information available. In more complex situations, when many facts need to be considered simultaneously, the decision-making process becomes more difficult. The process becomes even more difficult when one faces a human opponent, rather than nature. Even in those more complex instances, as in cost-benefit analysis, the technique is only an aid to decision making and to policy formulation. Decisions still must be made by individuals who consider ethical, economic, and political factors before making a judgment about what should be done. And as the results of policy formulation will be felt in the future, the exercise of judgment is especially important. When an issue is newly on the agenda, the first formulation of a solution will to some degree structure future attempts at solution and therefore will have an enduring legacy that must be considered very carefully.

Policy Design

All the aids that government can utilize when formulating policy still do not generate an underlying approach to policy design. That is, no technical means of addressing public problems relates the characteristics of those problems to the instruments that might be used to solve them, or to the values that would be used to evaluate the success of the policy.[57] Without such a comprehensive approach to design, much policy formulation in government is done by intuition or inertia, or by analogy with existing programs. This inertial pattern produces frequent mistakes and often much wasted time and effort. Thus, one of the many tasks of policy analysis is to develop a more comprehensive approach to the problems of formulating effective policies. This would require not only some idea of what "good" policies are but also some ideas about developing policymaking processes that might produce the more desirable policies.

In the United States, any more comprehensive approach to policy design is likely to be resisted. In the first place, the generally antistatist values of American politics will make such a planned and rationalistic approach unacceptable to many politicians and citizens. In addition, as pointed out earlier, American politics tends toward incremental solutions to problems rather than the imposition of any comprehensive frameworks or the use of design concepts for policy. Attempting to impose a design on a policy area may threaten the interests of agencies and committees that believe that they "own" the problem. Third, for many of the most important policy problems that American government now faces, there is yet inadequate agreement on the nature of the problem, much less on the nature of the solution to the problem. Important problems such as poverty, crime, and maleducation, and the like still lack any clear definitions of causes, much less solutions. These important political realities should not, however, prevent the student of policy from attempting to understand the problems of society in a less haphazard fashion than is sometimes used in government or from advocating innovative program designs for solving those problems.

Summary

This chapter has taken the policymaking process through its first stages: considering problems and then developing some mechanisms for solving them. Both activities—and indeed the entire activity of policymaking—are political exercises, but they can also involve the application of techniques and tools for analysis. The tools for agenda setting are largely political and require the "selling" of agenda items to authorized decision makers who may believe that they already have enough to do. Agenda setting also requires a detailed knowledge of the issue in question so that it can be related first to the known preferences of decision makers and second to existing policies and programs. Agenda setting is in some ways the art of doing something new so that it appears old.

The techniques that can be applied to policy formulation are more sophisticated technically, but they also require sensitive political hands that can use them effectively. To a great extent, the use of old solutions for new problems happens for formulation as well as in agenda setting. For both agenda setting and policy formulation, incremental solutions appear to be favored in the United States. Incrementalism produces a great deal of stability in the policy process, but it does make rapid response to major changes in the economy and society difficult. The solutions that emerge from these first stages of the policy process, then, are designed to be readily accepted by legislators and administrators who must authorize and legitimate the alternative policies selected. A more comprehensive approach to design might well produce better solutions to problems, but would face the barrier of political feasibility. The task of the analyst and advocate then becomes stretching the boundaries of feasibility to produce better public policies.

Notes

1. See Michael Harrington, *The Other America: Poverty in America* (New York: Macmillan, 1963). The huge number of more recent books explicitly on the topic of poverty include Judith A. Chafel, *Child Poverty and Public Policy* (Washington, D.C.: Urban Institute Press, 1993); Jonathan L. Freedman, *From Cradle to Grave: The Human Face of Poverty in America* (New York: Atheneum, 1993); Christopher Jencks, *Rethinking Social Policy* (Cambridge, Mass.: Harvard University Press, 1992).

2. James Agee, *Let Us Now Praise Famous Men* (Boston: Houghton Mifflin, 1941). This was a book of photographs and text about the plight of rural America during the Depression, funded by the Farm Security Administration. The book clearly had some impact, but that impact was more limited than a comprehensive attack on poverty.

3. Anthony Downs, "Up and Down with Ecology: 'The Issue Attention Cycle,'" *Public Interest* 28 (1972): 28–50; B. Guy Peters and Brian W. Hogwood, "In Search of the Issue-Attention Cycle," *Journal of Politics* 47 (1985): 238–53.

4. Peter Hennessy, Susan Morrison, and Richard Townsend, "Routines Punctuated by Orgies: The Central Policy Review Staff," *Strathclyde Papers on Government and Politics,* no. 30 (1985).

5. Frank Baumgartner and Bryan D. Jones, *Agendas and Instability in American Politics* (Chicago: University of Chicago Press, 1993).

6. Michael D. Cohen, James G. March, and Johan P. Olsen, "A Garbage Can Model of Organizational Choice," *Administrative Science Quarterly* 17 (1972): 1–25.

7. Joel Best, *Images of Issues* (New York: Aldine deGruyter, 1989).

8. Roger W. Cobb and Charles D. Elder, *Participation in American Politics* (Baltimore: Johns Hopkins University Press, 1983), 85.

9. This is what Peter Bachrach and Morton S. Baratz referred to as the "second face of power." See their "Decisions and Nondecisions: An Analytic Framework," *American Political Science Review* 57 (1964): 632–42.

10. Cobb and Elder, *Participation,* 86.

11. Ibid., 96

12. Jack L. Walker, "Setting the Agenda in the U.S. Senate: A Theory of Problem Selection," *British Journal of Political Science* 7 (1977): 423–45.

13. See A. Grant Jordan, "The Pluralism of Pluralism: An Anti-Theory," *Political Studies* 38 (1990): 286–301.

14. For another, similar setting, see B. Guy Peters, *Journal of European Public Policy* 1 (1994): 9–26.

15. C. Wright Mills, *The Power Elite* (New York: Oxford University Press, 1961); Charles E. Lindblom, *Democracy and the Market System* (New York: Oxford University Press, 1988).

16. E.E. Schattschneider, *The Semi-Sovereign People* (New York: Holt, Rinehart and Winston, 1969).

17. Lance deHaven Smith, *Philosophical Critiques of Policy Analysis: Lindblom, Habermas and the Great Society* (Gainesville: University of Florida Press, 1988); Habermas proposes the development of a more participatory "dialogical democracy" as a means of effectively including all interests. See also John Dryzek, *Discursive Democracy* (New York: Cambridge University Press, 1990).

18. Bachrach and Baratz, "Decisions and Nondecisions."

19. Ibid.

20. Martin J. Smith, *Pressure, Power and Policy* (Pittsburgh: University of Pittsburgh Press, 1993).

21. J. Leiper Freeman, *The Political Process: Executive Bureau–Legislative*

Committee Relations (New York: Random House, 1965).

22. Advisory Commission on Intergovernmental Relations, *The Federal Role in the Federal System* (Washington, D.C.: ACIR, 1980).

23. Nelson Polsby, *Policy Innovation in America* (New Haven: Yale University Press, 1984); John E. Schwarz, *America's Hidden Successes,* rev. ed. (New York: Norton, 1988).

24. See, for example, Baumgartner and Jones, *Agendas and Instability.*

25. Best, *Images of Issues;* Anne Schneider and Helen Ingram, "Social Construction of Target Populations: Implications for Policy and Politics," *American Political Science Review* 87 (1993): 334–47.

26. John W. Kingdon, *Agendas, Alternatives and Public Policy* (Boston: Little, Brown, 1984); Nancy C. Roberts, "Public Entrepreneurship and Innovation," *Policy Studies Review* 11 (1992): 55–73.

27. See James Q. Wilson, *The Politics of Regulation* (New York: Basic Books, 1980).

28. Robert H. Salisbury, "The Paradox of Interest Groups in Washington—More Groups, Less Clout," in *The New American Political System,* ed. Anthony King (Washington, D.C.: American Enterprise Institute, 1990).

29. Theodore R. Marmor, *The Politics of Medicare* (Chicago: Aldine, 1973).

30. Julie Kosterlitz, "All Together Now," *National Journal,* 13 November 1993, 2704–8.

31. Brian W. Hogwood and B. Guy Peters, *Policy Dynamics* (Brighton, England: Wheatsheaf, 1983).

32. Aaron Wildavsky, "Policy as Its Own Cause," *Speaking Truth to Power* (Boston: Little, Brown, 1979), 62–85.

33. Advocates for the victims of the disease would argue that there were significant delays in responding to the issue, in part because of "homophobia."

34. James M. Buchanan, *The Demands and Supply of Public Goods* (Chicago: Rand McNally, 1958): 3–7.

35. A classic statement of the issue is R.H. Coase, "The Problem of Social Cost," *Journal of Law and Economics* (1960): 1–44.

36. Charles Wolf, Jr., *Markets or Governments?* (Cambridge, Mass.: MIT Press, 1987).

37. The issue remains central to the political agenda, with politicians being evaluated very much on the performance of the economy.

38. Cohen, March, and Olsen, "A Garbage Can Model of Organizational Choice," 1–25.

39. Abraham Kaplan, *The Conduct of Inquiry* (San Francisco: Chandler, 1964).

40. On instruments see Christopher Hood, *The Tools of Government* (Chatham, N.J.: Chatham House, 1986); Lester M. Salamon with Michael S. Lund, *Beyond Privatization* (Washington, D.C.: Urban Institute Press, 1989; Stephen H. Linder and B. Guy Peters, "Instruments of Government: Perceptions and Contexts," *Journal of Public Policy* 9 (1989): 35–58.

41. Richard F. Elmore, "Instruments and Strategy in the Study of Public

Policy," *Policy Studies Review* 7 (1987): 174–86.

42. They are argued to be so by, among others, William Niskanen, *Bureaucracy and Representative Government* (Chicago: Aldine/Atherton, 1971). But see Andre Blais and Stephane Dion, *The Budget-Maximizing Bureaucrat* (Pittsburgh: University of Pittsburgh Press, 1991).

43. Kenneth J. Meier, *Politics and the Bureaucracy,* 3d ed. (Pacific Grove, Calif.: Brooks/Cole, 1993).

44. See Charles L. Heatherly, ed., *Mandate for Change: Policy Management in a Conservative Administration* (Washington, D.C.: Heritage Foundation, 1981).

45. The conservative end of the dimension of policy advice is also populated by the Cato Institute, which tends to advise from an almost philosophical libertarian position. On Bush, see Colin Campbell and Bert A. Rockman, eds., *The Bush Presidency: First Appraisals* (Chatham, N.J.: Chatham House, 1991).

46. See, for example, Robert Reich, *The Work of Nations: Preparing Ourselves for 21st Century Capitalism* (New York: Knopf, 1991); *Education and the Next Economy* (Washington, D.C.: National Education Association, 1988).

47. Michael Malbin, *Our Unelected Representatives* (New York: Basic Books, 1980). For a conservative critique, see Eric Felten, "Little Princes," *Policy Review* 63 (1993): 51–57.

48. See W. Kip Viscusi, "The Value of Risks to Life and Health," *Journal of Economic Literature* 31 (1993): 1912–46; Richard Zeckhauser and W. Kip Viscusi, "Risk within Reason," *Science* 248 (4 May 1990): 559–64.

49. Robert Eisner, *The Misunderstood Economy* (Cambridge, Mass.: Harvard Business School Press, 1994).

50. There have been a number of books and articles about "crises" in Social Security, but the pattern of decision making tends to be more incremental. See Theodore R. Marmor, *Social Security: Beyond the Rhetoric of Crisis* (Princeton: Princeton University Press, 1988); Peter J. Ferrara, *Social Security: Averting the Crisis* (Washington, D.C.: Cato Institute, 1982).

51. See Richard Topf, "Science, Public Policy, and the Authoritativeness of the Governmental Process," in *The Politics of Expert Advice,* ed. Anthony Barker and B. Guy Peters (Pittsburgh: University of Pittsburgh Press, 1993).

52. R. Kent Weaver, "Setting and Firing Policy Triggers," *Journal of Public Policy* 9 (1989): 307–36.

53. Paulette Kurzer, "The Politics of Central Banks: Austerity and Unemployment in Europe," *Journal of Public Policy* 8 (1988): 21–48.

54. See Henry J. Aaron, Thomas E. Mann, and Timothy Taylor, *Values and Public Policy* (Washington, D.C.: Brookings Institution, 1994).

55. Moshe F. Rubenstein, *Patterns of Problem Solving* (Englewood Cliffs, N.J.: Prentice Hall, 1975).

56. The political risks for the mayor may be different from the actual risks to the city and its people. The mayor does not want to be seen as panicking in the face of a crisis, but the unnecessary loss of life may be the most damaging possibility of all for a political leader.

57. Stephen H. Linder and B. Guy Peters, "From Social Theory to Policy

Design," *Journal of Public Policy* 4 (1984): 237–59; Davis Bobrow and John S. Dryzek, *Policy Analysis by Design* (Pittsburgh: University of Pittsburgh Press, 1987).

4. Legitimating Policy Choices

Once it has been decided that a certain program is required, or is feasible, as a response to a policy problem, that choice must be made a legitimate choice. It is almost certain that no matter what course of action is decided on, some citizens will believe themselves disadvantaged by the choice. At a minimum, any public program or project will cost money, and citizens who pay taxes and receive (or perceive) no direct benefits from the new program will frequently consider themselves to be harmed by the policy choice.

Because policy choices inevitably benefit some citizens to the detriment of others, a great deal of attention must be given in a democratic government to the process by which decisions are made. It is by means of these legitimate processes of government that substantive policy decisions are legitimated; that is, the policies have the legitimate authority of the state attached to them by the processes.

Legitimacy is a fundamental concept in the discipline of political science and is important in understanding policymaking. Legitimacy is conventionally defined as a belief on the part of citizens that the current government represents a proper form of government and a willingness on the part of those citizens to accept the decrees of the government as legal and authoritative.[1] The vast majority of Americans regard the government of the United States as the appropriate set of institutions to govern the country. And most Americans consequently accept the actions of that government as authoritative (as having the force of law) as long as the actions are in accordance with the procedures set forth in the Constitution, by procedures derived from the process described in the Constitution. It is understood that all policies adopted must be within the powers granted to the federal government by the Constitution. The boundaries of what is considered "constitutional" have expanded during the history of the United States, but the limits current at the time establish the boundaries of legitimate action.

Several things should be understood about legitimacy as it affects contemporary policymaking. First, legitimacy is largely a psychological property. It depends on the majority's acceptance of the appropriateness of a government. A government may come to power by all the prescribed processes, but if the population does not willingly accept that government or the rules by which it gained power, then in practice it has no legitimacy. For example, many constitutions (including those of France and Britain) give governments the right to suspend civil liberties and declare martial law, but citizens accustomed to greater freedom may find it difficult to accept such decrees.[2] Further, changes in a government may cause some citizens to question the legitimacy of a new government's actions.

Legitimacy has substantive as well as procedural elements. It matters not only how issues are decided but also what is decided. The government of the United States might decide to nationalize all oil companies operating in the country. (It will not do this, but just imagine so for a moment.) The decision could be reached with all appropriate deliberation as prescribed by the Constitution, but it would still not be acceptable to the majority of citizens. In a more realistic example, the war in Vietnam was conducted according to the procedures of the Constitution, but its legitimacy nevertheless was rejected by a significant share of the population. In addition, that conflict evoked a response from Congress, in the form of the War Powers Act, that would change the procedures by which the United States could become involved in any future foreign conflicts. The substantive question of legitimacy therefore produced a procedural response. At a somewhat less dramatic level, the attempts on the part of Congress to increase its own pay during 1989 and 1990 were procedurally correct but raised such an outcry from the public that they could not be implemented; the American public clearly regarded those actions as illegitimate.

Legitimacy is both a variable and a constant. It differs among individuals and across time. Some citizens of the United States may not accept the legitimacy of the current government. For example, some African American leaders have rejected the legitimacy of the U.S. government, and have called for the formation of a separate African American country within the country. On the other side, white supremacists have organized settlements in parts of the West that reject the authority of the constituted governments. A general decline in confidence in American institutions has been occurring, and that decline has been especially pronounced for government institutions other than the military (see table 4.1).[3] There was some upturn in confidence in the early 1980s but that has decayed and Americans now have less confidence in government than they have had in the past. In societies that are deeply divided ethnically or politically the rejection of the sitting government by one side or another is a constant fact of life. Even a government that is widely accepted may lose legitimacy, or strain its legitimate status, through its activities and its leaders. The Vietnam war and the Watergate scandal illustrate the low points to which the legitimacy of even a widely accepted political regime may fall. Nevertheless, the regime was able to survive

TABLE 4.1
CONFIDENCE IN AMERICAN INSTITUTIONS, 1973–94
(PERCENTAGE SAYING "GREAT DEAL" OR "QUITE A LOT")

	1994	1993	1991	1990	1989	1988	1987	1986	1985	1983	1981	1979	1975	1973
Military	64	68	85	68	63	58	61	63	61	53	50	54	58	n.a.
Organized religion	54	53	59	56	52	59	61	57	66	62	64	65	68	66
Supreme Court	42	44	48	47	46	56	52	54	56	42	46	45	49	44
Presidency	38	43	72	n.a.	n.a.	n.a.	n.a.	n.a.	n.a.	n.a.	n.a.	n.a.	n.a.	n.a.
Public schools	34	39	44	45	43	49	50	49	48	39	42	53	n.a.	58
Newspapers	29	31	32	39	n.a.	36	31	37	35	38	35	51	n.a.	39
Organized labor	26	26	25	27	n.a.	26	26	29	28	26	28	36	38	30
Big business	26	22	26	25	n.a.	25	n.a.	28	31	28	20	32	34	26
Congress	18	18	30	24	32	35	n.a.	41	39	28	29	34	40	42

SOURCE: *Gallup Poll Monthly*, April 1994, 6.

those problems, as well as such subsequent problems as the Iran-*contra* controversy, and continue to govern with legitimate authority.

Because of the variability of legitimacy, a fully legitimated government may gradually erode its legitimate status through time. A series of blatantly unpopular or illegal actions may reduce the authority of a government. That government may then become open to a challenge, whether of a revolutionary or more peaceable nature. Or a government may lose legitimacy through incompetence rather than unpopular activities. Citizens in most countries have a reservoir of respect for government, and governments can add to or subtract from that stock of authority. As a result, governments are engaged in a continuing process of legitimation for themselves and their successors.

Finally, government must somehow legitimate each individual policy choice. No matter how technically correct a policy choice may be, it is of little practical value if it cannot be legitimated. Policy analysts, in their pursuit of elegant solutions and innovative policies, frequently forget this mundane point, but their forgetfulness can present a real barrier to their success.[4] To design a policy that can be legitimated, a policy analyst must understand the political process, for that process will define the set of feasible policy alternatives in a more restrictive fashion than does the economic and social world. That is, more programs could work than could be adopted within the political values of the American system. Thus, the task of the policy analyst is to be able to "sell" his or her decisions to individuals who are crucial to their being legitimated. This does not mean that the analyst must advocate only policies that fit the existing definitions of feasibility, but it does mean that the analyst must have a strategy for expanding that definition if a highly innovative program is going to be proposed.[5]

In general, legitimation is performed through the legislative process, through the administrative process designed for the issuing of regulations (secondary legislation), through the courts, or through mechanisms of direct democracy. As shown in table 4.2, these modes of legitimation can be seen as combining characteristics of decisions—majoritarian and nonmajoritarian—and the range of actors involved. The nonmajoritarian mass cell is empty

TABLE 4.2

KINDS OF LEGITIMATION

Majority involvement	Majoritarian	Nonmajoritarian
Mass	Referenda	—
Elite	Congress	Courts; administrative regulations

in this table, but it might be filled by revolutionary or extreme interest-group activities. Indeed, the current political controversy over abortion policy may fall into this cell given that there is apparently no popular majority for the policies being pushed by an intense and active minority, and that minority is being successful in some states. We next discuss each kind of legitimation and its implications for the policy choices that might be feasible as a result of each process.

Legislative Legitimation

In the United States we traditionally have equated lawmaking with Congress, the principal legislative body at the federal level, or with similar bodies at the state level. As this section points out, that notion is now excessively naive, for the workload and technical content of many subjects on which decisions have to be made have overwhelmed Congress. This loss of capacity to legislate effectively is true despite the massive growth of legislative staffs and the availability of increased policy advice for congressmen. Governments are simply too large and involved in too many issues to permit a large and complex institution such as Congress to make all the decisions required to keep the society functioning (from a public policy perspective).

Of course, Congress remains the crucial source for primary legislation. That is, although administrative bodies are responsible for writing regulations in large numbers, Congress must supply the basic legislative frameworks within which other bodies can operate. Congress tends to pass legislation written in relatively broad language, allowing administrators latitude for interpretation. Thus, in the 1990s, despite the resurgence of congressional power in opposing the "imperial presidency" from the 1970s and the Reagan administration in the 1980s, it is best to think about legitimation in Congress as the legitimation of relatively diffuse statements of goals and structures. Those broad statements are then made operational by the executive branch, which fills in the details by writing regulations and using the implementation process.

Congress also retains its supervisory powers—oversight—so that if the executive branch strays too far in writing regulations (see below), Congress can reassert its powers to explain what its intentions were when it constructed the legislation.[6] Until 1983, Congress had at its disposal the "legislative veto," which required agencies issuing certain kinds of regulations to submit those regulations to Congress for approval. The Supreme Court, however, declared the legislative veto was excessive meddling by one branch of government into the affairs of another.[7] Despite the Court decision that the legislative veto in the one instance was not constitutional, Congress has continued to utilize similar instruments in other policy areas.[8]

Congress places a great deal of emphasis on procedural legitimation and has established elaborate sets of procedures for processing legislation.[9] In fact, its institutions and procedures have become so well developed that it is difficult for legislation to be passed. Typically, a bill must be passed by a subcommittee, by a full committee, and by floor action in each house. And as one house is unlikely to pass a bill in exactly the same form as the other house, conference committees will be necessary to reconcile the two versions. Given the possibility of using more arcane procedural mechanisms, such as filibusters, amendments, and recommitals, legislation can be slowed down or killed at a number of points by failure to attract the necessary majority at the proper time. Or, to put it the other way around, all that the opponents of a bill have to do is to muster a majority at one crucial point to prevent the passage of legislation.[10] Procedures are important as mechanisms to prevent unnecessary or poorly formulated legislation from becoming law, but they can also frustrate good and needed legislation. The ability of the opposition to postpone or block civil rights legislation during the 1950s and 1960s demonstrates the use of legislative procedures to thwart the apparent majority will of Congress. More recently, the continuing inability to produce a national health insurance bill indicates the difficulties of passing legislation even when a significant portion of the population favors some change from the status quo.

Legitimation through the legislative process is majoritarian. It depends on building either simple or special majorities at each crucial point in the process. The task of the policy analyst or legislative leader is to construct such majorities. In addition to appealing on the basis of the actual qualities of the proposed legislation, the needed majorities can be formed in several other ways. One method has been referred to as partisan analysis.[11] This involves convincing members of Congress that the piece of legislation that the analyst wants is also something that the member of Congress wants. The trick here is to design the legislation in such a way that it will appeal to a sufficient number of interests to create a winning coalition. For example, the National Defense Education Act of 1958 was passed by a coalition of congressmen interested in education and *defense*. The title of the bill indicates that it was intended to serve those two purposes, and it affects those two areas. It brought together liberals favoring a stronger federal role in education with conservatives favoring a stronger defense posture. Also, many social and housing programs have been "sold" to conservatives as benefiting business—as urban renewal certainly did—or as providing employment.[12]

Another strategy for forming coalitions that is not dissimilar to partisan analysis is logrolling.[13] In logrolling, coalitions are formed not around a single piece of legislation but across a set of legislative initiatives. In the simplest example, Congressman A favors bill A but is indifferent toward bill B.

Congressman B, in contrast, favors bill B but is indifferent to bill A. The logical thing for these two congressmen to do is to trade their votes on the two pieces of legislation, with A voting for bill B and B voting for bill A. The real world may not be so convenient, however, and several bills may be involved in vote trading across time. In some ways, logrolling is a rational activity because it allows the passage of legislation that some congressmen, and presumably their constituencies, favor intensely and that might not otherwise be able to gain a majority. But logrolling also has the effect of passing a great deal more legislation than would otherwise be passed, thus affecting public expenditures and taxation. It enables relatively narrow interests in the nation to develop coalitions for their legislation that may not be justifiable in terms of the broader "public interest."

As well as being a majoritarian body, Congress has universalistic norms that promote the spreading of government expenditures very broadly. This is commonly referred to as "pork-barrel" legislation, or as the parochial imperative in American politics. Pork-barrel legislation often concerns capital expenditures, with the classic examples being river and harbor improvements. Obtaining capital projects such as these has become a measure of the success of congressmen; some argue that it, instead of policymaking on broad national issues, has become the dominant activity of Congress.[14] Congressional representatives must demonstrate to their constituents that they can "bring home the bacon" and can produce tangible benefits for the voters of the district. Thus the tendency in designing legislation of this kind is to spread benefits as broadly as possible geographically and to create a majority by benefiting virtually anyone who wants a piece of the "pork." As with logrolling, this pattern of decision making tends to increase the costs of government. Douglas Arnold is quite correct in pointing out that pork-barrel legislation costs very little when compared with national defense or Social Security.[15] It may, however, stand as an example of the way in which government misuses money by funding projects with relatively low social benefit in order to ensure the reelection of incumbent congressmen. Politically, the importance of this style of decision making may outstrip the actual amount of money spent.

The description of legitimation through the legislative process does not give the most favorable impression of Congress. Actually, a good deal of congressional decision making is done on the basis of the merits of the legislation. To the extent that partisan analysis, logrolling, and pork-barrel legislation characterize the actions of Congress, however, the legislative process has certain effects on the kinds of rules that can be legitimated. It can be argued that the legislative process almost inevitably will produce broad and rather diffuse legislation. The necessity of building a coalition requires that one take care not to offend potential members, and that it does produce benefits for individual congressmen and their districts. As a consequence, legislation must be designed that is amenable to partisan analysis and is not so clearly worded as to reduce the number of possible coalition members. This, of course, allows administrators to make more difficult and politically charged decisions on cases, thus deflecting criticism from Congress.

Also, it can be argued that legislative decision making is associated with an expanding government. Both logrolling and pork-barrel legislation are perhaps related to the expansion of government beyond the bounds that could be set if there were no possibility of vote trading. There is a tendency to adopt public projects that are marginal in terms of their social productivity. We know quite well that the world of policymaking is by no means perfectly rational, but these patterns of institutional decision making seem to exacerbate the irrational character of much of politics. These patterns also make reducing the size of unneeded programs difficult. For example, the only effective way that Congress could find to have the closing of redundant military bases adopted in the early 1990s was to adopt, in advance, a rule that an independent commission recommend the closings and that they then be voted on as a group. Without that rule, logrolling might have meant that no bases would have been closed.

These difficulties in congressional decision making suggest more general points concerning problems of social decision making. In its simplest terms, the problem is this: how can a set of social preferences best be expressed in a single decision? Congress faces this problem when it attempts to combine the preferences of its members and their constituents in a single decision whether or not to adopt a piece of legislation; the same general problem arises in club, committee, and college faculty meetings.

One underlying problem facing decision makers is the issue of intensity of preferences. We faced this problem in discussing the logic of logrolling. In a majoritarian system, it may be possible to construct a majority composed of individuals who are not much interested in a proposal and who do not feel intensely about it. This is in part a function of having only one vote per person, whereas in the market setting, individuals have more than one dollar and can apply their resources differentially depending on their preferences and the intensity of those preferences. Logrolling is one means of attempting to overcome the intensity problem, but it can be successful only in a limited set of circumstances with a certain distribution of preferences.

In majoritarian institutions with one vote per member, it is difficult to reflect accurately the preferences of the participants in a decision in a manner that creates the greatest net satisfaction for the participants. Generating such an optimal decision is made more difficult if in a number of successive decisions (e.g., voting on amendments) the order in which options are eliminated affects the final preferences.[16] In examining problems about making choices of this type, the economist Kenneth Arrow argued that it is impossible to devise a social-choice mechanism that satisfies the logical conditions for rationality.[17] The only way in which such decisions can be arrived at, in Arrow's framework, is to impose them, which he rejects on philosophical grounds. But the imposition of administrative regulations as another means of legitimating decisions has some characteristics of imposed solutions, although the procedures for adopting regulations have been sanctioned legally.

Oversight

Once Congress has enacted legislation it has played its major role in legitimating policy, but its involvement is not over. We have already pointed out that the administrative agencies play a major role in translating legislation into specific regulations. The Congress then exercises some degree of oversight over the actions of the agencies.[18] The committees that initially adopted the legislation monitor the way in which the agencies implement that legislation and then can act legislatively to correct anything the agencies may do incorrectly. Congress may not even have to do anything directly, but can rely on its implicit authority over legislation and budgets to gain compliance from the agencies.

Oversight is in essence a second round of legitimation by Congress. They pass the initial legislation and then can look over the shoulders of the implementors to try to ensure that their intentions are followed. That having been said, Congress can be only so effective in this oversight activity. This is in part a function of the scarcity of time and the need for congressional attention to go forward to the next round of legislation. Further, there can be a scarcity of the necessary expertise to judge the numerous, complex, and technical regulations issued by administrative agencies, and the even more numerous administrative decisions taken by the agencies. This means that oversight tends to be more "fire alarm" (reaction to crises) than "police patrol" (routine scanning of the relevant environment).[19]

Regulations and the Administrative Process

Most rulemaking in the United States and other industrialized societies is now done through the regulatory process.[20] Here we are referring to the regulatory process in a rather broad context to include the rulemaking activities of executive branch agencies as well as those of independent regulatory commissions. We will be discussing the process by which administrative or independent regulatory bodies can issue binding regulations that are subsidiary to congressional legislation. These regulations are sometimes referred to as *secondary legislation,* and issuing such regulations is definitely a legislative or legitimating activity because it makes rules for the society. Nevertheless, those rules must be pursuant to primary legislation already adopted by Congress.

The volume of regulation writing in the federal government is immense. It can be judged by the size of the *Federal Register,* a weekly publication containing all regulations and proposed regulations (approximately 70,000 pages per year), and by the size of the *Code of Federal Regulations (CFR)* containing all the regulations currently in force. One example of the volume of regulatory activity is provided by the Occupational Safety and Health Administration (OSHA) in the Department of Labor. OSHA, which has been a frequent target of the critics of government regulation, issued 4,600 regulations during the first two years of its existence and continues to issue hundreds of new regulations each year. As of 1990, these regulations amounted to 3,617 pages of rather fine print in the *CFR.*[21] Taken together, three areas of public policy—agriculture, labor, and the environment—have rules equaling approximately 25,000 pages in the *Code of Federal Regulations.*[22]

Although conducted through a legal process, the decision making required for adopting regulations is not majoritarian. If it were, many of the regulations adopted by OSHA and many other regulatory bodies might never be adopted. Decision making in the regulatory process can be more technical and less tied to political considerations than can decision making in Congress, although political considerations cannot be neglected entirely. This is especially true for agencies that are a part of executive branch departments. Executive branch agencies are directly responsible to the president and consequently must issue regulations that address the political priorities of the president. Presidents Ford, Carter, and their successors have taken greater pains than previous presidents to know what regulations are being issued and to ensure that they match presidential priorities. Even the regulations issued by independent regulatory agencies cannot afford to stray too far from the basic political and ideological norms of the public; if they do, the agency threatens its own survival or at least its latitude to issue further regulations.

One of the ways in which government has attempted to keep regulatory activity in check is through regulatory analysis. President Carter, for example, required agencies to justify their choice of any one particular regulation against others, largely on economic grounds. President Reagan went further and required executive agencies to submit all new regulations for review by the Office of Management and Budget (OMB), and later to submit their plans for regulatory activity for the subsequent year. These regulatory reviews were as much political as economic, and they resulted in critics referring to the OMB as the "regulatory KGB."[23]

Although the OMB review of regulations was in many cases political and ideological, it also has served a legitimation function. In the first place, the elected presidency does have greater legitimacy than does the unelected bureaucracy, especially given the usual view that Americans have of the bureaucracy. Further, as the techniques used in regulatory analysis are "rational," the argument can be made that any regulations that survive it are perhaps more likely to make a positive contribution to the well-being of society.[24]

Even by the time of the Bush administration some analysts were arguing that deregulation had gone too far. So, for example, during that administration the Environmental Protection Agency began to issue a number of important new regulations, including imposing significant new air-pollution standards on five northeastern states. The Clinton administration has taken a somewhat more positive view of regulations and their impact on the economy and society. While proclaiming themselves to be "new Democrats," this administration has adopted a more activist position in environmental and economic regulations. They have, however, attempted to write those regulations with even greater amounts of consultation and negotiation than has been common in the past. For example, there are plans for substantially more public involvement and public disclosure during the regulatory processes than in the past, even though some of the tools of regulatory analysis will remain in place.[25]

Public Access to the Regulatory Process

The process of making regulations is open to the public's influence as well as that of the president and OMB. The procedures of the Administrative Procedures Act and several other laws affecting the issuing of regulations require that agencies accept advice and ideas from interested citizens as the process goes forward and requires time at each stage for affected interests in the society to respond to the agency initiatives.[26] For some segments of the economy, in fact, the regulatory process may be more democratic than decision making in Congress. The regulatory process permits direct access of affected interests to decision makers, whereas in Congress those affected interests may be excluded from effective involvement, especially if they represent an interest not widely considered "legitimate" by congressmen. Furthermore, the legislative outcomes may be more "in the public interest" than those in Congress, given that special-interest influences are funneled through an administrative process and frequently subject to judicial review.[27]

Access to the process does not, of course, mean that the ideas of the affected interests, or "public-interest groups," will be dominant in the decisions finally made. Simply granting access does not protect the interests of segments of the society that are not sufficiently well organized or alert to make their presentations to the agency. Access to agency decision making is by no means costless, so many less-well-funded groups may be excluded. This has led some agencies, such as the Federal Trade Commission, to provide funding for interests that might not otherwise have the lawyers and other resources needed to participate effectively.[28] Again, there are no guarantees of success, but the procedures do indicate the openness of the regulatory process to a range of ideas and opinions.

The Processes of Writing Regulations

There are two principal ways, referred to as formal and informal rulemaking, in which regulation writers collect ideas and opinions. Formal rulemaking has some of the appearance of a court proceeding, with a formal hearing, the taking of oral testimony from witnesses, and the use of counsel.[29] Formal rulemaking is a time-consuming and cumbersome process, but it is deemed necessary when the social and economic interests involved are considered sufficiently important. Examples of the use of formal rulemaking are approving new medications by the Food and Drug Administration and licensing nuclear power plants by the Nuclear Regulatory Commission. The written records generated in formal rulemaking are important, given that these rulings are important to many elements in society and may be the subject of subsequent discussion and litigation.

Informal rulemaking proceeds through three basic steps. First, the agency is required to publish (in the *Federal Register*) a notice of its intent to issue a certain regulation. Then a period of several months is allowed, during which individuals and groups who believe themselves potentially affected by the rule can offer opinions and make suggestions about the content of the regulation. After the designated time has passed, the agency may issue the draft regulation. This, as the name implies, is a draft of the regulation that the agency would ultimately like to see put into effect. The draft may be based on the suggestions received from affected interests, or it may be what the agency had been planning all along. Then there is another waiting period for responses to the draft regulation. Those responses may be directly to the agency or they may be indirect—by having a friendly congressman contact the agency with proposed alterations. Then, based on responses from interests, as well as its own beliefs about the appropriateness of the regulation, the agency issues the final regulation that will have the force of law.

In addition to the two principal forms of rulemaking, administrative law has been developing to include two other ways of adopting regulations. One is called "hybrid rulemaking," and represents an attempt at compromise between the thoroughness of the formal process and the relative ease of the informal process.[30] This form of rulemaking came about in part because of the courts[31] and in part because it was required by some acts of Congress, especially in environmental policy.[32] Although not requiring full-scale judicial proceedings, there may be requirements for the opportunity to cross-examine witnesses in order to create a full judicial record. This record can then be the basis for an appeal if further judicial proceedings are demanded.

The other emerging form of rulemaking is negotiated rulemaking. Given the complexity of many of the policy areas into which government must now venture, and the number of interests involved in each policy, it may be easier to negotiate rules than to attempt to make them administratively.[33] This process can save a great deal of future ill will among the affected interests and perhaps actually create superior policies to those that might emerge from a more centrally directed process. Congress has now recognized the validity of this form of rulemaking by passing the Negotiated Rulemaking Act of 1990 to specify the conditions under which this procedure can be used and the procedures required. They have also included language about negotiated rulemaking in the authorizing legislation for several executive agencies.[34]

The legitimate force of a regulation is derived from a statute passed by Congress and from following correct procedures in issuing the regulation. In general, issuing a regulation takes about eighteen months from beginning to end and allows for substantial representation of affected groups and individuals. Attempts to short-circuit the process will probably result in the regulation's being rejected, no matter how reasonable on its face, if appealed through the court system. The law does allow, however, some provisions for emergency rulemaking for some agencies.

The role assigned to affected interests in responding to issues in the regulatory process brings up another point about social decision making. This is the point made by John C. Calhoun, in part as a means of justifying slavery. Calhoun argued that a proper democracy would take into account not only the majority of individuals but also a majority of interests in society. His idea of "concurrent majorities" would have assigned greater importance to the role of pressure groups than is true in most of American political thought and would have made the opinions of the groups more central in the process of writing regulations.

The role permitted to interest groups in decision making about regulations also is similar to the development of "neocorporatism" in Western Europe.[35] The principal difference is that interest groups in the United States usually are not granted the quasi-official status as representatives of the economic or social group that they have acquired in much of Europe. Further, the affected interest groups are rarely brought together to negotiate a compromise decision, as they would be in many European systems.[36] One recent contrary example is the conference held in the Pacific Northwest to discuss differences between logging interests and conservationists over protection of the spotted owl.[37] Decision making in the United States is still done largely within the agency itself, with interest groups involved primarily as a source of information for making superior decisions. In addition to protecting the interests of their members, the interest groups frequently make substantive points about proposed regulations and can help prevent agencies from making serious substantive errors in their rules.

Finally, regulatory decision making is also threatened by the classical problem of the capture of regulatory agencies by the very interests they were designed to regulate.[38] Agencies that regulate a single industry have tended to become advocates of their industries, rather than impartial protectors of the public interest. Capture results from the agencies' needs to maintain political support when, especially with independent regulatory commissions, the only logical source of such support is the regulated industry itself. The public is usually too amorphous a body to offer the specific support an agency may need in defending its budget, or its very existence, before Congress. Thus, reforms intended to remove political pressures from regulatory decision making by making the agencies independent only succeed in making the agencies independent of one source of political pressure while making them dependent on another. In Lowi's terminology, the public interest is appropriated for private gain.[39]

The capture argument is less applicable to newer regulatory agencies, which operate across a number of industries, than it is to single-industry regulatory bodies.[40] For example, either the Consumer Products Safety Commission or the Occupational Safety and Health Administration regulates virtually every industry in the country; their advocacy and protection of any one industry might injure other industries. It is generally too difficult for an industry to capture these cross-cutting regulators, and they are therefore more likely to operate "in the public interest." Even then, the agency itself is permitted to define the public interest.

Regulation is a central process in the legitimation of policies, although it is one that many citizens would challenge. Many popular, and academic, writers comment negatively on laws being made by bureaucrats without the direct congressional involvement that those writers consider the essential processes for legitimation.[41] The procedures used are "due," however, and have been ordained by several acts of Congress. In addition, each regulation adopted must have a legislative peg to hang on. But unlike acts of Congress, these regulations tend to make specific judgments and decisions, and by so doing to affect individual interests more directly. Many regulations issued through this process have been criticized as impractical and unnecessary: everyone has his or her favorite silly regulation. Presidents have also been concerned about the effects of regulation on the economy and society and, going as far back as President Ford, have sought to have more deregulation than regulation.[42] But there is still the possibility of greater objectivity and the application of greater objective and scientific "rationality" in the regulatory process than in the more politicized arena of Congress. It may be, in fact, that the very attempt to apply strict criteria for decisions is the source of many objections.

The Courts

Another nonmajoritarian means of legitimating policies is through the courts. Along with the increasing role of the administrative process in legitimation, there has been an increasing involvement of the courts in issuing legitimate policy statements. Some critics have argued that public policy in the United States is indeed dominated by the court system, and not to the benefit of the policies generated.[43] Further, along with complaints against the administrative process, there have been complaints about "judge-made law" as being an illegitimate usurpation of congressional prerogatives. Of course, the courts have been involved in legitimating actions and issuing lawlike statements in the United States for some time. Nevertheless, perhaps because of the increasing litigation involving social issues (e.g., abortion) and the willingness of the courts to make declarations about remedies to remove violations of the Constitution for federal laws, there is a greater popular awareness of the role of the courts in making rules for society.

The courts have as their constitutional basis for making legitimating decisions the supremacy clause, which says that all laws and treaties made in pursuance of the Constitution are the supreme law of the land. In *Marbury* v. *Madison,* Chief Justice John Marshall decided that it was incumbent on the courts to decide whether or not a law conformed to the Constitution and to declare, if it did not, that the law was void. Following from that basic declaration of judicial power, the courts have been able to make rules based on their interpretation of the Constitution. Particularly crucial to their role in legitimating actions is their ability to accept or reject the remedies proposed by parties to particular disputes. If an action is declared unconstitutional, the courts frequently become involved in determining the actions needed to correct that unconstitutionality.

The most obvious examples of courts prescribing remedies to situations they find unconstitutional have been in cases involving school desegregation and prison overcrowding. In several cases, for example *Swann* v. *Charlotte-Mecklenburg Board of Education,*[44] the courts have declared that the existence of boundaries between school districts constitutes an intent on the part of local governments to maintain or create racial segregation of the schools. They then declared that cross-district busing was the logical remedy for the problem. In other cases, the courts have declared that seriously overcrowded prisons constituted cruel and unusual punishment, violating the Eighth Amendment to the Constitution. Judges then decided that they would take over the prison systems and run them directly in order to correct the situation, or they would make very specific policies that state administrators were obliged to follow.[45] These decisions represent greater involvement of the courts in mandating state and local government actions than many citizens consider proper.

The role the courts have accepted for themselves in legitimating action is twofold. In its simplest sense, the courts may further legitimate the actions of other decision makers by declaring that their actions are acceptable under the Constitution. As mentioned earlier, American society appears to be becoming increasingly litigious, so more and more issues are not fully decided until they have been ruled on by the courts. Litigation presents an important means of protecting individual rights in the policymaking process, but it can also slow down greatly the implementation of policy. Putting an issue into the court system is sometimes a means of winning a conflict simply by delay, as the largely successful attempts to block construction of nuclear power plants indicate.

In a second sense, the courts take part in policy legitimation by deciding that certain conditions existing in the society are in contradiction to the Constitution and by then offering a solution to those problems. The role of the courts in school desegregation is an example of this kind of legitimation. This role has been manifested not only in busing cases but also in the entire process of desegregation beginning with *Brown* v. *Board of Education* (1954). The courts have acted relatively independently of other political institutions and have been active in making decisions and offering remedies that they believe are derived from sound constitutional principles. Just as administrative agencies need a legal peg to hang their rulemaking on, so too do the courts need a constitutional peg on which to hang their interventions. Such phrases as due process and equal protection are sufficiently broad, however, to permit a wide scope for judicial involvement in legitimation activity.

Because the role of the courts is to judge the constitutionality of particular actions and to protect individual liberties against possible incursions by government or other individuals, decision making in the courts can be expected to be different from decision making through a legislative body. In many ways, the decisions made by courts are more legitimate than are other legitimating decisions, both because of the courts' connection to constitutional authority and because of the absence of any ready avenue of appeal once appeals through the court system are exhausted. The courts leave less room for compromise and vote trading than does a legislative body, and they have a less clearly defined constituency, if they have any constituency at all. Finally, a court decision is narrower, generally speaking to the particular case in question rather than a general principle of policy to be implemented in other specific cases. These court decisions legitimate certain actions but leave future decisions somewhat ambiguous, whereas decisions taken by both legislatures and administrative agencies are attempts to develop more general principles to guide subsequent actions and decisions.

Popular Legitimation

The three methods of legitimation discussed so far share one common feature: they are all performed by elites through political institutions. A number of American states provide mechanisms for direct democracy that allow voters to legitimate policy decisions.[46] The referendum device constitutes in part a way for state legislatures to "pass the buck" to the people on issues that the legislators believe might be too hot to handle for the good of their future political careers. Also, in some instances the public can use these mechanisms to bypass legislatures entirely or to prod them into action. Despite some agitation, these mechanisms for direct democracy have not been adopted at the federal level.

The majority of states in the United States employ referendums for some policy decisions. Typically, approval of the voters is required to pass bond issues and to change the state constitution. A referendum is a vote of the people on an issue put to them by the legislature or some other authoritative body. Approval by popular vote is required before the measure in question can become law. In some states, in addition to passing bond issues and constitutional changes, referendums are used to enact other legislation. An issue thought by the legislature to be sufficiently important, or highly charged politically, may be put to the voters for a decision. This practice certainly satisfies the tenets of democracy, but it may lead to small numbers—turnout on referendums is low—of relatively uninformed voters deciding about issues of great importance that might be better decided in more deliberative bodies.

The initiative is an even more extreme means of involving the public in policymaking. The initiative allows voters not only to pass on an issue put to them by government but also to place the issue on the ballot themselves. If the requisite number of signatures is obtained, an item can be placed on the ballot at the next election and, if approved by the voters, will become law. A number of significant policy issues—most notably Proposition 13 limiting property taxes and several important environmental laws in California—have been adopted through the initiative process. The initiative has many of the same problems that the referendum has. One difficulty is that complex policy issues such as nuclear power become embroiled in political campaigns so that the complex issues involved become trivialized and converted into simple yes–no questions. The initiative does provide an avenue for the expression of popular opinion, however, and it gives real power to the voters, who often think of themselves as absent from representative policymaking institutions.

In addition to these established mechanisms for popular involvement there is a continuing discussion of additional means of citizen involvement that would go beyond mere voting or public hearings. These mechanisms are usually discussed under the term "discursive democracy," or sometimes "strong democracy."[47] The basic idea is that a true democracy would not confine the role of citizens to selecting their leaders but should extend to the debate and selection of policies. This model has worked in the traditional New England town meeting, and the advocates of expanded participation would like to make it more general. The difficulty is in making it work in a country of 250 million people.

Legitimation is at once the most difficult and the simplest component of the policymaking process. On the one hand, it generally involves the least complex and technical forms of policy analysis, and the number of actors is relatively constrained, unless the initiative and referendum are used. On the other hand, the actors involved are relatively powerful and have well-defined agendas of their own. Consequently, the task of the policy analyst seeking to alter perceptions and create converts to new policies at this stage is difficult. The type of formal evidence used at other stages of the process may not carry much weight at this stage, while political factors become paramount.

The barriers that the policy analyst faces in attempting to push through his or her ideas are sometimes individual and political, as when congressmen must be convinced through partisan analysis or vote trading to accept the analyst's concept of the desirable policy alternative. Conversely, the task may be one of altering substantial organizational constraints, and turf wars, on a decision that would facilitate the appropriate policy response to a particular problem or a whole set of problems. Alternatively, the problem may be a legal one of persuading the courts to respond in the desired fashion to a set of facts and to develop the desired remedy for the perceived problem. Or, finally, the problem may be political in the broadest sense of persuading the voters (through the political masters of the analyst) to accept or reject a particular definition of an issue and its solution. This is a great range of problems for the analyst, and they demand an equally great range of skills.

No individual is likely to have all these skills, but someone must make strategic choices as to which skills are the most appropriate for a particular problem. If the problem is to get a dam built, then Congress is clearly the most appropriate arena; if the problem is a civil rights violation, the best place to begin is probably the court system. If the problem is a specialized environmental issue, then the regulatory process is the appropriate locus for intervention. Policies do not simply happen, they must be made to happen. This is especially true given the degree of inertia existing in American government and the number of points at which action can be blocked. As with so many issues, the major task of the policy analyst may be to define clearly the problem that must be solved. Once that is done, the solution may not be simple, but it is at least potentially analyzable, and a feasible course of action may become more apparent.

Notes

1. Peter G. Brown, *Restoring the Public Trust* (Boston: Beacon Press, 1994); Rodney Barker, *Political Legitimacy and the State* (Oxford: Clarendon Press, 1990).

2. The government of the United Kingdom has suspended civil liberties in Northern Ireland in response to sectarian violence there. For at least a portion of the population, this action has reduced the government's legitimacy. For others, the extreme crisis of sectarian violence and terrorism has justified the action.

3. See, for example, Alan Brinkley, "What's Wrong with American Political Leadership?" *Wilson Quarterly* 18, no. 2 (1994): 46–54.

4. This is to some degree what Aaron Wildavsky meant when he argued that policy analysts must engage in *Speaking Truth to Power* (Boston: Little, Brown, 1979).

5. Arnold J. Meltsner, "Political Feasibility and Policy Analysis," *Public Administration Review* 32 (1972): 859–67; Giandomenico Majone, "The Feasibility of Social Policies," *Policy Sciences* 6 (1975): 49–69.

6. Joel D. Aberbach, *Keeping a Watchful Eye: The Politics of Congressional Oversight* (Washington, D.C.: Brookings Institution, 1991).

7. *Immigration and Naturalization Service* v. *Chadha*, 462 U.S. 919 (1983); see also William West and Joseph Cooper, "The Congressional Veto and Administrative Rulemaking," *Political Science Quarterly* 98 (1983): 285–304.

8. Louis Fisher, "The Legislative Veto: Invalidated, It Survives," *Law and Contemporary Problems* 56 (1993): 273–92.

9. Walter J. Oleszek, *Congressional Procedures and the Policy Process* (Washington, D.C.: CQ Press, 1988).

10. There are, therefore, a number of "veto points," a concept not dissimilar to "clearance points" in implementation theory. See Ellen Immergut, *Health Care Politics* (Cambridge, England: Cambridge University Press, 1992).

11. Charles E. Lindblom and Edward J. Woodhouse, *The Policy-making Process*, 3d ed. (Englewood Cliffs, N.J.: Prentice Hall, 1993).

12. In many ways these programs were more successful in reaching these goals than in reaching the social and housing goals toward which they were nominally directed. See Clarence Stone and Heywood T. Sanders, eds., *The Politics of Urban Development* (Lawrence: University Press of Kansas, 1987).

13. James Buchanan and Gordon Tullock, *The Calculus of Consent* (Ann Arbor: University of Michigan Press, 1962), 120–44.

14. Morris P. Fiorina, *Congress: The Keystone of the Washington Establishment* (New Haven: Yale University Press, 1981).

15. R. Douglas Arnold, *Congress and the Bureaucracy* (New Haven: Yale University Press, 1979).

16. William R. Riker and Peter Ordeshook, *Positive Political Theory* (Englewood Cliffs, N.J.: Prentice Hall, 1973), 97–114.

17. Kenneth Arrow, *Social Choice and Individual Values,* 2d ed. (New York: John Wiley, 1963).

18. Aberbach, *Keeping a Watchful Eye.*

19. These terms come from Mathew McCubbins and Thomas Schwartz, "Congressional Oversight Overlooked: Police Patrols versus Fire Alarms," *American Journal of Political Science* 28 (1984): 165–79.

20. Cornelius M. Kerwin, *Rulemaking: How Government Agencies Write Law and Make Policy* (Washington, D.C.: CQ Press, 1994).

21. Cass R. Sunstein, *After the Rights Revolution* (Cambridge, Mass.: Harvard University Press, 1990), 109.

22. Kerwin, *Rulemaking,* 18–19.

23. Margaret T. Kriz, "Kibitzer with Clout," *National Journal* (30 May 1987): 1404–8.

24. Thomas O. McGarity, *Reinventing Rationality: The Role of Regulatory Analysis in the Federal Bureaucracy* (Cambridge, Mass.: Cambridge University Press, 1991).

25. Viveca Novak, "The New Regulators," *National Journal* (17 July 1993): 1801–4.

26. Martin Shapiro, "APA: Past, Present and Future," *Virginia Law Review* 72 (1986): 447–92.

27. Jerry L. Mashaw, "Prodelegation: Why Administrators Should Make Political Decisions," *Journal of Law, Economics and Organization* 5 (1985): 141–64.

28. Even then, there was a concentration of participation with only a few interest groups taking advantage of this opportunity. See Barry Boyer, "Funding Public Participation in Agency Proceedings: The Federal Trade Commission Experience," *Georgetown Law Journal* 70 (1981): 51–172.

29. See Glen O. Robinson, *American Bureaucracy: Public Choice and Public Law* (Ann Arbor: University of Michigan Press, 1991), 139–47.

30. Stephen Williams, "Hybrid Rulemaking under the Administrative Procedures Act: A Legal and Empirical Analysis," *University of Chicago Law Review* 42 (1975): 401–56.

31. *International Harvester Co. v. Ruckelshaus,* 478 F. 2nd 615 (1973).

32. William Gormley, Jr., *Taming the Bureaucracy* (Princeton: Princeton University Press, 1989), 94–97.

33. Philip Harter, "Negotiated Rulemaking: A Cure for the Malaise," *Georgetown Law Review* 71 (1982): 1–28; Thomas McGarrity, "Some Thoughts on Deossifying the Rulemaking Process," *Duke Law Journal* 41 (1992): 1385–1462.

34. David Pritzker and Deborah Dalton, *Negotiated Rulemaking Sourcebook* (Washington, D.C.: Administrative Conference of the United States, 1990).

35. Philippe C. Schmitter, "Still the Century of Corporatism?" *Review of*

Politics 36 (1974): 85–131.

36. Philippe C. Schmitter, "Corporatism Is Dead: Long Live Corporatism," *Government and Opposition* 24 (1990): 37–53.

37. Mike Mills, "President to Stage Timber Summit," *Congressional Quarterly Weekly Report* 51 (13 March 1993): 593.

38. See Colin S. Diver, "A Theory of Regulatory Enforcement," *Public Policy* 29 (1980): 295–96.

39. Theodore J. Lowi, *The End of Liberalism,* 2d ed. (New York: Norton, 1979).

40. Richard A. Harris and Sidney M. Milkis, *The Politics of Regulatory Change* (New York: Oxford University Press, 1989).

41. David Schoenbrod, *Power without Responsibility* (New Haven: Yale University Press, 1993).

42. Martha Derthick and Paul J. Quirk, *The Politics of Deregulation* (Washington, D.C.: Brookings Institution, 1985).

43. Robert A. Kagan, "Adversarial Legalism and American Government," *Journal of Policy Analysis and Management* 10 (1991): 369–406; Robert J. Samuelson, "Whitewater: The Law as Bludgeon," *International Herald Tribune,* 8 March 1994.

44. *Swann* v. *Charlotte-Mecklenburg Board of Education,* 402 U.S. 1 (1971).

45. Federal Judge Frank Johnson in Alabama literally took over the prisons and mental hospitals of that state. See *Wyatt* v. *Stickney,* 344 F.Supp. 373 (M.D. Ala. 1972) and *Pugh* v. *Locke,* 406 F.Supp. 318 (M.D. Ala. 1976).

46. Thomas J. Cronin, *Direct Democracy* (Cambridge, Mass.: Harvard University Press, 1989).

47. John S. Dryzek, *Discursive Democracy* (Cambridge, England: Cambridge University Press, 1990); Benjamin R. Barber, *Strong Democracy: Participatory Politics in a New Age* (Berkeley: University of California Press, 1984). For a less philosophical discussion, see Phil Duncan, "American Democracy in Search of Debate," *Congressional Quarterly Weekly Report* 51 (16 October 1993): 2850.

5. Organizations and Implementation

Once a piece of legislation or a regulation has been accepted as a legitimate public law, in some ways the easiest portion of the policymaking process has already transpired, for government must then put the legislation into effect. This requires the development of organizations that will apply the principles of the legislation to specific cases, monitor the performance of the policies, and, it is hoped, propose improvements in the content and method of administration of the policy. Even policies that are primarily self-administered or that rely on incentives rather than regulations require some organizational basis for administration, although the organizations can certainly be smaller than those needed for implementing programs that depend on direct administration and supervision. For example, the collection of the income tax, which is largely self-administered, requires many fewer persons for each dollar collected than does collecting revenues from customs duties, even leaving aside the role of customs agents in controlling smuggling.

Traditional American political thinkers have denigrated the roles of public administrators and bureaucrats in policymaking. The traditional attitude has been that policy was made by the legislative body and the administrators were merely to follow the guidelines set forth in the legislation. Such an attitude fails to take into account the important role of administrative decision making and especially the importance of decision makers at the bottom of the organization in determining the effective policies of government.[1] The "real" criminal justice policy of the nation or city is to a great extent determined by the way in which the police enforce the laws, just as the "real" social welfare policy is determined by decisions made by caseworkers or even by receptionists in social service agencies. We have noted that bureaucrats play an important role in interpreting legislation and making regulations; they also play an important role in making decisions while applying laws and regulations to individual cases.[2]

It is also customary to consider government as an undivided entity and to regard government organizations as rather monolithic. In fact, this is not true at all. We have mentioned that American government is divided horizontally into a number of subgovernments and vertically into levels of government in a federal system. But within the federal bureaucracy, and even within single cabinet-level departments, there exist a number of bureaus, offices, and sections, all competing for money, legislative time, and public attention. Each of these organizations has its own goals, ideas, and concepts about how to attack certain problems. As in the making of legislation, these ideas will influence the implementation of legislation. Implementation involves conflicts and competition, rather than neat coordination and control, and struggles over policy go on long after Congress and the president have enacted the legislation. Policies, as operating instruments, commonly emerge from these conflicts, as much as they do from the initial design of legislation. This does not mean that policies should necessarily be shaped in order to be implemented easily, but that anyone interested in policy outcomes must monitor implementation as well as formulation activities.

Dramatis Personae

The organization of the federal government is complicated not only because of the number of organizations but also because of the number of different kinds of organizations. There is no single organizational format for accomplishing the work of government, and the various organizations exist in different relationships to elective officials and even to government authority as a whole. In addition to the three constitutionally designated actors—the president, Congress, and the courts—there are at least eight different organizational formats within the federal government (see table 5.1).[3] One of these is a catchall category containing organizations that are difficult to classify with the other major types. This absence of a basic organizational format tends to lessen central coordination and to contribute to the incoherence of the policy choices made by the federal government. Further, the eight forms of organizations have a great deal of internal variation. As shown in table 5.1, they differ greatly in size; they can also differ greatly in their internal organization. For example, the Department of Agriculture is structured with almost fifty offices and bureaus, while the Department of Housing and Urban Development is structured more around several assistant secretaries and their staffs.

The most familiar forms of organization are the executive departments, such as the Department of Defense and the Department of Health and Human Services. Each of these fourteen departments is headed by a secretary who is a member of the president's cabinet and who is directly responsible to the president. These executive departments should not, however, be regarded as uniform wholes. Instead, they are collections or "holding companies" of relatively autonomous agencies and offices.[4] Departments vary in the extent to which their constituent agencies respond to central direction.

TABLE 5.1

EXAMPLES OF EMPLOYMENT IN FEDERAL ORGANIZATIONS

Kind of organization	Employment
Executive departments	
Department of Defense (civilian)	987,774
Department of Education	5,113
Executive Office of the President	
Office of Management and Budget	550
Office of National Service	1
Legislative organizations	
General Accounting Office	4,604
Biomedical Ethics Board	1
Independent executive agencies	
Environmental Protection Agency	18,196
Appalachian Regional Commission	29
Independent regulatory agencies	
Nuclear Regulatory Commission	3,528
Consumer Products Safety Commission	467
Corporations	
U.S. Postal Service	791,952
Neighborhood Reinvestment Corporation	226
Foundations	
National Science Foundation	1,248
National Endowment for the Arts	274
Other	
Smithsonian Institution	5,514
Office of Government Ethics	93

SOURCE: Office of Management and Budget, *Budget of the United States, 1995.*

Some, such as the Department of Defense, have relatively high degrees of internal coordination; others, such as the Department of Commerce, are extremely decentralized.[5] In some instances, the individual agency may have more political clout than does the department as a whole. One such agency is the Federal Bureau of Investigation (FBI), which is part of the Department of Justice but can often operate as if it were independent. And in some instances it is not entirely clear why agencies are located in one department rather than another, for example, why the U.S. Forest Service is best located in the Department of Agriculture rather than Interior, or why the U.S. Coast

Guard is located in the Department of Transportation rather than Treasury or Defense.[6]

Although the executive departments are linked to constituencies and provide services directly to those constituencies, the organizations within the Executive Office of the President exist to assist the president in carrying out his tasks of control and coordination.[7] The most important units within the Executive Office of the President are the Office of Management and Budget, the Council of Economic Advisers, the National Security Council, the Domestic Policy Council, and the White House Office. The first two assist the president in his role as economic manager and central figure in the budgetary process. The National Security Council provides advice and opinion on foreign and defense issues independent of that provided by the Departments of State and Defense, while the Domestic Policy Council performs a similar role for domestic policy. The White House Office manages the complexities of just being president of the United States and employs a number of personal advisers for the president. The units within the Executive Office of the President now employ almost 1,600 people—an insignificant number compared with a total federal civilian workforce of more than 2 million, but quite large when compared with the personal offices of the chief executives of other nations.[8]

Congress has also created organizations to assist it in its role in policymaking. The three most important legislative organizations are the General Accounting Office (GAO), the Congressional Budget Office, and the Congressional Research Service. Legislatures in democratic political systems generally audit the accounts of the executive to ensure that public money is being spent legally. The General Accounting Office, for most of its existence, has been strictly a financial accounting body. In the 1970s, however, the organization began to expand its concerns to the cost effectiveness of expenditures.[9] For example, in one report the GAO agreed that the Internal Revenue Service (IRS) had been acting perfectly legally in the ways it sought to detect income tax evaders, but recommended changing the IRS program to one the GAO considered more efficient. The Congressional Budget Office has its major policy impact on the preparation of the budget; its role is discussed thoroughly in chapter 6. The Congressional Research Service in the Library of Congress assists Congress in policy research and prepares background material for individual congressmen and committees.

In addition to the executive departments responsible to the president, there are a number of *independent executive agencies*. These organizations perform executive functions, such as implementing a public program, but are independent of the executive departments and generally report directly to the president. There are several reasons for this independence. Some independent executive agencies, such as the National Aeronautics and Space Administration, are mission agencies created outside existing departmental frameworks so as to have enhanced flexibility in completing their mission. Others, like the Environmental Protection Agency or the Small Business Administration, are organized independently to highlight their importance and in recognition of the political power of the interest groups supporting them. Other organizations, such as the General Services Administration and the Office of Personnel Management, provide services to a number of other government departments and locating them in any one department might create management difficulties.

The fifth form of organization is the *independent regulatory commission.* Three such organizations are the Interstate Commerce Commission, the Federal Trade Commission, and the Consumer Products Safety Commission. These commissions are different from independent executive agencies in that they do not perform executive functions but act independently to regulate certain segments of the economy.[10] Once the president has appointed the members of a commission, the application and formulation of regulations are largely beyond his control. The absence of direct political support often results, however, in the "capture" of the regulatory commissions by the interests they were intended to regulate.[11] Over time, lacking ties to the president or Congress, the independent agencies must seek the political support of the regulated interests in order to obtain their budgets, personnel, or legislation from the other institutions in government. The tendency toward capture is not so evident in agencies that cut across several industries—the Federal Trade Commission or Consumer Products Safety Commission, for example.[12] Also, it must be remembered that not all economic regulation is conducted through the independent commissions, and some of the more important regulatory agencies, such as the Occupational Safety and Health Administration (OSHA) and the Food and Drug Administration (FDA), are in executive departments; OSHA is in the Department of Labor, and the FDA is part of Health and Human Services.

The government of the United States has generally avoided becoming directly involved in the economy other than through regulations, but there are a number of *public corporations* in the federal government.[13] For example, since 1972 the U.S. Postal Service has been a public corporation rather than part of an executive department, which it was before. This public corporation employs about 700,000 people, or almost one-third of all federal civilian employees. Another public corporation, the Tennessee Valley Authority, has about 6 percent of the total electrical generating capacity of the United States. Some public corporations are very small, however. The Overseas Private Investment Corporation, for instance, employs only 100 people. Public corporations are organized much like private corporations, with a board of directors and stock issued for capitalization. The principal difference is that the board members are all public appointees and the stock is generally held entirely by the Department of the Treasury or by another executive department. There are several reasons for choosing the corporate form of organization. One is that these organizations provide marketed goods and services to the population and hence can be better managed as commercial concerns.[14] Also, this is a means of keeping some government functions at arm's length so that the president and Congress are not held directly responsible for their actions.

There are also several foundations within the federal government, the principal examples being the National Science Foundation, the National Endowment for the Humanities, and the National Endowment for the Arts. The foundation is intended primarily to separate the organization from the remainder of government. This is done because of a justifiable fear of creating a national orthodoxy in the arts or in science and thereby stifling creativity. The use of the more independent foundation enables government to support the activities while being removed from the decisions. This isolation is far from complete, as Congress has not been reluctant to intervene in the decisions of foundations, most notably in decisions of the National Endowment for the Arts that conservatives allege supported "pornography."[15]

In addition to the wholly owned government corporations described here, there is also a group of organizations described as "quasi governmental" or as being in the "twilight zone." Examples of these organizations are the National Railroad Passenger Corporation (Amtrak), the Corporation for Public Broadcasting, and the Federal Reserve Board. These organizations have some attributes of public organizations (most important, access to public funding), but they also have some attributes of private organizations. They are similar to public corporations except that a portion of their board of directors is appointed by private-sector organizations, just as the board of Amtrak is appointed in part by the member railroad corporations. Also, not all their stock may be owned by the public sector, as is true for wholly owned corporations; instead, some may be owned by the cooperating private-sector organizations. For example, a portion of the stock of COMSAT (Communications Satellite Corporation) may be held by communication common carriers.[16] Finally, employees of these quasi-governmental organizations are frequently not classified as public employees, and they generally are not subject to other regulations, such as the Freedom of Information Act.

The justification for the formation of quasi-governmental organizations such as these is, again, to allow government to become involved in a policy area without assuming any real or apparent direct control. The federal government clearly subsidizes certain activities—passenger railroad service would almost certainly have vanished in the United States without the formation of Amtrak—but this intervention is not as obvious as other forms of intervention. Also, intervention by an organization of this sort gives the public a greater role in decision making and provides greater representation of private interests such as the affected corporations. And, as with the Corporation for Public Broadcasting, this form of organization permits the federal government to become involved in an area from which it has traditionally been excluded.

It is important to understand just how vital these quasi-governmental organizations are to the federal government. For example, the Federal Reserve Board fits comfortably into this twilight zone, given its isolation from executive authority and its relationship to its member banks. But the Federal Reserve Board is responsible for making monetary policy for the United States and thereby has a significant—if not the most significant—influence on this nation's economic conditions. Similarly, Amtrak has received massive subsidies, and the public sector has no firm control over its policies, yet it is a significant element in national transportation, just as the Corporation for Public Broadcasting is a significant complement to commercial radio and television broadcasting.[17]

Finally, there is a catchall category of *other organizations*. One component of this category is the intergovernmental organizations—the Advisory Commission on Intergovernmental Relations, for example, or any one of the various regional commissions. Other organizations, including various claims commissions and the Administrative Conference of the United States, operate on the fringe of the judicial process. Finally, organizations such as the Smithsonian Institution, the National Academy of Sciences, and the American Red Cross are mentioned in federal legislation and receive subsidies, but they are far removed from the mainstream of government.

We should note several other points about the complexity of the organizational structure of the federal government. One is the redundancy that has been built into the system of organization. First, both Congress (through the Congressional Budget Office) and the Executive Office of the President (through the Office of Management and Budget) have offices to deal with budgeting and with many other aspects of government. Because of the doctrine of separation of powers, such duplication makes a great deal of sense, but this still conflicts with conventional managerial thinking concerning duplicative functions. Second, within the federal executive branch itself, we have seen that some units in the Executive Office of the President duplicate activities of the executive departments. Most notably, presidents appear to demand foreign policy advice other than that provided by the Departments of State and Defense, and they get it from the National Security Council. This demand may be justified, as those departments have existing policy commitments and ideas that may limit their ability to respond to presidential initiatives in foreign policy. But during at least every administration since Richard Nixon, conflicts have arisen between the two sets of institutions, and the management of foreign policy may suffer as a result. In most instances, this conflict has been perceived as a conflict between the experienced professionals in the Department of State and committed amateurs in the National Security Council. In other areas more than one federal organization may have a regulatory function. For example, both the Federal Trade Commission and the Antitrust Division of the Department of Justice are concerned with monopolies.[18] Some redundancy can be rationalized as a means of limiting error and providing alternative means for accomplishing the same tasks.[19] But if the redundant institutions are occupied by ambitious men and women, the potential for conflict and "gridlock" is great.[20]

It is also interesting to note that not all central management functions for the federal government are located in the Executive Office of the President. Several important central functions—monetary policy, personnel policy, debt management, and taxation—are managed by agencies outside the president's office and in one instance by an organization in the twilight zone. This is a definite limitation on the ability of the president to implement his policy priorities and consequently to control the federal establishment for which he is responsible.

Third, we have mentioned the variations in the "publicness" of organizations in the federal government. Some organizations are clearly public: they receive their funds from allocations in the federal budget; their employees are hired through public personnel systems; and they are subject to legislation such as the Freedom of Information Act, which attempts to differentiate public from private programs.[21] Other organizations described appear tied to the private sector as much as to government: they receive some or all of their funds as fees for service or interest on loans, they have their own personnel policies, and they are only slightly more subject to normal restrictions on public organizations than is General Motors. Again, for a president—who will be held accountable to voters and to Congress for the performance of the federal government—this presents an immense and perhaps insoluble problem. How can the president really take responsibility when so many of the organizations responsible for his policies are beyond effective control? This is but one of many difficulties a president encounters when he attempts to put his policies into effect; it also serves as a bridge to our discussion of implementation.

Implementation

All the organizations described earlier are established to assist in some way the execution of legislation or the monitoring of that execution. Once enacted, laws do not go into effect by themselves, as was assumed by those in the (presumed) tradition of Woodrow Wilson, who discussed "mere administration."[22] In fact, one of the most important things to understand about government is that it is a minor miracle that implementation is ever accomplished. There are so many more ways of blocking intended actions than there are of making results materialize that all legislators should be pleased if they live to see their pet projects not only passed into law but actually put into effect. Although this is perhaps an excessively negative attitude toward the implementation process, it should underline the extreme difficulties of administering and implementing public programs.

Policies do not fail on their own, however, and a large number of factors may limit the ability of a political system to put policies into effect. Rarely will all these factors affect any single policy, but all must be considered when designing a policy and attempting to translate that policy choice into real services for citizens. Further, any one of them may be sufficient to cause failure, or suboptimal performance by a policy, while all may have to be in good order for the policy to work. In short, it is much easier to prevent a policy from working than it is to make the policy effective.

The Legislation

The first factor that will affect the ability of a policy to be effectively implemented is the nature of the legislation. Laws vary according to their specificity, clarity, and the policy areas they attempt to influence. They also differ in the extent to which they bind the individuals and organizations charged with implementing them in the way the writers intended. Unfortunately, both legislators and analysts sometimes overlook the importance of the legislation. Also, laws that are easier to implement are, everything else being equal, more difficult to pass. Their specificity may make it clear who the winners and losers are and make building the necessary coalition that much more difficult.

Policy Issues

Legislators frequently choose to legislate in policy areas where there is not enough information about causal processes to enable them to make good policy choices. Although they may have the best intentions, their efforts are unlikely to succeed if they make only stabs in the dark in attempting to solve difficult problems. If we refer to the figure used in discussing policy formulation (figure 3.1, p. 65), we can estimate the likelihood of effective implementation of a policy. We anticipate that the highest probability of effective implementation will occur when we have both sufficient information about the policy area and an adequate knowledge of the causes of the problems. In such situations, governments can design legislation to solve, or at least ameliorate, the problem under attack. Likewise, we would expect little likelihood of effective implementation in policy areas where there is inadequate information and little knowledge of the causes of the problem.

The other two possible combinations of knowledge of causation and information may differ very little in their likelihood of effective implementation, although we would expect a somewhat better probability of implementation when there is a knowledge of the patterns of causation as opposed to more basic information. If the underlying process is understood, it would appear possible to formulate policy responses based on poor information, even if those responses involve a certain amount of overkill and excessive reaction. If the underlying process is misunderstood or is not understood at all, there is little hope of effectively implementing a policy choice, except by pure luck. In this instance, governments often wind up treating the symptoms, as they do with the problem of crime and delinquency, instead of dealing with the underlying social processes.

Perhaps the best example of a large-scale policy formulation and implementation in spite of inadequate knowledge of patterns of causation was the war on poverty in the United States. There were (and are) as many theories about the causes of poverty as there were theorists, but there was little real understanding even of the basics of the economic and social dynamics producing the problem. Thus, war was declared on an enemy that was poorly understood. Daniel P. Moynihan put it this way:

> This is the essential fact: The Government did not know what it was doing. It had a theory. Or rather a set of theories. Nothing more. The U.S. Government at this time was no more in possession of a confident knowledge as to how to prevent delinquency, cure anomie, or overcome that mid-morning sense of powerlessness than it was the possessor of a dependable formula for motivating Vietnamese villagers to fight Communism.[23]

Not only was it a war, but it was a war that appeared to be based on something approaching a dogma about the plan of attack—for example, the use of large-scale and rather expensive programs involving direct services to clients. Arguably, these programs were doomed to fail as soon as they were adopted because they were based on dubious assumptions about the operations of society and the mechanisms for approaching such problems. But they had the political appeal and visibility that smaller-scale efforts would have lacked.

An even more extreme example of a policy made without adequate knowledge was the Clean Air Act of 1970 (see chapter 12). The sponsors of this legislation were, in fact, quite sure that they did not understand the processes and that the technology for producing the environmental cleanup they legislated did not exist. This legislation was designed to force the development of the technology for improving the environment. To some extent, the same was true of the space program, which did not have a sure technology for accomplishing its goals when President John Kennedy pledged to place an American on the moon by the end of the decade. This is an interesting if somewhat novel approach to designing public programs, but it is not one that can be recommended as the usual strategy. It could work, in part because the problems being dealt with were part of the physical world, rather than the more complex social and economic realities that governments often face.[24] All this should not be taken to mean that governments should just keep to their well-worn paths and do what they have always done in the ways they have always done it. Instead, it is intended to demonstrate that if one expects significant results from programs based on insufficient understanding of the subject matter of the legislation, one's hopes are likely to be dashed frequently.

Political Setting

Legislation is adopted through political action, and the political process may plant within legislation the seeds of its own destruction. The very compromises and negotiations necessary to pass legislation may ultimately make it impossible to implement. The implementation problem becomes especially evident when the construction of the necessary coalition forces logrolling and tradeoffs among competing interests and competing purposes in the legislation.

The effects of the political process of legislation are manifested in different ways. One is the vagueness of the language in which the legislation is written. This lack of clarity may be essential to developing a coalition for the passage of legislation, as every time a vague term is made specific, potential coalition members are excluded. But by phrasing legislation in vague and inoffensive language, legislators run the risk of making their intent unclear to those who must implement the laws and of allowing the implementers to alter the entire meaning of the program substantially. Terms such as "maximum feasible participation," "equality of educational opportunity," "special needs of educationally deprived students," and that favorite vague term, "public interest," are all subject to a number of different interpretations, many of which could betray the true intent of the legislators. For example, the rather vague language of Social Security legislation from 1962 to 1972 provided for open-ended grants for "improved services" for citizens.[25] The assumption was that additional services would be provided with this money. Instead, quite contrary to the intent of the drafters of the legislation, the money was used to subsidize existing programs and provide fiscal relief for state budgets. These grants also grew much more rapidly than had been anticipated when states found ways of using them to shift a substantial portion of their social service expenditures to the federal government. Even words about which most citizens can agree may be sufficiently vague to produce problems during implementation, as when the Reagan administration attempted to include ketchup as a "vegetable" under the School Lunch Program.[26]

In addition to coalitions formed for the passage of a single piece of legislation, other coalitions may have to be formed across several pieces of legislation: the classic approach to logrolling. In order to gain support for one favored piece of legislation a coalition-building legislator may have to trade his or her support on other pieces of legislation. In some instances, this may simply increase the overall volume of legislation enacted. In others, it may involve the passage of legislation that negates or decreases the effects of desired legislation. Some coalitions that must be formed are regional, so it may become virtually impossible to give one region an advantage, which may be justified by economic circumstances, without making commensurate concessions to other regions, thereby nullifying the intended advantages. It is also difficult to make legislative decisions that are redistributive across economic classes; either the legislation will be watered down to be distributive (giving everyone a piece of the pie) or additional legislation will be passed to spread the benefits more broadly. Both General Revenue Sharing and the Elementary and Secondary Education Act are examples of this tendency.

Similar problems of vagueness and even logrolling can occur when other institutions make rulings that must be implemented. In a number of instances a judicial decision, intended to mandate a certain action, has been so vague as to be difficult or impossible to implement. One of the best examples of this lack of clarity is the famous decision of Brown v. Board of Education, which ordered schools to desegregate with "all deliberate speed." Two of those three words, "deliberate" and "speed," appear somewhat contradictory, and the decision did not specify exactly what the phrase meant. Similarly, the police are prohibited from searching an individual, an automobile they stop, or a home without "probable cause," but that term is left largely undefined. Further, the process of writing regulations in administrative agencies, intended to clarify and specify legislation, can itself create ambiguities that require more regulations to clarify and more delay in implementing the decisions.

In summary, politics is central to the formulation of legislation, but the results are such that the legislation cannot be implemented effectively. The compromises necessitated by political feasibility may result in just the reductions in clarity and purpose that make laws too diffuse to be implemented so as to have a real effect on society.

Interest-Group Liberalism

Related to the problem of vagueness and the problem of the involvement of government in policy areas about which it lacks knowledge of causation is Theodore J. Lowi's concern regarding government involvement in abstract aspects of human behavior.[27] Lowi's argument is that the United States has progressed from concerted and specific legislation such as the Interstate Commerce Act of 1887, which established clear standards of practice for the Interstate Commerce Commission, to abstract and general standards, such as "unfair competition" in the Clayton Act of 1914. This tendency has been extended through even more general and diffuse aspects of human behavior, in the attempts of social legislation following the 1960s to regulate what Lowi refers to as the "environment of conduct." It is simply more difficult to show that a person has discriminated against another person on the basis of race, color, or sex than it is to show that a railroad has violated prohibitions against discriminatory freight rates.

Lowi believes that the problems in these vague laws arise, not from their commendable intentions, but from the difficulties of implementing them. The diffuseness of the targets specified and the difficulty of defining standards open policies attempting to regulate those behaviors to errors in interpretation during implementation. Further, it becomes more difficult to hold government accountable when it administers ambiguous legislation. The interest-group liberalism inherent in American politics, in which the public interest tends to be defined in terms of many private interests, means that implementation of legislation will generally differ greatly from the intentions of those who framed the legislation. Implementation will be undertaken by agencies that are themselves tied to clients and to particular definitions of the public interest and that will not want to be swayed from their position by a piece of legislation. The difficulties in accountability and the deviations of policies in practice from the intentions of their framers can only alienate the clients and frustrate the legislator, and perhaps the administrators.

The Organizational Setting

As noted earlier, most implementation is undertaken by organizations, especially organizations in the public bureaucracy. Given the nature of public organizations, and organizations in general, the probability that such an organization will effectively implement a program is not particularly high—not because of any venality on the part of the bureaucracy or the bureaucrats but simply because the internal dynamics of large organizations often limit their ability to respond to policy changes and implement new or altered programs.

To begin to understand what goes wrong when organizations attempt to implement programs, a model of "perfect" administration may be useful. Christopher Hood points to five characteristics "perfect" administration of public programs would have:

1. Administration would be unitary; it would be one vast army all marching to the same drummer.
2. The norms and rules of administration would be uniform throughout the organization.
3. There would be no resistance to commands.
4. There would be perfect information and communication within the organization.
5. There would be adequate time to implement the program.[28]

Clearly these conditions are often absent in organizations attempting to implement programs, and almost never are all of them present. Governments depend on large organizations to implement their policies, and consequently, difficulties arise in administration and implementation. These difficulties need not be insurmountable, but they do need to be understood, and if possible anticipated, if successful implementation is to occur. Just what characteristics and difficulties in organizations lead to difficulties in implementation?

Organizational Disunity

Organizations are rarely unitary administrations. Instead, a number of points of disunity are almost inherent in organizational structures. One aspect of organizational disunity that affects implementation is the disjunction between central offices of organizations and their field staffs. Decisions may be made by politicians and administrators sitting in national capitals, but those decisions must be implemented by field staff members who may not share the same values and goals as the administrators in the home office. This disjunction of values may take several forms. A change in central values and programs may occur, perhaps as a result of a change in presidents or in Congress, and the field staff may remain loyal to the older policies. For example, the field staff, and indeed much of the central staff, of the Department of Health, Education, and Welfare regarded the Nixon administration as a temporary phenomenon and remained loyal to the more liberal social values of previous Democratic presidents.[29] This was true despite pressures from above for changes in policies. Much the same has been true of the staffs of the Environmental Protection Agency and the Department of the Interior under the Reagan and Bush administrations' apparent retreats on environmental issues.[30] More recently, the Clinton administration has inherited a government shaped for twelve years by Republican presidents.[31] Such problems with field staffs over policy changes produce frustration for politicians nominally in control of policies and make the implementation of policies that violate the norms of the existing field staffs extremely difficult.

A more common disparity between the goals of field staffs and those of the home office may occur as the field staff is "captured" by clients. Field staff members are frequently close to their clients, and they may adopt the perspective of their clients in their relationships with the remainder of the organization.[32] This is especially true when the clients are relatively disadvantaged and the organization is attempting either to assist them or to exercise some control over them. The identification of staff members with their clients is fostered by frequent contact, sympathy, empathy, and quite commonly by genuine devotion to a perceived mission that is in contrast to the mission fostered by the central office. For whatever reason, this identification does make the implementation of centrally determined policy difficult.

In many ways, government in recent years has promoted its own difficulties when using field staffs to implement policy. The requirement for community participation in decision making in many urban social service programs further lessens the control of central organizations over the implementation of programs. Developing community organizations that fulfill the requirements for participation is a major focus for pressures to divert the program toward more locally determined priorities, including successful efforts to say "Not in My Backyard" (NIMBY).[33] Even when community organizations are not used to implement programs, requirements for local participation can make it more difficult for agencies to do what they had planned.[34]

Arguably, community participation has been less effective than was intended and at worst has been a facade for control by bureaucracies, but to the extent that it has been successful, it may well have made implementation less successful. Further, even in policy areas where community participation has not been so directly fostered by government, either the lessons learned from community participation elsewhere or the general climate favoring participation has produced greater activity by individuals and communities affected by policies. A whole range of programs—including decisions by the Army Corps of Engineers about project siting, the construction of portions of the Interstate Highway System, and most dramatically the siting of nuclear waste facilities—have been seriously affected by local participation.[35]

Field staffs may also find that if they are to perform their tasks effectively, they cannot follow all the directives coming to them from the center of the organization. In such instances, in order to get substantive compliance the organization members may not comply with procedural directives. For example, in a classic study of the FBI, Blau noted that field agents frequently did not comply with directives requiring them to report the offering of a bribe by a suspect.[36] The agents had found that they could use the offer of a bribe to gain greater cooperation from the subject because at any time they could have the person prosecuted for offering the bribe. Their performance of the task of prosecuting criminals was probably enhanced, but it was done at the expense of the directive from the central office. More recently, Bardach and Kagan have argued that regulatory enforcement could be improved if the field staff were granted greater latitude.[37] They believe that rigidities resulting from strict central controls actually produce less compliance with the spirit of the regulations than would a more flexible approach.

Standard Operating Procedures

Organizations develop standard operating procedures (SOPs) to respond to policy problems. When a prospective client walks into a social service agency, the agency follows a standard pattern of response: certain forms must be filled out, certain personnel interview the prospective client, specific criteria are used to determine the person's eligibility for benefits. Likewise, if a "blip" appears on the radar screen of a defense installation, a certain set of procedures is followed to determine if the blip is real and, if so, whether it is friendly or hostile. If it should be hostile, further prespecified actions are taken.

Standard operating procedures are important for organizations. They reduce the amount of time spent processing each new situation and developing a response. The SOPs are the learned response of the organization to certain problems; they represent to some extent the organizational memory in action. SOPs may also be important for clients, as they are adopted at least in part to ensure equality and fairness for clients. Without SOPs, organizations might respond more slowly to each situation, they might respond less effectively, and they would probably respond more erratically.

Although SOPs are certainly important and generally beneficial, they can act as barriers to good implementation. This is most obvious when a new policy or a new approach to an existing policy is being considered. Organizations are likely to persist in defining policies and problems in their standard manner, even when the old definition or procedure no longer helps fulfill the mission of the agency. For example, when the Medicare program was added to the responsibilities of the Social Security Administration, the agency was faced with an entirely new set of concerns in addition to its traditional task of making payments to individuals. In particular, it assumed responsibility for limiting the costs of medical care. It chose, however, to undertake this responsibility in much the same way that it would have attempted to manage problems arising from pensions—by examining individual claims and denying those that appeared to be unjustified. It took the

Social Security Administration some time to focus attention on more fundamental and systemic problems of medical cost inflation and to develop programs like Diagnostic Related Groupings (DRGs) (see chapter 9). It required the Social Security Administration some time even to cope with adding the Supplemental Security Income program, which was much closer to its original portfolio of income-maintenance policies.[38]

Thus there is a need for designing programs and organizations that will more consistently reassess their goals and the methods they use to reach those goals. In some instances, for example the number of births and the future need for schools, the response should be programmed to be almost automatic; other situations will require more thought and greater political involvement. Organizations do not like to perform these reassessments; they threaten both the employees of the organizations and their clients. One reason for creating organizations with standard operating procedures is to ensure some stability and predictability, but that stability can become a barrier to success when problems and needs in the issue area change.

Standard operating procedures also tend to produce inappropriate or delayed responses to crises. Many stories about the slowness or apparent stupidity of the military came from the Cuban missile crisis, and similar stories probably would have come from other military encounters if they had been as well documented. The military, perhaps more than any other organization, tends to employ SOPs and to train its members to carry through with those procedures in the absence of commands to the contrary. In this way, the military can be sure of a certain reaction even when there is no direct link to the command structure. John Kennedy found that although he was nominally in charge of the armed forces of the United States, many things occurred that he had not ordered, and he realized that they were happening simply because they were standard procedures. In several instances, things that "just happened" threatened to generate overt conflict with the Soviets, while the president was doing everything possible to bring about a peaceful resolution of the crisis. More recently, the brief invasion of Grenada (1983) encountered difficulties when the communication SOPs of the navy and army did not correspond, and the soldiers on the island could not communicate with the ships providing them support. Soldiers found the best way to communicate was to use their telephone credit cards to call the Pentagon which would then communicate with the navy.

One standard means of avoiding the effects of SOPs in a new program is to create a new organization. When the Small Business Administration was created in 1953, it was purposely not placed in the Department of Commerce, whose SOPs tended to favor big business. The Office of National Drug Control Policy was established within the Executive Office of the President to ensure both its priority and its independence from other organizations, such as the Drug Enforcement Agency and the Customs Bureau. There are, of course, limits to the number of new organizations that can be set up, for the more that are created, the more chance there will be of interorganizational barriers to implementation replacing the barriers internal to any one organization. Drug policy, for example, suffers from coordination problems among the numerous agencies (the three mentioned above as well as the coast guard, the Department of Defense, the FBI, and so forth) all involved in the policy area.

Paradoxically, SOPs aid in the implementation of established programs, whereas they are likely to be barriers to change and to the implementation of new programs. Likewise, they may be too standard to allow response to nonstandard situations, or to nonstandard clients, thereby creating rigidity and extremely inappropriate responses to novel situations. Organizations tend to try to classify new problems as old problems as long as they can, and to continue to use familiar responses even when the problems are, to an outsider, demonstrably different.

Organizational Communication

Another barrier to effective implementation is the improper flow of information within organizations. Because government organizations depend heavily on the flow of information—just as manufacturers rely on the flow of raw materials—accurate information and the prevention of blockages of information are extremely important to the success of these public organizations. Unfortunately organizations, and particularly public organizations, are subject to inaccurate and blocked communication.

In general, information in bureaucracies tends to be concentrated at the bottom of the hierarchies.[39] The field staffs of organizations are in closer contact with the environment of the organization, and technical experts tend to be clustered at the bottom of organizations, with more general managers concentrated at the top. This means that if the organization is to be guided by changes in its environment and if it is to make good technical decisions, the information at the bottom must be transmitted to the top and then directions must be passed back down to the bottom for implementation. Unfortunately, the more levels through which information has to be transmitted, the greater the probability that the information will be distorted. This distortion may result from random error or from selective distortion. Selective distortion results when officials at each stage attempt to transmit only the information they believe their superiors wish to hear or the information they think will make them look good to their superiors. And the superiors, in turn, may attempt to estimate what sort of distortion their subordinates may have passed on and at least try to correct for that distortion.[40] The result of this transmitting of messages through a hierarchical organization frequently is rampant distortion and misinformation that limits the ability of the organization to take effective implementation decisions.

Certain characteristics of the organization may improve the transmission of information through its hierarchy. Clearly, if all members of an organization "speak the same language," less distortion of communication should occur. In other words, if organization members share common technical or professional backgrounds, their communication with one another should be less distorted. Their ability to communicate effectively with other organizations, however, may be diminished. In addition, attempts on the part of the organization to create internal unity through training and socialization should also improve internal patterns of communication. Finally, the "flatter" the organization (i.e., the fewer levels through which communication must go before being acted on), the less distortion is likely to occur.

Another way to improve communication in organizations is to create more, and redundant, channels. For example, President Franklin Roosevelt developed personal ties to lower-level members of organizations and placed his own people in organizations to be sure that he would receive direct and unvarnished reports from the operating levels of government.[41] Alternatively, a president or manager might build in several channels of communication in order to receive messages and to serve as checks on one another. Again, Franklin Roosevelt's development of parallel organizations (e.g., the Works Progress Administration and the Public Works Administration) provided him with alternative channels of information about the progress of his New Deal programs. In more contemporary times, the development of several channels of advice and communication to the president about national security policy and drug policy may be a way of ensuring that the information he receives is accurate and complete.

One particular threat to effective organizational communication is secrecy.[42] While a certain level of secrecy is understood to be important for some government organizations, secrecy also may inhibit both communication and implementation. Secrecy frequently means that a communication may not be transmitted because it has been classified; other parts of the organization or other organizations are consequently denied needed information. Again, the Cuban missile crisis offered numerous examples of how the military's penchant for secrecy prevented a rapid response to situations. Also, secrecy may produce inefficiency, as when FBI agents must spend a great deal of time reporting on one another when they infiltrate subversive organizations such as the Ku Klux Klan. Of course, to make themselves more acceptable to the organizations they have infiltrated, the agents tend to be among the most vociferous members and consequently are the subjects of a disproportionate share of reports from other agents. More recently, the Central Intelligence Agency's (CIA's) discovery of spies within its midst was slowed because different parts of the organization would not share information with other parts. Finally, secrecy may be counterproductive even when it is justified. For example, one argument holds that the interests of military deterrence are best served by fully informing an adversary of the full extent of one's arsenal, instead of masking its strength—uncertainty may only create a willingness to gamble on the strength of the opponent. Openness may thus prevent war. This logic may be particularly applicable in a nuclear age, when every major power has the ability to destroy the world several times over.

In modern organizations knowledge is power, and the inability of an organization to gather and process information from its environment will certainly be a serious detriment to its performance. Clearly the management of communication flows within an organization is an important component of taking raw information and putting it into action. Most organizations, however, face massive problems in performing even this simple, or apparently simple, task and as a consequence do not implement their programs effectively. Their own internal hierarchical structures, the differential commitment to goals, and the differences in professional languages all conspire to make organizational communication more difficult than it may appear from the outside.

Time Problems

Related to the problem of information management in the implementation of policies is the problem of time. Hood points to two time problems that inhibit the ability of public organizations to respond to situations in their policy environments. One is a linear time problem in which the responses of implementing organizations tend to lag behind the need for the response.[43] This often happens in organizations that have learned their lessons too well and that base their responses on previous learning rather than current conditions. This problem is somewhat similar to the problem of standard operating procedures, but it has less to do with processing individual cases and more to do with designing the mechanisms for putting new programs into effect. Organizations frequently implement programs to deal with a crisis that has just passed, rather than with the crisis they currently face or might soon face. To some degree the American armed forces in Vietnam used the lessons they had learned, or thought they had learned, in World War II and the Korean war. Unfortunately for them, a highly mechanized, technologically sophisticated, and logistically dependent fighting force broke down in a tropical, guerrilla war. Another example of this problem is the slow response of American elementary and secondary school systems to the baby booms that followed World War II and the Korean war. Virtually everyone knew that the children had indeed been born and would have to be educated, but few educators attempted to prepare for their arrival in the school systems or to construct the physical facilities or train the teachers they would require.

Other time problems are cyclical, and delayed implementation, instead of solving problems, may actually contribute to them. This is especially important in making and implementing macroeconomic policy in which, even if the information available to a decision maker is timely and accurate, a delay in response may exaggerate economic fluctuations. If a decision maker responds to a threatened increase in inflation by reducing money supplies or reducing expenditures, and if that response is delayed for a year, or even for a few months, it may only increase an economic slowdown resulting basically from other causes. Thus it is not sufficient merely to be right; an effective policy must be both correct and on time if it is to have the desired effect.

Horse-Shoe-Nail Problems and Public Planning

The final organizational problem in implementation arises when organizations plan their activities incompletely or inaccurately. Hood calls these "horse-shoe-nail" problems because the failure to provide the nail results in the eventual loss of the horse and, eventually, the battle.[44] And because government organizations often must plan for implementation with no access to information and no cues to the necessary choices, problems of this kind are likely to arise in the public sector. Examples of this problem abound: passing requirements to inspect coal mines, but failing to hire inspectors; requiring clients to fill out certain forms, but neglecting to have the forms printed; forgetting to stop construction of a $160 million highway tunnel leading to nowhere. There are countless examples of this political and policy version of Murphy's law.[45]

To ensure effective management and implementation, planners must identify the crucial potential blockages, or "nails," in their organization and allow for them in their planning. Clearly, with a new program or policy, this planning may be extremely difficult, as the problems that will arise are almost impossible to anticipate. Some planners use these difficulties to justify using incrementalism or experimentation when introducing new policies. Instead of undertaking large projects with the possibility of equally large failures, they may undertake smaller projects for which any failures or unanticipated difficulties would impose minimal costs but would help prepare the organization to implement full-scale projects. The problem, of course, is that the programs often are not permitted to grow sufficiently to reach an effective level but may remain small and "experimental."

But some programs will be effective only if they are on a large scale and comprehensive. Schulman's analysis of the National Aeronautics and Space Administration points out that a program like the space program—designed to reach a major goal within a limited amount of time and with an engineering as opposed to a pure research focus—must be large scale in order to be effective.[46] Similarly, it has been argued that the war on poverty, instead of being the failure portrayed in the conventional wisdom, actually was never tried on a scale that might have made it effective. In contrast, the so-called war on cancer was implemented as if it were a program that required a centralized, mission format. In reality, it required a more decentralized structure to allow scientific research to pursue as many avenues as possible.[47] Those who design programs and organizations must be very careful to develop programs to match the characteristics of the problem and the state of knowledge concerning the subject.

Interorganizational Politics

Few if any policies are designed and implemented by a "single lonely organization" in the 1990s.[48] Certainly individual organizations have their problems, but many more problems are encountered in the design of implementation structures or the pattern of interactions among organizations as they attempt to implement a policy. The problems of organizational disunity and communication become exaggerated when the individuals involved are not bound even by a presumed loyalty to a single organization but have competing loyalties to different organizations, not all of which may be interested in the effective implementation of a particular program. This may be exaggerated when private contractors are a central element in implementation, and their goals of profit and contract fulfillment conflict with goals of service delivery and accountability in the public sector.

Pressman and Wildavsky, who popularized the concern for implementation, speak of the problems of implementing policies through a number of organizations (or even within a single organization) as problems of "clearance points," defined as the number of individual decision points that must be agreed to before any policy intentions can be translated into action.[49] Even if the decision makers at each "clearance point" are favorably disposed toward the program in question, there may still be impediments to their agreement. Some problems may be legal, some may be budgetary, and others may involve building coalitions with other organizations or interests in the society. Statistically, one would expect that if each decision point is independent of the others and if the probability of any individual decision maker's agreeing to the program is 90 percent (.9), then the probability of any two agreeing is 81 percent (.9 × .9); and for three points, the probability would be 73 percent (.9 × .9 × .9); and so forth. Pressman and Wildavsky determined that there were at a minimum seventy clearance points in the implementation of the Economic Development Administration's decision to become involved in public works projects in Oakland, California.[50] With this number of clearance points, the probability of all of them agreeing, given an average probability of 90 percent for each clearance, is less than one in a thousand. Only if there were a probability greater than 99 percent at each clearance point would the odds in favor of implementation be greater than 50–50. Of course, implementation is not just a problem of statistics, and the political and administrative leaders involved in the process can vastly alter the probabilities at each stage. With so many independent clearance points and limited political resources, however, a leader may well be tempted to succumb to the inertia inherent in the implementation system.

Judith Bowen has argued that the simple statistical model proposed by Pressman and Wildavsky may understate the probabilities of successful implementation.[51] She points out that if persistence is permitted, and each clearance point can be assaulted a number of times, the chances for successful implementation increase significantly. She also explains that the clearance points may not be independent, as assumed, and that success at one clearance point may produce an increased probability of success at subsequent steps. Similarly, the clever implementer can make strategic choices about which clearance points to try first, and how to package the points so that some success can be gained even if the whole campaign is not won. Thus, while successful implementation is still not perceived to be a simple task, it is subject to manipulation, as are other stages of the policy process. The clever policy analyst therefore can improve his or her probabilities of success by understanding how to intervene most effectively.

Vertical Implementation Structures

One problem in implementation occurs vertically within the hierarchical structures of government. I have described some problems of intergovernmental relations in the United States associated with the several levels of governments, all of which may well be involved in the implementation of a single piece of legislation. The impact of intergovernmental relations is especially evident for federal social and urban legislation in which all three levels of government may be involved in putting a single piece of federal legislation into effect. For example, Title XX of the Social Security Amendments of 1972 called for the availability of day-care services for poor working mothers. These services were to be funded through the Social Security Administration in Washington but implemented through state and local governments. For the typical poor child to receive day care supported by the federal government, the Social Security Administration must agree to give a grant for the proposed program to a local government. But this money will be channeled through the state government, which will issue regulations to carry out the intentions of the program within the structure of the particular state government. The grant money is then transferred to the local government. But the local government can rarely provide the day care itself; instead, it contracts with day-care providers (usually private) to provide the services. The local government will have to monitor the standards and contract compliance of the private-service providers and ensure that no federal policy guidelines are violated. Even that regulation may differ substantially from state to state or local government to local government.[52]

Such a vertical implementation structure can give rise to several possibilities for inadequate implementation or no implementation. One problem could result from simple partisan politics, when the local government and the federal government are controlled by different political parties and consequently have different policy priorities. Or localities may, for other reasons, have different policy priorities than does the federal government and may choose to implement programs differently than the federal government desires. Two good examples of these differences can be seen in the resistance of local governments to federally mandated scattering of public housing projects in middle-class neighborhoods and in the resistance of most state and local governments to federal proposals to locate nuclear waste disposal facilities in their territory. Even if local governments want to do what the federal government would have them do, they sometimes lack the resources to do so. For example, local governments have attempted to resist various federal mandates, such as the Water Pollution Control Act of 1972 and day-care quality standards, claiming they lacked the funds to meet the standards imposed.[53] Also, the states and localities may have few incentives to comply with federal directives. For example, in the Elementary and Secondary Education Act of 1965 the states were to receive their grants merely for participating in the program, without having to do anything in particular to improve education. When easy money is available, there is little or no reason, other than good faith and a desire to encourage good government, to comply with federal regulations.

Horizontal Implementation Structures

In addition to difficulties in producing compliance across several levels of government, difficulties may occur in coordinating activities and organizations horizontally. That is, the success of one agency's program may require the cooperation of other organizations, or at least the effective coordination of their activities. One classic example of the difficulties in bringing about this kind of coordination was the Model Cities program of the war on poverty. A major purpose of the Model Cities program was to coordinate the activities of the numerous social service agencies serving the model neighborhoods. Even with the existence of an umbrella organization such as the Model Cities agency in each city, coordination was difficult to achieve. And in the absence of such a coordinating mechanism, effective coordination may be virtually impossible.

The breakdown of coordination can come about in several ways. One is through language and encoding difficulties. Individual agencies hire certain kinds of professionals and train all their employees in a certain manner. As a result, the housing experts in the Model Cities program decided that the problems of residents resulted from substandard housing, whereas employment experts thought that the problems arose from unemployment. Psychiatric social workers, however, perceived the problems as resulting from personality problems. Each group of professionals, in other words, found it difficult to understand the perspectives of the other groups, and consequently found it difficult to cooperate in treating the "whole client"—one of the stated objectives of the program. This was strongly demonstrated in the pattern of referrals among agencies. The vast majority of referrals of clients from one agency to another occurred within policy areas rather than across policy areas.[54] A client who visited an agency seeking health-care services would frequently be referred to another agency, most commonly another health-care agency. Clients would much less frequently be referred to social welfare agencies for assistance in receiving funds to provide better nutrition, which might have been as effective as medical care in improving clients' health. Agencies tend to label and classify clients as belonging in their own policy areas; they often do not refer clients broadly or provide services for the client's whole range of needs. The perceptual blinders of organizations and their members prevent them from seeing all the client's needs, and their training as professionals makes it difficult for service providers to shake off their blinders.

The lack of control among agencies and the consequent deficiencies in the implementation of programs may also occur because the objectives of one organization conflict with those of one or more other organizations. Agencies have to live, and to live they require money and personnel. Thus, at a basic level an organization may not be willing to cooperate in the implementation of a program simply because the success of another agency may threaten its own future prospects. On a somewhat higher plane, organizations may disagree about the purposes of government and about the best ways to achieve the goals about which they do agree. Or an agency may simply want to receive credit for providing a service that inevitably involves the cooperation of many organizations and, by insisting on receiving credit, may prevent anything from happening. For example, several law enforcement agencies knew about a major drug shipment, but they allowed it to slip through their fingers simply because they could not agree about which of the "cooperating" agencies would make the actual arrest and receive the media attention.

Finally, a simple failure to coordinate may prevent effective implementation. This is the result of oversight and failure to understand the linkages among programs; it is not a result of language problems or an attempt to protect an organization's turf. Even if a program can be implemented without adequate coordination with other agencies, its effectiveness may be limited, or substantial duplication of efforts may result. Most citizens have heard their share of horror stories about the same streets being dug up and repaired in successive weeks by different city departments and by private utilities. Equally horrific stories are told of reporting requirements issued by a variety of federal agencies that use contradictory definitions of terms or that involve excessive duplication of effort by citizens. Venality is rarely at the root of these problems, but that does not prevent the loss of efficiency or make citizens any happier about the management of their government.

Coordination of programs appears to have become more difficult during the 1980s and 1990s. As the public sector has begun to rely more on the private sector to deliver public programs, and to use state and local governments to deliver these services, it has become more difficult to provide integrated services. This is true despite widespread pressure to make the public sector more "user friendly" and "customer oriented."[55] Further, effective coordination is becoming increasingly important as their interactions become more evident. For example, social programs are becoming increasingly dependent on effective job-training programs, and economic success is becoming increasingly dependent on educational policy.

From the Bottom Up?

It has been argued that many of the problems encountered with implementation are a function of their being considered from a "top-down" perspective.[56] That is, the person judging evaluation looks at what happens to a law and considers that the bureaucracies have failed because they have not produced outcomes exactly like those intended by the framers of the legislation. The assumption here, rather like Hood's, is that bureaucracies should march to a single drummer, and that the drummer should be Congress or the president. Expecting such an orderly approach to governance and implementation may be expecting too much from American government, given its complexity and the multiple and competing interests organized into the system. Indeed, the appropriate question may be in what policy areas can we accept the slippage between goals and outcomes, and what can be done to produce greater compliance in the most sensitive areas.[57]

An alternative to the "top-down" perspective is to think of implementation from the "bottom up," or through "backward mapping."[58] This argues that the people who design public programs should think about the ease, or even possibility, of implementation as they design the program. Also, programs should take into account the interests of the lower echelons of the bureaucracy, their contacts with the program's clients, and indeed the values and desires of the clients themselves. With these factors in mind, policy-makers should then design a set of policies that can be readily implemented. Such a program may not fulfill all the goals that the policy formulators had originally, but it will be able to gain a high degree of compliance and, in the eyes of the advocates of this approach, ultimately gain more than a program based on strict legal norms of compliance and autonomy of policy formulators.

The "bottom-up" concept of implementation and program design is appealing. It promises rather easy victories in the complicated wars involved in making programs work. Even if these promises could be fulfilled, however, and there must be some reasonable doubts, there are other important problems with this approach. The most important is the normative problem that political leaders and their policy advisers have the responsibility (and usually the desire) to formulate programs that meet their political goals and fulfill the promises made in political campaigns.[59] Programs that are easily implementable may not meet those goals. This is perhaps especially true when conservative administrations attempt to implement changes in social programs through field staffs committed to more liberal goals, or when liberals attempt to implement expansionary economic policies through more conservative economic institutions inside and outside government. Governments may wind up doing what they can do, or what they have always done, rather than what they want to do.

In addition, the ability of agency field staffs to define what is "feasible" may allow them substantially greater control over policy than may be desirable within a democratic political system. Their definition of feasibility also may be excessively conservative and with proper design the options available for government may be much greater. Finally, there is as yet little reliable evidence about what really is feasible in implementation terms and what is really impossible.[60] Too facile definitions of feasibility may undervalue the abilities and leadership of politicians and administrators alike.

Summary

American government is a massive, complex, and often confusing set of institutions. It has many organizations, but lacks any central organizing principle. Much of the structure of American government was developed on an ad hoc basis to address particular problems at particular times. Even with a more coherent structure, many of the same problems might still arise when there is an attempt to implement a program. Many problems are inherent in any government, although they are certainly exacerbated by the complexity and diffusion of the structure of American government. For public policy, implementation is a vital step in the process of governing because it involves putting programs into action and producing effects for citizens. The difficulty in producing desired effects, or indeed any effects, then, means that policy is a much more difficult commodity to deliver to citizens than is commonly believed. The barriers to effective implementation commonly discourage individuals and organizations from engaging in the activities devised for their benefit. Public management then becomes a matter of threatening or cajoling organizations into complying with stated objectives, or a matter of convincing those organizations that what they want to accomplish can best be accomplished through the programs that have been authorized.

Notes

1. Michael Lipsky, *Street Level Bureaucracy* (New York: Russell Sage, 1980).

2. Gary Bryner, *Bureaucratic Discretion* (New York: Pergamon, 1987).

3. See U.S. Senate, Committee on Governmental Affairs, *The Federal Executive Establishment: Evolution and Trends* (Washington, D.C.: Government Printing Office, 1980), 23–63.

4. Harold Seidman and Robert S. Gilmour, *Politics, Position and Power,* 4th ed. (New York: Oxford University Press, 1986).

5. The degree of central control in Defense can be exaggerated. See C. Kenneth Allard, *Command, Control, and the Common Defense* (New Haven: Yale University Press, 1990).

6. At various times in its history the coast guard has been in those other two departments.

7. John Hart, *The Presidential Branch,* 2d ed. (Chatham, N.J.: Chatham House, 1995).

8. George W. Jones, *West European Prime Ministers* (London: Frank Cass, 1991).

9. Frederick C. Mosher, *The GAO* (Boulder, Colo.: Westview, 1979); Ray C. Rist, *Program Evaluation and Management of Government* (New Brunswick, N.J.: Transaction, 1990).

10. Marc Allan Eisner, *Regulatory Politics in Transition* (Baltimore: Johns Hopkins University Press, 1993).

11. The classic statement is Samuel P. Huntington, "The Marasmus of the ICC," *Yale Law Review,* April 1952, 467–509. For a very different perspective, see Jonathan R. Mezey, "Organizational Design and Political Control of Administrative Agencies," *Journal of Law, Economics and Organization* 8 (1992): 93–110.

12. In addition, the growth of the consumer movement has placed additional pressures on regulatory agencies to escape capture. See Michael D. Reagan, *Regulation: The Politics of Policy* (Boston: Little, Brown, 1987).

13. Annemarie Hauck Walsh, *Managing the Public's Business* (Cambridge, Mass.: MIT Press, 1980), 41–44.

14. Richard Rose et al., *Public Employment in Western Nations* (Cambridge, England: Cambridge University Press, 1985).

15. Michael Dorf, "Artifactions: The Battle over the National Endowment for the Arts," *Brookings Review* (Winter 1993): 32–35.

16. Herman Schwartz, "Governmentally Appointed Directors in a Private Corporation—the Communications Satellite Act of 1962," *Harvard Law Review*, December 1961, 341–65.

17. Seidman and Gilmour, *Politics, Position and Power*, 274.

18. Marc Allan Eisner, *Antitrust and the Triumph of Economics* (Chapel Hill: University of North Carolina Press, 1992).

19. Martin Landau, "The Rationality of Redundancy," *Public Administration Review* 29 (1969): 346–58; Jonathan R. Bendor, *Parallel Politics* (Berkeley: University of California Press, 1985).

20. James L. Sundquist, "Needed: A Political Theory for a New Era of Coalition Government in the United States," *Political Science Quarterly* 108 (1988): 613–35.

21. U.S. Senate, Committee on Governmental Affairs, *Federal Executive Establishment* (Washington, D.C.: Government Printing Office, 1980), 27–30.

22. Woodrow Wilson, "The Study of Administration," *Political Science Quarterly* 1 (1887): 197–222.

23. Daniel Patrick Moynihan, *The Politics of Guaranteed Income* (New York: Vintage, 1973), 240.

24. That difference is discussed well in Richard R. Nelson, *The Moon and the Ghetto* (New York: Norton, 1977).

25. Robert B. Stevens, ed., *Income Security: Statutory History of the United States* (New York: McGraw-Hill, 1970), 639–59.

26. That decision eventually was rescinded.

27. Theodore J. Lowi, *The End of Liberalism,* 2d ed. (New York: Norton, 1979), 42–63.

28. Christopher Hood, *The Limits of Administration* (New York: Wiley, 1976).

29. Ronald Randall, "Presidential Power versus Bureaucratic Intransigence: The Influence of the Nixon Administration on Welfare Policy," *American Political Science Review* 73 (1979): 795–810.

30. Paul R. Portney, "Natural Resources and the Environment," in *The Reagan Record,* ed. John Palmer and Isabel Sawhill (Washington, D.C.: Urban Institute Press, 1984).

31. Burt Solomon, "'Twixt Cup and Lip," *National Journal* (24 October 1992): 2410–15.

32. A classic description of the dangers of this occurring is found in Herbert Kaufman, *The Forest Ranger* (Baltimore: Johns Hopkins University Press, 1960).

33. Jan Horah and Heather Scott, *NIMBYs and LULUs (Not-in-My-Back-Yard and Locally-Unwanted-Land-Use)* (Chicago: Council of Planning Librarians, 1993).

34. See Jack DeSario and Stuart Langton, *Citizen Participation in Public Decision Making* (New York: Greenwood, 1987).

35. See Ortwin Renn, Thomas Webler, Horst Rakel, Peter Dienel, and Branden Johnson, "Public Participation in Decision Making: A Three-Step Procedure," *Policy Sciences* 26 (1993): 189–214.

36. Peter M. Blau, *The Dynamics of Bureaucracy* (Chicago: University of Chicago Press, 1955), 184–93.

37. Eugene Bardach and Robert A. Kagan, *Going by the Book: The Problem of Regulatory Unreasonableness* (Philadelphia: Temple University Press, 1982).

38. Martha A. Derthick, *Agency under Stress: The Social Security Administration in American Government* (Washington, D.C.: Brookings Institution, 1990).

39. Arthur Stinchcombe, *Information and Organizations* (Berkeley: University of California Press, 1990).

40. James G. March and Herbert A. Simon, *Organizations* (New York: John Wiley, 1958).

41. James MacGregor Burns, *Roosevelt: The Lion and the Fox* (New York: Harcourt, Brace, 1956).

42. Harold Wilensky, *Organizational Intelligence* (New York: Basic Books, 1967), 130–45.

43. Hood, *The Limits of Administration*, 85–87.

44. Ibid., 192–97.

45. For a good compilation, see Peter Hall, *Great Planning Disasters* (London: Weidenfield and Nicolson, 1980).

46. Paul R. Schulman, *Large-Scale Policy Analysis* (New York: Elsevier, 1980).

47. Richard A. Rettig, *Cancer Crusade* (Princeton: Princeton University Press, 1977).

48. Benny Hjern and David O. Porter, "Implementation Structures: A New Unit of Organisational Analysis," *Organisation Studies* 2 (1981): 211–28.

49. Jeffrey L. Pressman and Aaron Wildavsky, *Implementation* (Berkeley: University of Calfornia Press, 1979).

50. Ibid.

51. Judith Bowen, "The Pressman-Wildavsky Paradox," *Journal of Public Policy* 2 (1982): 1–22; Ernst Alexander, "Improbable Implementation: The Pressman-Wildavsky Paradox Revisited," *Journal of Public Policy* 9 (1989): 451–65.

52. Peter J. May, "Mandate Design and Implementation: Enhancing Implementation Efforts and Shaping Regulatory Policy," *Journal of Policy Analysis and Management* 12 (1993): 634–63.

53. William T. Gormley, "Regulating Mr. Rogers's Neighborhood: The Dilemmas of Day Care Regulation," *Brookings Review* 8 (1990): 21–28.

54. R. Lewis Bowman, Eleanor C. Main, and B. Guy Peters, "Coordination in the Atlanta Model Cities Program," Department of Political Science, Emory University, 1971. Mimeo.

55. Jon Pierre, "The Marketization of the State: Citizens, Consumers and the Emergence of Public Markets" in *Governance in a Changing Environment,* ed. Donald Savoie and B. Guy Peters (Montreal: McGill/Queens University

Press, 1995).

56. Richard F. Elmore, "Backward Mapping and Implementation Research and Policy Decisions," in *Studying Implementation,* ed. Walter Williams (Chatham, N.J.: Chatham House, 1984).

57. M. Kiviniemi, "Public Policies and Their Targets: A Typology of the Concept of Implementation," *International Social Science Quarterly* 108 (1986): 251–65.

58. Elmore, "Backward Mapping"; Paul A. Sabatier, "Top-Down and Bottom-Up Models of Policy Implementation: A Critical Analysis and Suggested Synthesis," *Journal of Public Policy* 6 (1986): 21–48; Stephen H. Linder and B. Guy Peters, "Implementation as a Guide to Policy Formulation: A Question of 'When' Rather Than 'Whether,'" *International Review of Administrative Sciences* 55 (1989): 631–52.

59. Linder and Peters, "Implementation as a Guide."

60. Giandomenico Majone, "The Feasibility of Social Policies," *Policy Sciences* 6 (1975): 49–69.

BUDGET

BUDGET OF THE UNITED STATES GOVERNMENT

Fiscal Year 1996

6. Budgeting: Allocation and Public Policy

To implement public policies, government requires money as well as institutional structures. The budgetary process provides the means of allocating the available resources of government among the competing interests to which they could be applied. In principle, all resources in the society are available to government, although in the United States a politician who openly advocated such a position probably would not last a day. Likewise, all the purposes for which politicians and administrators wish to spend the money have some merits. The question is whether those purposes are sufficiently meritorious to justify using the resources in the public sector instead of putting them to other possible uses in the private sector. Finding answers to questions requires economic and analytical judgment, as well as political estimates of the feasibility of the actions being approved.

Two different aspects of budgeting sometimes merge. One is the question of system-level allocation between the public and private sectors: How many activities or problems justify government intervention into the economy for the purpose of taxing and spending?[1] Could the best interest of society as a whole be served by keeping the money in the hands of businesses or individuals for investment decisions and allowing some potentially beneficial programs in government to go unfunded? Or do the equity, equality, and economic growth potentially produced through a public project justify the use of political capital by officials to pass and collect an additional tax or to increase an existing tax? During the 1980s and 1990s the system-level questions also came to include the extent to which government should finance its expenditures with taxes and fees, or, to say it another way, how large a deficit can the United States afford to run?

The second major budgeting question is this: how should available public-sector resources be allocated among competing programs? When they devise a budget, decision makers function within definite resource constraints and must base their decisions on the assumption that no more revenues will come in (or that no larger deficit will be accepted). Decision makers must therefore attempt to apportion the available amount of money for the greatest social, economic, and political benefit. This is not an easy task, of course, because of differing opinions about what uses of the money would be best. In addition, decision makers are often constrained by commitments to fund existing entitlement programs, such as Social Security, before they can begin to allocate the rest of the funds to other worthy programs. Because money can be divided almost infinitely, however, it offers a medium for resolving social conflicts that indivisible forms of public benefit, such as rights, often do not. Therefore, although there are a number of possible justifications for budgetary decisions, we must be aware that political considerations tend to dominate and that many of the most effective arguments revolve around votes and coming elections.

Characteristics of the Federal Budget

Before we discuss the budget cycle through which the federal budget is constructed each year, several fundamental features of that budget should be explained. These features have a number of benefits for decision makers in the federal government but also constrain them and at times help create undesirable outcomes. There are, therefore, attempts at one time or another to reform almost all these features of the budgetary process. Those reform efforts also encounter resistance by the interests advantaged by the status quo, and the process as well as the content of budgeting as part of the political debate.

An Executive Budget

The federal budget is an executive budget, prepared by the president and his staff, approved by Congress, and then executed by the president and the executive branch. This has not always been the case; before 1921, the federal budget was a legislative budget, prepared almost entirely by Congress and then executed by the president. One major tenet of the reform movement in the early twentieth century was that an executive budget was a necessity for more effective management in government. In that doctrine, no executive should be required to manage a budget that he or she had no part in planning.

The passage of the Budget and Accounting Act of 1921 marked the beginning of a conflict between the executive and legislative branches over their respective powers in the budgetary process.[2] In general, budgetary power has accumulated in the executive branch and in the Executive Office of the President, in large part because of the analytical dominance of the Office of Management and Budget (called the Bureau of the Budget until 1971). The excesses of the Nixon administration, and to some degree those of the Johnson administration during the Vietnam war, led to the development of the Congressional Budget Office as a part of the Congressional Budget and Impoundment Control Act of 1974. This office provides Congress with much of the analytical capability of the executive branch, just as the development of the budget committees in both houses gives Congress greater control over budgeting than it had before the passage of the act in 1974. More recently, negotiations with President Bush over the fiscal year 1991 budget gave Congress more responsibility in framing budget options.[3] Congress, however, is still very much in the position of responding to budgetary initiatives from the White House.

Line Item

Despite several attempts at reform, the federal budget remains a line-item budget. That is, the final budget document appropriating funds allocates those funds into categories—wages and salaries, supplies, travel, equipment, and so forth. These traditional categories are extremely useful in that they give Congress some control over the executive branch. Moneys are appropriated for agencies and are allocated for specific purposes within the agency. It is then rather easy for the legislature, through the General Accounting Office, to make sure that the money is spent under legal authority.[4] But it is difficult to determine if the money was spent efficiently and effectively. Also, the rigidities of the line-item budget may prevent good managers in government from managing effectively by limiting how they can spend the money. It may be that more equipment and less personnel can do the same job better or more cheaply or both, but managers generally are not given that option. Critics have argued that it would be better to give a manager a relatively unrestricted budget and then judge him or her on the achievement of program goals with that money. Congress, however, tends to want to maximize its oversight over the executive instead of managerial flexibility.

An Annual Budget

The federal budget is primarily an annual budget. Agencies are now required to submit five-year expenditure forecasts associated with each of their expenditure plans, but this is primarily for management purposes within the Office of Management and Budget (OMB). The budget presented to Congress and eventually the appropriations bills of Congress together constitute only a one-year expenditure plan. The absence of a more complete multiyear budget makes planning difficult for federal managers and does not necessarily alert Congress to the long-term implications of expenditure decisions made in any one year. A small expenditure in one year may result in much larger expenditures in subsequent years and create clientele who cannot be eliminated without significant political repercussions. Conversely, a project that would have to run several years to be truly effective may be terminated after a single year. Many state and local governments in the United States now operate with multiyear budgets, but the federal government still does not. The annual advice from OMB to the agencies as a guide for preparing budgets provides some information about expectations for five years, but the information for the four "out years" is speculative at best.

One of the several recommendations of the Gore Commission (the National Performance Review) was to go to a biennial budget.[5] The logic behind this is to enable organizations to plan more effectively and therefore to deliver services more efficiently. Further, this reform might enable Congress to reduce the amount of time it has to spend on the budget and enable it to spend more time performing its other legislative duties. Again, however, Congress does not appear to be very excited about this reform, one that might lessen its control over the organizations within the executive branch. Likewise, there has been little enthusiasm for capital budgeting.[6]

The Budget Cycle

Each year there must be a new budget, and an annual cycle has evolved for the appropriation and expenditure of available public moneys. The repetitive nature of the budget cycle is important, for the agency officials involved might behave differently if they did not know that they have to come back year after year to get more money from the same OMB officials and the same congressmen. In addition to the emphasis this repetition places on trust and dependability, it allows policy entrepreneurs multiple opportunities to build their cases for new programs and changes in budgetary allocations.

Setting the Parameters: The President and His Friends

Most of this chapter discusses the micro-level allocation of resources among programs rather than the setting of broad expenditure and economic management policy. It is necessary, however, to begin with a brief discussion of decisions concerning overall levels of expenditures and revenues. The budget process is initiated by a number of decisions about total spending levels, and those decisions about parameters influence subsequent decisions about programs. Inevitably changes in particular programs and socioeconomic conditions (wars, recessions, etc.) will influence the overall spending levels of government, so this stage is largely one of setting targets, not making final decisions.

One of the first official acts of the budget cycle is the development, each spring, of estimates of the total size of the federal budget to be prepared for the fiscal year. Although the agencies and the OMB will already have begun to discuss and prepare expenditure plans, the letter from the president through the OMB (usually in June) is an important first step in the formal process. This letter is a statement of overall presidential budgetary strategy and of the financial limits within which the agencies should begin to prepare their budgets. In addition to setting the overall parameters, this letter will present more detailed information on how those parameters apply to individual agencies. Also, the past experience of budgeting officials in each agency should give them some idea of how to interpret the general parameters.

Alice Rivlin

Defense agencies, for example, knew during the era of the Cold War that they were not necessarily bound by those parameters, whereas planners of domestic programs with little client support and few friends on Capitol Hill could only hope to do as well as the letter had led them to believe they might.

The overall estimates for spending are prepared some sixteen months before the budget is to go into effect. For example, the fiscal year 1992 budget went into effect on 1 October 1991, but the planning for that budget began in June 1990 or earlier. For any budget, this means that the economic forecasts on which the expenditure estimates are based may be far from the prevailing economic reality when the budget is actually executed. Changes away from those economic forecasts are important. The recession of 1991, for example, meant a reduction in revenues and an increase in expenditures; people who are out of work do not pay income and Social Security taxes and they demand unemployment insurance payments and perhaps welfare. As well as being important, these economic forecasts are not entirely the product of technical considerations; they are also influenced by political and ideological considerations. For example, during the first years of the Reagan administration the belief that "supply side" economics would produce larger revenues through an upswing in economic activity led to a serious overestimation of the amount of revenues. This, in turn, was the beginning of the large federal deficits that have come to be a continuing feature of American public finance.[7] In the early 1990s the belief by the Bush administration that the recession would be short-lived also produced larger actual deficits than those promised in budget documents.

The preparation of economic and expenditure estimates is the result of the interaction of three principal actors: the Council of Economic Advisers (CEA), the OMB, and the Treasury. Collectively, these three are referred to as the "troika."[8] The CEA is, as the name implies, a group of economists who advise the president. Organizationally, they are located in the Executive Office of the President. The role of the CEA is largely technical, forecasting the state of the economy and advising the president on the basis of these forecasts. They also mathematically model the probable effects of certain budgetary choices on the economy. Of course, the economics of the CEA must be tempered with political judgment, for mathematical models and economists do not run for office—but presidents must. One chairman of the Council of Economic Advisers in the Reagan administration said that he relied on his "visceral computer" for some of the more important predictions.[9]

The OMB, despite its image as a budget-controlling organization, comes as close to a representative of the expenditure community as exists within the troika. Even though the agencies whose budgets OMB supervises find it difficult to perceive the OMB as a kindly benefactor, some of its personnel may be favorably disposed toward expenditures. They see the huge volume of agency requests coming forward, and they are aware of the large volume of "uncontrollable" expenditures (e.g., Social Security benefits) that will have to be appropriated regardless of changes in economic circumstances. These considerations of commitments and inertia were not as important under the Reagan and Bush administrations as during previous administrations, in part because of the political commitment of several directors of the OMB to the cause of reducing federal expenditures. The Clinton administration is also grappling with the problem of entitlement spending.[10] This in part reflects the fear that these programs will swamp the entire budget process and in part because the administration wants some latitude to launch new programs.

Finally, the Treasury represents the financial community, and historically it has been the major advocate of a balanced budget within the troika. The Treasury, through issuing government bonds, must cover any debts created by a deficit. The principal interest of the Treasury in troika negotiations may be to preserve the confidence of the financial community at home and abroad in the soundness of the U.S. economy and the government's management of that economy. Some particular (and increasing) concerns of the Treasury may be relationships with international financial organizations, such as the International Monetary Fund, that are important for the funding of the continuing deficits in the federal budget.

Even at this first step in the budgetary process, a great deal of hard political and economic bargaining occurs. Each member of the troika must compete for the attention of the president as well as protect the interests of the particular professional, organizational, and political community it represents. But this is just the beginning of a long series of bargains as agencies attempt to get the money they want and need from the budgetary process.

Agency Requests

As in so much American policymaking, the agency is a central actor in the budgetary process.[11] Whether working independently or in a cabinet-level department, the agency is primarily responsible for the preparation of estimates and requests for funding. The agency makes these preparations in conjunction with the OMB and, if applicable, with the agency's executive department budgeting personnel. During the preparation of estimates, OMB provides guidance and advice concerning total levels of expenditures and particular aspects of the agency's budget. Likewise, the agency may have to coordinate its activities with those of other agencies of the executive department in which it is located. It would do this through a departmental budget committee and the secretary's staff. This coordination is necessary to ensure that the agency is operating within the priorities of the president and the cabinet secretary and to ensure support from the secretary in defending the budget to OMB and Congress.

The task of the agency in the budgetary process is to be aggressive in seeking to expand its own expenditure base but at the same time recognize that it is only one part of a larger organization.[12] In other words, the agency must be aggressive but reasonable, seeking more money but realizing that it operates within the constraints of what the federal government as a whole can afford. Likewise, the executive department must recognize its responsibilities to the president and his program and to agencies under its umbrella. The cabinet secretary must be a major spokesperson for his or her agencies in the higher levels of government, but at the same time agencies often have more direct support from interest groups and perhaps from Congress than does the department as a whole. Thus, a cabinet secretary may not be able to go far in following the president's program if that would seriously jeopardize ongoing programs, and their clienteles, in the department. This problem is reflective of the general fragmentation of American government, with much of the real power and the operational connections between government and the interest groups being at the agency, rather than the department, level.

An agency may employ a number of strategies in seeking to expand its level of funding, but the use of these strategies is restrained by the knowledge that budgeting is an annual cycle. Any strategic choice in a single year may preclude the use of that strategy in later years and, perhaps more important, may destroy any confidence that OMB and Congress had in the agency.[13] For example, an agency may employ the "camel's nose" or "thin wedge" strategy to get a program funded at a modest level in its first year with the knowledge that the program will have rapidly increasing expenditure requirements. Even if that strategy is successful once, that agency may be assured that any future requests for new spending authority will be carefully scrutinized. Therefore, agencies may be well advised to pursue careful, long-term strategies and develop trust among the political leaders who determine their budgets.

Executive Review

After the agency has decided on its requests, it passes them on to the OMB for review. The OMB is a presidential agency, and one of its principal tasks is to amass all the agency requests and make them conform to presidential policy priorities and to the overall levels of expenditures desired. This may make for a tight fit, as some spending programs are difficult or impossible to control, leaving little space for any new programs the president may consider important. The more conservative presidents of the past decade also have found it difficult to make overall spending levels conform with their views that government should tax and spend less.[14]

After OMB receives the estimates, it passes them on to its budget examiners for review. In the rare case in which an agency has actually requested the amount, or less than the amount, that OMB had planned to give it, there is no problem. In most cases, however, the examiners must depend on their experience with the agency in question, as well as whatever information about programs and projected expenditures they can collect, to make a judgment concerning the necessity and priority of any requested expenditure increases. And, as with so many decisions about public finance, much depends on the trust that has developed among individuals across time. In this case, the examiners spend a great deal of their time in the agencies they supervise and may adopt a stance more favorable to the agency than might be expected, given the image of OMB as a tough budget-cutting organization.

On the basis of agency requests and the information developed by the examiner, OMB holds hearings, usually in October or November. At these hearings the agency must defend its requests before the examiner and other members of the OMB staff. Although OMB sometimes seems to be committed to cutting expenditures, several factors prevent it from wielding its ax with excessive vigor. First, it is frequently not difficult for the agency to pull an "end run" on the hearing board and to appeal to the director of OMB, the president, or ultimately to its friends in Congress. Also, some budget examiners tend, over time, to favor the agencies they are supposed to control, so at times they may be advocates of an agency's requests rather than the fiscal conservatives they are expected to be. This is a pattern not dissimilar to that of regulatory "capture," described in chapter 4.

The results of the hearing are forwarded to the director of OMB for the "director's review," which involves all the top staff of the bureau. At this stage, through additional trimming and negotiation, the staff tries to pare the final budget down to the amount desired by the president. After each portion of the budget goes through the director's review, it is then forwarded to the president for final review and then for compilation into the final budget document. This stage necessarily involves final appeals from agency and department personnel to OMB and the president as well as last-minute adjustments to take into account unanticipated changes in economic fore-casts and desired changes in the total size of the budget. The presidential budget is then prepared for January delivery to Congress within fifteen days after it convenes. Presidents differ in the amount of time they devote to budgeting, but the budget is perceived as a statement of the priorities of the president and his administration, even if it is really prepared by OMB.

In this way the presidential budget is made ready to be reviewed for ap-propriations by Congress, but the two branches will already have begun to communicate about the budget. By 10 November of each year the president must submit to Congress the "current services budget," which includes "proposed budget authority and estimated outlays that would be included in the budget for the ensuing fiscal year . . . if all programs and activities were carried on at the same level as the fiscal year in progress."[15] This is a form of "volume budgeting" inasmuch as it budgets for a constant volume of public services.[16] Given the rate of inflation in the 1970s and early 1980s, this con-stant-service budget gives Congress an early warning of the anticipated size of current expenditure commitments if they are extended. But these esti-mates are subject to substantial inaccuracy, either purposive or accidental. They provide Congress with a rough estimate for planning purposes, but only that.

Congressional Action

Although Congress is specifically granted the powers of the purse in the Constitution, by the 1960s and 1970s it had clearly ceased to be the domi-nant actor in making budgetary decisions. Congress has attempted a coun-terattack, largely through the Congressional Budget and Impoundment Con-trol Act of 1974. Among other provisions, this act established in each house of Congress a budget committee to be responsible for developing two con-current resolutions each year outlining fiscal policy constraints on expendi-tures, much as the troika does in the executive branch. The act also estab-lished the Congressional Budget Office to provide the budget committees with a staff capacity analogous to that which OMB provides the president.[17] This enhanced analytic capacity is important for Congress in understanding its budgetary activity, but the need to implement somewhat more immediate and less analytic expenditure reforms has tended to make these changes less important than they might otherwise have been.

Decisions on how to allocate total spending among agencies and programs are made by the appropriations committees in both houses.[18] These are extremely prestigious and powerful committees, and those serving on them are veteran members of Congress. Members tend to remain on these committees for long periods, thereby developing not only budgetary expertise but also political ties with the agencies they supervise as well as with their own constituencies.[19] These two committees, and especially the House Appropriations Committee, do most of their work in subcommittees. These subcommittees may cover one executive department, such as Defense, or a number of agencies, such as Housing and Urban Development and independent executive agencies, or a function, such as public works. Most important, the whole committee does not closely scrutinize the decisions of its subcommittees, nor does the House of Representatives as a whole frequently reverse the decisions of its appropriations committee.

Scrutiny by the whole House has increased, in large part because of the general opening of congressional deliberations to more "sunshine," or public scrutiny. In addition, the politics of deficit reduction has tended to place greater restraints on committee and subcommittee autonomy. The committees must now submit appropriation levels that correspond to the total spending levels permitted under the joint resolutions on taxing and spending. Provided that the committees can stay within those predetermined levels, they have substantial autonomy; once an agency's budget has been agreed to in a subcommittee, that budget, in all probability, has been largely decided.[20]

Beginning with the presidential recommendations, each subcommittee develops an appropriations bill, or occasionally two, for a total of thirteen or fourteen each year. Hearings are held, and agency personnel are summoned to testify and to justify the size of their desired appropriation. After those hearings, the subcommittee will "mark up" the bill—make such changes as it feels are necessary from the original proposals—and then submit it, first to the entire committee and then to the House of Representatives. In accordance with the Congressional Budget Act, the appropriations committees are expected to have a completed mark-up of all appropriations bills before submitting the first for final passage, so as to have a better overall idea of the level of expenditure that would be approved. The Senate follows a similar procedure, and any differences between the two houses are resolved in a conference committee. This procedure needs to be finished by 15 September in order for the budget to be ready to go into effect on 1 October; but the Congressional Budget Act also requires the passage of a second, concurrent resolution setting forth the budget ceilings, revenue floors, and overall fiscal policy considerations governing the passage of the appropriations bills. Because there will undoubtedly be differences in the ways in which the two houses make their appropriations figures correspond with the figures in the concurrent resolution, the reconciliation bill, in which both houses agree on the spending totals, must be passed by 25 September. While the reconciliation bill appears to be a technicality, the Reagan administration used this opportunity to impose its budgetary will at the beginning of the administration.[21] The budget is then ready to go to the president for his signature and execution.

Budget Execution

After the executive branch has been appropriated money, the agencies must develop mechanisms for spending that money. An appropriations warrant, drawn by the Treasury and countersigned by the General Accounting Office, is sent to each agency. The agency then makes plans for its expenditures for the year, on the basis of this warrant, and submits a plan to OMB for apportionment of the funds. The funds appropriated by Congress are usually made available to the agencies on a quarterly basis, but for some agencies there may be great differences in the amounts made available each quarter. For example, the U.S. Park Service spends a very large proportion of its annual appropriation during the summer because of the demands on the national parks at that time. Two principal reasons for allowing agencies access to only a quarter of their funds at a time are to provide greater control over spending and to prevent an agency from spending everything early in the year and then requiring a supplemental appropriation. This still happens, but apportionment helps control any potential profligacy.

The procedures for executing the budget are relatively simple when the executive branch actually wants to spend the money it has been appropriated. Procedures become more complex when the president decides he does not want to spend the appropriated funds. Prior to the Congressional Budget Act of 1974, a president had at least a customary right to impound funds, that is, to refuse to spend them.[22] Numerous impoundments during the Nixon administration (e.g., half the money appropriated for implementing the Federal Water Pollution Control Act Amendments of 1972 was impounded from the 1973 to 1975 budgets) forced Congress to take action to control the executive and reassert its customary powers over the purse.

The Congressional Budget and Impoundment Control Act of 1974 was designed to limit the ability of the president to use impoundment as an indirect means of overruling Congress, even when he was not able to achieve this through the normal legislative process (the water-pollution-control legislation had been passed over a presidential veto). The 1974 act defined two kinds of impoundment. First, rescissions are cancellations of budgetary authority to spend money. A president may decide that a program could reach its goals with less money or simply that there were good reasons not to spend the money. The president must then send a message to Congress requesting the rescission. Congress must act positively on this request within forty-five days; if it does not, the money is made available to the agency for obligation.

Deferrals, in contrast, are requests merely to delay making the obligational authority available to the agency. In this case, if either house of Congress does not exercise its veto power, the deferral is granted. The comptroller general (head of the General Accounting Office) is given the power to classify specific presidential actions, and at times the difference between a deferral and a rescission is not clear. For example, attempting to defer funds for programs scheduled to be phased out is, in practice, a rescission. These reforms in the impoundment powers of the president have substantially increased the powers of Congress in determining how much money will indeed be spent by the federal government each year.

Budget Control

After the president and the executive branch spend the money appropriated by Congress, the Congress must check to be sure that the money was spent legally and properly. The General Accounting Office (GAO) and its head, the comptroller general, are responsible for the postexpenditure audit of federal expenditures. Each year the comptroller general's report to Congress outlines deviations from congressional intent. Requests from individual congressmen or committees may produce earlier and perhaps more detailed evaluations of agency spending or policies. Each year the GAO provides Congress and the interested public with hundreds of evaluations of expenditures.

The GAO has undergone a major transformation from a simple accounting organization into a policy-analytic organization for the legislative branch.[23] It has become concerned not only with the legality of expenditures but also with the efficiency with which the money is spent. Although the reports of the GAO on the efficiency of expenditures have no legal authority, any agency that wishes to maintain its good relations with Congress would be well advised to take those findings into account. Congress will certainly be cognizant of those recommendations when it reviews an agency's budget the following year and would expect to see some changes. These GAO recommendations would also form one part of the ongoing process of congressional oversight of administration. The problem with GAO controls —whether of an accounting or a more policy-analytic nature—is that they are largely ex post facto. This means that the money will probably have been spent long before the decision that it had been spent either illegally or unwisely is made.

Summary

A long and complex process is required to perform the difficult tasks of allocating federal budget money among competing agencies. The process takes almost eighteen months and involves many bargains and decisions. From this process of bargaining and analysis emerges a plan for spending billions of dollars. But even this complex process, now made more complex by numerous reforms of congressional budgeting procedures and deficit fighting procedures, cannot control all federal expenditures as completely as some would desire, nor can it provide the level of fiscal management that may be necessary for a smoothly functioning economic system. Let us now turn to a few problems that presidents and congressmen alike face in making the budgetary process an effective allocative process. The process may never be as "rational" as some would like because it is inherently a political as well as an economic process, but there are identifiable problems that cause particular difficulty.

Problems in the Budgetary Process

The major problems arising in the budgetary process of the federal government affect the fiscal management function of budgeting as well as the allocation of resources among agencies. It is difficult, if not impossible, for any president or Congress to make binding decisions as to how much money will be spent in any year, or even as to who will spend it for what, and this absence of basic controls makes the entire process subject to error. Those elected to make policy and control spending frequently find themselves incapable of producing the kinds of programs or budgetary changes they campaigned for, and this can result in disillusionment for both leaders and citizens.

Uncontrollable Expenditures

Many expenditure programs in the federal government cannot be controlled in any one year without policy changes that may be politically unpalatable.[24] For example, a president or the Congress can do very little to control the level of expenditure for Social Security in any year without either changing the criteria for eligibility or altering the formula for indexation (adjustment of the benefits for changes in consumer prices or workers' earnings) of the program. Either choice may produce a major political conflict and might well be impossible. Some minor changes, such as changing the tax treatment of Social Security benefits for beneficiaries with other income, may be entertained, but this category of expenditure is essentially uncontrollable.

Much of the federal budget is uncontrollable in any one year (see table 6.1). The most important uncontrollable expenditures are the large entitle-

TABLE 6.1

CHANGES IN "UNCONTROLLABLE" FEDERAL EXPENDITURES

	1976	1980	1990	1991	1992	1993
Controllable	63.7	46.8	40.0	40.4	38.7	37.2
Uncontrollable	36.3	53.2	60.0	59.6	61.3	62.8

SOURCE: Office of Management and Budget, *Special Analyses of the FY 1995 U.S. Budget* (Washington, D.C.: Government Printing Office, 1994).

ment programs of social welfare spending such as Social Security, Medicare, and unemployment benefits. These expenditures are uncontrollable both because they cannot be readily cut by a government and because the government cannot accurately estimate, while planning the budget, exactly how much money will be needed for the programs. The final level of expenditures will depend on levels of inflation, illness, and unemployment, as well as on the number of eligible citizens who actually take advantage of the programs. In addition, outstanding contracts and obligations constitute a significant share of the uncontrollable portion of the budget, although these can be altered over a number of years, if not in any single year. The major controllable component of the federal budget is the defense budget. The end of the Cold War makes this a particularly attractive target for budget cutting, although the apparent shift from large strategic forces to more tactical (personnel-intensive) forces may reduce the overall savings.

The uncontrollable element of the budget has meant that even a president committed to the goals of reducing federal expenditures and producing a balanced budget will find it difficult to determine where the expenditure reductions will come from. Congress has begun to grapple with these expenditures but finds the political forces of entitlements difficult to overcome.[25] Some discretionary social expenditures have been reduced over the past decade, but the bulk of federal expenditures have continued to increase (see table 6.1) and are likely to continue to increase. Thus, any president coming into office with a desire to balance the budget or reduce federal spending will soon find it difficult to do so.

Back-Door Spending

Linked to the problem of uncontrollable expenditures is "back-door spending"—expenditure decisions that are not actually made through the formal appropriations process. These expenditures to some degree reflect an institutional conflict within Congress, between the appropriations committees and the substantive policy committees. There are three principal kinds of back-door spending: borrowing authority, contract authority, and permanent appropriations.

BORROWING AUTHORITY

Agencies are sometimes allowed to spend public money not appropriated by Congress if they borrow that money from the Treasury—for student-loan guarantees, for instance.[26] It has been argued that these are not actually public expenditures because the money will presumably be repaid eventually. In many instances, however, federal loans have been written off, and even if the loans are repaid, the government may not know when that repayment will occur. Further, the ability of government to control expenditure levels for purposes of economic management is seriously impaired when the authority to make spending decisions is so widely diffused.

CONTRACT AUTHORITY

Agencies also may enter into contracts that bind the federal government to pay a certain amount for specified goods and services without going through the appropriations process. Then, after the contract is let, the appropriations committees are placed in the awkward position of either appropriating the money to pay off the debt or forcing the agency to renege on its debts. While this kind of spending is uncontrollable in the short run, any agency attempting to engage in this circumvention of the appropriations committees probably soon will face the ire of those committees when attempting to have its annual budget approved. Also, Congress has been developing rules that make spending of this type increasingly difficult for agencies.

PERMANENT APPROPRIATIONS

Certain programs have authorizing legislation that requires the spending of certain amounts of money. The largest expenditure of this kind is payment of interest on the public debt; this expense constituted over 13 percent of total federal expenditures in fiscal year 1995 and is projected to continue to increase as a result of continuing large federal deficits. Likewise, federal support of land-grant colleges is a permanent appropriation that began during the administration of Abraham Lincoln. In the case of a permanent appropriation, the appropriations committees have little discretion, unless they choose to renege on these standing commitments of the government.

The Overhang

Money appropriated by Congress for a fiscal year need not actually be spent during that fiscal year; it must only be obligated. That is, the agency must contract to spend the money, or otherwise make commitments about how it will be spent, with the actual outlay of funds coming perhaps some years later. In 1995 there was a total budget authority of about $2.5 trillion (see figure 6.1) with only $1.5 trillion being appropriated during that year.[27] Thus, in the 1995 fiscal year the "overhang" is two-thirds as large as the amount of money appropriated by Congress during that fiscal year. The president and the executive agencies could not actually spend all that over-hang in the single fiscal year (a good deal of it is in long-term contracts), but it represents a substantial amount in unspent obligations for the agencies and the government as a whole.

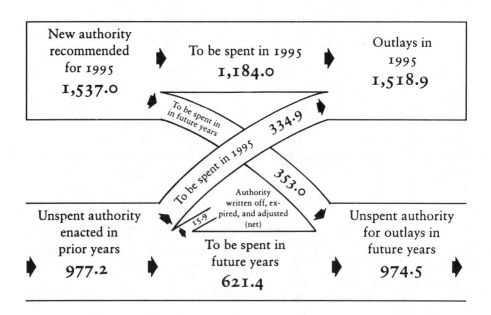

FIGURE 6.1

RELATIONSHIP OF BUDGET AUTHORITY TO OUTLAYS — 1995
(VALUES IN BILLIONS OF DOLLARS)

SOURCE: Office of Management and Budget, *Budget of the United States, FY 1994* (Washington, D.C.: Government Printing Office, 1992), appendix 1, p. 142. Updated by the author.

The major problem is that the overhang makes it difficult for a president to use the budget as an instrument of economic management. One principal component of economic management, even in a post-Keynesian era, is the amount of public expenditures; because of the overhang, the president and Congress cannot always control the actual outlay of funds. The agencies may have sufficient budget authority, convertible into actual outlays, to damage presidential forecasts of outlays. They would do this, not out of malice, but out of a perceived need to keep their programs operating as they thought best, especially if the president was seeking to restrict the creation of new obligational authority.

Intergovernmental Budget Control

Although it does not specifically affect the federal budgetary process, the lack of overall fiscal control in the public sector of the United States makes it impossible for the federal government to control total public expenditures and hence to exercise the kind of fiscal management it might like. Just as a president cannot control the overhang within the federal government, he cannot control the taxing and spending decisions of thousands of state and local governments.

The federal government itself spends only about two-thirds of the total amount of money spent by governments in the United States. The federal government has the capacity to stimulate state and local government expenditures through matching grants, but encouraging reductions in expenditures is more difficult. The federal government has even less control over revenue collection. For example, in 1963 the Kennedy administration pushed through a tax cut for the federal government, only to have almost the entire effect of that cut negated by state and local tax increases. The federal tax cut in the 1980s was also offset (albeit somewhat more slowly) by increases in state and local taxation.[28]

The principles of federalism would appear to reserve to state and local governments a perfect right to decide on their own levels of revenues and expenditures. But in an era in which the public budget is important for economic management as well as for the distribution of funds among organizations, there may be a need for greater overall control of expenditures. This control need not be imposed unilaterally by the federal government, but could perhaps be decided by "diplomacy" among representatives of the several levels of government, as it is in Germany and to some extent Canada.[29] The potential effects on economic performance of uncoordinated fiscal policies were to some degree reflected by the presence of large state and local government surpluses in the mid-1980s, at the same time that the federal government was running large deficits.[30] Depending on one's point of view, this was either a good thing (helping to reduce total public borrowing) or a bad thing (counteracting the economic stimulus of the deficit). In either event, it represented the absence of an integrated fiscal policy within the United States.

Reprogramming and Transfers

The first four problems we have identified in the federal budgetary process affect primarily the total level of expenditures. The next two problems, reprogramming and transfers, affect levels of spending by individual agencies and the purposes for which the agencies spend their money.

Reprogramming refers to the shifting of funds within a specific appropriations account. When Congress passes an appropriations bill, that bill contains a number of appropriations accounts, which in turn contain a number of program elements. For example, the appropriations bill for the Department of Agriculture contains an appropriations account for crop supports, with separate program elements for cotton, corn, wheat, and so on. Reprogramming involves shifting obligational authority from one program element to another. The procedures for making reprogramming decisions has been thoroughly developed only in the Department of Defense. In general, there is a threshold (variable by agency) below which agencies are relatively free to reprogram funds, but above which they require approval from appropriations committee or subcommittee personnel, although not from the entire Congress. There are also requirements for reporting reprogramming decisions to the appropriations committees.

Transfers are more serious actions, for they involve transferring funds from one appropriations account to another. In our Department of Agriculture example above, this might involve shifting funds from crop supports to the Farmers Home Administration or to rural electrification. Transfer funds have been subject to significant abuse and circumvention of congressional authority, especially during the Nixon administration and the Vietnam war. And, as with reprogramming—outside the Department of Defense—few established procedures exist for controlling the use of transfer funds other than those that specifically forbid the use of such funds for certain functions.

Both reprogramming and transfer funds are important in providing the executive branch with some flexibility in implementing its programs and in using public funds more effectively. These opportunities have been the subject of many abuses, however, and are ripe for reform and improvement. In particular, they frequently allow an agency to circumvent the judgment of the entire Congress through an appeal to the appropriations committee, or perhaps even to its chairman.

Supplemental Appropriations

Even with the apportionment of funds mentioned earlier, agencies may require supplemental appropriations—those made outside the normal budget cycle—to cover shortfalls during the fiscal year. Agencies sometimes simply run out of money. This can result from improper management, but more often it happens because of changes in the demand for services or because of a poor estimate of the demand for a new service. For example, during a recession, the demand for unemployment assistance will naturally increase, and supplemental funding will be required. Likewise, a year of poor weather may force additional funding for crop supports and crop insurance in the Department of Agriculture. Or a new program, such as food stamps, may acquire more clients than anyone anticipated during the early years of its existence. When we are talking about supplemental appropriations, we are not talking about insignificant amounts of money. In 1994 a net of some $3.52 billion was appropriated through supplementals. While a few of the supplemental actions were to reduce the amounts appropriated, the additions to agency obligational authority ranged from $1.8 million for land acquisition for the U.S. Fish and Wildlife Service to almost $500 million for the Department of Defense for the additional expenses incurred in operations in Somalia and Bosnia. There was also $225.5 million for the Soil Conservation Service to help recovery from disastrous floods in the Midwest. The changes in budget procedure required by deficit reduction strategies (see p. 140) have reduced the size of supplemental appropriations, but they still constitute a potential avenue for additional funding for an agency.

The request for supplemental appropriations may be a useful strategy for agencies attempting to expand their funding. The agency may be able to initiate a program with minimal appropriations through the usual budgetary process, anticipating a wide acceptance of its program by prospective clients, and then return to Congress for a supplemental appropriation when clients do indeed materialize and demand benefits. Supplemental appropriations frequently are not scrutinized as carefully as regular appropriations are, and this relative invisibility may permit friendly congressmen to hide a rapidly expanding program. The level of scrutiny has increased because of the requirements for expenditures proposals to be "deficit neutral" (see below), but supplementals usually still are easier to push through than regular appropriations are. But obvious and frequent abuse of the supplemental appropriations process will almost certainly damage the relationship between the agency and Congress. That may hurt more than help the agency, in the long run, in expanding its expenditure base, given the importance of trust in the politics of the budgetary process.

Assessing the Outcomes: Incrementalism or What?

One standard word used to describe changes in budgetary allocations in the United States is *incremental*. Any number of meanings have been attached to this word.[31] Broadly, incrementalism means that changes that appear in an agency's budget from year to year tend to be predictable. More specifically, incrementalism has taken on several additional interpretations. First, incremental decision making is described as a process that is not "synoptic," or not fully "rational."[32] That is, incremental decision making does not involve examining sweeping alternatives to the status quo and then making a decision about the optimal use of budgetary resources. Instead, incremental decision making involves "successive limited comparisons" or the sequential examination of marginal changes from the status quo and decisions about whether to make these marginal adjustments to existing policies.[33] An incremental decision-making process tends to build on earlier decisions and then seek means to improve the existing situation rather than alter current policies or budgetary priorities completely. In budgetary terms this means an agency can expect to receive in any year approximately what it received the previous year, plus a little bit more to adjust for inflation or expanded services.

Advocates of incremental decision making argue that this method of making policy choices is actually more rational than the synoptic method. Because it provides an experiential base from which to work, the incremental method offers a greater opportunity to make good policy choices than does the apparently more rational synoptic method. In addition, any errors that are made in an incremental decision-making process can be more easily reversed than can major changes made in a synoptic process. In many ways incremental decision making is a cost-minimizing form of rationality rather than a benefit-maximizing approach. Incrementalism reduces costs, first, by limiting the range of alternatives and thereby limiting the research and calculation costs for decision makers; and, second, by reducing the costs of change, particularly of error correction. Because in an incremental world few choices involve significant deviations from existing policies or appropriations, there is little need to make major adjustments either in the actual programs or in the thought patterns of decision makers about the policies. Given the limited calculative capacity of human beings, even with the aid of modern technology, and given the resistance of most individuals and organizations to change, incrementalism can be argued to be a rational means for making choices.

Incrementalism has also been used to describe the pattern of outcomes of the budgetary process. In particular, Davis, Dempster, and Wildavsky demonstrated a great deal of stability in the increases in appropriations granted to agencies from year to year by the president and the Congress.[34] The changes in budgets are not only small but also quite stable and predictable, so the best estimate of an agency's budget in one year would be the previous year's budget plus a stable percentage increase. Some agencies grow more rapidly than others, but each will exhibit a stable pattern of growth.

Several factors contribute to the pattern of incremental budgeting found in the United States. One factor is that such a large percentage of the budget is uncontrollable that few significant changes in appropriations can be made from year to year. Also, most empirical examinations of incremental budgeting have been made during periods of relative economic stability and high rates of economic growth; as less favorable economic conditions have become more common in the United States, the level of incrementalism appropriate for rich and predictable budgeting systems has become less appropriate for one that is prosperous and less stable.[35] These changes in the economic climate of budgeting are to some degree reflected in the reform efforts described below (pp. 153–64).

Most important, the repetitive and sequential nature of the budgeting process tends to produce incremental outcomes in budgeting. A budget must be passed each year, so minor adjustments can be made from year to year as the need arises, thus avoiding the need to attempt to correct all the problems of the policy area at once. Also, the annual cycle prevents an agency from trying to "shoot the moon" in any one year—trying to expand its budget base greatly, perhaps with flimsy evidence. Agency leaders know that they will have to return for more money next year, and any attempt to deceive only invites future punishment. The sequential nature of the process, in which several different actors make several different decisions one after another, also tends to produce incremental outcomes. Many decisions have to be made, and many bargains must be struck. The incremental solution not only provides a "natural" choice but also helps to minimize bargaining costs among institutions. Once a decision rule of a certain percentage increase for a particular agency each year has been established, it is far simpler to honor that rule than to seek a "better" decision for one year and then have to do the same hard bargaining and calculation in each subsequent year.

CRITIQUES OF INCREMENTALISM

A number of criticisms have been leveled at incrementalism, both in its prescriptive capacity (decisions should be made incrementally) and in its descriptive capacity (decisions are made incrementally). The basic argument against incrementalism as a prescription for policymaking is that it is excessively conservative, so the status quo is perpetuated long after better solutions are available. This is true for certain kinds of program decisions as well as for expenditure decisions. Incrementalism may be a perfectly rational means of policymaking as long as all parties agree that a policy or program is functioning well and is well managed. But how many policies currently fall in that happy category in the United States? Budgeting may be especially in need of more comprehensive reform, given the tendency of the process to produce so many huge deficits over the past decade.

In addition, even the incrementalist might agree that at times (e.g., during periods of crisis) nonincremental decisions are required, but the approach provides no means of identifying when and how those nonincremental decisions should be made.[36] If one uses the incremental approach to provide a prescriptive model of governmental decision making, then one must be able to specify what a "big" change would be, when it would be appropriate, and how it might be made.

Several problems also relate to incrementalism as a description of budgetary decision making. In the first place, the majority of empirical examinations of incremental budgeting have been performed at the agency level. This is certainly justifiable, given the importance of those organizations in American public policy, but it is perhaps too high a level of aggregation for examining incremental budgeting.[37] When other researchers have disaggregated agency budgets into program-level budgets, they have found a great deal of nonincremental change, although, as pointed out, it is sometimes difficult to define just what an incremental change is or is not.[38] Thus, while public organizations may have a stable pattern of expenditure change, the managers of these organizations may drastically alter priorities among the operating programs within the agency and produce more rapidly shifting fortunes for the programs.

In addition, when the uncontrollable elements of public expenditures are removed from the analysis, the pattern of expenditure change for the controllable portion is anything but incremental.[39] As budgets have been squeezed by inflation and citizen resistance to taxation, and by presidents committed to a smaller public sector, budgetary increments have not been granted as usual, and at times the base has also been cut—that is, there have been real reductions in the amount of new obligational authority for the agency compared with the preceding year. Incrementalism may therefore now be descriptive of only certain kinds of expenditures and not of the budget process as a whole. Of course, since uncontrollable expenditures accounted for approximately 75 percent of total federal expenditures in 1991, the incrementalist approach may still be a useful description.

Also, incrementalism may apply only to certain kinds of agencies and programs, such as those whose existence has been fully accepted as a part of the realm of government activity; it may not apply to newer or more marginal programs. For example, the budgets of programs such as Aid to Families with Dependent Children (AFDC, or "welfare") are always more subject to change than are programs such as veterans' benefits or Social Security, although all would be broadly classified as social service expenditures. Although AFDC has been in existence for a number of years, it still does not have the legitimacy that other programs have developed. In addition, incrementalist theory does not explain how and when programs make big gains—or big losses—in their appropriations. Even if the approach is successful in explaining a great deal of the variance in normal times, it seems incapable of explaining the most interesting and most important aspects of budgeting: who wins and who loses.

Finally, the prescriptive appeal of incrementalism is based in part on the reversibility of small changes. In the real world of policymaking, many changes may not be reversible.[40] Once a commitment is made to a client, or a benefit is indexed, it is difficult to go back and take away the benefit. This is especially true of programs that have a "stock" component, that is, involve the development of a capital infrastructure or the development of a financial base.[41] Once a program such as Social Security is introduced, individuals covered under the program take the benefits under the program into account when making their financial plans for retirement; thus, any reduction or elimination of benefits may create a hardship.

Whether incrementalism accurately describes the budgeting process in the United States or its results, it has certainly become the conventional wisdom. And, in turn, it has prompted a number of proposals for reform of the budgetary process to make it more "rational" and to try to reduce the tendency of a program, once authorized, not only to remain in existence forever but to receive steadily increasing appropriations. It is to those attempts at reform that we now turn our attention.

Reform Budgeting

Numerous criticisms have been directed at the budgetary process in the United States. For most of our contemporary history these criticisms have focused on the incremental, "irrational," and fragmented nature of the process. More recently, however, the focus has shifted from imposing rationality toward finding somewhat simplistic means of correcting the outcomes of the process. These negative results are in part the incremental nature of the decisions, but more directly the huge federal deficits of the 1980s and 1990s. During the first stage of reforms, several methods sought to make the consideration of expenditure priorities more comprehensive and to facilitate governments making the best possible use of their limited resources. The two most important budgeting reforms of that type were program budgeting and zero-base budgeting. We discuss those two reforms briefly. Even though they were implemented several decades ago, the ideas contained in the reforms are still important. After that, we discuss the less rational but perhaps more effective reforms of the 1980s and 1990s.

Program Budgeting

Program budgeting was largely a product of the Johnson administration, although in some agencies it had been tried previously. Whereas traditional budgeting allocates personnel costs, supplies, equipment, and so forth, among organizations, program budgeting allocates resources on the basis of the activities of government and the services that government supplies to society.[42] It also places a pronounced emphasis on the analysis of programmatic expenditures and the most efficient use of scarce resources.

Underlying program budgeting, or more specifically the planning, programming, budgeting system (PPBS), is a systems concept. That is, it is assumed that the elements of government policy are closely intertwined, and so a change in one type of policy may affect all others. For example, if one wants to improve the quality of health for citizens in the United States, it may be more efficient to improve nutrition and housing than to invest money in medical care. Program budgeting is always looking for interactions among policy areas and for means of producing desired effects in the most efficient manner.

There are six basic characteristics of program budgeting as it was, and is, practiced in the federal government. First, the major goals and objectives of government must be identified. We must be able to specify what government is attempting to do, but this identification is made high in the hierarchy of government, usually by the president and Congress. Whereas traditional line-item budgeting is initiated by the agencies, program budgeting must begin with a specification of the central goals and priorities of government, which can be supplied only by the principal political leaders.

Second, programs must be developed according to the specified goals. How will government attempt to attain the goals that have been chosen for it? These programs are analytically defined and may not exist as organizational entities. For example, when Robert McNamara—who with his "whiz kids" was largely responsible for introducing program budgeting into the Defense Department and thence into the federal government as a whole —developed the program structure for Defense, one of the programs developed was "strategic deterrence." This program was actually spread among all three services. The air force had its manned bombers and some missiles, the navy had Polaris submarines, and the army had Intermediate Range Ballistic Missiles located in Europe. Strategic deterrence certainly described one set of activities of the defense establishment, but no organization was specifically responsible for that program.

Third, resources must be allocated among programs. Although many traditional line items were used in developing the program budget, the final budget document was presented in terms of overall costs for the achievement of certain objectives. These costs would then be justified as being an efficient and effective means of reaching the desired goals. Program budgeting then places its emphasis on the costs of reaching certain objectives, whereas line-item budgeting emphasizes the costs of keeping organizations or programs in operation.

Fourth, organizations are not sacrosanct in program budgeting, and there is no assumption that each program is housed within a single agency or that each agency provides only a single program. As with the defense example mentioned above, program budgeting attempts to expand the framework of budgeting and planning to include all actors who contribute to the achievement of the goals. This is obviously a realistic attitude toward the interaction of several activities and organizations in producing the final effects on the society, but it does make budgeting more difficult in an environment perhaps best regarded as composed of many organizations, each of which is attempting to sustain its own interests.

Fifth, program budgeting extends the time limit on expenditures found in line-item budgeting. It attempts to ask and answer questions about the medium- and long-term implications of programs. Some programs that appear efficient in the short run may actually be less desirable when their long-term implications are considered. For example, most publicly supported health programs concentrate on curative medicine, whereas it may be more efficient in the long run to emphasize preventive medicine.

Sixth, alternative programs are systematically analyzed. Agencies examine alternatives to existing program structures with the hope of finding more effective and efficient programs. Agencies are expected to present their justifications for programs—to show, in other words, that the chosen program is superior to the other programs investigated. Also, this aspect of program budgeting relates to our previous discussion of policy formulation, for agencies are expected to develop alternatives and to examine their relative merits, using techniques such as cost-benefit analysis.

CRITICISM OF PROGRAM BUDGETING
Advocates of program budgeting point with pride to the enhanced rationality and analytic rigor associated with this form of budgeting and to the way that it breaks down organizational control over budgetary outcomes. Despite these apparent advantages, program budgeting has not been especially successful in most of its applications. There are some technical reasons for these apparent failures, but the most severe problems in the implementation of program budgeting are political.

Technically, applying program budgeting successfully requires a great deal of time and effort; it also requires an almost certain knowledge of unknown relationships of spending to program success. The systems concept built into the method implies that if one aspect of the system is altered, the entire system must be rethought. This in turn may mean that program budgeting may actually institutionalize the rigidity it was designed to eliminate. Also, it is difficult if not impossible to define programs, measure their results, and evaluate the contributions of individual agencies and activities to the achievement of those results. One major problem in public policy analysis and budgeting is the difficulty, or impossibility, of measuring the effects of government, and such measurement occupies a central place in program budgeting.[43]

Program budgeting also has several political disadvantages. First, as mentioned, the method forces decisions to a higher level of government.[44] Agencies dislike this centralizing tendency, as do congressmen who have invested a considerable amount of effort in developing relationships with clientele groups supporting the agency. Likewise, the assumption that organizations are not the most appropriate objects of allocation runs counter to all the folkways of American government. Finally, the need to analyze systematically alternative strategies for achieving ends forces the agency to expose its program to possible attack, as it may develop and eliminate alternative programs that others might prefer, and the explicit nature of the process brings those alternatives up for active consideration. The discussion of alternative policies reduces the maneuverability of the agency, as it must justify its policy choice in writing and consequently cannot play games with OMB, or even with Congress if the information developed from the planning, programming, budgeting system is passed on to the legislative branch. In short, PPBS was a dagger pointed toward the central role of the agency in policymaking in the federal government, and as such it could not really have been expected to succeed, except perhaps in organizations such as the Department of Defense. That organization had a strong leader committed to the concept of program budgeting, and it produced extremely nebulous results that could be tested only against simulations or scenario-building exercises; it also had few potent political enemies. For other agencies, with considerably greater political opposition and with real clients demanding real services, PPBS was apparently doomed to failure from the beginning.

Zero-Base Budgeting

If program budgeting required an almost superhuman analytical capability and rafts of data, the conceptual underpinnings of zero-base budgeting (ZBB) were extremely simple. The idea was that whereas traditional incremental budgeting operates from the assumption that the previous year's budget was justified (the "base") and it is principally increments that need examination, a more comprehensive examination of all expenditures should be made. That is, there should be no base, and the entire spending plan should be justified. It was assumed that weaker programs, which were being extended largely through inertia, would be terminated or at least severely cut, and more meritorious programs would be fully funded. This form of budgeting came to Washington with the Carter administration, after having been tried by President Carter while he was governor of Georgia.

Zero-base budgeting is done on the basis of decision units, which may be agencies but which frequently are smaller components such as operating programs within an agency. Each budget manager is expected to prepare a number of decision packages to reflect his or her priorities for funding. These packages are presented in rank order, with a "survival package" presented first. This package is the lowest level of funding on which the unit can continue to exist. On top of the survival package are additional decision packages, reflecting, first, the continuation of existing programs at existing levels of service and then expansions of services. Each decision package is justified in terms of the services it would provide at an acceptable cost.

Decision packages prepared by lower-level budget managers are then passed up the organizational hierarchy to higher-level managers, who prepare consolidated decision packages that reflect a ranking of priorities among the several decision units that they may supervise. These rankings are then passed along and consolidated further, ending up in the Office of Management and Budget. All the rankings from the lower levels are passed along with the consolidated packages so that higher levels can examine the preferences of lower-level managers and their justifications of those preferences. Like program budgeting, zero-base budgeting is geared toward multiyear budgeting to better understand the implications of budget choices made during any one budget cycle.

Zero-base budgeting, again like program budgeting, has several apparent advantages. Obviously, the method is intended to eliminate incremental budgeting. The agency's base is no longer protected but must be defended—although in practice the survival level may function as a base. Also, the method focuses on cost effectiveness in the justification of the rankings of decision packages and even of the survival level of funding. One principal advantage of zero-base budgeting appears to be the involvement of managers at relatively low levels of the organization in the consideration of priorities and goals for the organization. Also, this method considers the allocation of resources in package terms, whereas the incremental budget tends to assume that any additional amount of money can be effectively used. It makes greater sense to think of adding meaningful amounts of money that can produce additional services, rather than simply adding more money without regard for the threshold values for service provision and efficiency.

Nevertheless, there are a number of glaring difficulties with zero-base budgeting. For example, in theory this form of budgeting is an obvious threat to the existence of some agencies. In practice, however, a number of factors, such as clientele groups and uncontrollable expenditures, may negate the concern that many administrators may have had about the method. It is nevertheless clear that the intent of the method is to bring the existence of each program into question each year.

To some degree the enormity of the task of examining each program carefully each year is a major weakness of this method. There is no means by which OMB, held to a reasonable size, or a Congress with its other commitments, can carefully consider the entire budget each year. Therefore, either there is a superficial analysis of each program under the guise of a zero-base review—probably with incremental results—or there is a selective review of a number of more controversial programs. Either is an acceptable means of reducing the workload, but neither would constitute a significant departure from the incremental budget or justify the massive outlay of effort required to prepare the necessary documents.

In addition, zero-base budgeting threatens established programs by allowing the reopening of political conflicts during each budget cycle. One virtue of traditional incremental budgeting is that once a program is agreed to, it is accepted and is not subject to significant scrutiny unless there are major changes in the environment or serious administrative problems in the agency. With zero-base budgeting, the existence of the program is subject to question each year, and the political fights that authorized the existence of the agency may have to be fought again and again. This is, of course, no problem for well-established and popular programs, but it is certainly a problem for newer and more controversial programs. Also, zero-base budgeting tends to combine financial decisions with program decisions and to place perhaps an excessive burden on budgetary decision makers.

From Scalpels to Axes: Budget Reform in the 1980s and 1990s

To a greater degree than the analytic methodologies proposed in program budgeting and, to some extent, zero-base budgeting, the fundamental incrementalist patterns have been more challenged by the continuing fiscal problems of government. These problems have spawned a number of "solutions."[45] Some of these solutions have already been implemented, including the Gramm-Rudman-Hollings Act (technically the Balanced Budget and Emergency Deficit Control Act of 1985) and the budget agreement between Congress and the president made in 1990. Other proposed reforms include ideas such as the balanced-budget amendment and the line-item veto. Most of these reforms are incrementalism turned around. As with incrementalism, there is a tendency to substitute minimization of decision-making costs for maximization of benefits resulting from expenditures. They are, for the most part, "no-think solutions," just as incrementalism has been a nonanalytic means for making budgetary decisions. But even as incrementalism has been successful and acceptable, these methods for dealing with complex problems have been acceptable to some because of their simplicity. Simple policies are not always, and perhaps only rarely, the best solutions for complex problems, but they are very often the most acceptable in the political world.

Gramm-Rudman-Hollings

As the magnitude of the deficits created by the Reagan tax cuts became apparent to Congress, it began to find means to staunch the budgetary "hemorrhaging" that was occurring. This was difficult to do by traditional means because of the logrolling and pork-barrel legislative styles so typical of Congress. Therefore Congress adopted a method, commonly referred to as "Gramm-Rudman-Hollings" after its sponsors, that would remove some of the discretion from its hands and force cuts in spending if the president and Congress could not reach agreement on how to do so. The idea at the outset was to reduce the federal deficit to zero within five years (fiscal year 1991). This target is indicative of the totemic status of a balanced budget in American thinking about public finance,[46] but it soon proved to be an unattainable and perhaps unwise target.

The basic idea behind Gramm-Rudman-Hollings was that if Congress and the president did not expect to meet the declining budget target in any year, they could cut spending, raise taxes, or do some combination of the two. If no agreement could be reached on those actions, then automatic cuts in spending (called sequestrations)—half from defense and half from domestic programs—would be instituted. Certain expenditures (interest on the federal debt, Social Security, veterans' retirement, etc.) were excluded so that any cuts made would have to come from only 30 percent of the budget. That, in turn, meant that those cuts would have to be severe. The scorekeeper in the process was to be the General Accounting Office.

The role assigned to the GAO proved to be the downfall of the initial version of the process. The Supreme Court ruled[47] that the GAO as a legislative organization could not perform an executive act—order cutting of budgets for specific executive agencies. After considerable discussion, the scorekeeper was changed to the Office of Management and Budget in the Executive Office of the President. Although Congress feared that its interests might be slighted by this change, it appeared to be the only possible compromise if the original mechanisms of the act were to be maintained at all.

But the original intentions of the act proved to be extremely difficult and painful politically, so Congress agreed to several changes in 1987-88. First, the time period for reducing the deficit to zero was extended to fiscal 1993. Second, Congress decided to postpone most of the truly significant cuts until after the 1988 presidential and congressional elections, thereby confirming the adage that future budget cuts are always more acceptable than current ones, especially for incumbents. Congress attempted to restore the deficit reductions to their original trajectory after the election, but it was deterred by economic and political circumstances.

The principal factor hampering the ability of the president and Congress to reach their targets was the sluggish, then decelerating, economy. President Bush proposed a budget that would meet the Gramm-Rudman-Hollings target of a $64 billion deficit for fiscal 1991, but as the budget process progressed in 1990 it became clear that the actual deficit would be closer to $300 billion because of the slowed economy. The sense of crisis emerging from these negotiations produced a new program for deficit reduction, or at least deficit management. This was adopted in the Budget Enforcement Act of 1990. The provisions of the Budget Enforcement Act included

1. Separation of mandatory spending from discretionary spending.
2. Differentiation of three types of discretionary spending: defense, international, and domestic, with separate spending targets for each.
3. A "pay as you go" plan for mandatory spending and revenues, so any increase in spending or reduction in revenues must have another spending reduction or tax increase associated with it to keep the package deficit neutral.
4. Elimination of overly optimistic or unrealistic targets for deficit reduction.
5. Inclusion of loan programs in the budgetary calculations (they had been excluded previously).
6. The Office of Management and Budget is the scorekeeper.[48]

Gramm-Rudman-Hollings and all the other legislative manifestations of fiscal control represent a major effort at reform of the budgetary process to eliminate the federal deficit and to force government to live within its revenues. They also point out the extreme difficulties of making and implementing such an agreement. Not only were unrealistic future targets set and then dismissed, but important segments of federal financial operations, such as credit (initially) and the savings-and-loan bailout, were ignored. Further, the cuts imposed fell on a relatively small proportion of the budget and therefore fell very heavily in those areas. In many ways, the Gramm-Rudman-Hollings enterprise has helped add to the already high level of cynicism that the American people have about government. The 1990 agreements offered a somewhat more realistic proposal for change in budgeting, but it was not clear how long this agreement could last in the face of continuing poor performance by the economy and the impending presidential election.

The incoming Clinton administration used the provisions of the Budget Enforcement Act to begin to implement its own budgetary and economic strategy. Changes in timing contained in the Budget Enforcement Act allowed a new administration to submit that year's budget. The first proposed Clinton budget contained a very modest increase in expenditures over that previously projected, but a much larger increase in revenues, thereby producing some reduction in the deficit.[49] Congress did change the budget but left intact much of the administration's plans for economic change and some reduction in the deficit.

The Balanced-Budget Amendment

The size of the federal budget deficit has elicited a number of proposed solutions in addition to the Gramm-Rudman-Hollings machinery and its sequel. Among the most commonly discussed solutions has been the balanced-budget amendment. This amendment to the Constitution would require Congress to pass a balanced budget each year, unless an extraordinary majority of Congress declared that a sufficient economic emergency existed to justify running a deficit.[50] Somewhat like the situation under the 1990 budgetary process, the amendment would force a more explicit comparison of revenue and expenditure figures and would further require those involved in the budgetary process to be responsible for the amount of money they appropriate. The difference, of course, is that this arrangement would be constitutional and therefore permanent.

The balanced-budget amendment has substantial political appeal and has gained some support. It was voted on again in 1993 and again in 1995 and each time came close to receiving enough votes in Congress to send it to the states. Like so many simple "solutions" to complex problems, however, it has some major difficulties. First, as already noted, the planning for a budget begins over a year before the start of its execution and over two years before the completion of the budget year. Further, both revenue and expenditure projections on which a budget is based are to some degree influenced by the condition of the economy and the projected state of the economy during the time the budget is to be executed.[51] It is easy to get the projections wrong; over the past twenty years, the official figures have overestimated revenues by an average of 3.9 percent and underestimated expenditures by an average of 4 percent.[52] Even if Congress acts in good faith and attempts to comply with the spirit of the amendment, it could easily miss the target of a balanced budget badly—an average of almost 8 percent.

Laura D'Andrea Tyson / Lloyd Bentsen / Leon Panetta

As well as the potential economic problems caused by such an un-planned deficit, the deficit may seem to some a violation of the Constitution and may further undermine already weakened public respect for Congress. A more cynical scenario would have Congress passing a budget that, although balanced on paper, would be known to have little chance of being balanced when executed. In either case, there could be substantial political damage to the legitimacy of Congress and to the government as a whole. The difficulties already encountered in implementing the Gramm-Rudman-Hollings plan to limit spending give some idea of how such an agreement would, or would not, work.

In addition, deficits are not necessarily a public evil. When adopted for economic reasons, as opposed to the political unwillingness to impose the true costs of government on citizens, budget deficits can be an important tool for economic management, following the Keynesian tradition. Passing a balanced-budget amendment would only remove one important tool of economic management from the federal government, without any certainty that economic benefits sufficient to justify that loss would be generated.

The Line-Item Veto

In his 1985 budget submission, President Reagan proposed that the line-item veto be adopted for the president, especially for appropriations bills. He was not the first president to make this recommendation—Ulysses Grant was —nor was he the last, for Bill Clinton also has advocated this instrument of presidential power. Similar to the powers that governors in forty-three states already have, the line-item veto would allow the president to veto a portion of a bill while permitting the rest to be put into effect.[53]

This selective veto is seen as a weapon for the president in dealing with the tendency of congressmen to add their pet projects to appropriations bills, placing the president in the awkward position of having to refuse money for a large segment of the federal government in order to prevent one or two small, and often wasteful, projects from being funded. Also, as noted earlier, the majority of appropriations for the federal government are contained in a dozen or so appropriations acts. In order to eliminate a few items the president would have to veto the entire act and create potential disruption and hardships.

One of the justifications for this change in the budgetary process (it would have to be a constitutional amendment) is that it would attack the problem of growing federal deficits. This may be so; but the veto, as proposed, could not be applied to many uncontrollable programs, such as debt interest and Social Security. Further, with the powers of rescission the president can achieve some of the same ends, although he does need the agreement of Congress (see above). In 1992, for example, President Bush attempted to rescind $7.9 billion but by the time Congress had finished with the proposal there was a rescission of $8.2 billion containing few of the items the president had proposed to cut.[54]

The line-item veto might actually encourage Congress to add more pet projects onto appropriations acts, placing the onus of removing those projects on the president. It might also give the president independent powers over public spending not intended by the framers of the Constitution or desired by the public. Thus, as with the balanced-budget amendment, there are few magic solutions for solving the deficit problems, but there is the continuing need for political will and courage to solve those problems.

Decrementalism

The preceding discussion of the balanced-budget amendment and the line-item veto is indicative of the general problem facing American government and the governments of other industrialized countries: the control of public expenditures. While incrementalism has become the conventional wisdom for describing budgeting, large numbers of politicians are looking for means of enforcing decrementalism, or the gradual reduction of expenditures, on government.[55] The majority of these political leaders are from the political right—as exemplified by President Bush—but even some on the political left are seeking to reduce expenditures while maintaining levels of service. The word *reform* has been heard often coming from national capitols around the world, but there has been little agreement on how much reform is needed and whether simple procedural reforms will be sufficient to address the deep and abiding difficulties faced in budgeting.[56]

In addition to the rationalistic approaches to budgeting and the Gramm-Rudman-Hollings machinery discussed earlier, somewhat more blunt instruments have been employed to try to reduce federal expenditures. One of these was the president's Private Sector Survey on Cost Control (the Grace Commission). This survey, similar to ones conducted in most state governments, brought to Washington some 2,000 volunteers from business and other private-sector organizations to examine the management of the federal government. The volunteers prepared 2,478 distinct recommendations projected to save the government $424 billion a year if they were all implemented.[57] Many of these proposals for cost reduction have been criticized as being politically naive or simply impossible, given the political realities of Washington and the connection of the agencies with powerful clientele groups.[58] Nevertheless, the survey gave those in Washington something to think about.

Other efforts at controlling the costs of government have been even more crude. These efforts have included across-the-board reductions in staffing levels and budgets and moratoria on the implementation of new programs and regulations. In addition, President Reagan and his advisers decided to attempt to reduce the pay of public employees to a level of 94 percent of comparable employees in the private sector—the 6 percent difference was to be made up by the greater job security and fringe benefits associated with federal employment.[59] The Clinton administration had few proposals for changing the mechanisms for budgeting, other than the familiar proposals for a line-item budget and the proposals for a biennial budget contained in the National Performance Review.[60]

Reaction to these reform efforts has been almost opposite that of proposals such as program budgeting and zero-base budgeting. The more recent across-the-board reform exercises have been criticized as mindless, as simply attacking government without regard to the real benefits created by some agencies and the real waste created by others. This contrasts with the large-scale analytic exercises that would have been required to implement program or zero-base budgeting. Perhaps sadly, the across-the-board exercises (such as those contained in the Gramm-Rudman-Hollings procedures) have a much greater chance of being implemented than do the more analytic methods.

Is Budget Change Its Own Reward?

All the attempts at budget reform we have mentioned have had some impact on the way in which the federal budget is constructed. Both program budgeting and zero-base budgeting were significant rationalistic efforts at reforming the budgetary process, and although both methods have a great deal to commend them, neither was particularly successful in producing changes in the behavior of budgetary decision makers. The less rationalistic methods such as Gramm-Rudman-Hollings have had a greater impact on the budget, in part because they did not attempt to change the basic format of the process or the outcomes. Despite the real problems in both the budget process and budget outcomes, why does the traditional line-item incremental budget persist?[61]

There appear to be several reasons for the resistance of traditional budgeting. One is that the traditional budget gives the legislature an excellent means of controlling the executive branch. It allocates funds to identifiable organizations for identifiable purposes (personnel, equipment, etc.), not to nebulous "programs" or "decision units." Those who manage the real organizations can then be held accountable for the expenditures of money appropriated to them. The blunt instruments now tacked onto the process, such as the Budget Enforcement Act, can enhance the control elements of the budgetary process without altering its basic elements.

More important, while the benefits promised by both program and zero-base budgeting were significant, so too were the costs. These costs are in terms of both the calculations required to reach decisions and the political turmoil created by nonincremental changes. Incremental budgeting provides ready guidelines for those who must make budget decisions, minimizing the necessity for them to engage in costly analysis and calculation. In addition, as most political interests are manifested through organizations, the absence of threats to those organizations in incremental budgeting means that political conflicts can be confined to marginal conflicts instead of conflicts over the very existence of those organizations.

In short, although incremental budgeting does nothing very well, neither does it do anything very poorly. Incrementalism is a convenient means of allocating resources for public purposes. It is not an optimal means, but it is a means that works and one in which those who must use it have great confidence. This in itself is enough to explain perpetuation of the incremental processes in the face of so many challenges by presumably superior systems of budgeting.

Notes

1. Jan-Erik Lane, *The Public Sector: Concepts, Models, and Approaches* (London: Sage, 1994).

2. Louis Fisher, *Presidential Spending Power* (Princeton: Princeton University Press, 1975).

3. Donald F. Kettl, *Deficit Politics* (New York: Macmillan, 1992).

4. Frederick C. Mosher, *The GAO: The Quest for Accountability in American Government* (Boulder, Colo.: Westview, 1979), 65–96.

5. General Accounting Office, *Biennial Budgeting for the Federal Government*, GAO/T-AIMED-94-4 (Washington, D.C.: GAO, 7 October 1993).

6. "Federal Capital Budgeting," *Intergovernmental Perspective* 20 (1994): 8–16.

7. Charles L. Schultze, "Paying the Bills," in *Setting Domestic Priorities*, ed. Henry J. Aaron and Charles L. Schultze (Washington, D.C.: Brookings Institution, 1992).

8. Paul E. Peterson and Mark Rom, "Macroeconomic Policymaking: Who Is in Control?" in *Can the Government Govern?* ed. John E. Chubb and Paul E. Peterson (Washington, D.C.: Brookings Institution, 1989).

9. This official was Murray Weidenbaum. See David Stockman, *The Triumph of Politics* (New York: Harper & Row, 1986), 104.

10. David E. Rosenbaum, "Answer: Trim Entitlements. Question: How Do You Do It?" *New York Times*, 8 June 1993.

11. Terry M. Moe, "The Politics of Bureaucratic Structure," in Chubb and Peterson, *Can the Government Govern?*

12. Aaron Wildavsky, *The New Politics of the Budgetary Process* (Glenview, Ill.: Scott, Foresman, 1986), 100–118.

13. Ibid, 81–82.

14. John H. Makin, Norman Ornstein, and David Zlowe, *Balancing Act* (Washington, D.C.: American Enterprise Institute, 1991).

15. Office of Management and Budget, *Preparation and Submission of "Current Services" Budget Estimates*, Bulletin 76-4 (Washington, D.C.: OMB, 13 August 1975), 2–4.

16. Maurice Wright describes volume budgeting in "From Planning to Control: PESC in the 1970s," *Public Spending Decisions*, ed. Maurice Wright (London: Allen and Unwin, 1980), 88–119.

17. See Thomas W. Wander, F. Ted Hebert, and Gary W. Copeland, *Congressional Budgeting* (Baltimore: Johns Hopkins University Press, 1984); Robin Toner, "Putting Prices on Congress's Ideas," *New York Times*, 21 August 1994.

18. John W. Ellwood and James A. Thurber, "The Politics of the Congressional Budget Process," in *Congress Reconsidered*, 2d ed., ed. Lawrence C. Dodd and Bruce Oppenheimer (Washington, D.C.: CQ Press, 1981).

19. Paul Starobin, "Bringing It Home," *National Journal*, 27 March 1993.

20. D. Roderick Kiewiet and Mathew D. McCubbins, *The Logic of Delegation* (Chicago: University of Chicago Press, 1991).

21. John R. Gilmour, *Reconcilable Differences: Congress, the Budget Process and the Deficit* (Berkeley: University of California Press, 1990), 115–23.

22. Fisher, *Presidential Spending Power.*

23. Mosher, *The GAO,* 169–200; Ray C. Rist, "Management Accountability: The Signals Sent by Auditing and Evaluation," *Journal of Public Policy* 9 (1989): 355–69.

24. Barry M. Blechman, Edward M. Gramlich, and Robert W. Hartman, *Setting National Priorities: The 1976 Budget* (Washington, D.C.: Brookings Institution, 1975), 192–202.

25. Jeff Shear, "The Untouchables," *National Journal,* 16 July 1994.

26. A variety of federal loan programs account for over $200 billion in outstanding direct loans and over $700 billion in guaranteed loans. The Tax Foundation, *Facts and Figures on Government Finance, 1993* (Washington, D.C.: Tax Foundation, 1994).

27. Office of Management and Budget, *Budget of the United States, FY 1995* (Washington, D.C.: OMB, 1995).

28. Peter Passell, "Despite All the Talk about Tax Cuts, People Can Expect to Pay More," *New York Times,* 17 November 1991.

29. For Canada, see Richard B. Simeon, *Federal Provincial Diplomacy* (Toronto: University of Toronto Press, 1974). For Germany, see Russell J. Dalton, *Politics in Germany,* 2d ed. (New York: HarperCollins, 1993), 372–77.

30. These surpluses tended to be on average 11 percent of total state revenues, although some 13 percent of total state revenues came from grants from the federal government.

31. William D. Berry, "The Confusing Case of Budgetary Incrementalism: Too Many Meanings for a Single Concept," *Journal of Politics* 52 (1990): 167–96.

32. M.A.H. Dempster and Aaron Wildavsky, "On Change: Or, There Is No Magic Size for an Increment," *Political Studies* 28 (1980): 371–89.

33. See David Braybrooke and Charles E. Lindblom, *A Strategy for Decision* (New York: Free Press, 1963).

34. Otto A. Davis, M.A.H Dempster, and Aaron Wildavsky, "A Theory of the Budgetary Process," *American Political Science Review* 60 (1969): 529–47.

35. Aaron Wildavsky, *Budgeting: A Comparative Theory of the Budgetary Process,* rev. ed. (New Brunswick, N.J.: Transaction, 1986): 7–27.

36. Michael T. Hayes, *Incrementalism and Public Policy* (New York: Longman, 1992), 131–44.

37. Peter B. Natchez and Irvin C. Bupp, "Policy and Priority in the Budgetary Process," *American Political Science Review* 64 (1973): 951–63.

38. Dempster and Wildavsky, "On Change."

39. John R. Gist, "'Increment' and 'Base' in the Congressional Appropriation Process," *American Journal of Political Science* 21 (1977): 341–52.

40. Robert E. Goodin, *Political Theory and Public Policy* (Chicago: University of Chicago Press, 1983): 22–38.

41. Brian W. Hogwood and B. Guy Peters, *The Pathology of Public Policy* (New York: Oxford University Press, 1985), 124–26.

42. David Novick, *Program Budgeting: Program Analysis and the Federal Budget* (Cambridge, Mass.: Harvard University Press, 1967).

43. Robert H. Haveman and Burton A. Weisbrod, "Defining Benefits from Public Programs: Some Guidance from Policy Analysts," in *Public Expenditure and Policy Analysis,* 3d ed., ed. Robert H. Haveman and Julius Margolis (Boston: Houghton Mifflin, 1983); Philip G. Joyce, "Using Performance Measures for Federal Budgeting: Proposals and Prospects," *Public Budgeting and Finance* 13 (1993): 3–17.

44. Aaron Wildavsky, "Political Implications of Budgetary Reform," *Public Administration Review* 21 (1961): 183–90.

45. These solutions are examples of "formula budgeting" that substitute formulas for political judgment and political will. See Eric A. Hanushek, "Formula Budgeting: The Economics and Politics of Fiscal Policy under Rules," *Journal of Public Analysis and Management* 6 (1986): 3–19.

46. James D. Savage, *Balanced Budgets and American Politics* (Ithaca, N.Y.: Cornell University Press, 1988).

47. *Bowsher v. Synar,* 478 U.S. 714 (1986); see also Lance T. LeLoup, Barbara Luck Graham, and Stacey Barwick, "Deficit Politics and Constitutional Government: The Impact of Gramm-Rudman-Hollings," *Public Budgeting and Finance* 7 (1987): 83–103.

48. Congressional Budget Office, *The Economic and Budget Outlook,* 1992–96 (Washington, D.C.: Government Printing Office, 1991).

49. Karl O'Lessker, "The Clinton Budget for FY 1994: Taking Aim at the Deficit," *Public Budgeting and Finance* 13 (1993): 7–19.

50. Alvin Rabushka, "Fiscal Responsibility: Will Anything Less Than a Constitutional Amendment Do?" in *The Federal Budget,* ed. Michael J. Boskin and Aaron Wildavsky (San Francisco: Institute for Contemporary Studies, 1982), 333–50. See also Henry J. Aaron, "The Balanced Budget Blunder," *Brookings Review,* Spring 1994, 41.

51. Rudolph G. Penner and Alan J. Abramson, *Broken Purse Strings: Congressional Budgeting 1974–1988* (Washington, D.C.: Urban Institute Press, 1989), 95–100.

52. Updated by author from Rudolph G. Penner, "Forecasting Budget Totals: Why We Can't Get It Right," in Boskin and Wildavsky, *Federal Budget,* 89–110. See also Donald F. Kettl, *Deficit Politics,* 109–17.

53. U.S. House of Representatives, Committee on the Budget, *The Line-Item Veto: An Appraisal* (Washington, D.C.: Government Printing Office, 1984).

54. Viveca Novak, "Defective Remedy," *National Journal,* 27 March 1993.

55. Daniel Tarschys, "Rational Decremental Budgeting: Elements of an Expenditure Policy for the 1980s," *Policy Sciences* 14 (1982): 49–58.

56. Allen Schick, "Micro-Budgetary Reform," *Public Administration Review* 48 (1988): 523–33.

57. President's Private Sector Survey on Cost Containment (Grace Commission), *Report to the President* (Washington, D.C.: PPSSCC, 1984).

58. Charles T. Goodsell, "The Grace Commission: Seeking Efficiency for the Whole People?" *Public Administration Review* 44 (May-June 1984): 196–204; B. Guy Peters and Donald J. Savoie, "Civil Service Reform: Misdiagnosing the Patient," *Public Administration Review* 54 (1994): 418–25.

59. Sar A. Levitan and Alexandra B. Noden, *Working for the Sovereign* (Baltimore: Johns Hopkins University Press, 1983), 85.

60. *From Red Tape to Results* (The Gore Report) (Washington, D.C.: The National Performance Review, 1993).

61. Aaron Wildavsky, "A Budget for All Seasons: Why the Traditional Budget Lasts," *Public Administration Review* 38 (1978): 501–9.

7. Evaluation and Policy Change

The final stage of the policy process is to assess what has occurred as a result of the selection and implementation of public policy and, if it is found necessary, to produce some change in the current policies of government. Critics of government tend to believe that these evaluative questions are extremely easy to answer, that the activities of government are rather simple, and that inefficiencies and maladministration could be corrected easily, if only government really wanted to do so. As this chapter points out, however, producing a valid evaluation of government programs is a difficult and highly political process in itself. That evaluation is much more difficult than for activities in the private sector. Further, if the evaluation determines that change is necessary or desirable, the policymaking process involved in making the change is perhaps even more difficult to implement successfully than is the process of policy initiation—the first adoption of a policy. Government organizations have a number of weapons to protect themselves against change, so any attempts to alter existing policies and organizations are almost certain to engender conflict.

Nevertheless, we must not be too quick to assume that government organizations are always wedded to the status quo. Change is threatening to any organization, but most organizations also know their own strengths and weaknesses and want to correct the weaknesses. The difficulties these organizations encounter in producing change arise as often from Congress and from the organizations' clients as they do from internal conservatism. Most organizations, public as well as private, are engaged in continuous evaluation of their performance. What they must find is the means to bring out effective change in that performance.

Problems in Evaluating Public Programs

Evaluation is an important need of programs and organizations in government. Like other enterprises, they need to know how they are performing. In its simplest form, evaluating a public program involves cataloging the goals of the program, measuring the degree to which these goals have been achieved, and perhaps suggesting changes that might bring the performance of the organization more in line with the stated purposes of the program. Although these appear to be simple things to do, it is actually difficult to produce unambiguous measurements of the performance of a public organization. Several barriers stand in the way of anyone who attempts to produce such valid evaluations.

Goal Specification and Goal Change

The first step in an evaluation is to identify the goals of the program, but even this seemingly simple task may be difficult, if not impossible.[1] The legislation that establishes programs or organizations should be the source of goal statements, but we have already seen (chapter 4) that legislation is frequently written in vague language to avoid offending potential members of the coalition necessary to pass that legislation. As a result, it is difficult to attach any readily quantifiable goals to programs or organizations. In addition, the goals specified in legislation may be impossible or contradictory. For example, one program had as its goal to raise all students to the mean reading level (think about it), while the expressed aim of one foreign aid program was to assist those nations in greatest need as well as those that would most likely use the money to produce significant developmental effects. When an organization is faced merely with impossible goals, it can still do something positive, but when it is faced with contradictory goals, its own internal political dynamics will become more important in determining ultimate policy choices than will any legislative statement of purpose. Further, as organizations do not function alone in the world, the contradictions existing across organizations—as when the government subsidizes tobacco production and simultaneously discourages tobacco consumption—make the identification of the goals of government as a whole that much more difficult.

Of course, internal political dynamics are still important in organizations with clear and unambiguous goals stated in their legislation. An initial statement of goals may be important in initiating a program, but once that program is in operation, the goals may be modified. These changes may be positive, as when programs adapt to changing environmental conditions in order to meet real societal needs. These positive changes in goals most often have been noted in the private sector, as when the March of Dimes shifted its goal from serving victims of polio to helping children with birth defects, but they also occur in the public sector.[2] For example, the Bureau of Indian Affairs has been transformed from an organization that exercised control over Native Americans into one that now frequently serves as an advocate of the rights and interests of those people. Also, the Army Corps of Engineers transformed its image from one of gross environmental disregard to environmental sensitivity and even environmental advocacy.[3]

Goal transformations are, of course, also negative at times. The capture of regulatory bodies by their regulated industries is a commonly cited example of negative goal change.[4] A more common example is the "displacement of goals" among the employees of an organization.[5] Although members may have been recruited on the basis of public service goals, over time the individuals' goals may become more focused on personal survival and aggrandizement. Similarly, the goals of the organization as a whole may shift toward its own maintenance and survival. Downs describes organizations (as well as the individuals within them) as going through a life cycle, beginning as zealots or advocates of certain social causes, but over time becoming more interested in surviving and maintaining their budgets than in doing anything for clients.[6] In these instances the operating goals of the program deteriorate, even if the stated goals remain the same. The organization may not even realize that the change has occurred, but the clients almost certainly will.

We should be aware that organizational transformation of goals and individual transformations have very different implications for policy and for evaluation (figure 7.1). If an individual member of the organization attempts to impose his or her own goals, whether when implementing policy or when attempting to protect his or her position, the evaluative problem is more in identifying those personal deviations. The problem is in motivating or sanctioning individuals instead of making an assessment of the performance of the organization (other than in its management). When the organization itself makes such deviations, there is more reason to evaluate the policies of the organization and the actual goals that undergird them.

	Individual	*Organization*
Reflexive	Displacement	Empire building
Operational	Street-level	Adaptation

FIGURE 7.1
TYPES OF GOAL CHANGE

Even when the goals are clearly expressed, they may not be practical. The Preamble to the Constitution, for instance, expresses a number of goals for the American government, but few, if any, are expressed in concrete language that would enable a researcher to verify that these lofty goals are or are not being achieved. Specifying such goals and putting them into operation would require further political action within the organization or the imposition of the values of the researcher in order to make it possible to compare performance with aspiration. For example, the Employment Act of 1946 pledged the government of the United States to maintain "full employment." At the time the act was passed, full employment was declared to be 4 percent unemployment. Over time, the official definition crept upward to 4.5 percent and then to 5 percent unemployed, and some economists now argue that 6 percent is an appropriate level of unemployment. Obviously, it is to the advantage of political leaders to declare that full employment has been achieved, and therefore pressure is applied to change the definition of "full employment." In this case, an admirable goal has been modified in practice, although the basic concept has remained part of national policy. This is but one instance of government playing the "numbers game" to attempt to prove that goals have been reached.[7]

In addition, most public organizations are serving multiple constituencies and therefore may have different goals with respect to those different groups in society. For example, the Comprehensive Employment and Training Act (CETA) performed a number of different functions for different segments of the society and was differentially successful at serving those constituencies. For people employed by the program, it was a source of employment and potentially of training for a better job. For individuals concerned about unemployment and whose political careers may have depended on reducing unemployment, it was a means of reducing unemployment without undertaking the more difficult task of stimulating the entire economy or altering the economic structure to supply more jobs for unskilled and semi-skilled workers. Finally, for mayors and other local government officials, the program served as a source of cheap labor that enabled them either to balance their city budgets or to prevent even more rapid tax increases than otherwise would have been necessary to maintain services. To the extent that the program kept the mayors happy by providing cheap labor in unskilled jobs such as garbage collection, it could never fulfill the goals of training the participants in the program for better jobs in the private sector. Thus, when programs are being evaluated, it is important to ask whose goals, as well as what goals, are being achieved.

Finally, it should be noted that goals may be either straitjackets or opportunities for an organization. In addition to telling an organization what it should be doing, specific goal statements tell it what it is not supposed to be doing. This may limit the creativity of the organization and may serve as a powerful conservative force within the organization. Further, the specification of goals may limit the efficiency and effectiveness of government as a whole. It may divide responsibilities in ways that are less meaningful, given an expansion of knowledge and information or a change in values. So, for example, locating the U.S. Forest Service in the Department of Agriculture may mean that trees are treated more as a crop than as a natural resource as they might be if the Forest Service were within the Department of the Interior. Giving one program or organization a goal may mean that other, more efficient means of delivering the same service will not be explored or that existing duplication of services will not be eliminated.

Measurement

Once goals have been identified and expressed in clear, concrete language, the next task is to devise a means to measure the extent to which those goals have been attained. In the public sector, measuring results or production is frequently difficult. In fact, one fundamental problem that limits the efficiency and effectiveness of government is the absence of any ready means of judging the value of what is being produced.

One of the best examples of this measurement problem occurs in one of government's oldest functions: national defense. The product called "defense" is, in many ways, the failure of real or potential enemies to take certain actions. Logically, the best defense force would never do anything, for there would be no enemy willing to risk taking offensive actions; in fact, to some degree, if a defense force is called into action, it has already failed. But measuring nonevents and counterfactual occurrences is difficult, so defense is frequently measured by surrogate measures. Thus, the megatonnage of nuclear weapons available and capable of being launched in fifteen minutes and the number of plane-hours of flight time logged by the Strategic Air Command have been used as measures of defense.

The illustration from defense policy helps to make the point that frequently activity measures are substituted for output measures when attempting to evaluate performance in the public sector. Some scholars, as well as some politicians and analysts, despair of finding more adequate means to measure the benefits of many public-sector programs. For example, Byatt argues that "it is not possible to measure benefits from defense by any known techniques, nor is it easy to even begin to see how one might be developed." He goes on to say that "it is quite impossible to allocate costs to the final objectives of education."[8] Scholarly pessimism aside, the perpetuation of activity measures serves the interests of existing organizations. First, it can shield them from stringent evaluations on nonprocedural criteria. Perhaps more important, action becomes equated with success. This will have a predictable upward impact on levels of government expenditures. It may have the less obvious effect of giving program personnel incentives to keep people on programs when they might be able to survive without the benefits.

Several factors inhibit the adequate measurement of government performance. One is the time span over which the benefits of many public programs are created. For example, although the short-term goal of education is to improve reading, writing, and computation, the long-term and perhaps ultimate goals of education can be achieved only in the future. They cannot be measured or even identified during the time in which the child is actually attending school. Among other things, education is supposed to improve the earning potential of individuals, make society more stable, and simply improve the quality of life for the individuals who receive it. These are elusive qualities to measure when an evaluation must be done quickly. This time problem in evaluation is also illustrated by Lester Salamon's analysis of the "sleeper" effects of the New Deal programs in the rural South, where it was widely believed these programs were failures while in operation but where significant results were apparent thirty years after the programs were terminated.[9]

The other side of the time problem is that any effects produced by a program should be durable.[10] Some programs, for example, produce effects only after they have been in existence for years, whereas other programs produce demonstrable results in the short term but have no significant effects in the long run. It has been argued that the latter is true of the Head Start program. Participants in the program tend to enter school with skills superior to those of non–Head Start children. After several years, however, no significant differences can be discerned between those who were in the program and those who were not. It seems that without reinforcement in later years, the effects of Head Start decay.[11] The program per se therefore may not be unsuccessful or ineffective; it simply is not carried through for a sufficient amount of time.[12]

The time element in program evaluation also produces significant political difficulties. Many individuals responsible for making policy decisions are short of time, and they must produce results quickly if their programs are to be successful. Congressmen, for example, have a tenure of only two years before facing reelection, and any program they advocate should show some "profit" before those two years have passed. Thus the policy process tends to favor short-term gains, even if they are not durable, over long-term successes. Some actors in the policy process, most notably the permanent public bureaucracy, can afford to take a longer time perspective, but most politicians cannot and do not. Thus, time itself can be crucial in evaluation.[13] The cycle of policymaking is largely determined by the political calendar, but the effects of policies have their own timetables. Part of the job of the analyst and evaluator is to attempt to make the two coincide.

The evaluation of public programs is also confounded by many other factors affecting the population. If we are to evaluate the effectiveness of a health program on a poor population, for example, we may find it difficult to isolate the effects of that health program from those of a nutrition program or those of a housing program. All these programs may have the effect of improving the health of the population, and we may find it difficult to determine which program caused the observed changes. In fact, all the programs mentioned may be related to those changes, in which case it becomes difficult to determine which program is the most efficient means of affecting the health of that community. We may be able to isolate the effects of an individual program with a more controlled social experiment, but few people want to be the subjects of such an experiment. Further, it is difficult to hold constant all the social and economic factors that also might affect the success of a public program independent of any policy; health may have improved because more people are employed and can afford more nutritious food for their families. All these problems point out that measurement in policy analysis is not as simple as the measurement that a scientist can make of a passive molecule or an amoeba.

In addition, measurement of the effects of public programs can be confounded by the history of the program and of the individuals involved.[14] Few truly new and innovative policies are initiated in industrialized countries such as the United States, and programs that have existed in the same policy area for some years may jeopardize the success of any new program. Clients may well become cynical when program after program promises to "solve" their problems. Likewise, administrators may become cynical and frustrated after changing the direction of their activities several times. Any number of policy areas have gone through cycles of change and contradiction, with inevitable effects on the morale and cooperation of clients and administrators alike. The numerous attempts to "solve" the problems of the poor are the best example of endless change and confusion.[15] In addition to creating frustration over the ability of government to make up its collective mind, one policy may not be successful after another policy has been in place. For example, if a policy of lenient treatment and rehabilitation has been tried in a prison, it may be difficult for jailers to return to more punitive methods without disruption. Interestingly, the reverse may also be true.

Another problem in the measurement of policy effects is that the organizational basis of much evaluation limits excessively the scope of the inquiry, and many unintended consequences of the program are not included in the evaluation. For example, highway engineers probably regard the interstate highway system as a great success. Many miles of highways have been built in a relatively short period, and these highways have saved many lives and many millions of gallons of gasoline, assuming that Americans would have driven the same number of miles if these superhighways had not been built. The mayor of a large city or members of the Department of Energy, however, may regard the program as a crashing failure. They realize that the building of highways in urban areas has facilitated urban sprawl and the flight of whites to the suburbs. They also know that this in turn reduced the tax base of the city and resulted in social and economic problems in the city (and the costs of urban programs) while the surrounding suburbs grew afflu-ent. Likewise, the rapid automobile transportation promised by the high-ways encouraged people to move to the suburbs and consequently to use millions of gallons of gasoline each year in commuting to their jobs. This one program and its effects show that measures used by any single agency to evaluate its programs may be too narrow and will frequently ignore many important unintended social or economic effects of the programs.

Finally, if experimentation is used as a means of attempting to ascertain the possible utility of a program, the danger that the "reactive effects of test-ing" will influence the results becomes an important consideration.[16] If citi-zens are aware that a certain policy is being tried "as an experiment," they may well behave differently from the way they would if the policy was de-clared to be "the policy." In other words, those who favor the policy may work especially hard to make the program appear effective, whereas those who do not support the program may attempt to make it appear ineffective. Even those who have no definite opinions on the policy may not behave as they would if the policy was thought to be a true attempt at change instead of an experiment. For example, if a voucher plan for educational financing is being experimented with, neither parents nor educational providers are likely to behave as they would if a voucher plan were said to be fully in op-eration. Parents may be reluctant to place their children in private schools for fear the voucher program will be terminated, and providers are unlikely to enter the marketplace if the number of parents capable of paying for their services is apt to decrease soon.

The simple knowledge that a policy initiative is considered to be a test will alter the behavior of those involved and consequently influence the re-sults of the experiment, or quasi experiment. There have been some very successful experimental evaluations of programs, such as the New Jersey In-come Maintenance Experiment, but most have required some strong incen-tives to gain the effective participation of the subjects.[17] Researchers then may have difficulty knowing if the participants are behaving "normally" or simply responding to the unusual, and often exciting, opportunity to be a guinea pig.

In evaluation research, there are problems encountered with research designs, experimental or not, that reduce the analyst's ability to make defini-tive statements about the real worth of policy. The importance and expense of public programs have led to more experimental evaluations of programs before they are implemented; nearly 100 have been instituted since 1991.[18] These experiments are concentrated very heavily in the area of social policy, in part because of the controversy surrounding many of those programs. These experiments are expensive, but not as expensive perhaps as imple-menting a poorly designed program. Conversely, not using an experimental method means that a large number of mainly unmeasured social and economic factors, not the program in question, can be the cause of any observed effects on the target population.

Targets

Related to the problem of goals is the question of the targets of a program.[19] It is important for the evaluator to know not only what the program is intended to do but also on whom it is intended to have an impact. Programs that have significant effects on the population as a whole may not have the desired effects on the more specific target population. For example, the Medicare program was intended, among other things, to benefit less affluent older people, although all the elderly were declared eligible for the program. But although the health of the elderly population in general has improved, probably at least in part as a result of Medicare, the health of the neediest portion of the elderly population has not improved commensurately.[20] As the program has been implemented, substantial coinsurance has been required along with substantial deductibles if the insured enters a hospital. As a consequence, it is difficult for the neediest elderly citizens to participate in the Medicare program.

A similar problem was encountered with the Elementary and Secondary Education Act of 1965 (ESEA). The principal intent of this program was to improve the educational attainment of underprivileged children. The evidence of the success of this legislation is mixed, but the access of all children to educational materials and facilities has increased substantially, whether or not their educational attainment has improved. In this instance as well as the Medicare example, the general population has benefited, while the target population most in need has not particularly benefited. In one instance, the target group benefited very little, while in the other it has not benefited differentially compared to the total population.

One problem in defining a target population and the program's success in reaching that population is that participation in many programs is voluntary and depends on individuals who are potential beneficiaries "taking up" the benefit. Voluntary programs directed at the poor and the less educated frequently face difficulties in making the availability of the program widely known among the target population. Even if it is made widely known to potential beneficiaries, pride, real and perceived administrative barriers, and real difficulties in consuming the benefits produced may make the program less effective than intended. An extreme example may be taken from the United Kingdom and its experience with National Health Service. One ostensible purpose of the National Health Service was to equalize access to medical care for members of all social classes. The evidence after three decades of the National Health Service does not indicate that such equalization has taken place.[21] Instead, the disparities in health status that existed before the adoption of the NHS and that in fact existed in the early twentieth century have not been narrowed by an almost completely free system of medical care. Noneconomic barriers such as education, transportation, free time, and simple belief in the efficacy of medical care have served to ensure that although there has been a general improvement in health status among the British population, little or no narrowing of class differentials has occurred. The less affluent simply have not availed themselves of the services offered to the extent that they might, especially given their relatively greater need for medical services. Although the evidence is less dramatic, it appears that social programs in the United States have suffered many of the same failures in equalizing access to, and especially utilization of, some basic social services.

Programs may create a false sense of success by "creaming" the segment of the population they serve.[22] Programs that have limited capacities to serve clients and that use stringent criteria for eligibility may select clients who actually need little help instead of those who have the greatest need. This can make the programs appear successful, although those being served did not need the program in the first place, and a large segment of the neediest go unserved. This pattern has been observed, for example, in many drug-treatment programs that take addicts who are already motivated to rid themselves of their habits. These programs can show a high rate of success when they argue for additional public funding. Such programs are successes, but only of a limited nature. Further, it would be a mistake for policymakers to generalize from the "successes" of such programs and assume that similar programs would work if applied to a general population, many of whom would not have the same level of motivation. Of course, excessively negative results may be produced by including too many people, many of whom may be inappropriate, as members of the population selected for treatment.[23]

As with so much of policy evaluation, defining the target population is a political exercise as much as an exercise in rational policy analysis. As we noted when discussing legitimation, one tendency in formulating and adopting policies is to broaden the definition of the possible beneficiaries and loosen eligibility requirements for the program. This helps build the political coalition necessary to adopt the program. This political broadening frequently makes the target population of the program more diffuse and consequently makes the program more difficult to evaluate. It is therefore often unfair to blame program managers for failing to serve the target population when those who constructed the legislation provided broad and unworkable definitions of that target. Further, with the increasing strains on the public budget it may become more politically feasible to target programs more tightly simply to reduce program costs.

Efficiency and Effectiveness

A related problem is the search for the philosopher's stone of efficiency in government, a search that often leads to a dead-end street. Measuring efficiency requires relating the costs of efforts to results and then assessing the ratio of the two. As noted, measuring results is difficult in many policy areas; it is often equally difficult to assign costs to particular results, even if those results were measurable. For much the same reasons, equal difficulties may arise in attempting to measure effectiveness. Surrogate measures of the intended results are frequently developed for public programs and policies, but all require the suspension of disbelief to be accepted as valid and reliable descriptions of what is occurring in the public sector.

As a consequence of these difficulties in measuring the substantive consequence of government actions, much of the assessment of performance in government depends on the evaluation of procedural efficiency. That is, what is assessed is not so much what is produced as how the agencies go about producing it. Some of this proceduralism depends on the legal requirements for personnel management, budgeting, and accounting; but attempts to assess procedural efficiency go beyond those formal requirements. The efficiency of public agencies may be assessed by determining the speed with which certain actions occur or by ensuring that every decision goes through all the appropriate procedural stages specified for a process. The important point here is that goals may be displaced when evaluations are made on such a basis, so the process itself, rather than the services that the process is intended to produce, becomes the measure of all things.[24] The concern with measuring efficiency through procedures may, in fact, actually reduce the efficiency of the process in producing results for citizens, because of the proliferation of procedural safeguards and their associated "red tape."

Values and Evaluation

Finally, the analyst who performs an evaluation requires a value system to enable him or her to assign valuations to outcomes. But value systems are by no means constant across the population, and the analyst who evaluates only a single program may perceive very different purposes and priorities within its policy area. Thus there may be no simple means of determining the proper valuation and weighting of the outcomes of a program. This is especially true when the program has significant unintended effects (usually negative) that must be weighed against the intended consequences.[25]

One point for consideration is that the analyst brings his or her own values to the evaluation process. Despite their rational and neutral stance, most analysts involved in policymaking have proceeded beyond the "baby analyst" stage to the point at which they have values they wish to see manifested through the policy process.[26] And as the analyst is in a central position in evaluation, he or she may have a substantial influence over the final evaluation of outcomes. Nevertheless, the analyst's values will be but one of several sets of values involved in making that final assessment of a program or policy. The organizations involved will have their own collective values to guide them in evaluating outcomes, or at least their own activities. The professions with which members of the organization or external service providers identify will also provide sets of well-articulated values that may affect the assessment of policies. Frequently, all these different sets of values conflict with one another, or with the values of clients or the general public. Thus, assessing a policy is not a simple matter of relating a set of known facts about outcomes to a given set of values. As in almost all aspects of the policy process, the values themselves may be the major source of conflict, while rational argumentation and policy analysis are merely the ammunition.

Politics

Finally, we must always remember that evaluations of public programs are performed in a political context. There may well be a sharp difference between the interpretation that an analyst might make about the success or failure of a program and the interpretation that political officials might make of the same data. Most evaluation schemes, for example, may be based on total benefits for the society, but political leaders may be interested only in the benefits created for their constituents; if that benefit is significant, the overall inefficiency of a program may be irrelevant. Political leaders may also be supportive of programs that their constituents like, whether or not the programs have any real impact on the social problems for which they were intended.

It is also important to remember that evaluations may not be done for the purpose of evaluating a program. Their ultimate purpose may be to validate a decision that has already been made for very different reasons. Thus, evaluations are often performed on very short notice, and the evaluators may be given little time to do their work. The purpose then may be simply to produce some sort of a justification for public consumption, not to produce a "real" answer about the quality of the program. That is, in part, why institutionalized forms of evaluation, such as the General Accounting Office, are so important in the public sector.[27]

Summary

Policy evaluation is a central political process and although it is also an analytic procedure, the central place of politics and value conflict cannot be ignored. The Government Performance and Results Act of 1992 is placing even more pressure on agencies to develop indicators of their performance. As increasing pressures are brought to bear on the public sector to perform its role more effectively and efficiently, evaluation will probably become even more a center of conflict. Negative evaluations of the effectiveness and efficiency of a program will be more likely to lead to the termination of the program than would have been true in more affluent times. The content of an evaluation, the values that are contained in it, and even the organization performing the evaluation will all affect the final assessment. Evaluation research is now a major industry involving numerous consulting firms ("beltway bandits"), universities, and organizations within government itself. Even these evaluative organizations will have their own perspectives on what is right and wrong in policy and will bring those values with them when they perform an analysis.

The latter point is demonstrated clearly by the evaluation of a CETA program performed by both the John F. Kennedy School of Government at Harvard University and the School of Public Policy at the University of California, Berkeley. These two schools stressed different values and approaches in their evaluations of the program. The JFK researchers concentrated on the costs and benefits of the program in strict economic terms, reflecting more utilitarian values. They found the program to be failing, with the costs surpassing the value of the benefits created. The Berkeley researchers, in contrast, stressed the political and participatory aspects of the program.[28] They found the program to be a great success, with the participants being pleased with the outcomes. The difficulty is, of course, that they were both right.

Policy Change

After evaluation, the next stage of the policy process is policy change. Rarely are policies maintained in exactly the same form over time; instead, they are constantly evolving. This change may be the direct result of an evaluation, but more often it is the result of changes in the socioeconomic or political environment, learning on the part of the personnel administering the program, or simple elaboration of existing structures and ideas. Further, a great deal of policymaking in industrialized countries such as the United States is the result of attempts at policy change rather than the result of new issues coming to the public sector for the first round of resolution.[29] Most policy areas in industrialized democracies are already populated by a number of programs and policies, so what is usually required is policy change rather than totally new policies. Policy succession, or the replacement of one policy by another, is therefore an important way of examining the development of contemporary public policies.

When a policy or program is reconsidered or evaluated, three outcomes are possible: policy maintenance, policy termination, or policy succession.[30] Policy maintenance occurs rarely as a conscious choice, but it happens as a result of simple failure to make decisions. It is possible, but unlikely, that a policy will be considered seriously and then maintained in exactly the same form. In the first place, politicians make names for themselves by advocating new legislation, not by advocating the maintenance of existing programs. Less cynically, few policies or programs are so well designed initially that they require no changes after they begin operation. The implementation of programs frequently demonstrates the weaknesses in the original design of programs that then require modification. Through what might be considered almost continuous experimentation, programs can be made to match changes in society, in the economy, and in knowledge, and can thus be made to work more effectively.

It is also unlikely that many public programs will be terminated. Once begun, programs have a life of their own. They develop organizations, and those organizations hire personnel. Programs also develop a clientele, who come to depend on the program for certain services. Once clients use the services of a program, they may find it difficult ever to return to the market provision of goods or services, or to do without. This is especially true for programs that create a "stock" of benefits, as opposed to those that are merely a flow of resources. For example, Social Security created a stock of future benefits for its recipients, so once the program was initiated, future recipients began to plan differently for their retirement. Any reduction in benefits would thus create a severe hardship that the participants in the program could not have anticipated. Programs such as AFDC or food stamps, which involve no planning by recipients, create hardships if they are reduced, but the planning or "stock" element is not involved, and so it may be possible to move clients back into the market system. Public programs, policies, and organizations may not be immortal, but relatively few are ever fully terminated.[31] Even the Reagan administration, which came into office with promises to terminate organizations like the Department of Education and the Small Business Administration, found those promises difficult to keep as the support for existing programs tended to keep them running.[32]

Dismissing the other two options leaves policy succession as the most probable outcome for an existing policy or program. Policy succession may take several forms:

1. *Linear.* Linear successions involve the direct replacement of one program, policy, or organization by another, or the simple change of location of an existing program. For example, the replacement of earlier manpower programs by the Comprehensive Employment and Training Act is an example of a linear succession.

2. *Consolidation.* Some successions involve placing several programs that have existed independently into a single program. The rolling together of a number of categorical health and welfare programs into a few block grants in the Reagan administration, as well as reflecting a change in the delivery system, was a consolidation.

3. *Splitting.* Some programs are split into two or more individual components in a succession. For example, the Atomic Energy Commission was split in 1974 into the Nuclear Regulatory Agency and the Energy Research Development Agency, reflecting the contradictory programs of regulation and support of nuclear energy that had existed in the earlier organization.

4. *Nonlinear.* Some policy and organizational successions are complex and involve elements of other kinds of successions. The complex changes involved in creating the Department of Energy from existing programs (including the two nuclear energy agencies mentioned above) are examples of nonlinear succession.

Although they entail much of the same process described for making policy (chapters 3–6), policy successions are processed in a distinctive manner. First, the agenda-setting stage is not so difficult for policy succession as it is for policy initiation. The broad issue at question has already been accepted as a component of the agenda and therefore needs only to be returned to a particular institutional agenda. Some issues, such as debt ceilings and annual reauthorizations of existing programs, automatically return to an agenda every year or even more frequently. More commonly, dissatisfaction with the existing programs returns an issue for further consideration. But returning the issue to the institutional agenda is easier than its initial introduction because there are organizational manifestations of the program and identified clients who are in a better position to bring about the consideration. Furthermore, once organizations exist, it is more likely that program administrators will learn from other, similar programs and will find opportunities for improving the program or that they will simply think of better "solutions" to the problems.

The legitimation and formulation processes will also be different from those used in policy initiation. But instead of fewer obstacles, as in agenda setting, there are likely to be more barriers. As noted, the existence of a program produces a set of client and producer interests that may be threatened by any proposed policy change. This is especially true if the proposed succession involves a "policy consolidation" (combining several programs) or a change in the policy instrument delivering the program in a direction that will demand less direct administration. For example, using policy consolidation to combine a number of categorical grants into block grants during the

Reagan administration provoked outcries from both clients (primarily big-city mayors) and producers (administrators who had managed the categorical programs). And part of the conflict over the negative income tax proposed in President Nixon's Family Assistance Plan, as well as over some of President Carter's welfare reforms, concerned the change in the instruments used to deliver the benefits, as well as ideological conflicts over the level of benefits.[33] Thus, once a policy change of one of these kinds enters an institutional arena, it is quite likely to encounter severe resistance from the affected interests. This may be true even if the threat to those interests is not real. The mere threat of upsetting established patterns of delivering services may be sufficient to provoke resistance.

Of course, some policy successions may be generated within the organization administering the program rather than imposed from the outside. An array of external political forces may be strong enough to effectuate the change, and the organization and the clientele will "gladly" accede. They may even publicly cosponsor the change. Also, some program managers may be risk takers, rather than risk avoiders like most public bureaucrats. They may be willing to gamble that the proposed change will produce greater benefits for the organization, so they need not attempt to hang on to what they have. Finally, some programs may have expanded too far; their personnel may wish to pare off some of the peripheral programs to target their clientele more clearly and protect the organizational "heartlands."[34] This does not necessarily imply that the pared-off programs will be terminated, only that they will change their organizational locations.

Clientele groups may seek to split a program from a larger organization in order to develop a clearer target for their political activities. Pressures from the National Educational Association and other educational groups to divide the Department of Health, Education, and Welfare and establish an independent Department of Education illustrate this point. It was argued that HEW did not give educational interests the direct attention they deserved. In addition, because the education budget had the greatest flexibility of all the budgets in HEW (the remainder being primarily entitlement programs), any cutting that was done was likely to be in education.[35] Although there were pressures on the Reagan administration to eliminate the Department of Education, once established it has proven difficult to alter its independent status. To some degree the Bush administration, by virtue of its increased interest in education, placed the Department of Education in a more central position.

Forming a coalition for policy change requires careful attention to the commitments of individual congressmen to particular interests and ongoing programs. As with the initial formulation and legitimation of a policy, an attempt at policy succession requires the use of the mechanisms of partisan analysis, logrolling, and the pork barrel, in order to deliver that change (see chapter 4). Again, this stage of the policy process may be even more difficult than it is for policy initiation. While the implications of a new policy are often vague, the probable effects of a change in an existing policy may be more readily identifiable. It may be easy to persuade legislators of the benefits of a new policy on the basis of limited information, but once the program has been running for some time, information will become available to the legislator. Persuading legislators to change a program that is "good enough" may be much more difficult.

There may, however, be many clients, administrators, and legislators who are dissatisfied with the program as it is being implemented, and those individuals can be mobilized to advocate the change. A coalition of this kind may involve individuals from both the right and left who oppose the existing policy. The coalition built around the 1986 tax reform illustrates this process rather well. The coalition was formed of liberals who wanted more equitable treatment of the working and middle classes and greater equity in the tax system, combined with some conservatives who wanted greater fairness in the tax code for all types of businesses.[36] Managing a policy succession by organizing such a broad coalition runs the risk that termination of the policy may be the only thing on which the coalition can agree as an alternative to the status quo. Therefore, before beginning the process, it is crucial for the analyst to have in mind the particular policy succession that he or she would like to have implemented. Otherwise, allowing political forces to follow their own lead may threaten the existence of the program.

Finally, implementing a policy succession may be the most difficult aspect of the process. That is, of course, much the same as was true for the initiation of the policy, for putting a policy into effect in the intended manner is problematic at best. But several features of policy succession as a process may make it that much more difficult. First, it is important to remember that organizations exist in the field as well as at headquarters.[37] People working in the field may have policy preferences as strong as do those working in the home office, but they may not be consulted about proposed changes. Yet the field workers must put the policy change into effect and ultimately decide who will get what as a result of the change. Thus, if policy change does not involve significant and clear modification of the existing policies, then the field staffs may well be able to continue doing what they were doing prior to the nominal change and subvert the intention of the succession legislation. This subversion need not be intentional; it may be only the result of inertia or inadequate understanding of the intentions of headquarters and the legislation.

In addition, it is important to remember that organizations do not exist alone in the world, nor do policies.[38] Instead, each organization exists within a complicated network of other organizations, all of which must cooperate in order for any of them to be successful.[39] Any change in the policies of one organization may reduce the ability of other organizations to fulfill their own goals. Education and job training may now be as important for economic performance, especially in the long run, as is formal economic policy. This interaction is perhaps especially evident in the field of social policy, where a variety of policies are necessary to meet the many and interrelated needs of poor families and in which changes in any one policy may influence the success of all the programs. Terminating food stamps, for example, would mean that AFDC payments would not be sufficient for families to buy the amounts of food they used to buy. As a consequence, housing, education, and even employment programs would be adversely impacted by increasing demands.

Finally, implementing policy succession is almost certain to be disappointing. The massive political effort required to bring about a policy succession is unlikely to be rewarded the first month, or even the first year, after the change. This is almost certain to create disappointment in the new program and perhaps cynicism about the entire policy area. As a consequence, one policy succession may generate enough disruption to engender a rapid series of changes. Further, once a stable set of policies and organizations has been disturbed, there will no longer be a single set of entrenched interests with which to contend, so forming a new coalition in favor of policy change or termination may be easier. The advocate of policy change must be cognizant that he or she may produce more change than was intended once the possibility of reform becomes apparent to participants in the policy area.

Since we now understand that implementing policy succession will be difficult, we should address the problem of designing policy changes that would be easier to implement. The ease with which change can be brought about is a function at least in part of the design of previous organizations and programs. In an era of increased skepticism concerning government and bureaucracy, policies are being designed with built-in triggers for evaluation and termination.[40] The interest in "sunset laws" means that any administrator joining such an organization, or any client becoming dependent on its services, should have reason to question the stability of those arrangements.[41] If the declining conception of entitlement to either employment or benefits from an organization can make future policy successions more palatable to those already connected with the program, then one major hurdle to policy change will have been overcome. But this declining sense of entitlement may be related to a declining commitment of workers to the program, and that can have negative consequences for the organizations that exceed the costs of change.

It is not possible to reverse history and redesign programs and organizations that are already functioning without such built-in terminators. The analyst or practitioner of policy change must therefore be prepared to intervene in existing organizations in order to produce the smooth transition from one set of policies to another. One obvious trigger for such change would be a change in the party in office, especially in the presidency. Until the Reagan presidency, however, the alternation of parties in office had produced little significant policy change.[42] That administration injected very substantial doses of ideology and policy change into American politics, with the question now being whether the subsequent Democratic administration could undo the "Reagan revolution."[43] It has been extremely difficult for the Clinton administration to assert a more activist agenda for government, given the legitimation of the antigovernment perspective during twelve years of Republican presidents.

Rapid change in demand and environmental conditions may also trigger attempts at policy succession, but organizations have proved to be remarkably effective in deflecting attempts at change and in using change for their own purposes. At present it is fair to say that there is no available technology for implementing policy succession, just as there is no reliable technology for implementation in general. A common finding is that organizations are able to interpret new policy initiatives in ways that fortify their current approaches. As with the discussion of the social construction of issues on the agenda (see pp. 47–48), organizations also socially construct the meaning of policy and law, and do so in ways that will benefit them.

Summary

Policies must be evaluated, and frequently policies must be changed. But neither task is as easy as some politicians, and even some academicians, make it appear. Identifying the goals of policies, determining the results of programs, and isolating the effects of policies compared with the effects of other social and economic forces all make evaluating public policies tricky, and at times impossible. The surrogate measures that must be used at times may be worse than no measures at all, for they emphasize activity of any sort rather than actions performed well and efficiently. The method of evaluation then places pressure on agencies merely to spend their money rather than always to spend it wisely.

Evaluation frequently leads to policy change, and the process of producing desired changes and implementing those changes in a complex political environment will tax the abilities of the analyst as well as the politician. All the usual steps in policymaking must be gone through, but they must be gone through in the presence of established organizations and clients. The implications of the proposed policy changes may be all too obvious to those actors, and they may therefore strenuously oppose the changes. As often as not, these entrenched forces will be successful in deflecting pressures for change. American government often then is a great machine that will proceed onward in its established direction without the application of significant and skillful political force. Those whose interests are already being served benefit from this inertia, but those on the outside may continue to be excluded.

Notes

1. J.N. Noy, "If You Don't Care Where You Get To, Then It Doesn't Matter Which Way You Go," in *The Evolution of Social Policy,* ed. C.C. Abt (Beverly Hills, Calif.: Sage, 1976), 97–120.

2. David L. Sills, *The Volunteers* (Glencoe, Ill.: Free Press, 1956), 253–68.

3. Daniel A. Mazmanian and Jeanne Nienaber, *Can Organizations Change?* (Washington, D.C.: Brookings Institution, 1979).

4. There is a growing literature on the means of minimizing and controlling changes in the mission of regulatory agencies. See Mathew D. McCubbins, Roger G. Noll, and Barry R. Weingast, "Structure and Process, Politics and Policy: Administrative Arrangements and the Political Control of Agencies," *Virginia Law Review* 75 (1989): 431–82; Jonathan R. Mezey, "Organizational Design and the Political Control of Regulatory Agencies," *Journal of Law, Economics and Organization* 8 (1992): 93–110.

5. Robert K. Merton, "Bureaucratic Structure and Personality," *Social Forces,* 1940, 560–68.

6. Anthony Downs, *Inside Bureaucracy* (Boston: Little, Brown, 1967), 92–111.

7. William Alonzo and Paul Starr, *The Politics of Numbers* (New York: Russell Sage Foundation, 1987).

8. I.C.R. Byatt, "Theoretical Issues in Expenditure Decisions," in *Public Expenditure: Allocation among Competing Ends,* ed. Michael V. Posner (Cambridge, England: Cambridge University Press, 1977), 22–27.

9. Lester M. Salamon, "The Time Dimension in Policy Evaluation: The Case of New Deal Land Reform," *Public Policy,* Spring 1979, 129–83.

10. See Robert E. Goodin, *Political Theory and Public Policy* (Chicago: University of Chicago Press, 1983), 26–29.

11. Debra Viadero, "'Fade-Out' in Head Start Gains Linked to Later Schooling," *Education Week* 13 (20 April 1994): 9.

12. For a discussion of this point, see Henry J. Aaron, *Politics and the Professors* (Washington, D.C.: Brookings Institution, 1978), 84–85. More recent research indicates that there may be some more durable effects. See Edward Zigler and Susan Muenchow, *Head Start: The Inside Story of America's Most Successful Educational Experiment* (New York: Basic Books, 1992).

13. Gerald Schneider, *Time, Planning and Policymaking* (Bern, Switzerland: Peter Lang, 1991).

14. Donald T. Campbell and Julian C. Stanley, *Experimental and Quasi-Experimental Design for Research* (Chicago: Rand McNally, 1966); Richard E. Neustadt and Ernest R. May, *Thinking in Time: The Uses of History for Decision-Makers* (New York: Free Press, 1986).

15. See, for example, Edward D. Berkowitz, *America's Welfare State: From Roosevelt to Reagan* (Baltimore: Johns Hopkins University Press, 1991).

16. Campbell and Stanley, *Experimental and Quasi-Experimental Design for Research*, 44–53.

17. For a discussion of the role of experimentation in assessing social policy, see R.A. Berk et al., "Social Policy Experimentation: A Position Paper," *Education Research* 94 (1985): 387–429.

18. Peter Passell, "Like a New Drug, Social Programs Are Put to the Test," *New York Times*, 9 March 1993.

19. Helen Ingram and Anne Schneider, "The Choice of Target Populations," *Administration and Society* 23 (1991): 149–67; Anne Schneider and Helen Ingram, "Social Construction of Target Populations: Implications for Politics and Policy," *American Political Science Review* 87 (1993): 334–47.

20. Karen Davis, "Equal Treatment and Unequal Benefits," *Milbank Memorial Fund Quarterly*, 1975, 449–88.

21. Peter Townsend, ed., *Inequalities in Health* (The Black Report) (London: Penguin, 1988).

22. Brian W. Hogwood and B. Guy Peters, *The Pathology of Public Policy* (Oxford: Oxford University Press, 1985).

23. Barbara J. Holt, "Targeting in Federal Grant Programs: The Case of the Older Americans Act," *Public Administration Review* 54 (1994): 444–49.

24. Peter H. Rossi and Howard E. Freeman, *Evaluation: A Systematic Approach*, 4th ed. (Newbury Park, Calif.: Sage, 1989), 135–37.

25. Sam D. Sieber, *Fatal Remedies* (New York: Plenum, 1980).

26. Arnold Meltsner, *Policy Analysts in the Bureaucracy* (Berkeley: University of California Press, 1976).

27. Eleanor Chelimsky, "The Politics of Program Evaluation," *Society* 25 (November 1987): 24–32.

28. Michael Nelson, "What's Wrong With Policy Analysis," *Washington Monthly*, September 1979, 53–60. See also Dan Durning, "Participatory Policy Analysis in a Social Service Agency: A Case Study," *Journal of Policy Analysis and Management* 12 (1993): 297–322.

29. Brian W. Hogwood and B. Guy Peters, *Policy Dynamics* (Brighton, England: Wheatsheaf, 1983).

30. Ibid.

31. Peter DeLeon, "A Theory of Policy Termination," in *The Policy Cycle*, ed. Judith V. May and Aaron Wildavsky (Beverly Hills, Calif.: Sage, 1978), 279–300; Janet E. Franz, "Reviving and Revising a Termination Model," *Policy Sciences* 25 (1992): 175–89.

32. Kirk Victor, "Uncle Sam's Little Engine," *National Journal* 23 (November 1991).

33. Laurence E. Lynn, Jr., and David deF. Whitman, *The President as Pol-*

icymaker: Jimmy Carter and Welfare Reform (Philadelphia: Temple University Press, 1981).

34. Downs, *Inside Bureaucracy.*

35. Rufus E. Miles, "Considerations for a President Bent on Reorganization," *Public Administration Review* 37 (1977): 157.

36. Gary Mucciaroni, "Public Choice and the Politics of Comprehensive Tax Reform," *Governance* 3 (1990): 1–32; Timothy J. Conlan, Margaret T. Wrightson, and David R. Beam, *Taxing Choices: The Politics of Tax Reform* (Washington, D.C.: CQ Press, 1990).

37. Jean-Claude Thoenig and Eduard Friedberg, "The Power of the Field Staff," in *The Management of Change in Government,* ed. Arne F. Leemans (The Hague: Martinus Nijhoff, 1976).

38. E.H. Klijn and G.R. Teisman, "Effective Policymaking in a Multi-Actor Environment" in *Autopoeisis and Configuration Theory,* ed. L. Schap et al. (Dordrecht: Kluwer, 1991).

39. On the network concept, see Edward O. Laumann and David Knoke, *The Organizational State: Social Change in National Policy Domains* (Madison: University of Wisconsin Press, 1987); R.A.W. Rhodes, *Beyond Westminster and Whitehall* (London: Unwin Hyman, 1988).

40. R. Kent Weaver, "Setting and Firing Policy Triggers," *Journal of Public Policy* 9 (1989): 307–36.

41. William T. Gormley, Jr., *Taming the Bureaucracy: Muscles, Prayers and Other Strategies* (Princeton: Princeton University Press, 1989), 205–7.

42. John L. Palmer and Isabel V. Sawhill, eds., *The Reagan Record: An Assessment of America's Changing Domestic Priorities* (Washington, D.C.: Urban Institute Press, 1984).

43. Gary Orfield, "Refurbishing a Rusted Dream," *Change* 25 (March 1993): 10–15.

PART THREE

Substantive Policy Issues

8. Making Economic Policy

The performance of the economy in Western societies was once considered something like the weather: everyone talked about it, but no one was able to do anything about it. Economic cycles and fluctuation were considered natural, acts of God, beyond the control of governments or human beings. That concept of the economy was altered during the Great Depression in the 1930s and the postwar economic boom.[1] The magnitude and duration of the depression were such that even conservative governments were forced to pay some attention to its effects.[2] Perhaps more important, the work of John Maynard Keynes and other economists gave governments the economic tools, and the intellectual justification for using those tools, to control an economy. The confidence of governments in their ability to manage economies is perhaps best exemplified in the postwar full-employment acts in both the United States and the United Kingdom, pledging the governments of the two nations never again to allow mass unemployment. This confidence was bolstered during the economic miracles of the 1950s, 1960s, and early 1970s in which most Western nations experienced rapid and consistent economic growth, very low levels of unemployment (the United States being a notable exception), and relatively stable price levels. In the early 1960s advisers to President Kennedy spoke of the government's ability to "fine tune" the economy and to manipulate economic outcomes by pulling a few simple economic levers.[3]

Anyone reading the above account must regard it as curious.[4] The American economy since the late 1970s and early 1980s has been characterized by unreliable and usually slow growth, high unemployment, extremely high trade deficits, and relatively high, if now declining, inflation (see table 8.1). This "stagflation" has resulted in an extremely diminished public faith in the capacity of governments to manage their national economies effectively; politicians who promise a bright economic future are now regarded with some skepticism.[5]

The Reagan administration to some degree was able to produce some economic growth during part of the 1980s with its "supply-side economics," but it did so at the cost of a greater public deficit, increased income inequal-

TABLE 8.1

PERFORMANCE OF THE U.S. ECONOMY

	1950–59	1960–69	1970–79	1980–89	1990–93
Average unemployment rate	4.5	4.8	6.2	7.2	6.6
Average GNP growth	4.0	4.1	2.8	2.7	1.5
Average price change	2.1	2.3	7.1	5.6	3.8
Average real wage growth	3.6	2.9	0.8	−0.2	−0.3

ity, and increased unemployment. The administration's efforts and those social costs still produced an average annual rate of economic growth (3.2 percent) substantially lower than the postwar average (3.6 percent). The economic growth rate during the Bush administration (2.1 percent) was even lower, and that fact played a significant role in President Bush's defeat in the 1992 election. Despite their conservatism and appeals to free-market values, Republican administrations could not escape responsibility for economic policy and attempted to ameliorate economic miseries as much as possible.

The Clinton economic proposals during the 1992 campaign were more expansionist, focusing on the creation of jobs and economic growth. Although more interested in using the power of government than his immediate predecessors, Clinton's emphasis on growth and "growing down the deficit" did well politically in a country facing numerous uncertainties about its economic future. The Clinton plans are not explicitly Keynesian, but they do depend on increasing government activity to help move the economy forward. The Clinton economic strategy also depends heavily on microeconomic tools, for example, industrial policies, job training and similar policies, to achieve the desired results.[6] Finally, the strategy depends on free trade, including the passage of the North American Free Trade Agreement (NAFTA), a strategy that continued unabated from Republican administrations. The economic indicators so far have been positive for the Clinton administration, but many underlying structural problems remain in the American economy, perhaps the most important being the continuing trade deficits and continuing, if not increasing, levels of economic inequality.

Economic policy is a central concern of government; as Bill Clinton was reminded during the 1992 campaign, "Its the economy, stupid." Economic policy is also a by-product of many other policy choices. One important step that a government must take is to form a set of policies intended to manage the economy. Factors important in that policy are the results of decisions about matters such as spending for public programs, patterns of taxation, and the interest rate charged by the central bank (the Federal Reserve System in the United States). Economic policy also depends heavily on the actions of people over which governments have little or no control. In the basic Keynesian concept of fiscal policy, an excess of public expenditures above revenues is supposed to stimulate the economy because citizens will spend the additional money, creating additional demand for goods and services. But if citizens will not spend the additional money, then the intended stimulation effect will not be created. Only when governments choose to regulate the economy directly through instruments such as wage and price controls can they be reasonably confident that their actions will generate desired behaviors. Even then, policing compliance with a wage and price policy presents severe administrative difficulties of its own.

The Goals of Economic Policy

Economic policy has a number of goals, all of which are socially desirable but some of which are not always mutually compatible. Political leaders frequently must make decisions that benefit some citizens and impose burdens on others. For example, although it is by no means as clear as it once was, there is a tradeoff between inflation and unemployment.[7] To the extent that governments attempt to reduce unemployment, they may increase the rate of inflation. The results of such a decision may benefit the worker about to be laid off but harm the senior citizen on a fixed income, as well as all citizens who hold fixed-rate investments. In general, economic policy has four fundamental goals, which German political economists have labeled "the golden quadrangle." These goals are economic growth, full employment, stable prices, and a positive balance of payments from international trade. To these may be added an additional intermediate goal: positive structural change in the economy.

Economic Growth

Economic growth has been a boon to both citizens and governments. Although it is popular among the ecologically minded in the 1990s to question the benefits of economic growth and to praise smaller and less technologically complex economic systems, most American citizens still want more of everything.[8] They became accustomed to receiving more and more income each year during the postwar period. All this economic growth translated into massive increases in the availability of consumer goods, and items such as television sets and automobiles, which were not widely available in 1950, are owned almost universally today. In material terms, economic growth has produced a standard of living in 1994 much higher than that of 1950, or perhaps even of 1970, and almost all Americans like that.

Economic growth has also been important in the political history of the postwar era. It acted as a political "solvent" to ease the transition of the United States from a "warfare state" to a "welfare state." Economic growth was sufficiently great that virtually every segment of the society could be given its own government programs without exhausting all the newly created wealth. Public programs grew along with private affluence, so individuals did not feel particularly disadvantaged by their taxes or by government benefits granted to others.[9] Further, economic growth aided the redistribution of income to the less advantaged. One calculation is that 90 percent of the postwar improvement in the economic status of American blacks has been the result of economic growth rather than redistributive public programs. The best welfare program is still a good job (see pp. 305–6).

Yet American economic growth has not compared well with the majority of our major trading partners during the postwar period. Average annual growth in per capita GNP for the United States from 1960 to 1980 was 2.2 percent, while it was 3.1 percent for Germany, 3.8 percent for Italy, and over 6.3 percent for Japan. In addition, American economic growth has been falling (although not as rapidly as growth in most other industrialized countries); average economic growth in the 1980s was less than half what it was during the 1950s, becoming even slower, or negative, in the early 1990s.

The United States may be entering a "zero-sum society" in which the gains achieved by one segment of the society must come at the expense of some other segment.[10] That to some degree already has happened. During the economic growth of the Reagan years, the middle and upper classes gained at the expense (at least relatively) of the poor and working classes. The relatively slow rate of growth is highlighted by the real (adjusted for price changes) income of the average American worker from 1970 to 1990. This important indicator of economic well-being for individuals hardly changed at all over these two decades (table 8.1). Whereas previous generations could expect to do better than their parents economically, the future for young people entering the labor market in the 1990s appears somewhat bleak. Increasing benefits for the elderly through Social Security also may mean a direct loss in the income of working-age citizens, and programs for the poor may mean a reduction in the income of the middle and upper classes through taxes. The decline of, and continuing uncertainty about, economic growth may well make politics more contentious and more difficult in the 1990s.

Full Employment

The benefits of full employment are obvious. Most adults want to work and use their talents. The welfare state has provided a floor for those who are made unemployable so that they and their families are unlikely to starve or do without medical care. These benefits, however, cannot match the income that can be earned by working, nor can social programs replace the pride and psychological satisfaction that comes from earning one's own living. These psychological benefits are perhaps especially pronounced in the United States, where the social and political culture attaches great importance to work and self-reliance. These values are reflected in the significantly higher rates of family problems, suicides, and alcoholism found among the unemployed than among the employed.

In addition to its effects on individuals, unemployment has some influences on government budgets. When individuals are not working, they do not contribute to Social Security or pay income taxes. Also, they cost the government money in unemployment benefits, Medicaid payments, food stamps, and the services of other social programs. Thus, increasing unemployment may upset the government's best plans to produce a balanced budget or a deficit of a certain size. Even if the level of unemployment is accurately anticipated, revenues are still lost and expenditures required. Also, other important programs may be underfunded because of the need to assist the unemployed through public programs. Compared to many of its major trading partners, the United States has achieved relatively low rates of unemployment since the late 1980s.

What is perhaps more important than the aggregate performance of the United States on this indicator is the concentration of unemployment by race and age. Blacks and young Americans bear by far the highest rates of unemployment; among young blacks, the rate of unemployment approaches 50 percent. And even though aggregate employment figures appear good, there has been a shift in the types of jobs being created in the economy. There were over 15 million more nonfarm jobs in the United States in 1992 than in 1980. During that time, the number of goods-producing jobs declined by 400,000, while the number of service-producing jobs increased by almost 15.5 million. Of the new service jobs created, at least one-third were in restaurants, hotels, and other relatively low-wage industries, while the other two-thirds were in a variety of more lucrative service occupations—in financial services, computer firms, and the like.[11] The same pattern of employment change is projected to continue for at least the next decade.[12]

The changing pattern of job creation to some degree reflects changes in the structure of the U.S. economy. The whole economy has been shifting toward a service base. This shift poses a very great problem for some regions of the country (the industrial Northeast), and for the traditional industrial labor force (see table 8.2). Many dozens of new jobs are created in the United States every day, but they tend to be either suited for those with technical skills (computer programming) or to pay relatively little (clerking in fast-food restaurants). Industrial workers accustomed to earning high wages in unskilled or semiskilled occupations have found the structural shift in

TABLE 8.2

UNEMPLOYMENT IN THE UNITED STATES

Across time

1970	1975	1980	1986	1988	1990	1991	1992	1993
4.4	4.8	7.0	6.9	5.4	5.4	6.6	7.4	6.8

By state (March 1994)

High		Low	
West Virginia	11.0	Nebraska	3.2
Alaska	9.1	South Dakota	3.5
California	8.9	Utah	3.6
Maine	8.6	Iowa	4.2
New Jersey	8.4	North Carolina	4.5

SOURCE: Bureau of Labor Statistics, *Monthly Labor Review,* June 1994.

the economy very disturbing, but they are almost powerless to change it.[13] The increased prevalence of low-wage jobs often makes two incomes necessary to maintain a reasonable family lifestyle; this increases demands for improved social (family leave) and educational (early childhood) programs from the public sector. In this instance, as in almost any area of social or economic life, it is impossible to contain the effects of change within a single policy area.

Stable Prices

Unlike unemployment, inflation affects all citizens through increases in the prices they pay for goods and services.[14] Increased rates of interest are also a form of inflation because they increase the costs of borrowing money, which is then passed on in higher prices. Inflation affects different portions of the community differently, however, and may even benefit some people. On the one hand, inflation particularly hurts those living on fixed incomes, such as the elderly who live on fixed pensions. It also adversely affects those (such as college professors) who are not sufficiently well organized to gain wage increases equal to increases in price levels.

On the other hand, inflation benefits individuals and institutions that owe money. The significance of a debt is reduced as inflation eats away at the real value of currency. As the biggest debtor in the society, government is perhaps particularly benefited by inflation. The amount governments owe, relative to the total production of their economies, can diminish if inflation makes everything cost more. Governments with progressive tax structures also benefit from inflation as people whose real incomes (i.e., incomes adjusted for changes in purchasing power) have not increased see their money incomes increase. These people are moved into higher tax brackets and pay a larger portion of their income in taxes; as a consequence, government receives a relatively painless (politically) increase in its revenues. Many tax changes undertaken in the 1980s had as one purpose reducing the progressivity of taxation or requiring governments to relate the thresholds of tax brackets to inflation so that government would not receive an automatic "fiscal dividend."

Inflation is by no means an unqualified boon for governments. Many benefits paid out by governments now are indexed, or adjusted for changes in the price level.[15] As a consequence, much of any increase in revenues from inflation must be paid out directly as increased benefits. The things that a government must buy, most notably the labor of its employees, increase in price during inflationary periods. This is especially important because government work tends to be so labor intensive that its costs increase more rapidly than other labor costs in the society. Consequently, government revenues must increase more rapidly than those of the rest of the economy in order for the government to be able to supply the same quantity of goods and services.[16]

The performance of the American economy in maintaining a stable price level during the postwar period has been better than that of most of its major trading partners. Only Germany and Japan have been more success-

TABLE 8.3

INFLATION RATE OF UNITED STATES
AND MAJOR TRADING PARTNERS

	1988	1989	1990	1991	1992
United States	4.0	4.7	5.3	3.0	3.0
Canada	4.0	4.8	4.8	1.5	1.8
Japan	0.6	2.3	3.1	1.7	1.2
France	2.6	3.7	3.4	2.4	2.0
Germany	1.3	2.8	2.7	4.0	4.2
Italy	5.1	6.3	6.5	5.4	4.2
Sweden	6.8	6.1	6.9	2.2	4.7
United Kingdom	4.9	8.0	9.4	3.7	1.6

SOURCE: Organization for Economic Cooperation and Development, *Main Economic Indicators* (Paris: OECD, monthly).

ful in the postwar period in holding down price increases, and countries such as Italy have had more than double the rate of inflation of the United States. The relatively superior performance of the U.S. economy in this area can be explained by several factors, including its relatively poorer performance on unemployment during much of the postwar period. It is also argued that the Federal Reserve Board's independence from political interference has allowed it to use monetary policy to regulate the price level.[17] Also, the relative weakness of the labor movement in the United States has meant fewer strong pressures to push wages upward than have been brought to bear in other Western countries, although the power of large corporations might have been expected to be related to increasing prices.[18]

For whatever reason, in comparison with other nations the United States has been a low-inflation country during most of the postwar period, although many Americans may be far from pleased with the price increases that have occurred. That record began to become less positive relative to the rest of the industrialized world during the late 1980s. This has been in part because of the inflationary effects of large-scale budget deficits, but the recession of the early 1990s helped keep prices virtually stable for the first years of this decade. Even with the return to economic growth in the mid-1990s inflation has remained very low, in part because of the active intervention of the Federal Reserve. Still, with economic growth being more rapid than in most other countries, inflation has also been more rapid.

For the 1990s, inflation may not be the threat it once was, and central banks and politicians now run the risk of overreacting to the threat of inflation. If the money supply is restricted too much, economic growth and employment will be threatened. A number of economic factors appear to be conspiring to make inflation a less significant economic threat than in the past. One factor is the expansion of energy sources, with greater access to oil in the former Soviet Union and a number of new sources, which should stabilize or lower those prices. Further, the prices for other raw materials (including agricultural products) are stable or decreasing as Third World countries are stressing exports of primary commodities rather than rapid industrialization. Also, wage rates in the United States have been dropping (in real terms) for the last five to ten years so that a major cost of production is also dropping. In short, deflation may be possible and price stability a very real possibility.

A Positive Balance of Payments

The economy of the United States is relatively autarkic, and the U.S. economy is relatively less involved in international trade than are the economies of most other industrialized countries.[19] It is still important for the United States to regulate the balance of payments from trade. The balance of payments is the net result of the cost of imports and the cost of exports. If a country spends more money abroad than it receives from abroad, it has a negative balance of payments. Naturally, a country that spends less overseas than it receives has a positive balance of payments. The final figure for the balance of payments is composed of the balance of trade (payment for real goods traded) and the balance on "invisibles," such as insurance, banking, and shipping fees.

Over the past decade, the United States has generally had a large negative balance of trade but a positive balance on invisibles, and these have added up to a negative balance of payments. A number of factors were included in the large negative balance of payments. For much of the 1980s, world oil prices were low, but prices began to increase in the early 1990s. The United States had learned little from earlier oil crises and had again become heavily dependent on foreign oil. America's demand for other foreign products, such as Japanese automobiles and electronics, continued to increase. By the mid-1990s the relatively rapid recovery of the American economy (when compared to the rest of the industrialized world) meant that demand in the United States for foreign goods tended to increase more rapidly than did foreign demand for American goods. This increasing demand also contributed to the continuing negative balance of payments.

The effects of a net negative balance of payments are generally detrimental to a country's economy. In the first place, a negative balance of payments indicates that the country's products are not competitive with those from other countries. This may occur because of the price, because of quality, or because a country cannot produce a commodity, such as oil. More important, a negative balance of payments tends to reduce the value of the country's currency in relation to that of other nations. If a country continues to trade its money for commodities overseas, the laws of supply and demand dictate that the value of the country's currency eventually will decline, as more money goes abroad than is returned. This effect has been especially difficult for the United States because the dollar has been the "top currency" in international trade for some years and because so many dollars are held overseas and used in international transactions.[20] Finally, as in the case of trading for raw materials, a negative balance of payments may indicate a country's dependence on the products of other nations, with the potential for international "blackmail." And holding a great deal of a country's currency abroad may mean that the value of that currency is especially vulnerable to the actions of others.

For the United States in the 1990s, international flows of capital have also become a difficulty. Money flowed into the United States, in part because of political stability and high interest rates, but this has meant that a number of businesses and a large amount of property is now owned outside the country.[21] This is in part offset by the large amount of property and industries overseas owned by American firms and individuals. Further, as the world economy becomes less national and more international, the issues of capital flows may become more a fact of economic life.

Structural Change

The final goal of economic policy is structural change, or changing the industrial and regional composition of production. Some regions of a country may be less developed than others; the South traditionally has been the depressed section of the United States, but it is now relatively prosperous compared to the Great Lakes states. In addition, the composition of production makes some regions extremely vulnerable to economic fluctuations. The experience of Michigan during the continuing slump in automobile production and that of Louisiana due to declining oil prices in the late 1980s are graphic evidence of the danger of relying too heavily on a single product. In addition, government may want to alter the structure of the entire economy. The most common manifestation of this is the effort of Third World countries to industrialize their agricultural economies. This was, of course, also true of the United States in the nineteenth century, and industrialized countries still want to shift their economies into the most profitable sectors possible.

In the United States, the federal government has been relatively little involved in promoting structural change. Major exceptions have been regional programs such as the Tennessee Valley Authority and the Appalachian Regional Commission. Also, the federal government has been active in supporting and protecting defense industries. If anything, the federal government has tried to use trade policies such as quotas as a means of slowing the structural change of the economy. But state and local governments have been extremely active in attempting to promote economic development and structural change, particularly through their tax systems.[22] States will permit industries moving in to receive tax credits for their investments and to write off a certain percentage of their profits against taxes for some years. Local governments have fewer tax options (property tax relief being most important), but they can give grants for industrial sites and other infrastructural developments to make themselves attractive to industries.

Southern states have been especially active in promoting economic development through tax incentives; these policies, combined with a favorable climate, more available energy, and low rates of unionization, have tended to reverse the traditional imbalance in economic growth between the North and the South.[23] The Frostbelt states have become economically depressed, while many Sunbelt states have grown rapidly. The northern industrial states have appealed to the federal government for assistance but have yet to receive any substantial help. They also are using their own incentives to convince industries to remain where they are instead of moving south, and have actively sought new investments. In the 1980s some northern states generated a (brief) turnaround in their economies, relying on their educational and technological resources instead of their industrial labor force.[24] This strategy is likely to become more effective as the United States continues to lose manufacturing jobs overseas and must compete primarily with educational and technological capacity.

The Instruments of Economic Policy

Governments have a number of weapons at their disposal to try to influence the performance of their economies. Analysts often speak of a dichotomy between monetary policy and fiscal policy.[25] These are certainly two of the more important policy options, but other options are available. This section discusses fiscal policy, monetary policy, regulations and control, financial support, public ownership, incentives, and moral suasion as instruments of economic management. Most governments use a combination of all these tools, although the government of the United States tends to rely most heavily on the indirect instruments of fiscal and monetary policy.

Fiscal Policy

We have discussed the importance of the budgetary process as a means of allocating resources among government agencies and between the public and private sectors of the economy. These decisions are also central to the Keynesian approach to economic management, which stresses the importance of the public budget in regulating effective demand. Simply stated, if government wants to stimulate the economy (i.e., to increase economic growth and reduce unemployment), it should run a budget deficit. Such a deficit would place in circulation more money than the government had removed from circulation, thereby generating more demand for goods and services as citizens found more money to spend. This additional money, as it circulates through the economy, multiplies in magnitude to an extent that depends on the propensity of citizens to spend their additional income rather than save it. Likewise, if a government seeks to reduce inflation in an "overheated" economy, it would run a budget surplus, removing more money from circulation in taxes than it put back through public expenditures. This budget surplus would leave citizens with less money than they had before the government's action and should lessen total demand.

The theory of fiscal policy is rather straightforward, but the practice presents several important difficulties. Perhaps the most important of these is that deficits and surpluses are not politically neutral. It is a reasonable hypothesis that citizens like to receive benefits from government but do not like to pay taxes to finance those benefits. Consequently, despite the rhetoric in American politics lauding the balanced budget,[26] there were forty-two budget deficits in forty-five years from 1950 through 1994. Deficits occurred even during the 1950s and 1960s when the economy performed very well. Politicians have practiced "one-eyed Keynesianism," reading the passages Keynes wrote about running deficits but apparently not reading the passages about running surpluses in good times.[27] The tendency toward running deficits was accentuated during the Reagan administration, when the administration's belief in supply-side economics produced large tax cuts without commensurate reductions in expenditure (see pp. 209–11). Although Keynes has been disavowed by many, or even most, economic policymakers, his ideas are still considered when the budget is made, and the influence of deficits (and at least in theory, surpluses) must be considered.

Also, as noted, estimating the amounts of revenues to be received, or the outlays of public programs, is not a simple task. Even with the best budget planning it is not possible to adjust precisely the level of a deficit or surplus (see table 8.4). The automatic stabilizers built into the revenue and expenditure programs of government help regulate the deficit. For example, when the economy begins to turn downward, government revenues will decline as workers become unemployed and cease paying income and Social Security taxes. Also, the unemployed workers and their families will begin to place demands on a variety of social programs. The declines in revenues and increases in expenditures will automatically push the budget toward a deficit without political leaders making any conscious choices about fiscal policy. Of course, if the recession is very deep or continues for a very long time, government may have to act with new programs that will further increase the deficits.

To assist in making decisions about the right-size budget deficit or surplus to aim for, the "full-employment budget" has been suggested, and to some extent used, as a decision-making aid.[28] The idea is that the budget should be in balance during the periods of full employment, defined as 5 percent unemployed. Naturally, during times of higher unemployment there would be a deficit, given the fundamental Keynesian paradigm. A budget is calculated that would be in balance at full employment, and then the added costs of unemployment in social expenditures and lost revenues are added to determine the full-employment deficit. That deficit is deemed justifiable because it results not from the profligacy of governments but from economic difficulties. Any deficit higher than that is seen as a political decision to spend money that will not be raised as taxes and as expenditures giving incumbent politicians an advantage in reelection. A deficit also may be accepted for ideological reasons, as in the case of the very large deficits of the

TABLE 8.4

FEDERAL DEFICIT AND DEBT, 1970–93

IN BILLIONS OF DOLLARS

Year	Deficit	Debt
1965	−1,411	322,318
1970	−2,342	380,921
1975	−53,242	541,925
1980	−73,835	908,503
1981	−78,976	994,928
1982	−127,989	1,136,798
1983	−207,818	1,371,164
1984	−185,388	1,564,110
1985	−212,344	1,816,974
1986	−221,245	2,120,082
1987	−149,769	2,345,578
1988	−155,187	2,600,768
1989	−153,477	2,867,537
1990	−220,470	3,206,347
1991	−268,746	3,598,993
1992	−290,160	4,002,669
1993	−327,347	4,410,475

SOURCE: Tax Foundation, *Facts and Figures on Government Finance, 1993* (Washington, D.C.: Tax Foundation, 1994).

Reagan/Bush administrations resulting largely from tax cuts. Of course, in an overheated economy, there would be a full-employment surplus, with the additional revenues being taken out of circulation.

MAKING FISCAL POLICY

Most fiscal policy decisions are made through the budgetary process outlined in chapter 6. When the president and his advisers establish the limits under which expenditure decisions of the individual agencies must be made, they make these decisions with a particular budget deficit or surplus in mind. Given the rhetoric and conventional wisdom of American politics, it appears that most presidents initiate the process with the intention of producing a balanced budget, but few if any actually do so. They are overwhelmed by the complexity of the calculations and, more important, by political pressures to spend but not to tax. They may also be overwhelmed by their own belief in economic policies intended to produce rapid economic growth that cannot do so once they are implemented.

Fiscal policy is primarily a presidential concern, and it is a primary one for most presidents. Only at the level of the entire budget can global decisions about economic management be made and somewhat shielded from special interests that demand special expenditures or tax preferences. But budgetary decisions cannot be purely presidential. Within the executive branch the president is subject to advice and pressures—largely in the direction of spending more. Although the president can attempt to rise above special interests, his cabinet secretaries certainly cannot; they may press appeals from special interests on him and his budget director. Furthermore, the president cannot make expenditure and taxation decisions alone. The Congress is involved in these decisions, and its involvement has been increasingly important since the mid-1970s. The formation of the Congressional Budget Office, combined with the increasing vigor of the Joint Economic Committee and the Joint Budget Committee, has given Congress a greatly enhanced capacity to compete with the president over fiscal policy decisions. The negotiations between the Bush administration and congressional leaders during the budget crisis of 1990 indicated the extent to which budgetary decisions, and decisions about fiscal policy, have become joint decisions.[29]

Similarly, the negotiations between the Clinton administration and Congress over the FY 1994 budget pointed to the importance of Congress as an economic policymaker.[30] The Clinton administration began with the budget originally proposed by the outgoing Bush administration and attempted to change that budget in order to reduce the deficit. They attempted to adapt that budget to conform to the economic proposals made by President Clinton during the 1992 campaign. In particular, there was some increase in taxes and other revenues ($36 billion net), and some reduction in expenditures (over $50 billion net) in an attempt (to some degree successful) to reduce the size of the federal budget deficit.

Despite the competition of Congress, the budget is labeled a presidential budget, and the economic success or failure it produces (or at least with which it is coincident) generally is laid at the president's doorstep politically.[31] As a consequence, even if the budget is not the dominant influence on economic performance it is sometimes made out to be, a president will want to have his ideas implemented in the budget and at least be judged politically on the effects on his own policies, rather than those of Congress. Further, leadership in economic policy has become as much a part of the role of a president as being commander-in-chief of the armed forces. Any president who attempts to avoid responsibility for the economy will find difficulty in doing so, and might be perceived as a weak domestic leader. President Bush, for example, attempted to blame Congress for the recession of the early

1990s, but he received most of the blame from the public and the media, and that was a major factor in his loss of the 1992 election.

SUPPLY-SIDE ECONOMICS

With the election of President Reagan in 1980 there came something of a revolution in fiscal policy in the United States, usually referred to as "supply-side economics."[32] Basically, this approach states that, instead of inadequate demand in the American economy (the standard Keynesian critique), there was a dearth of supply, especially a dearth of investment. The fundamental idea of supply-side economics is to increase the supply of both labor and capital so that economic growth will take place. Further, this approach argues that the intervention of government, especially through high taxes, is the major barrier to full participation of labor and capital in the marketplace, and therefore any measures to reduce that role will in the (not very) long run produce rapid economic growth.

Some of the analysis supporting the supply-side policies had a great deal of face validity. In particular, the U.S. economy has had a dearth of savings and investment compared with other industrialized countries (see table 8.5). Savings are the assets from which business can borrow for new factories and

TABLE 8.5

FIXED CAPITAL FORMATION AS A PERCENTAGE
OF GROSS DOMESTIC PRODUCT

	1974	*1980*	*1988*	*1993*
Australia	23.5	23.5	24.9	14.9
Belgium	22.7	20.7	17.8	18.0
Canada	23.7	23.1	22.0	18.9
France	25.8	22.4	20.1	20.6
Germany	21.6	21.8	19.9	19.6
Italy	25.9	22.8	20.7	18.9
Japan	34.8	31.7	30.5	23.3
Netherlands	21.9	21.0	21.4	19.9
Spain	28.0	21.8	22.0	21.9
Sweden	21.5	19.8	19.7	16.1
Switzerland	27.6	21.8	26.6	26.5
United Kingdom	20.9	18.6	19.2	18.3
United States	18.6	20.4	17.1	15.7

SOURCE: Organization for Economic Cooperation and Development, *Main Economic Indicators* (Paris: OECD, monthly).

equipment, but Americans have chosen to spend, and to borrow to spend more, rather than save and invest.[33] This is a real problem in the economy, although the record of cutting taxes appears to be that the public simply takes the savings and spends more. This is another example of a tool of economic policy that depends on the behavior of the public to be effective and that does not appear to have had much cooperation from the public.

The major instrument for implementing supply-side economics was the Economic Recovery Tax Act of 1981 (ERTA) which, over four years, reduced the average income tax of Americans by 23 percent. The tax reductions were not across the board, but especially advantaged those in higher income brackets, presumably those most likely to invest if they had additional after-tax income. The fundamental assumption of ERTA was that if individuals had increased incentives to work and invest they would do so, and economic growth would occur as a result. Thus, Keynesian economics believed in providing people (usually the less affluent) with increased income through government expenditures, with the expectation that they would spend the money and create more demand for goods and services. The supply-side solution, in contrast, argued for providing people (usually the more affluent) with a greater incentive to work and invest because they could retain more of what they earned.

The impact of the Economic Recovery Tax Act was a massive increase in the federal deficit (table 8.4, p. 207). Taxes were reduced significantly, but despite the best efforts of some members of the administration, federal expenditures were not reduced nearly as much. The deficit was largely ignored at first by the Reagan administration, despite protests by administration members such as David Stockman (who later left the administration at least in part because of questions about the deficit). This absence of concern by a fiscally conservative administration was justified by the belief that the reduction in taxes would so stimulate economic growth that, over time, more revenues would be generated by lower tax rates; this sharp response of government revenues to tax reductions is referred to as the "Laffer curve," after the economist Arthur Laffer.[34] Even after the optimistic Laffer curve did not work, taxes were not increased by the Reagan administration, and low taxation became a central feature of its (and the succeeding Bush administration's) economic policies and political appeals to the public.

The deficits generated by the Reagan tax plan have continued at historically high levels. The Reagan administration did little to increase revenues when it became apparent that economic growth was not occurring as rapidly as expected. In addition, expenditures have proven more difficult to reduce than expected. The Tax Equity and Financial Responsibility Act of 1982, initiated by Congress, was directed at increasing revenues by closing some tax loopholes and increasing some indirect taxes, but the problem of the deficit persisted. George Bush had once referred to supply-side economics as "voodoo economics," but once in office he continued most of the economic policies of the Reagan administration.

The problem of the deficit came to a head during the construction of the 1990-91 (FY 1991) federal budget in the Bush administration. The deficit projected for that year was a great deal more than that permissible under the Gramm-Rudman-Hollings law passed by Congress (see chapter 6), but neither President Bush nor Congress wanted to take responsibility for raising taxes or reducing popular benefits. Also, congressional Democrats had a very redistributive plan for increasing taxes that the president and even some conservatives in their own ranks could not accept. President Bush was especially reluctant to increase taxes after making his campaign pledge of "No new taxes," but in the end he did have to propose some increased taxation. After several continuing resolutions to keep government operating without passing a formal budget and one failed budget bill, a compromise was finally reached in mid-October 1990. This compromise called for increasing some taxes (largely excise taxes on tobacco, alcohol, and gasoline) and reducing a few spending programs, but nothing of a magnitude that would have eliminated the deficit, or even reduce it significantly. Further, the deficit figure being discussed was actually a low estimate of the true federal deficit. It did not include, for example, the costs of "bailing out" failed savings-and-loan institutions insured by the federal government and several other "off budget" expenditure programs.[35]

Budget deficits appear to be a continuing problem for the federal government and therefore a potential economic problem for all Americans. The deficits have had a number of potentially negative consequences for the economy. One is that a great deal of foreign capital was needed to fund the debts created, and the United States became the world's largest debtor nation in the space of a single decade. Further, the need to borrow so much money may make interest rates too high for businesses and individuals to borrow the money they need and may slow economic growth. Finally, government debt, like private debt, must be repaid; at a minimum, the interest on the debt must be paid. The need to pay so much debt interest is placing a severe restriction on the capacity of the federal government to fund other programs. The continuing conservative impact of the Reagan administration may be that debt interest keeps government from spending money on social programs for years in the future.

Monetary Policy

Whereas the basic fiscal policy paradigm stresses the importance of demand management through varying levels of revenues and expenditures, the monetary solution to economic management stresses the importance of the money supply in controlling economic fluctuations. Like the presence of additional public expenditures, increasing the amount of money in circulation is presumed to stimulate the economy. The extra money lowers interest rates, making it easier for citizens to borrow for investments or for purchases, and this in turn encourages economic activity. Likewise, reducing the availability of money makes it more difficult to borrow and to spend, thus slowing down an inflationary economy.

In the United States, the Federal Reserve Board and its member Federal Reserve banks are the primary makers of monetary policy. The Federal Reserve Board and the banks are intentionally independent from the executive authority of the president, and because their budget is only appended to the federal budget, it is also independent from congressional control through the budgetary process.[36] The Federal Reserve is independent intentionally, so its members exercise their judgment as bankers rather than submit to the control of political officials who might want to manipulate the money supply for political gain. And the Federal Reserve has exercised its independence and has refused several times to accede to presidential requests. For example, during the Johnson administration, Federal Reserve Chairman William McC. Martin turned down the president's request to increase the money supply more rapidly to ease the financial pressures created by the simultaneous expansion of domestic social programs and the Vietnam war. More recently, the Federal Reserve Board would not cooperate with the Bush administration in its efforts to fund the continuing deficits with a minimum of tax increases, nor with President Clinton in his efforts to keep the economy recovery moving as rapidly as possible during 1994.

The Federal Reserve has a variety of tools at its disposal to influence the economy. Its three principal tools are open-market operations, the discount rate, and reserve requirements. Open-market operations are the most commonly used mechanisms for monetary control. These involve the Federal Reserve going into the money markets to buy or sell securities issued by the Federal Reserve. If it wishes to reduce the supply of money, the Federal Reserve attempts to sell securities, exchanging the bonds for a quantity of cash that was in circulation before the purchase. If it wants to expand the money supply, it will purchase securities on the market, exchanging money for the bonds. The success or failure of these operations depends, of course, on the willingness of citizens to buy and sell the securities at the time and at the rate of return the Federal Reserve offers.

A more drastic option available to the Federal Reserve is to change the discount rate. The discount rate is the rate of interest at which member banks can borrow money from the Federal Reserve bank. Obviously, this rate will affect interest rates in the economy as a whole, as member banks will have to increase their interest rates to compensate for the increased cost of borrowing money from the Federal Reserve. And with the basic monetary paradigm, making money more difficult (or at least more costly) to borrow will slow down economic activity and, presumably, inflation. The discount rate changes relatively infrequently and then only by a very small amount. For example, the rate had not changed for months prior to December 1990 when the Federal Reserve reduced the rate slightly to attempt to minimize an apparent recession. As that recession continued well into 1991, the Federal Reserve continued to make downward adjustments in the discount rate to attempt to stimulate investment and growth, and the rate reached its lowest level for over a decade. During 1994 and 1995, however, the Federal Reserve raised the discount rate several times in attempting to prevent a return to inflation, despite fears that this action would slow down the economic recovery.

Finally, the Federal Reserve Board can change the reserve requirement. Member banks of the Federal Reserve system are required to keep reserves on deposit at the Federal Reserve banks to cover their outstanding loans. This is a percentage of the total amount they have out in loans, normally around 20 percent. If the Federal Reserve raises the reserve requirement from 20 to 25 percent, then for each dollar a bank had out in loans before the change, it can lend only 75 cents. The bank will have to deposit more money, call in some loans, or reduce the pace at which it grants new loans. Any of these measures will reduce the amount of money in circulation and should slow down economic activity. Conversely, if the Federal Reserve reduces the reserve requirement, banks can make more money available for loans and increase economic activity. Changing the reserve requirement is a drastic action and is undertaken only if there is a perceived need to influence the economy dramatically and quickly.

The Federal Reserve has been a paragon of conservative economic policy. Its members traditionally have been bankers or businessmen who have tried to please a constituency composed of the same. The Federal Reserve's tight money policies have been criticized frequently for producing economic hardship and slow growth, as when it raised interest rates during the early days of the economic recovery in 1993. On the other hand, actions of the Federal Reserve have also been defended as appropriate, given threats of inflation fueled in part by federal fiscal policy. What is most important, however, is the possibility that a lack of coordination of fiscal and monetary policy will cause the two to cancel each other's effects and produce little or no real benefit, or the possibility that their coordination may produce an excessive amount of correction to the economy so that changes constantly overshoot the mark and the fluctuations of the economy are exaggerated rather than minimized.

Regulation and Control

In general, regulation has been used, not for the purpose of general economic management, but for the sake of achieving other economic and social goals. Regulations have been associated with cleaning up the environment, making workplaces safer, or making consumer products safer. Obviously such regulations also have an effect on overall economic growth because they make it more or less profitable to engage in certain economic activities. In addition, some regulatory activities, such as antitrust regulation, do have a pervasive impact on the economic structure of the society and perhaps on consumer prices for a range of goods.

Antitrust regulation has been one of the most important forms of government control of the economy. Beginning with the Sherman Act in 1890, the federal government has sought to ensure that a few firms did not control an industry and then extract excessive profits.[37] The criminal nature of the sanctions in the Sherman Act, and the vagueness of its definitions of illegal actions, made enforcement difficult, and the Clayton Act was passed in 1914 at the same time that the Federal Trade Commission was created. This legislation gave clearer (although still far from unambiguous) definitions of actions that constituted "combinations in restraint" of trade and provided an enforcement mechanism that could act administratively rather than entirely through the courts.[38]

Antitrust regulation as a mechanism for fostering competition has been a significant tool in American economic policy, but it is possible that it has outlived its utility. The concern in the 1990s is for external *competitiveness*, rather than for internal *competition*. It may be that to be competitive with many foreign firms American firms will have to be larger and have a larger market share. Further, there may be needs for greater protection of patent rights and intellectual property rights that, in turn, may create natural monopolies in certain areas. There will still be a need to protect consumers and nascent firms from the economic power of big business, but antitrust may not be the best tool.

One form of regulation that does have more pervasive effects on the economic goals outlined previously is wage and price controls, otherwise referred to as incomes policies. American experience with this regulation is rather limited, although it has been used during wartime. But even in peacetime wage and price policies have been proposed and even adopted. The New Economic Policy of the Nixon administration was a wage and price policy adopted during a time when there was no declared war, although Vietnam certainly did have some influence on the economy of the time. The fundamental idea behind wage and price controls is to mandate rates at which those two crucial factors in the economy can change. These policies are directed primarily at problems of inflation but have effects on a variety of economic indicators. Wage and price policies are dramatic steps, especially in countries such as the United States with a dominant free-market ideology, and they are even more dramatic when adopted by presidents with conservative images. At least in the short run, these policies can buy time to allow other policies to work to slow inflation.

Perhaps the most remarkable thing about the limited experience of the United States with wage and price controls is that they were very popular when in place, especially given the prevailing economic ideology of the country.[39] Citizens apparently believed that at last the government was attempting to do something to control inflation and was attempting to make equitable decisions about price increases. There is some evidence that citizens would have welcomed a more direct effort at price control during the rapid inflation of the late 1970s and early 1980s. Wage and price controls involve massive administrative efforts, but because inflation is built as much on psychology as it is on economics, the act of attempting to control inflation may be as important as the accuracy of the determinations made in implementing policy.

Public Support for Business
In addition to regulating the conduct of business and providing support through tax incentives, governments provide a number of more direct subsidies to industry. In the United States the federal government has a share of the action in providing such subsidies, but a great deal of support also comes from state and even local governments. The majority of the direct expenditures benefiting business and industry are for research and development and for the subsidization of credit. Other forms of support for industry include promotion of inland water transportation by allowing use of locks and dams on rivers at below-market prices, services such as free weather reports and other economic information, and a variety of grants and loans for small business. Federal credit facilities are available for a host of business projects, including the facilitation of international trade through the Export-Import Bank and a variety of supports for agriculture and housing. Taken together, the federal government in 1990 supplied over $70 billion in support for business and industry.[40]

State and local governments tend to provide supports for business and industry in a competitive environment. Just as they compete with one another with tax incentives in order to attract industries to their localities, so too can state governments use direct services and credits to attract industry.[41] In fact, there is some evidence that government services are more important than tax breaks in attracting industries. The services of state and local governments need not be extraordinary; they may need only do things that they usually do, such as supplying transportation, water, sewers, and similar services, and do them well. Of course, some expenditures of subnational governments are more extraordinary; they may even include the building of plants for industries that agree to come to the locality.

All these supports for business must be examined in the context of the "industrial policy debate" in the United States. As the United States has fallen behind Japan, West Germany, and even such smaller countries as South Korea and Taiwan in the production of basic commodities such as steel and finished products such as automobiles, the question "What is wrong with American industry?" has become a central policy issue.[42] There are numerous possible answers to that question, including inept management, avaricious unions, and meddlesome government. Another answer is that government does not do enough to support American industry, and what it does is often poorly organized. The implication is that a more comprehensive approach to the problems of American industry and its competitiveness in the international marketplace should be adopted. Such a program might include some or all of the following elements:

1. *Direct government grants for the modernization and expansion of industry.* Much of the machinery of American industry is outdated in comparison with that of its competitors. Government could help by supplying grants, loans, or both.
2. *Trade policy.* American government has followed free-trade policies during most of the postwar period and has used tariffs and other restrictions on imports infrequently. Another option for government would be to impose tariffs and other trade barriers until American industry "gets back on its feet." There are voluntary arrangements with Japan over the import of automobiles, but some advocate broader use of these powers. The United States attempted to "get tough" with the members of the European Community in trade talks in late 1990 and the talks collapsed, but many citizens believe that our government still does not do enough to protect industry from "unfair" competition. Even the free-trade agreements with neighboring Canada and Mexico are believed by some citizens and politicians to have the potential to undermine the American economy.[43]
3. *Deregulation.* Some sections of the business community argue that the numerous safety and environmental regulations of the federal government make it difficult for American industry to produce products at a price that is competitive on the world market. In particular, businessmen and unions alike are concerned with the number of jobs that are being lost to low-wage and low-regulation countries such as Mexico and Brazil. They believe that deregulation would improve the competitiveness of business; even after a decade of Reagan and

Bush, American industry was more heavily regulated than that in many competitor countries.[44] In addition, the United States tends to pursue regulatory policies such as antitrust with much greater vigor than is true for most of the rest of the world. This policy also may inhibit the competitiveness of American industry in world markets.

4. *Research and development.* American industry has a tradition of being the most advanced technologically in the world. Unfortunately, this has become more of a tradition than a reality; except for a few industries, such as computers, American industry appears to be falling behind many countries. Government could make a major contribution to American industry by making more funds available for research.

5. *Regional policy.* The effects of the declining industrial fortunes of the United States have not been spread evenly over the country but have been concentrated in the older industrial regions, especially in the Great Lakes area. Thus, as well as dealing with the direct problems of industry, there is a need to address some of the human problems created by a changing industrial base in many states and localities. In turn, these efforts may make those localities more attractive to industries considering relocation. More recently, the decline in defense industries have made Southern California one of the more economically depressed areas of the American economy.

Government has been involved in supporting industry for most of the history of the United States. Many of the great industrial ventures in this country, for example the spread of the railroad westward, were undertaken with the direct or indirect support of government.[45] There may now be an even greater need for government support for business and industry than in the past, given the declining industrial position of the United States. Yet too much dependence on government to "bail out losers" may mean that American industry ceases to be responsible for its own revitalization and will simply wait for the public sector to rescue it. That "bail out" may come through direct subsidies or through protectionist trade policy.[46] Use of the trade policy avenue is, however, increasingly constrained by international agreements such as NAFTA and GATT.[47]

Public Ownership

Although it is not common in the United States, public ownership of certain industries may be important for economic management, especially influencing the location of those industries. Even in the United States a number of public and quasi-public corporations are involved in the economy. In 1976 there were twenty wholly publicly owned and seven partly owned corporations in the federal government, and the general movement toward managerialism and privatization in government has led to an increased use of corporate forms of organization. At the state and local levels many public enterprises are organized to carry out economic functions. These enterprises range from publicly owned utilities, such as electricity, gas, and transportation, to functions usually associated with the private sector, such as insurance and banking.

These public corporations perform a variety of functions for government. One is to provide revenues. For example, local government utilities can buy electricity at commercial rates and then distribute it at rates that yield a profit. Also, public corporations can be used to regulate prices and certain essential services. Although many publicly owned transportation corporations run with a deficit, they maintain relatively low costs and provide greater service than could be given by a private firm, and local government considers those objectives important. At the federal level, corporate structures have been used for regional development in the Tennessee Valley Authority in an attempt to transform the economy of a backward region through public action and public ownership of electrical power production. Also, federal corporations have been active in promoting U.S. foreign trade through the Export-Import Bank and the Overseas Private Investors Corporation (related to the goals of having a positive balance of payments) and in providing transportation to promote economic growth through the St. Lawrence Seaway and Amtrak.

One interesting variation on public ownership is the use of loan guarantees and insurance to attempt to guarantee continuing employment and economic growth. One notable example of this policy option was the Loan Guarantee Board, which was charged with developing financing to keep the Chrysler Corporation in business and its workers in jobs. The federal government did not buy one share of Chrysler stock, but used its economic powers to keep the company alive. Also, the federal government spent billions of dollars to make good on its insurance commitments to account owners of failing savings and loans and banks in the early 1990s. These activities helped preserve employment and enabled one corporation to reverse its economic fortunes. They also protected the savings of millions of citizens and helped preserve confidence in the financial institutions of the country. It might be argued that public involvement in moribund corporations is disguised social policy and may actually slow economic growth. At least for the short-term, however, it represents an important economic policy instrument.

Incentives

Governments can also attempt to influence economic change through providing incentives for desired behaviors. Most incentives are made available through the tax system and are directed primarily at encouraging investment and economic change. The tax reforms of the 1980s eliminated many of these incentives, but they still constitute a powerful economic weapon for government. We have already mentioned the role that state government tax incentives play in encouraging structural change in their individual state economies. The federal government also provides special incentives for selected industries and general incentives for businesses to invest, especially in research and development.

The major incentives for structural change in the U.S. economy have been the oil depletion allowance and similar allowances for other depletable natural resources. The allowances permit investors to write off against profits a portion of the investments they made in searching for oil. The decontrol of "new oil" under President Carter's energy program was another means of encouraging exploration for domestic energy supplies. A variety of provisions of the federal tax code also serve to encourage investment in general by both corporations and individuals. The capital gains provisions of the tax laws permit profits made on investments held for over six months to be taxed at half the individual's normal tax rate, and in no case at higher than 25 percent. Likewise, industries are given extensive tax credits for new investments and allowed higher-than-average depreciation on investments during the first year. All these policies make it easier and more profitable for industries to invest and for economic growth to follow that investment, but none mandates that the industry make the investments. The administrative costs of incentive programs are comparatively small when subsidy programs are considered as an alternative, and those programs are perceived as less intrusive into the free-market economy. But the dollar an industry saves from taxes is worth exactly the same as the dollar given as a subsidy, and perhaps even more, since there are fewer restrictions on how the dollar saved from taxes can be spent.

Moral Suasion

When all else fails, or perhaps before anything else is tried, governments can try to influence citizens and industries by persuasion. Persuasion works best in times of national emergency, but economic circumstances may be sufficiently dire to create the perception of an emergency. Presidents, using their power as spokesmen for the nation, are central to the use of suasion to control economic behavior. They can use a variety of symbols to influence citizens. A number of recent examples illustrate the appeals that presidents can make. Lyndon Johnson exerted the power of the office in "jawboning" industries into restraining price increases. He attempted to speak for the nation as president and appealed to patriotism to get what he wanted. Gerald Ford used more subtle methods in trying to influence citizens through his

WIN (Whip Inflation Now) program, complete with buttons and other advertising. Ronald Reagan used his gifts as the "great communicator" to get citizens to accept his economic and tax policies. Even George Bush's buying a pair of socks in a shopping mall can be seen as an attempt to manipulate symbols to get Americans buying again and lift the country out of the recession.

The effects of persuasion depend on the nature of the problem being addressed and the character of the political leader attempting to use the persuasion. Industrialists are unlikely to continue to provide jobs for workers in an unprofitable factory simply because they are asked to, but citizens may well try to "buy American" in order to improve the balance of payments. Political leaders who are trusted and respected may find it relatively easy to influence their fellow citizens, whereas those who are less popular may find more direct mechanisms for economic management more effective. Also, some economic problems may simply be too big (the current deficit) to be attacked with words alone.

Tax Policy

Another major component of economic policy is tax policy. The process of public budgeting involves decisions about raising enough revenues to meet expenditure demands, or the acceptance of a deficit. Here we are more concerned with the choice of revenue instruments used to collect the needed money. Raising the same amount of tax revenues by different means may have very different economic and political effects, and those effects should be understood when discussing tax policies. For example, raising money by an income tax is more favorable to the poor than is raising that same money through a sales tax. Also, raising money by different means may be more or less difficult administratively, so governments may choose ease of collection rather than other values—equity or impacts on economic growth—when selecting their tax policies.

Table 8.6 shows the tax profile of the United States in comparison with other major Western countries. The table shows the proportion of total tax revenues in each country derived from a number of possible revenue sources. The United States stands out from its major trading partners in several ways. First, there is substantially less reliance on taxes on goods and services in the United States than in the other countries. Although most states and many localities have sales and excise taxes, there is no national sales tax comparable to the value-added tax (VAT) used in most European countries.[48] Fiscal pressures, especially on the Social Security system (see chapter 10), may one day make such a tax necessary, but it has been delayed longer in this country than elsewhere.

Second, the United States derives substantially more of its total tax

TABLE 8.6
KINDS OF TAX REVENUES, 1991 (AS PERCENTAGE OF TOTAL)

	Personal income tax	Corporate income tax	Employees' Social Security	Employers' Social Security	General consumption tax	Selective commodity taxes	Property tax	Customs	Other
Australia	41.4	14.5	0.0	0.0	8.1	14.6	9.8	0.7	10.9
Belgium	30.3	6.0	11.1	21.8	16.0	7.8	2.5	0.9	3.6
Canada	40.7	5.5	4.8	10.2	14.1	10.1	9.5	1.9	3.2
Denmark	53.4	3.3	2.4	0.7	20.6	10.9	3.7	0.8	4.2
France	13.5	4.5	13.0	27.1	17.8	8.3	5.8	1.2	7.8
Germany	27.1	4.3	17.1	20.1	16.4	9.3	2.8	0.9	2.0
Italy	26.4	9.6	6.6	23.2	14.3	11.0	2.5	1.4	5.0
Japan	26.9	20.0	11.4	15.6	4.4	7.4	9.3	2.3	2.7
Netherlands	26.2	7.3	22.8	7.1	15.6	7.5	3.6	1.8	12.1
Norway	25.7	9.7	8.4	16.3	17.4	15.9	2.9	2.1	1.6
Spain	23.4	7.7	5.7	25.4	15.9	10.5	5.1	1.9	4.4
Sweden	34.2	3.1	0.0	26.9	16.7	9.2	4.1	2.2	2.6
Switzerland	34.3	6.3	7.6	10.8	9.7	7.0	7.2	5.2	11.9
United Kingdom	28.5	8.9	6.7	10.4	18.5	12.8	8.2	1.8	4.2
United States	34.9	7.3	11.8	16.5	7.6	7.1	11.2	1.9	1.7

SOURCE: Organization for Economic Cooperation and Development, *Revenue Statistics of OECD Member Countries, 1965–1992* (Paris: OECD, 1993).

revenues from property taxes than most other countries do. Property taxes are collected by state and local governments and are the principal revenue source for most local governments. This pattern appears to reflect an Anglo-Saxon tradition in revenue collection, for the United Kingdom, Canada, and New Zealand all use the property tax more heavily than most other industrialized countries.[49] Britain had dropped the local property tax in favor of a per capita "poll tax," but public opposition rather quickly forced a reversal of that policy innovation by the Thatcher government.[50]

Third, there is a relatively high reliance on corporate taxes in the United States. Given the characterization of American politics as dominated by special interests (especially business interests), that reliance may require some explanation. Corporations rarely bear the full burden of corporate taxation; the real tax burden falls on consumers of firms' products or on the companies' workers. Under many economic circumstances, firms can add taxes as a cost of doing business on to the price of their products. This practice is also reflected in the relatively high rate of corporate taxation in Japan, resulting in higher prices for consumer goods. A more political explanation for high corporate taxes involves the tradition of populism in many states in the United States; these states place a relatively heavier burden of taxation on corporations than on individuals, and even conservative politicians on the national level must remember that corporations do not vote but individual taxpayers do.

One thing that table 8.6 cannot show is the complexity of the tax system in the United States. Some of this complexity is a function of federalism and the numerous different tax systems existing at state and local levels (table 8.7). At the federal level, as the tax system has evolved, numerous deductions, exemptions, and other special treatments ("tax expenditures" or "loopholes") have been written into the tax laws (see table 8.8).[51] The tax reform of the 1980s (pp. 228–31) closed some of the more egregious loopholes in the tax system, but a number still remain. While many of these remaining exclusions have good economic and social justifications (e.g., the deductibility of mortgage interest stimulates homeownership as well as the construction industry), some loopholes (capital gains or oil depletion allowances) appear to benefit primarily the wealthy and the well organized. The apparent unfairness of many aspects of the tax system helped produce tax reform, but a number of apparent inequities remain.

Choices in Tax Policy

The United States obviously has made a number of choices concerning taxation that are different from policy choices made in other industrialized countries, although tax reform in many countries has tended to make their tax policies increasingly similar. The aggregate figures presented above represent taxation decisions made by many thousands of individual governments, although the federal government alone accounts for approximately three-quarters of all taxes. What criteria might these governments be employing when they make their decisions about taxes?

TABLE 8.7

VARIATIONS IN TAX RATES BY STATE

	Personal income[a]	*Sales*[a]	*Motor fuel*	*Distilled spirits*[b]
Maximum	12%	7%	32.5 cents/gal	$6.70/gal
Minimum[b]	0.4%	3%	7.5 cents/gal	$1.50/gal
Number of states using tax	41	45	50	50

a. Of the states that use this form of taxation.

b. Does not include markup in state stores in 19 states that have a public monopoly on the sale of distilled spirits.

TABLE 8.8

REVENUE LOSSES FROM MAJOR TAX
EXPENDITURES, FY 1995
(IN MILLIONS OF DOLLARS)

Exclusion of employer contributions to medical insurance programs	56,265
Exclusion of employer pension contributions	55,540
Deductability of mortgage interest on owner-occupied houses	54,800
Accelerated depreciation of capital equipment	27,495
Exclusion of interest on state and local government debt	19,865
Deductibility of charitable contributions	19,330
Deductibility of state and local property tax on owner-occupied houses	14,655
Deferral of capital gains on homes	14,620
Net exclusion of individual retirement account	5,290

SOURCE: Office of Management and Budget, *Special Analyses of the FY 1995 U.S. Budget* (Washington, D.C.: Government Printing Office, 1994).

COLLECTIBILITY

One criterion that must be considered is the ability of government to collect a tax, and even more the ability of that tax to yield large amounts of revenues for the investment made in collecting it. The administration of taxes is expensive and has political costs in addition to its economic costs. Therefore, a government should be sure that it can generate enough revenues from a tax to justify those costs.

The two major tax "handles" for modern, industrialized governments are income and expenditure. By definition, almost all money in an economy is both income and expenditure, and governments can raise revenues by tapping either or both streams of economic transactions. Further, given that in modern economies most income is earned as salaries and wages in relatively large organizations, and most purchases are made through relatively large and identifiable organizations, governments can employ private bodies to do much of the tax collection for them. Employers typically withhold a portion of their employees' incomes for income and Social Security taxes and are required to submit detailed accountings of sales and profits for their own taxes. These collection procedures impose a cost on the private sector—one estimate is that it costs businesses over $7 billion to comply with tax laws —but they make the collection of revenues easier and less expensive for government.[52] Individual citizens also do a great deal of the work for government. The Internal Revenue Service estimates that the average taxpayer requires 9.4 hours a year to keep records and fill out and file the forms for the federal income tax; this amounts to over 1 billion hours of work a year for all taxpayers.[53]

FISCAL NEUTRALITY

As well as being collectible, a "good" tax is one that does not produce any significant distortions in the economy.[54] That is, the tax system should not give preference to one kind of revenue or expenditure, unless there is a very good reason to do so. If the tax system does advantage certain economic activities, it could direct resources away from their most productive economic use and probably reduce the rate of economic growth in the society. Prior to tax reform in 1986, the tax system in the United States was not fiscally neutral but contained a large number of special-interest provisions ("loopholes") that had been written into the law. These provisions provided citizens and corporations alike with incentives to use their money in ways that might be unproductive on economic grounds (investing in race horses or loss-making businesses) but that were quite lucrative given the character of the existing tax system. Tax reform in 1986 has made the tax system more fiscally neutral, but there are continuing efforts by special interests to gain special tax benefits for themselves. Every year since the passage of the major tax reform has seen some special preferences creep back into the tax laws.[55] Also, state and local tax systems provide a number of tax benefits that can distort economic activity, most importantly the numerous tax incentives used to attract new industry to one place or another.

BOUYANCY

Raising revenues is unpopular politically, so any tax that can produce additional revenues without any political activity is a valuable tax for government. A buoyant tax is one for which the yield keeps pace with, or exceeds, the pace of economic growth and/or inflation. In principle, the progressive income tax is a buoyant tax. As individuals earn more income, they pay not only higher taxes but higher rates of tax, so there is a fiscal dividend from the tax, with government automatically receiving a higher proportion of national income. Taxes that require reassessments or adjustments in rates in order to keep pace with inflation (e.g., the property tax) are not buoyant and hence may generate political difficulties if the real value of their yield is to be maintained. This was very evident in the "tax revolt" against the property tax in a number of states.

The fiscal dividend associated with the progressive income tax during inflationary periods has led to legislation that indexed tax brackets. That is to say, as inflation increases the money income of citizens without increasing their real income, the income level at which taxes are first charged and at which tax rates change are increased so that tax rates change at the same real income. Everything else being equal, real tax income for government would therefore remain constant without legislative action to increase rates. This kind of change was a major part of tax reform during the first Reagan administration. In addition, the tax reform of 1986 reduced the progressivity of the tax system; the number of tax brackets was reduced from fourteen to five, and then effectively to three (two rates plus a surcharge) in 1990.

DISTRIBUTIVE EFFECTS

Another thing that taxes can do for government is to alter the income distribution in society. This change is usually thought of as benefiting the less affluent at the expense of the more affluent. Nevertheless, many taxes used by governments may be regressive, that is, they may take a larger proportion of income from the poor than from the rich. These regressive taxes (e.g., the Social Security tax or sales taxes) must be justified on other grounds, such as ease of collection.

Analyses of the net impacts of taxes on income distribution are difficult to calculate, especially if attention is given to the effects of expenditures that the taxes finance. Nevertheless, there does seem to be a general finding in the United States that both the poor—especially the working poor—and the rich pay a higher rate of tax than the majority of citizens do, while the large majority of citizens pay approximately the same rate of tax.[56] This is true when federal, state, and local taxes are added together; the federal tax structure has been at least moderately progressive, although some of the changes made during the Reagan years have made it less so. It is especially interesting that the working poor pay such a high rate of tax. This is explained by their higher propensity to consume, rather than save their income, so almost all their income is subject to sales and excise taxes. All their income also is covered by Social Security taxation, whereas the more affluent can earn substantial amounts of money above the threshold rate of Social Security income and pay no additional tax. Finally, the working poor may be unable to take advantage of many of the "loopholes" in the tax system that the more affluent can use. Even if they can, the loopholes are worth less for the less affluent at their lower tax rates.

Changes in the federal tax system over the past decade have tended to make the system somewhat less progressive. The top rates of income tax were reduced significantly (70 percent to 33 percent) during the Reagan and Bush years, and the tax burden has been shifting slightly away from income taxation and toward excise and Social Security taxes, as well as toward user fees.[57] These changes have been offset in part by eliminating a number of the less defensible loopholes in the tax laws that primarily did benefit the rich. The decreased progressivity of the tax system was in large part done very consciously. Part of the "supply side" strategy of President Reagan was to place more money in the hands of the affluent so they would invest. Further, the Bush administration found that its pledge of "No new taxes" meant in practice no new income taxes. Excise taxes were more palatable, both to the administration and to most citizens.[58]

The Clinton administration has reversed somewhat this trend toward a less redistributive tax. Early in his term of office President Clinton put through an economic reform package and a budget bill. This bill shifted some of the tax burden back on to the more affluent, although critics argue that it was not the middle-class tax cut promised in the campaign.[59] This increased the tax rate on taxable incomes over $140,000 for couples ($115,000 individuals) to 36 percent. While this tax change affected only a rather small percentage of the American public, it did raise approximately $27.5 billion in 1994. Another $7.5 billion was raised by increasing the top rate of corporation tax to 36 percent. The Clinton package was not entirely redistributive, however, and heavier taxes also were imposed on alcohol, tobacco, and energy, taxes that tend to fall disproportionately on the less affluent. Still, an estimated 70 percent of the new tax revenues came from households with incomes over $100,000 a year (4.4 percent of all households).[60]

VISIBILITY

Finally, public officials making political decisions about taxes must be concerned about the political acceptability of taxes. To some degree this factor is crucial, for low taxes are related to the historical traditions of the country or even a state: in many states with populist political cultures, the property tax is regarded as a threat to the "little man" who owns a house. The political acceptability of taxes also may be a function of the visibility of the taxes. Everything else being equal, the less visible a tax is, the more acceptable it will be.[61] Even though income tax is withheld from employees' checks at each pay period, the citizen is still required to file a statement each year on which he or she must see the total tax account for the year. Similarly, property tax bills are typically sent to homeowners each year; in states and localities with high property taxes, the bill may seem huge. Both taxes are obvious to the taxpayer and therefore may be resisted. The Social Security tax is less visible. Even though it is deducted from paychecks along with the income tax, there is no annual reckoning that might bring the total tax bill to the citizen's attention, and in addition half of the total Social Security bill is paid by the employer.

The lack of a total tax bill is a very important element in a country (such as the United States) with several levels of government, all of which levy taxes. These taxes are levied at different times and in different ways, so only the better-informed citizens are likely to know their total tax bills.[62] Even though the United States is a low-tax country, the division among taxes and taxing units may make the total bill appear even lower. The United States is a low-tax country in part because Americans want it that way, and the maintenance of the "fiscal illusion" created by multiple taxing units helps make such taxes as do exist more palatable.[63] This is especially true because citizens tend to focus their ire on the federal level of government and permit state and local taxes to creep upward.

The problem of tax visibility is one reason for considering a value-added tax (VAT) for the United States,[64] perhaps as a means of reducing the continuing federal deficit. Unlike a sales tax, which is levied as the consumer pays for the commodity and is added on as a separate item, the VAT is levied at each stage of the production process and included in the price of the product when sold. As a result, the actual amount of the tax—and even the fact that a tax is being levied—may be largely hidden from the consumer; consequently, there may be less political mobilization opposing the tax. It is just that invisibility, however, that makes many fiscal conservatives extremely wary of the VAT, fearing that government could expand its activities without citizens' understanding what the real increases in their tax bill had been.

The Politics of Tax Reform

Taxation is different from other kinds of policy in that it is essentially something that no one really wants and everyone seeks to avoid when possible. Former Senator Russell Long of Louisiana, long a power on the Senate Finance Committee responsible for tax legislation, encapsulated the nature of tax politics in this little ditty: "Don't tax you, don't tax me, tax that fellow behind the tree." The nature of tax politics is to try to divert the burden of taxation on to others and to build in special privileges for oneself. Because virtually no one in contemporary economic systems can avoid taxes, the next-best strategy is to ensure that everyone pays his or her fair share of the costs of government. This helps explain why sales taxes are popular among all segments of society, even though they are regressive.[65]

Compared with other forms of policymaking, tax policymaking has also been relatively technical and legalistic.[66] The tax code is an extremely complex set of laws, and it is made even more complex by rulings made by the Internal Revenue Service and tax courts concerning just what the tax code really means. In Congress, tax policymaking has been the preserve of a relatively few powerful and knowledgeable congressmen and senators (e.g., Senator Long and former Congressman Wilbur Mills).[67] The perceived complexity of tax policymaking allowed many special interests to have desired provisions written into the tax code with little awareness on the part of the general public. The many special interests are also represented by members of Congress whose constituencies may contain large concentrations of one kind of industry or another. Adding loopholes to a tax law often was an exercise in coalition building through logrolling, with every congressman adding his or her provision in return for support of the legislation as a whole. All this has resulted in a federal tax system, especially an income tax, perceived as highly unfair by many citizens. Harris surveys taken before tax reform indicated that an average 90 percent of respondents thought that the federal income tax was unfair.[68] Polls taken after the reform were almost as negative about the tax structure.

Any number of proposals for tax reform have been made in the United States. It was surprising to most observers that a major tax reform was actually passed in 1986. What is perhaps even more surprising is that the reform passed was as sweeping and as comprehensive as it was.[69] It is relatively easy to criticize the reform and point out its weaknesses. Still, given the history of tax policy in the United States, and indeed most other countries, the package actually put into effect was remarkable. The tax system was simplified for the average taxpayer, a large number of the more egregious "loopholes" were removed, and there was a somewhat more equitable impact of the tax system on the less affluent. A year, or a few months, before passage such a change in the tax laws would have been thought impossible.

What happened to produce this major reversal of tax policymaking as usual? There is no simple answer to that question; instead, there was a confluence of forces, liberal and conservative, business and labor, producers and consumers, that all wanted change. President Reagan wanted change to reduce the progressivity of taxes and allow the more affluent to keep more of what they earned. Some of his conservative allies wanted to eliminate many special preferences for certain industries to produce a more level playing field for all industries as a means of stimulating economic growth.[70] Liberals also wanted the elimination of the special preferences built into the tax laws as a means of attempting to help middle- and low-income groups that could not take advantage of many of these "loopholes." In addition, several policy entrepreneurs—Senator Bill Bradley, Congressman Dan Rostenkowski, Secretary of the Treasury Donald Regan, and others—made heavy political investments to bring about this major policy change.[71] There was, for one of the few times, a "policy window" through which advocates of tax reform could jump along with their proposals and produce significant change in the tax structure.[72]

Naturally, those interests whose particular benefits were affected by tax simplification were skeptical about the legislation. Among the first to question the efficacy of the legislation were mayors and governors. They argued that ending the deductibility of some state and local taxes makes it more difficult for subnational governments to increase taxes. Mayors and governors were followed closely by business interests, who argued that the repeal of special investment credits, accelerated depreciation, and other benefits going to investment would further slow the rate of capital formation in the United States and thereby slow economic growth. A standard place to begin any political analysis is to ask "whose ox is gored," and a large number of oxen would be gored by this tax reform legislation.[73]

Despite public discontent with many aspects of the prevailing tax system, tax reform was a difficult undertaking. Making tax policy has traditionally been the preserve of the special interests, and it may be difficult to prevent them from continuing their role in the process. In addition, many of the arguments advanced by those special interests may have social and economic validity. The repeal of credits for business investment may indeed have some negative impact on economic growth in the United States. In short, tax reform was a desirable policy goal, but like almost any policy change, it was not without its critics and its negative consequences.

The management of the economy is a central concern of government. It is one area of policymaking on which governments are frequently judged by their citizens. This is true not only because of the central importance of the issues for citizens but also because of the frequent reporting of standard indicators such as the inflation rate and the unemployment rate. Even if an individual has a job and an income that keeps pace with the cost of living, he or she may believe the president is not doing a good job because of the aggregate numbers that regularly appear in the newspapers. It is interesting to notice the extent to which the performance of the economy is laid at the feet of government, especially the president. This is a marked contrast to the era before the depression, when the economy was not believed to be controllable by government. The president clearly plays a crucial role in economic management. This is true in part because of his role as spokesman for government. It is also true because of the central role of the presidential budget in controlling the economy and because of his importance in other areas of economic policy such as taxation.

It is also important to understand that the condition of the economy is not solely a presidential responsibility. Congress is involved with the president in determining the budget, which is the central instrument of presidential intervention in the economy. The actions of the Federal Reserve Board are almost totally beyond the control of the president. Furthermore, the federal structure of the United States is such that state and local government taxing and spending decisions have a significant impact on not only the overall stimulative or depressive effects of public expenditures but also the attempts to move industries and labor geographically. Also, increasingly the success of national economic policies depend on the decisions made by other nations, by international organizations such as the International Monetary Fund, and by global markets.

Finally, we citizens have a substantial impact on the state of the economy. Many presidential decisions on fiscal policy and some Federal Reserve decisions on monetary policy depend on citizens responding in the predicted fashion. Even major aggregates such as economic growth depend to a great extent on the perceptions and behaviors of citizens. If citizens and businesses believe that prosperity is coming, they will be willing to invest and thus may make their belief a self-fulfilling prophecy. For example, the slow return of consumer confidence after the recession in the early 1990s has been one factor preventing more rapid recovery. Government can do everything in its power to try to influence the behavior of citizens, but ultimately most decisions are beyond its control. Nevertheless, the success of an economic policy is a major factor in determining whether citizens believe that government is doing a good job.

Notes

1. See Michael Stewart, *Keynes and After* (Harmondsworth, England: Penguin, 1972); Peter A. Hall, *The Political Power of Economic Ideas: Keynesianism Across Nations* (Princeton: Princeton University Press, 1989).

2. Robert Skidelsky, *Politicians and the Slump* (London: Macmillan, 1967).

3. Walter Heller, *New Dimensions of Political Economy* (Cambridge, Mass.: Harvard University Press, 1966).

4. Paul Ormerod, *The Death of Economics* (London: Faber and Faber, 1994).

5. On the other hand, politicians who tell the truth about the economic future, and especially about higher taxes, are regarded with even greater skepticism.

6. Jonathan Rauch, "The Visible Hand," *National Journal*, 9 July 1994, 1612–17.

7. This tradeoff is refered to as the "Phillips Curve." See "A Cruise Around the Phillips Curve," *The Economist*, 19 February 1994, 82–83; A.J. Hallett-Hughes and M.L. Petit, "Stagflation and Phillips Curve Instability in a Model of Macroeconomic Policy," *Manchester School of Economic and Social Studies* 59 (1991): 123–45.

8. In fairness, they often have been promised more of everything by politicians, and often without any associated costs. See Isabel V. Sawhill, "Reaganomics in Retrospect" in *Perspectives on the Reagan Years*, ed. John L. Palmer (Washington, D.C.: Urban Institute Press, 1986).

9. For a discussion of this "treble affluence," see Richard Rose and B. Guy Peters, *Can Government Go Bankrupt?* (New York: Basic Books, 1978).

10. Lester Thurow, *The Zero-Sum Society* (New York: Basic Books, 1979).

11. Service industries include a wide range of activities: insurance, medical care, computer services, banking, in addition to dry cleaners, restaurants, etc.

12. William B. Johnston and Arnold H. Packer, *Workforce 2000: Work and Workers in the 21st Century* (New York: Hudson Institute, 1987).

13. Paul Starobin, "Unequal Shares," *National Journal*, 11 September 1993, 2176–79.

14. Fred Hirsch and John H. Goldthorpe, *The Political Economy of Inflation* (Cambridge, Mass.: Harvard University Press, 1978).

15. R. Kent Weaver, *The Politics of Indexation* (Washington, D.C.: Brookings Institution, 1988.)

16. This is "Baumol's disease," named after the economist William J. Baumol, "The Macroeconomics of Unbalanced Growth: The Anatomy of Urban Crisis," in *Is Economics Relevant?* ed. Robert L. Heilbroner and A.M Ford (Pacific Palisades, Calif.: Goodyear, 1971).

17. John T. Woolley, *Monetary Politics: The Federal Reserve and the Politics of Monetary Politics* (Cambridge, England: Cambridge University Press, 1986).

18. Gøsta Esping-Andersen, *The Three Worlds of Welfare Capitalism* (Princeton: Princeton University Press, 1990).

19. In 1991 imports equaled just under 20 percent of gross national product in the United States.They averaged 46.4 percent of GNP in Western Europe and 32.5 percent of GNP in all OECD countries.

20. William S. Harat and Thomas D. Willett, eds., *Monetary Policy for a Volatile Global Economy* (Washington, D.C.: AEI Press, 1991).

21. Martin Tolchin and Susan Tolchin, *Buying into America: How Foreign Money Is Changing the Face of Our Nation* (New York: Times Books, 1988).

22. Susan B. Hansen, *The Politics of State Economic Development* (Pittsburgh: University of Pittsburgh Press, forthcoming).

23. Robert J. Reinshuttle, *Economic Development: A Survey of State Activities* (Lexington, Ky.: Council of State Governments, 1984).

24. Fox Butterfield, "New England's Siren Call of the 1980s Becomes Echo of Depression," *New York Times*, 15 December 1991.

25. Paul E. Peterson and Mark Rom, "Macroeconomic Policymaking: Who is in Control?" in *Can the Government Govern?* ed. John E. Chubb and Paul E. Peterson (Washington, D.C.: Brookings Institution, 1989).

26. James D. Savage, *Balanced Budgets and American Democracy* (Ithaca, N.Y.: Cornell University Press, 1988).

27. Rose and Peters, *Can Government Go Bankrupt?* 135–41; James M. Buchanan and Richard Wagner, *Democracy in Deficit: The Political Legacy of Lord Keynes* (New York: Academic Press, 1978), 38–48.

28. Henry Aaron et al., *Setting National Priorities: The 1980 Budget* (Washington, D.C.: Brookings Institution, 1979). For a critique, see William H. Buiter, "A Guide to Public Sector Deficits," *Economic Policy* 1 (1985): 3–15.

29. See chapter 6. See also Lawrence J. Haas, "Deficit Doldrums," *National Journal*, 7 December 1991.

30. "Budget Resolution Embraces Clinton Plan," *1993 CQ Almanac* (Washington, D.C.: CQ Press, 1994), 102–21.

31. Douglas A. Hibbs, *The American Political Economy: Macroeconomics and Electoral Choice* (Cambridge, Mass.: Harvard University Press, 1987).

32. Paul Craig Roberts, *The Supply-Side Revolution: An Insider's Account of Policymaking in Washington* (Cambridge, Mass.: Harvard University Press, 1984), esp. 27–33.

33. B. Douglas Bernheim, *The Vanishing Nest Egg: Reflections on Saving in America* (New York: Twentieth Century Fund, 1991).

34. Bruce Bartlett and Timothy P. Roth, eds., *The Supply-Side Solution* (Chatham, N.J.: Chatham House, 1983).

35. James T. Bennett and Thomas J. DiLorenzo, *Underground Government: The Off-Budget Public Sector* (Washington, D.C.: Cato Institute, 1983); Bruce R. Bartlett, *The Federal Debt: On-Budget, Off-Budget and Contingent Liabilities*, Study Prepared for Use of Joint Economic Committee (Washington, D.C.: Government Printing Office, 1983).

36. Donald F. Kettl, *Leadership at the Fed* (New Haven: Yale University Press, 1986). For a more muckraking account, see William Greider, *Secrets of the Temple: How the Federal Reserve Runs the Country* (New York: Simon and Schuster, 1987).

37. Marc Allan Eisner, *Antitrust and the Triumph of Economics* (Chapel Hill: University of North Carolina Press, 1991).

38. The Department of Justice had been the only enforcement agency. It retained its powers after the passage of the Clayton Act and both it and the Federal Trade Commission enforce antitrust legislation.

39. Lawrence C. Pierce, "Wage and Price Controls: Economic Necessity or Political Expediency," in *What Government Does*, ed. Matthew Holden and Dennis L. Dresang (Beverly Hills, Calif.: Sage, 1977).

40. Author's calculation based on the federal budget documents.

41. J.C. Gray and D.A. Spina, "State and Local Government Industrial Location Incentives: A Well-Stocked Candy Store," *Journal of Corporation Law* 5 (1980): 517–687.

42. William S. Dietrich, *In the Shadow of the Rising Sun: The Political Roots of American Economic Decline* (University Park, Pa.: Penn State University Press, 1991).

43. The most famous was Ross Perot and his prediction of a large loss of jobs to Mexico under NAFTA as a "large sucking sound." See also G. Bruce Doern and Brian W. Tomlin, *Faith and Fear: The Free Trade Story* (Toronto: Stoddard, 1991).

44. Jonathan Rauch, "The Deregulatory President," *National Journal*, 30 November 1991, 2902–6.

45. Jonathan T.R. Hughes, *The Governmental Habit Redux: Economic Controls from Colonial Times to the Present* (Princeton: Princeton University Press, 1991).

46. See David B. Yoffie, "American Trade Policy: An Obsolete Bargain," in Chubb and Peterson, *Can the Government Govern?*

47. North American Free Trade Agreement and General Agreement on Tariffs and Trade.

48. Charles E. McClure, *The Value Added Tax: Key to Deficit Reduction?* (Washington, D.C.: American Enterprise Institute, 1987).

49. B. Guy Peters, *Taxation: A Comparative Perspective* (Oxford: Blackwell, 1991).

50. John Gibson, *The Politics and Economics of the Poll Tax: Mrs. Thatcher's Downfall* (Warley, West Midlands, England: EMAS, 1990).

51. Stanley S. Surrey and Paul R. McDaniel, *Tax Expenditures* (Cambridge, England: Cambridge University Press, 1985).

52. F. Vaillancourt, "The Compliance Costs of Taxes on Businesses and Individuals: A Review of the Evidence," *Public Finance* 42 (1989): 395–414.

53. Even at the minumum wage of $4.25 per hour, this will amount to over $4 billion in free work by citizens.

54. Richard A. Musgrave, *Fiscal Systems* (New Haven: Yale University Press, 1969).

55. For somewhat different views, see Robert S. McIntyre, "Thrown for a Loop," *New Republic* 208 (15 March 1993): 17, 19ff; Laura Sanders, "The Campeau Coup and the May Maneuver," *Forbes* 142 (31 October 1988): 98–99.

56. Joseph A. Pechman, *Who Paid the Taxes, 1966–85?* (Washington, D.C.: Brookings Institution, 1986).

57. Paul E. Peterson and Mark Rom, "Lower Taxes, More Spending and Budget Deficits," in *The Reagan Legacy,* ed. Charles O. Jones (Chatham, N.J.: Chatham House, 1988).

58. B. Guy Peters, *The Politics of Taxation* (Oxford: Blackwell, 1992), 166–73.

59. See the extended analysis of the Clinton proposals in the *New York Times,* 18 February 1993.

60. Gwen Ifill, "President Assures Middle Class over Income Taxes," *New York Times,* 17 February 1993.

61. Harold Wilensky, *The "New Corporatism," Centralization and the Welfare State* (Beverly Hills, Calif.: Sage, 1976).

62. The author, for example, pays four separate income taxes, three property taxes, sales and excise taxes, etc. Some of these taxes are small, but they do add up.

63. W.W. Pommerehne and F. Schneider, "Fiscal Illusion, Political Institutions and Local Public Spending," *Kyklos* 31 (1978): 381–408.

64. McClure, *Value-Added Tax.*

65. Peters, *Politics of Taxation,* 165–67.

66. Sven Steinmo, *Taxation and Democracy* (New Haven: Yale University Press, 1992).

67. J.M. Verdier, "The President, Congress and Tax Reform: Patterns over Three Decades," *The Annals,* 1988, 114–23.

68. Even after reforms, the federal income tax is considered the least fair tax by a plurality of respondents in surveys. See Advisory Commission on Intergovernmental Relations, *Changing Public Attitudes on Government and Taxes* (Washington, D.C.: ACIR, annual).

69. Timothy J. Conlan, Margaret T. Wrightson, and David R. Beam, *Taxing Choices: The Politics of Tax Reform* (Washington, D.C.: CQ Press, 1989); J.H. Birnbaum and A.S. Murray, *Showdown at Gucchi Gulch* (New York: Random House, 1987).

70. Gary Mucciaroni, "Public Choice and the Politics of Comprehensive Tax Reform," *Governance* 3 (1990): 1–32.

71. Conlan, Wrightson, and Beam, *Taxing Choices.*

72. John W. Kingdon, *Agendas, Alternatives and Public Policies* (Boston: Little, Brown, 1984).

73. See Cedric Sandford, *Successful Tax Reform* (Bath, England: Fiscal Publications, 1993).

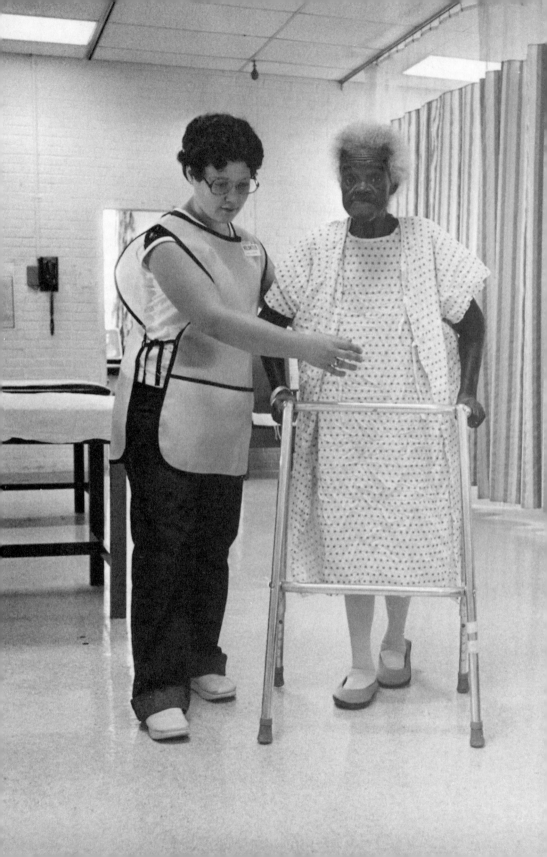

9. Health-Care Policies

One of the great myths about American political life and public policy is that we have a private health-care system. In fact, in 1992, over 42 percent of all health-care expenditures in the United States were made by government agencies of some sort,[1] and many physicians who so loudly proclaim the virtues of private medical care receive a substantial portion of their income from public medical programs such as Medicare and Medicaid. Over half of all payments to hospitals and over one-third of all payments to physicians come from public sources (see table 9.1). The public sector makes a much smaller proportion of total health expenditures in the United States than in most other industrialized countries, but there is a significant involvement of government in the provision of health care.

The extent of involvement of American government in health care can be seen in part in the health-care programs listed in table 9.2. All three levels of government are to some degree involved in health care, and at the federal level a wide variety of public agencies are involved. Almost all cabinet-level departments of the federal government are to some degree involved with health care, as are a number of independent executive agencies. Their involvement ranges from directly providing medical care to some segments of the population (e.g., through the Department of Defense, the Department of the Interior, or the Department of Veterans Affairs), through regulating some aspects of medical care, to subsidizing medical research. Without public involvement, American health care would certainly be very different and probably would not be as good as it is. It certainly would not be as accessible for the poor and the elderly, and the overall technical quality would probably not be as high as it currently is for those who nominally pay all their medical expenses. For one thing, the federal government is a major source of funds for medical research ($7.7 billion in 1990), without which many of the advances in medicine with which the average citizen is now familiar would not have happened or would have been delayed.

Although the role of government in health care is larger than most American citizens believe it to be, that role is still not as great as many people believe it should be. Rather than opt for greater involvement in medi-

TABLE 9.1

SOURCES OF PAYMENT TO HEALTH CARE PROVIDERS,
1992 (IN PERCENTAGES)

	Hospitals	*Physicians*	*Other*
Government			
Federal	39.9	27.4	20.1
State	15.3	6.7	11.1
Direct payments	5.0	19.1	47.6
Private insurance	35.1	46.8	17.7
Other private payers	4.7	0.1	3.5

SOURCE: Sally T. Sonnefeld et al., "Projections of National Health Expenditures through the Year 2000," *Health Care Financing Review*, 13 (Fall 1991).

TABLE 9.2

MAJOR HEALTH PROGRAMS

Federal	*State*	*Local*
Department of Agriculture	State hospitals	City hospitals
Meat inspections	State mental	Sanitation and
	hospitals	public health
Department of Health and Human	Substance abuse	
Services	Medicaid	
Food and Drug Administration		
Community Health Services		
Indian Health Services		
National Institutes of Health		
Substance abuse programs		
Health education		
HMO loan funds		
U.S. Public Health Service		
Medicare		
Medicaid		
Department of the Interior		
Territorial health programs		
Department of Veterans Affairs		
VA hospitals		

cal care, the Reagan and Bush administrations cut back the federal role. These actions included cutting back on federal health funding and converting former categorical programs supporting health care at state and local levels into block-grant programs. This type of grant program depends much more on the priorities of state governments for implementation, and there is some evidence that health care for the very poor has been significantly reduced in quantity and quality.[2] Medicaid has become an extremely expensive program for the states, and they have been looking for means to limit their financial exposure.[3] In the 1990s, even much of the middle class is encountering difficulty in financing adequate medical care for themselves and their families (see pp. 242–43): in 1994 approximately 40 million Americans had no medical insurance, public or private.

The problems of cost and access to care have helped produce increasing demands for more public involvement in health, including growing interest in a national health insurance program. Some surveys indicate that well over half the American population would support some form of national health insurance. For example, a survey in mid-1994 indicated that 77 percent of the population wanted some form of universal medical care, although they disagreed on the exact nature of the program.[4] Health care is one policy area in which the conservative policy ideas of the past decade appear to be encountering strong opposition. Yet, with typical ambivalence about the role of government, Americans appear to want universal access to medical care without a large-scale government program.

President Clinton placed health-care reform at the top of his policy agenda when he came to office in 1993. He took a strong personal interest in this policy and put Hillary Rodham Clinton in charge of a task force to draft the reform. After a series of consultations around the country and hearings before congressional committees, the administration drafted a bill that proposed a complex arrangement of purchasing organizations ("alliances") that would operate somewhat like existing Health Maintenance Organizations (HMOs, discussed later). The most important aspect of the bill for the administration was that it guaranteed universal coverage to all citizens. The Clintons' proposal generated several other proposals, ranging from a single-payer plan similar to that found in Canada (detailed later in this chapter) to very modest extensions of existing public and private-sector programs relying on voluntary acceptance and tax subsidies.[5] The bill that was finally proposed (but never even voted on formally) called for a complex system of health alliances to function, very much like HMOs now do, as providers of all medical services for their subscribers.

Although the major emphasis is now on creating a national program of health insurance, the states have already begun to put their own programs into place. For example, Hawaii has a public health-care system that, along with private insurance, covers almost the entire population of the state; Massachusetts has tried a similar plan.[6] Minnesota also has adopted a health program using HMOs that approaches comprehensive coverage; other states, such as Pennsylvania, provide health coverage for all children if not all adults.[7] Individual states also have innovated in the manner in which they deliver Medicaid services to improve coverage and lower costs (see pp. 249–51). The major question in the public role in health care appears to be the extent of the role of the federal government, rather than whether the public sector will be involved.

Problems in Health Care

The United States is one of the richest countries in the world, and it spends by far a larger proportion of its economic resources (as measured by gross national product) on health care than does any other industrialized nation (see table 9.3). The results of all those expenditures, however, are not so impressive. In infant mortality, a commonly used indicator of the quality of medical care, the United States is tied for thirteenth in the world, behind most Western European countries and Japan.[8] Depending on one's perspective, these figures are made better or worse if the total figure is disaggregated by race. For the white population in the United States, the infant mortality rate is as low as that of many Western European countries, but for minority populations, the infant mortality rate is closer to that of many Third World countries (see table 9.4).

Health care of the finest kind is available in the United States, but it may be available only to a limited (and declining) portion of the population.

TABLE 9.3

HEALTH EXPENDITURES AS A PERCENTAGE OF GROSS NATIONAL
PRODUCT, SELECTED COUNTRIES, 1991

United States	13.4	Italy	8.3
Canada	10.0	Belgium	7.9
France	9.1	New Zealand	7.6
Sweden	8.6	Norway	7.6
Germany	8.5	Japan	6.8
Australia	8.4	United Kingdom	6.6
Austria	8.4	Denmark	6.5

SOURCE: Organization for Economic Cooperation and Development, *OECD Health Systems: Facts and Trends* (Paris: OECD, 1993).

TABLE 9.4

INFANT MORTALITY RATES[a]

Japan	4.3	Italy	7.8
Iceland	5.4	United States (total)	8.4
Taiwan	5.7	Slovakia	8.4
Sweden	5.8	Greece	8.9
Hong Kong	5.9	Bulgaria	9.4
Netherlands	6.2	Czech Republic	9.7
Switzerland	6.6	Portugal	9.8
Germany	6.6	Cuba	10.5
Brunei	6.8	Slovenia	10.8
France	6.8	Bosnia	12.6
Canada	7.0	Hungary	13.1
Austria	7.3	Chile	15.9
Australia	7.4	United States (blacks)	17.0
United Kingdom	7.4	Belarus	19.0
Norway	7.7	Ukraine	21.0
United States (whites)	7.7		

SOURCES: World Health Organization, *World Health Statistics Annual, 1993* (Geneva: WHO, 1994); U.S. Bureau of the Census, *Statistical Abstract of the United States, 1994* (Washington, D.C.: Government Printing Office, 1994).
   a. Deaths in the first year of life per 1000 live births.

Vast disparities exist among racial, economic, and geographical groups in the United States; and even with Medicare, Medicaid, and other public programs, the poor, the elderly, and those living in rural areas receive less medical care than do white middle-class urban citizens. They also report that their health is poor compared to that of more advantaged Americans (see table 9.5). And an increasing number of middle-class citizens are beginning to be squeezed out of the medical-care market by rapidly increasing prices and declining insurance benefits provided by employers. The problems that Americans now face in medical care are basically three: access, quality, and cost.

Access to Medical Care

For any medical-care system to function effectively, prospective patients must have access to that system. A number of factors can deter citizens from becoming patients, and one purpose of public involvement in the medical marketplace must be to equalize access for all citizens. Americans still differ on the extent to which they believe that equal access to medical care should

TABLE 9.5
PERSONAL ASSESSMENT OF HEALTH STATUS
(IN PERCENTAGES)

	Excellent	Very good	Good	Fair or poor
Race				
White	42.8	34.8	21.7	10.1
Black	28.3	21.7	29.8	19.5
Family income				
Under $10,000	28.9	21.7	27.5	21.1
$10,000–14,999	34.0	24.7	27.0	13.7
$15,000–19,999	36.9	26.7	25.5	10.4
$20,000–34,999	43.7	27.1	21.9	6.9
$35,000 or more	52.8	26.1	15.9	4.6

SOURCE: U.S. Department of Health and Human Services, *Health Status of the Disadvantaged: Chartbook, 1986* (Washington, D.C.: Public Health Service, 1986).

be a right of citizenship, but most are willing to accept that all citizens require some form of protection for at least serious illnesses.[9]

The most commonly cited barrier to access to health care is economics. As the majority of medical care in the United States is still paid for privately, those who lack the income or insurance to pay for medical care may not have that medical care. Even with several public medical-care programs, medicine is still not as available to the poor as it is to the more affluent. As of 1990, almost 30 percent of all the poor (those with incomes below the official poverty line) were not eligible to receive Medicaid benefits. They were poor, but not sufficiently poor to qualify under the means-testing criteria of Medicaid.[10] Only 20 percent of the poor have any privately financed health insurance, and only 10 percent of the poor have any nonhospital coverage.[11] Among all Americans, approximately 40 million people do not have health insurance (see table 9.6). The elderly poor, who have access to Medicare as a result of their age, must still pay for parts of their insurance, at a rate that may well deter some from taking full advantage of the program.

Even the middle class may find that the rising cost of medical care and the possibility of catastrophic illness may make all but the very wealthy medically indigent. The federal government made a very brief foray into catastrophic coverage for Medicare recipients, but financing, administrative, and political difficulties led to the program's termination in 1989 after only one year.[12] Further, the absence of medical insurance is not a problem just

TABLE 9.6

PERCENTAGES OF GROUPS COVERED BY HEALTH INSURANCE,

1991

Group	Percentage
Total	86.6
Race	
White	87.5
Black	81.5
Hispanic	71.0
Other	80.5
Employment status	
Full-time, full year	87.5
Part-time, full year	72.3
Some unemployment	68.9
Nonworker	77.4
Age	
Under 16	86.0
16–24	78.6
25–34	81.7
35–44	86.6
45–54	88.3
55–64	89.1
65+	99.5

SOURCE: U.S. Bureau of the Census, *Current Population Reports*, 1992, p. 74.

for the poor. In 1992 almost 30 percent of all uninsured had incomes over $30,000 a year, and one in eight uninsured had incomes over $50,000. More than 84 percent of the uninsured live in families headed by people who work, usually for small firms in service industries, at least part of the year.[13] Over half the uninsured had someone in the family who worked full-time.[14] These facts help to explain why there is a demand to reform the health care system of the United States (see pp. 264–70).

In the contemporary American medical-care system, having insurance, as well as not having it, can present troubles. The principal problem is that it can minimize mobility in the economy. If a person has a job that provides health benefits, it is difficult for him or her to leave that job for one that may be better in other respects but does not offer insurance. In some instances, even if the new job does provide insurance, it will not cover preexisting conditions. If a prospective employee or family member has been diagnosed with a serious condition that cannot be covered by the new insurance, then moving between jobs may be impossible.

Even if direct economic barriers to access to medical care were removed, there might still be significant noneconomic barriers to equal access. Interestingly, even with the almost entirely free medical-care system of the United Kingdom, the differences in health status by social or economic class have not been narrowed significantly.[15] Each social class is on average healthier, but the disparities between the wealthy and the poor have been maintained, indicating that there are other barriers to consuming health care and, perhaps more important, other barriers to creating health, which cannot be removed simply by providing free access. Members of the poor and working classes tend to lose hourly wages if they go to the doctor, whereas salaried employees either do not lose pay or have personal-business leaves. Transportation is generally easier for the more affluent, whereas the poor must rely on public transportation. Perhaps most important, the more affluent and educated know better how to get what they want from professional and bureaucratic organizations than do the poor, and they are more likely to be well treated by individuals and institutions than are the less-well-off. A doctor is likely to pay more serious attention to the description of symptoms of a middle-class person than to those of a poor person, and the middle-class person is more likely to demand extra diagnostic and curative procedures. So even if all direct economic barriers were removed, there might still be serious barriers to gaining equality in medical care, especially as the poor are generally not as healthy as the more affluent to begin with, and as a consequence may require greater medical care.

In addition to economic conditions, geography plays a significant dual role in defining access to medical care. First, urban areas are generally better served with doctors and especially with hospitals than rural areas are. For example, in Standard Metropolitan Statistical Areas (SMSAs) in the United States, the average number of physicians per 100,000 population is 215, and the average number of hospital beds per 100,000 is 459. This contrasts with 97 physicians per 100,000 and 425 hospital beds per 100,000 in non-SMSA regions of the country. Another example of the disparity in medical-care resources is that eighteen rural counties in Texas alone do not have a single physician, although there are more doctors in the United States than ever before. The geographical disparities in medical services would be even more pronounced if the areas of specialization of physicians and the standards and equipment of the hospitals were also considered.

Second, there are marked regional imbalances in access to medical care.[16] These can be related in part, but not entirely, to urban-rural differences. The places in the United States best served by physicians and hospitals are the Middle Atlantic states and the states of the Far West. The worst served are the Upper Midwest and the Deep South. There are, for example, 337 physicians per 100,000 people in Massachusetts and 334 per 100,000 in Maryland, but only 125 per 100,000 in Idaho and 133 per 100,000 in Mississippi.[17] A variety of programs, public and private, have been tried to equalize the distribution of personnel but these imbalances persist. This maldistribution does not exist so clearly for hospital beds. Many small communities have been able to maintain hospitals, in part as a means of attempting to attract physicians and other health workers.[18]

Thus, in some parts of the United States, high-quality medical care may not be available, even for someone who can afford it, without a substantial investment in travel. For any serious emergency, this puts the affected individual at even greater risk. Several pilot programs to encourage young doctors to practice in rural, "underdoctored" areas have been tried, and more are being advocated, but there are still pronounced inequalities. Many rural areas have tried on their own to attract physicians and may be willing to finance the medical education of a young person willing to come to their town. These issues of access must be addressed along with economic issues if there is to be greater equality in access to health care.

Finally, we should note that access alone may not be sufficient to ensure that medical care is successful. The relatively high rate of infant mortality is often taken as a indicator of poor access to medical care, although there is some evidence that other factors may be as important in determining those health outcomes. For example, the highest rates of infant mortality (by state) tend to be less related to the availability of medical personnel and facilities, or even per capita income, than to the family situations into which children are born. Illegitimate births, for example, tend to have a much higher rate of infant mortality.[19]

Cost

The second fundamental problem that has troubled health-care consumers and health policymakers is the rapidly rising cost of medical care. Table 9.7 shows changes in prices for some components of medical care compared with the overall consumer price index (CPI), and the composite medical-care price index. It is clear from these data that medical costs as a whole have increased more rapidly than have total consumer costs and that, among the components of medical costs, hospital costs have increased most rapidly. These costs have increased 210 percent more over a twenty-eight-year period than have total consumer prices, while those for total medical care have increased "only" 57 percent more rapidly than the CPI. The rates of increase in medical costs slowed slightly in the early 1990s, but they still are outpacing general price increases.

TABLE 9.7

CHANGES IN MEDICAL CARE COSTS COMPARED

WITH CONSUMER PRICE INDEX (1967 = 100)

Year	CPI	Total medicine	Hospital	Physicians	Commodities
1960	88.7	79.1	57.3	77.0	104.5
1965	94.5	89.5	75.9	88.3	100.2
1970	116.3	120.6	145.4	121.4	103.6
1975	161.2	168.6	236.1	169.4	118.8
1980	246.8	265.9	418.9	269.3	168.1
1985	326.6	413.0	722.5	407.9	262.7
1988	359.1	504.0	895.5	494.2	332.5
1990	421.8	592.9	1,096.1	533.1	388.4
1991	439.5	645.7	1,199.1	565.1	420.2
1992	452.7	694.7	1,309.7	600.7	447.1

SOURCE: U.S. Bureau of the Census, *Statistical Abstract of the United States* (Washington, D.C.: Government Printing Office, annual).

The importance of these data on costs is that medical care is becoming more difficult for the average person to afford. Even if an individual's income keeps pace with the CPI, it will still fall behind the increase in the costs of even general medical care. With these rapidly increasing prices, few people can afford to pay for a catastrophic illness requiring long-term hospitalization and extensive treatment. Even the best medical insurance available will frequently be exhausted by such an illness. Thus it has become increasingly possible that even those with substantial incomes will be financially destroyed by a major illness. There is an additional problem that all the concern about the cost of medicine will undermine the quality of medical care, something that may be especially problematic with "prospective reimbursement" and Diagnostic Related Group (DRGs, see pp. 253–54).

Medical-care costs are a problem for government as well as for private citizens, as almost half the total medical-care bill in the United States is paid by government. But even such a large share of the medical marketplace has not enabled government to exercise any significant control over health costs, perhaps because decisions about health-care spending are made, not by one government, but by several. And within each government there are several agencies interested in health care. Government's attempts to control medical costs have been diffuse and have encountered difficulty overcoming the technical and political power of health-care providers. As we discuss later, however, government is attempting to move more effectively to assist citizens —both as taxpayers and as patients—to cope with the costs of health care.

To be able to control costs, we must understand why medical costs have been increasing so rapidly. A number of factors have been identified as causing at least part of the increase in medical-care costs.[20] For hospitals, one factor has been a rapid increase in the cost of supplies and equipment. This has been true of large capital investments such as CAT scanners, as well as more mundane items such as dressings and surgical gloves. In addition, labor costs for hospitals have been increasing rapidly, as many professional and nonprofessional employees unionize to bargain for higher wages. Also, there may be too many hospital beds for the number of available patients. Empty hospital beds have capital costs and even some running costs that must be met, and these costs are spread among the patients who occupy beds through increases in room rates. The same thing may be said for over-investment in technology; every hospital that buys a CAT scanner, for example, must pay for it, whether or not it is used very often. For example, the United States has over 2,000 magnetic resonance imaging (MRI) systems (at about $2 million each), while Canada is able to get by with less than 20.[21] Finally, the complex system of funding medical care in the United States costs a great deal of money. Some studies find that 25 percent of total hospital costs are in administration—about twice that in Canada with a single-payer public insurance program.[22]

In the early 1990s hospitals reacted to increasing pressures from insurers (including government agencies) and began to anticipate changes from national health reform. They attempted to reduce their operating costs by reducing their number of employees, managing their patient loads more effectively, and consolidating expensive services such as CAT and MRI scanning units. Managed competition programs also have been used to establish maximum payments for certain procedures, and to encourage the insured to make the best use of their insurance dollars.[23] Hospital costs continue to increase, but the rate of increase has slowed.

Physician costs also have been rising, although not as rapidly as hospital costs. In addition to the general pressures of inflation in the economy as a whole, increases in equipment and supply costs, increased insurance paperwork, the increasing cost of medical malpractice insurance, and the practice of "defensive medicine" to protect against malpractice suits by ordering every possible diagnostic procedure have all produced increases in doctors' fees.[24] Some of the relatively high cost of physicians' services in the United States results from the high level of specialization of American doctors.[25] Only 16 percent of private physicians in office-based practice in the United States are in general practice, down from 27 percent in 1970.

In part as a reaction to public pressures, and to reduce the possibility of controls being mandated by government, the American Medical Association (AMA) proposed to its member physicians that they impose a one-year moratorium on new price increases. Somewhat surprisingly, a large majority of physicians surveyed supported such a cost-reducing (or cost-maintaining) action. Further, physicians have cooperated increasingly with "managed care" programs in which large insurance carriers such as Blue Cross negotiate fees for their clients below the fees usually charged by physicians, and monitor the charges imposed by physicians. The insurers also require second opinions for expensive procedures or for procedures that are often performed unnecessarily. Physicians sometimes resent this interference in their clinical freedom, but the programs ensure them access to large pools of patients, all of whom by definition have insurance and who therefore present fewer problems in collecting fees than might other patients.[26]

The federal government has undertaken another program to attempt to control physician costs for Medicare patients, called the "resource-based relative value scale" (RBRVS).[27] This plan assigns reasonable costs to procedures based on the time involved, as well as the direct costs to the physician and malpractice premiums. Medicare then reimburses 80 percent of those "reasonable costs." As designed, this program assigns somewhat higher relative values to services provided by general practitioners than it does to specialists, which should also tend to reduce medical costs. There is relatively little experience with this program, but estimates are that it could save 12 percent of physicians' charges under Medicare.[28]

Finally, the method of payment for most medical care, especially hospital care, may influence increasing costs. Over 76 percent of all hospital costs and approximately 60 percent of all medical expenses are paid by third-party payers.[29] These third-party payers may be private (e.g., Blue Cross) or public (Medicaid or Medicare). As a result, neither doctors nor patients have an incentive to restrict their consumption of medical care; it is perceived as "free." Individuals may, in fact, want to use all the insurance benefits they can in order to recover the amount they have paid as premiums over the years. Of course, the increased consumption of medical care will be reflected in higher insurance premiums for all consumers in the future. This is a "tragedy of the commons" in which the rational behavior of individuals creates a pattern of irrationality for the society as a whole.[30] To rectify some of the problems with third-party payment, the Reagan administration included in the 1985 budget a program to tax employer-financed health insurance above a certain value. This made it more expensive to have so-called first-dollar coverage (i.e., coverage from the first dollar spent for treatment and all subsequent dollars). The change was intended to make the consumer of medical care more conscious of the costs of medicine, something that third-party payment does not do.

The states have the primary responsibility for administering Medicaid, the public medical program for the poor, and have been encountering large increases in their costs. In addition to the usual programs for managed care and scrutiny of costs, at least one state, Oregon, has adopted a more radical plan for cost containment. The state government decided that it wanted to be able to continue to provide care to all persons who could not afford private care, rather than lower the amount of income at which individuals lost eligibility for the program. But the state also decided that it could not pay for everything for everybody.[31] It therefore decided that Medicaid in Oregon would pay only for a range of diseases—selected by cost, seriousness, and effectiveness of treatment—that fell above a line determined by the amount of money available. Medicaid would not pay for treatment of other conditions. So, for example, in 1991 Medicaid would pay for inflammation of the stomach (number 587 on the list of disorders) but not for lower back pain (number 588).[32] Also, the program would not pay for "heroic treatments" for extremely difficult cases, such as babies born weighing less than 500 grams.

This policy has had its critics, who argue that this program of rationing prevents the poor from getting equal treatment and that the selection of the cutoff point in care is arbitrary.[33] It was particularly attacked by groups representing the disabled and chronically ill. Advocates, however, argue that this program enables the state to continue serving all the poor and to continue providing routine and cost-effective diagnostic procedures free of charge. At least in the short run, the critics of the program were able to win, and the program was curtailed because it was alleged to violate legal protections for the disabled.[34] This is but one of many difficult choices that rising medical costs may soon impose on American society and its government.

Quality

Finally, both citizens and government must be concerned with the quality of medical care being provided. Citizens' obvious expressions of concern about quality have been the increased number of malpractice suits and complaints against physicians and hospitals. Governments' concerns about quality extend from the general social responsibility for regulating the safety and effectiveness of medicines and medical devices on the market to the quality of care provided to Medicare and Medicaid patients to perhaps a more philosophical concern with the efficacy of modern medical care as a remedy for the health problems of American citizens.[35] Medical care is, however, a difficult product for which to judge quality.

When a patient—regardless of whether the resulting bill will be paid by Blue Cross-Blue Shield, by Medicaid, or out of pocket—enters a physician's office, he or she has the right to expect, at a minimum, competent medical care that meets current standards. Unfortunately, many patients do not receive such care. Many patients complain about receiving poor-quality care or medical treatment that they believe is delivered without any genuine humanity. The AMA's own statistics document a significant rate of error in diagnosis and treatment. A more subtle manner in which the quality of treatment is eroded appears in a number of studies documenting excessive use of medical technology and drugs as a means of earning more money for physicians and hospitals. For the public sector, complaints of overtreatment mean increased costs for Medicare and Medicaid patients, as well as more human costs for the patients.

The medical profession itself is supposed to be the first line of defense in the quality of medical care. State medical associations and their review boards are supposed to monitor the practice of medicine and handle complaints about incompetent or unethical practitioners. Other professional organizations are supposed to perform the same task for their members. While these organizations do have an interest in maintaining the integrity of the medicine, they also find it difficult to discipline their fellow professionals and friends.

A more important philosophical question has been injected into the discussion of the quality of care. Former Colorado Governor Richard Lamm commented that "we all have the duty to die," meaning that the terminally ill perhaps should not be kept alive by heroic means when that intervention only "prolongs dying" rather than saves life.[36] Is it high-technology medicine that sustains a semblance of life that has lost most human qualities, or is it a high-technology ego trip for the physician? The physicians' first commandment, *primum non nocere* (first, do not harm), has always been taken to mean preserving life at all costs; modern technology has made that an expensive and possibly inhumane interpretation. Some patients' families have gone to court to have their loved ones removed from life-support systems, but the techniques available to sustain life appear to have outpaced the ethical, legal, and policy capacity to cope with the changes.[37]

The question of what care is appropriate for the very elderly and the terminally ill raises the question of rationing of health care (see chapter 15). While this is sometimes discussed primarily as a problem of cost, it also has a number of implications for a definition of quality. Some countries have already begun to impose rather strict rationing of care—not performing organ transplants for patients over certain ages, for example. This has, in turn, produced fears that a more extensive public role in American medical care will also mean a greater possibility for rationing. For people used to being able to purchase what they want (provided they have good insurance) in the medical marketplace, the imposition of rationing is also prima facie a reduction of quality.

Public Programs in Health Care

As we have demonstrated, government is deeply involved in health services, despite the rhetoric concerning a free-enterprise medical-care system in the United States. Existing public programs provide direct medical services for some segments of the population, offer medical-care insurance for others, and support the health of the entire population through public health programs, regulation, and medical research. Many citizens question the efficacy of these programs, especially the regulatory programs, but they are evidence of the large and important role the government plays in medicine. We now proceed to discuss several major government programs in medical care, with some attention to the policy issues involved in each, and the possibilities of improving the quality of health through public action.

Medicare

The government medical-care program with which most citizens are familiar is almost certainly Medicare, adopted as part of the Social Security Amendments of 1965. The program is essentially one of medical insurance for the elderly and the disabled who are eligible for Social Security or Railroad Retirement benefits. The program has two parts. Part A, financed principally through payroll taxation, is a hospitalization plan. It covers the first 60 days of hospitalization but requires the patient to pay the first $676 (1993). The program also covers hospitalization during the 61st to 90th days, but requires a copayment of $169 per day (1993). This portion of the plan also covers up to 100 days in a nursing-care facility after release from the hospital, with this coverage being subject to a $84.50 copayment by the insured after the first 20 days (1993).

Part B of Medicare is a supplementary insurance program covering doctors' fees and other outpatient services. These expenses are also subject to deductibles and coinsurance, with the insured paying the first $100 each year, plus 20 percent of the allowable costs. This portion of the Medicare program is financed by the insured, who pay a monthly premium of $41.10 (1994). Insured persons bear a rather high proportion of their own medical expenses under Medicare, given that it is a publicly provided insurance program. The program is certainly subsidized, however, and is still a bargain for the average retired person, who might not be able to purchase anything like the coverage provided in the private market. This is true in part because the elderly have, on average, significantly higher medical expenses than the population as a whole.

Medicare is a better program than would be available to most of the elderly under private insurance programs; it requires no physical examination for coverage, covers preexisting health conditions, is uniformly available throughout the country, and provides some services that might not be available on private plans. The plan does have some problems. Perhaps the greatest difficulty is that the program requires those insured to pay a significant amount out of their own pockets for coverage, even when they are hospitalized. Purchasing Part B of the plan requires an annual outlay of $493.20 (1994) which, although it is not much money for health insurance, may be a relatively large share of a pensioner's income. In addition, the costs of deductibles and coinsurance in both parts of Medicare may place a burden on less affluent beneficiaries of the program.

In addition to the costs to the recipient of covered expenses, Medicare does not cover all the medical expenses that most beneficiaries will incur. For example, it does not pay for prescription drugs, eye or dental examinations, eyeglasses or dentures, preventive examinations, or immunizations. Nor does the program cover very extended care. In short, Medicare does not cover many medical problems that plague the elderly population the program was intended to serve, and as a result it does not really meet the needs of the elderly poor, who are most in need of services. In fact, at least one study shows that the gap between the health status of rich and poor elderly people has widened since the introduction of Medicare.[38] The more affluent can use the program as a supplement to their own assets or private health insurance programs, while the less affluent are incapable of providing adequately for their medical needs, even with Medicare.

One attempt to solve the "medigap" problem has been the introduction of a number of private health insurance programs to fill in the lacunae of Medicare coverage. Unfortunately, most existing policies of this type do not cover the most glaring deficiencies of Medicare—for example, the absence of coverage for extended nursing-home care. In addition, the policies do not cover preexisting health problems and frequently have long waiting periods for eligibility. In short, these policies often cost more money without providing the protection required. The 96th Congress passed legislation in 1980 imposing some standards on such insurance policies, but the law was directed more at outright fraud than at providing a means of making useful policies available to cover the gaps in Medicare coverage. Additional legislation, passed in 1990, tightened the controls on insurers, but often there is still duplication and waste.[39]

On the government's side of the Medicare program, the costs of funding medical insurance for the elderly impose a burden on the working-age population and on government resources. The basic hospitalization coverage under Medicare is financed by a payroll tax collected as a part of the Social Security tax, taking 1.45 percent of each worker's salary in 1991. Employers matched that 1.45 percent. After the policy was changed in 1991, the health insurance portion of the Social Security tax was extracted on all earned income, unlike the pension and disability portion, which is extracted only up to $60,600 per year (1994). With increasing opposition to the Social Security tax have come suggestions to shift the financing of Medicare to general tax revenues such as the income tax, leaving the entire payroll tax to fund Social Security pensions.[40] But with the increasing costs of medical care and the growing number of Americans eligible for Medicare, difficulties are likely to arise in financing the program for some years to come.

Finally, problems of quality and fair pricing for Medicare patients are also likely to persist. Medicare regulations allow the Health Care Financing Administration to pay "reasonable" costs to physicians and hospitals for services rendered to beneficiaries and, of course, require that the providers give adequate and "standard" treatment. In some instances, physicians have charged more than the amount designated as "reasonable," thereby imposing additional costs on the patient. In other instances, physicians have employed tests and procedures generally considered unnecessary, knowing that the costs would be largely covered by Medicare. In 1972 Congress established Professional Standards Review Organizations (PSROs) to police the quality and pricing of services rendered to Medicare and Medicaid patients. These PSROs are composed primarily of physicians, and the results of their efforts have been mixed. Some have reported substantial savings as a result of their efforts, while others have been almost totally ineffective in enforcing any discipline on physicians or hospitals.[41] PSROs are also increasingly involved in detecting and exposing outright fraud on the part of a few physicians who bill for patients they do not see or otherwise abuse the system. Their actions have been supplemented by efforts of private insurance firms, who also lose money through fraud.[42] But with the increasing costs of all medical care, the need for effective cost control for these programs is likely to remain an important issue for some time to come.

One move to control costs for public medical programs is called Diagnostic Related Groups (DRGs) and is a form of prospective reimbursement. This program, adopted 1 October 1983, has hospitals reimbursed for Medicare and Medicaid patients according to one of over 400 specific diagnostic groups (e.g., appendicitis).[43] The hospital is guaranteed a fixed amount for each patient according to the DRG to which his or her complaint is assigned. A hospital that is able to treat a patient for less can retain the difference, but if the hospital stay costs more than allowed under the DRG, the hospital must absorb the loss. Despite some experience with DRGs, a number of questions remain about how it affects medical care. For example, the doctor, more than the hospital, determines how much a course of treatment will cost, and there has been increased conflict between hospital administrators and physicians about how patients are to be treated. Also, this program may tend to reduce the quality of care provided to Medicaid and Medicare patients, or cause too-early dismissals of patients with associated cost shifting onto home medical-care programs and community medicine; patients are discharged "quicker and sicker," and too often they must be readmitted soon after discharge. Also, DRGs do not easily accommodate the multiple diseases and infirmities characteristic of so many Medicare patients. Nevertheless, the DRG program is an interesting attempt to impose greater cost consciousness on hospitals and physicians that has been copied by some private health insurers. This approach to cost control may be preferable to rationing approaches such as that imposed in Oregon for Medicaid patients (see p. 249).

Medicaid

While Medicare is directed toward the elderly and disabled, Medicaid, the second major public health-care program, is directed toward the indigent. Medicaid was passed at the same time as Medicare, to provide federal matching funds to state and local governments for medical care of welfare recipients and the "medically indigent," a category intended to include those who do not qualify for public assistance but whose income is not sufficient to cover necessary medical expenses. Unlike Medicare, which is a uniform national program, Medicaid is administered by the states, and as a consequence the benefits, eligibility requirements, and administration vary considerably. But if a state chooses to have a Medicaid program (two states do not), it must provide benefits for all welfare recipients and for those who receive Supplemental Security Income because of categorical problems—age, blindness, and disability.

Medicaid regulations require states to provide a range of services to recipients of the program: hospitalization, laboratory and other diagnostic services, X-rays, nursing-home services, screening for a range of diseases, and physicians' services. The states may also extend benefits to cover prescription drugs and other services. For each service, the states may set limitations on the amount of care covered and the rate of reimbursement. Given increasing costs, states have tended to provide little more than the minimum benefits required under federal law, and several have left, or are considering leaving, the system. Federal laws, however, are becoming increasingly stringent and are imposing additional costs on the states, which the states are finding difficult to fund.[44] Some are reacting by using alternative service systems such as HMOs for their Medicaid clients.

In addition to the problems of variance in the coverage and benefits across the country, Medicaid has other policy problems. The ones most commonly cited are fraud and abuse. It is sometimes estimated that up to 7 percent of total federal outlays for Medicaid are accounted for by abuse.[45] Almost all this abuse is by the service providers, rather than by the beneficiaries of the medical treatments, in part because of the complex eligibility requirements and procedures for reimbursement. But this fraud still presents a negative image of the public program to the public.[46] With a continuing strain on public resources, any program that has a reputation for fraud is likely to encounter difficulties in receiving its funding. This is true whether the fraud is committed by such respected providers as physicians or by their indigent clients.

The general strain on fiscal resources at all levels of government and increased medical costs also have produced serious problems for the Medicaid program. States have been forced to cut back on optional services under the program and to reduce coverage of primary (physician) care in order to be able to finance hospital care for recipients. Also, some states have set limitations on the amount of physicians' reimbursements for each service. These reimbursements are significantly lower than the rates doctors would receive from private or even Medicare patients; the result is that an increasing number of physicians refuse to accept Medicaid patients. In part because of these trends, Medicaid has increasingly become a program of institutional medical care—paradoxically, this is the most expensive way of delivering medical services. As with Medicare, however, institutional care through hospitals, hospital emergency rooms, and nursing homes is the one kind of medical care almost sure to be covered under the program. So, today less than 2 percent of all Medicaid spending goes to home health services, while over 40 percent of all expenditures goes to extended-care facilities, many of which do not meet federal standards.

Like Medicare, the Medicaid program has done a great deal of good in making medical care available to people who might not otherwise receive it. Nevertheless, some significant Medicaid problems will be political issues for years. Proposals for solutions range from the abolition of both Medicare and Medicaid to the establishment of national health insurance, with a number of proposals for internal readjustments of the programs or the use of private health insurance in between the more radical alternatives.

Health Maintenance Organizations

A fundamental criticism frequently is made of American medical care: it is, or at least has been, fee-for-service medicine. Medical practitioners are paid for each service they perform, and as a consequence they have an incentive to practice their skills on patients; surgeons make money by wielding their scalpels, and internists make money by ordering diagnostic procedures. Furthermore, critics charge that American medical care is primarily acute care. The system is oriented toward treating the ill rather than toward preventing illness. The most money is to be made through curing illness, not through promoting health. This point is to some degree substantiated by the relatively low levels of immunizations found among American children (see table 9.8). With all the money being spent on medical care in the United States, there are still millions of children who are not fully immunized against normal childhood diseases.

The Health Maintenance Organization (HMO) is at least a partial attack on these two characteristics of the health-care system.[47] First, the HMO provides prepaid medical care. Members of an HMO pay an annual fee in return for which they receive virtually all their medical care. They may have to pay ancillary costs (e.g., a small set fee for each prescription), but the vast majority of medical expenses are covered through the HMO by the annual fee. Under this prepayment scheme, doctors working for the HMO have no incentive to prescribe additional treatments. If anything, given that the doctors commonly share in the profits of the organization or frequently own the HMO themselves, they have an incentive not to prescribe treatments. Any surgery or treatment that would cost the organization money without providing additional income reduces profits. With the same reasoning, doctors in an HMO have an incentive to keep the members healthy and to encourage preventive medicine. A healthy member is all profit, while a sick member is all loss. It is argued that by reversing the incentives usually presented to physicians, HMOs can significantly improve the quality of health care and reduce the rapid escalation of medical-care costs. Critics argue that the incentives have been altered too far and that members of HMOs may not receive the treatment they need because of the owners' desire to maintain levels of profit. At a minimum, the HMO is an interesting and potentially significant innovation in American health care.

The formation of HMOs has been supported by the federal government. In 1973 President Nixon signed into law a bill directed at improving

TABLE 9.8

PERCENTAGE IMMUNIZED, CHILDREN AGES ONE TO FOUR
YEARS, 1991

	Total	White	Nonwhite
Diptheria-pertussis-tetanus	65.8	68.6	54.8
Polio	50.6	52.7	42.1
Measles, etc.	77.6	77.9	76.4
Haemophilus B	56.9	58.5	50.4
All up to date	42.1	44.6	31.7

SOURCE: U.S. Bureau of the Census, *Statistical Abstract of the United States, 1993* (Washington, D.C.: Government Printing Office, 1994), table 200.

choice in the health marketplace.[48] The legislation provided for planning and development grants for prospective HMOs, but at the same time placed a number of restrictions on any HMO using federal funding. Most important, all HMOs had to offer an extensive array of services including psychiatric care. Any employer offering group insurance to employees had to make the same amount of money available to any employee who wanted to join an HMO. The federal involvement in HMOs was reauthorized in 1978 for another three years, with additional support for the development of outpatient care facilities—important in eliminating expensive hospitalization. The HMO movement has also been assisted by federal efforts restricting the actions of physicians and private insurers who sought to reduce the competition offered by HMOs.

Several successful HMOs now operate in the United States, the best-known being the Kaiser-Permanente organization with more than 3 million members and 3,000 physicians. The American Medical Association resisted these organizations as unfair competition because HMOs are subsidized by the federal government and as not providing adequate medical care. Although they appeal to many people, HMOs must overcome several obstacles if they are to make a significant impact on American health care. One important obstacle is the capital required to start a large-scale medical-care facility. The federal government has yet to underwrite these expenses; it provides funds only for planning. A good deal of skepticism continues about the quality of medical care provided by HMOs, and some citizens seem unwilling to adopt this rather significant departure from the traditional means of delivering health services.

Although the concept does have critics—most of them members of the medical profession—it also has supporters. HMO plans have been supported by organized labor as one means of reducing medical inflation, and they appear to be increasingly acceptable to businesses as a means of reducing costs, a mechanism that is more palatable than direct government regulation. In one vote of confidence, the Reagan administration in 1984 allowed Medicare and Medicaid patients to opt to join HMOs for their medical care, believing that this option could reduce the government's costs for these programs with no loss of medical quality.[49] As the pressures on medical costs have increased, and employers and individual consumers have sought lower-cost alternatives, an increasing proportion of the medical profession has moved into HMOs and similar organizations.[50]

Health-Care Regulation

Perhaps the most pervasive impact of government on the delivery of health-care services in the United States has been through regulation. There are many kinds of health-care regulations, and this section briefly discusses four: facilities, costs, quality, and pharmaceuticals.

Facilities and Planning

In addition to attempting to influence health-care delivery indirectly by providing financial support for certain activities, government is involved in more direct attempts to move resources around in the health industry. One such attempt is through the regulation of health-care facilities and more comprehensive planning for the health needs of communities. Another basic criticism that has been made of American medicine is that it overuses and overpurchases high technology. The symbols of this medical technology are the CAT scanner and the MRI machine, both sophisticated, computer-assisted devices for imaging the interior of the human body.[51] One hears anecdotal evidence of these extremely expensive machines being used only a few hours a day, and of several hospitals in the same area having the same expensive and underused equipment. But why would presumably rational hospital administrators purchase such a machine when they know that one exists just down the street? The answer is that hospitals do not have patients; doctors do. Hospitals must compete among themselves to attract doctors who have patients so that the hospitals can fill their beds and meet their budgets. One common means of competing for doctors is making sure that your hospital has the most up-to-date equipment available. Costs are rarely a consideration for the doctors or even the patients, as the majority of expenses are paid by a third party, such as Blue Cross or Medicare or Medicaid. Therefore, the hospital can afford to purchase a CAT scanner or any other piece of equipment and then simply pass the cost along to patients through the room rate and other charges.

The 1974 Health Planning Act was an attempt on the part of the federal government to address this cause of medical-care inflation, as well as the more fundamental question of the underuse of resources in the health-care industry. The money used to purchase the CAT scanner not only drives up the cost of medical care but also means that the money cannot be used for another program, such as a broad-scale screening for hypertension or diabetes, which might benefit a much larger number of people. The 1974 act created a series of local planning agencies to monitor the development of medical-care facilities. Each of these Health Systems Agencies (HSAs) covers between 1 million and 3 million people, with statewide agencies coordinating the activities of local agencies. Associated with the federal regulations are state certificate-of-need laws, which establish guidelines on what needs must be manifest before the local HSA can allow the construction of a health-care facility. By 1980, all states except Louisiana had passed certificate-of-need legislation. These laws covered new hospital facilities and all capital equipment with a value of $150,000 or more. Interestingly, the new facilities of an HMO were exempt from these certificate-of-need regulations, as a means of ensuring that these rules will not prevent new HMOs from being established.

The health-planning legislation was extended until 1986, at which time it was more closely related to the whole DRG approach to reimbursement of hospitals. The idea is that capital as well as operating costs of hospitals would be reimbursed based on their patient mix, classified by the DRGs.[52] Thus a hospital with relatively few complex surgical cases might have little justification for purchasing, and little federal money to support purchasing, capital equipment such as CAT scanners. As with much of the thrust of the Reagan administration, this program substitutes a competitive, market incentive for direct regulation. The program has been somewhat beneficial to hospitals that have relatively low capital costs (e.g., inner-city hospitals), but it may slow the growth of new, and especially new proprietary, hospitals. Although it is essentially a market incentive, many in the industry would like to have even that degree of control removed from their capital decisions.

Hospital Costs

Cost increases are a major consideration in health care in the 1990s, and hospital costs have been the most rapidly increasing component of medical costs. Further, as hospitals constitute a major component of the total health-care bill (44 percent) and are readily identifiable institutions with better recordkeeping than the average physician, it seems sensible to concentrate on them as a locus for controlling medical-care costs.[53] The approaches to controlling hospital costs have been varied. The Carter administration proposed direct regulation of hospital costs. This was not passed, but it seemed to frighten the hospital industry sufficiently to introduce its own voluntary effort (VE) program to slow increases in costs. Spokesmen for the industry claimed that this program reduced the rate of inflation to 12.8 percent per year, below the target figure of 13.6 percent. Yet these figures were significantly higher than the 9 percent proposed by the Carter administration.

Another major approach to controlling hospital costs, begun in New Jersey, has been prospective reimbursement. The federal version of this approach for Medicare patients is the Diagnostic Related Group mentioned earlier. In essence DRGs constitute a market approach to cost containment, for they allow hospitals that are efficient to make a profit, while those that are not well run can sustain losses. This is more in line with the thinking of the Reagan administration than the direct price controls proposed by the Carter administration.

Although both the Carter program and DRGs attack the problem of hospital costs, neither attempts to attack some fundamental problems causing prices to escalate. One problem is the fundamental principle of fee-for-service medicine, which gives hospitals and doctors an incentive to provide more services. Related to that is the tendency of the medical profession to use high-cost hospital treatment when lower-cost options would be as effective. This is done for the convenience of the physician and because many health insurance policies will pay for hospital treatments but not for the same treatments performed on an outpatient basis. The regimen of DRGs and preferred provider plans limiting costs in private insurance have helped change this somewhat, but American medical care remains more centered on the hospital than care in many other countries. Finally, it is important to remember that hospitals do not have patients, doctors do; and hospitals must compete for doctors in order to fill hospital beds. This competition takes place largely through the acquisition of high-cost technology (CAT scanners, magnetic resonance imaging systems, etc.), which must be amortized through the higher price of hospital care.

Health Quality

The regulation of health-care quality is one of the most controversial areas of government intervention in the health field. First, it comes up directly against long-established canons of clinical freedom and the right of members of the medical profession to regulate their conduct. The medical profession, and probably most of the public, assumes that the only person qualified to judge the professional conduct of a physician is another physician.

In addition, private mechanisms have been established for rectifying any harm done by a physician in the conduct of his or her profession. There are, of course, tort and malpractice lawsuits. These legal proceedings have themselves generated problems for medicine, however, and have been cited as one of the factors causing the rapid increases in medical-care costs. Some effects of malpractice litigation are direct, as physicians pass the doubled or tripled malpractice insurance costs on to patients in higher fees. The direct impact of malpractice insurance fees on medical costs appears minimal, but the indirect effects, the practice of "defensive medicine," appear more substantial.[54] A doctor, fearing a malpractice suit, will prescribe additional diagnostic procedures, extra days in the hospital, or extra treatments to lessen his or her chances of being declared legally negligent. The costs of these extra procedures are passed on to all consumers through increased medical insurance premiums or higher taxes.

As I mentioned when discussing Medicare, the major public instruments for regulating the quality of medical care are the Professional Standards Review Organizations (PSROs). These organizations are designed in part to monitor costs of services provided to Medicare patients, but they necessarily become involved in the issue of appropriate and effective treatment as well.

Treatments that are ineffective or dangerous can also be costly. Some PSROs have gone so far as to establish standard profiles of treatment for certain rather common conditions and then to question physicians whose treatment differs significantly from those patterns. Physicians who are using more extensive treatments may be imposing additional costs on the program, while those who are using unusual or less extensive treatments may be threatening the health of the patient. Other effects of malpractice as a control device for quality are more systemic, as doctors in specialties such as obstetrics and neurosurgery that are subject to frequent suits simply change to other specialties. This condition is leaving small towns and even small cities without certain types of medical care.

Most PSROs are not so diligent, however; the standard complaint against PSROs has been that they are not sufficiently aggressive in monitoring the practice of Medicare and Medicaid physicians. This is generally said to result from the domination of PSROs by physicians and from doctors' tendency to protect one another from outsiders' attempts to impose any regulations on their practice of medicine. The growth of malpractice litigation and its attendant costs, however, may produce pressures on the profession to adopt more stringent internal policing of professional practices, as well as the development of administrative rather than legal mechanisms for redressing grievances.

Drug Regulation

The federal government is also deeply involved in the regulation of the pharmaceutical industry and in the control of substances in food and water that are potentially harmful to health. The federal government began to regulate food and drugs in 1902, with extensive increases in its powers in 1938 and again in 1962. The issues surrounding drug regulation have been more heated since the early 1980s than at any time since the initial passage of the legislation. The Food and Drug Administration (FDA), which is responsible for most drug regulation, has been under attack from all sides. Some argue that its regulations have been excessively stringent and have prevented useful drugs from coming to the market. The AIDS epidemic has brought this complaint to the fore and has actually produced some changes in the procedures for licensing new drugs.[55] Other critics of the FDA believe that its regulations have been too lax and excessively dominated by the pharmaceutical industry and that, as a result, potentially dangerous drugs have been certified for sale.

The basic regulatory doctrine applied to pharmaceuticals is that a drug must be shown to be both safe and effective before it can be approved for sale. Several problems arise from this doctrine. First, almost any drug will have some side effects, so that proving its safety is difficult, and some criteria must be established for weighing the benefits of an individual drug against the side effects it may produce. The example commonly cited here is that because of a range of known side effects, common aspirin might have considerable difficulty being certified for use under the standards prevailing in the 1990s. The safety and effectiveness of a drug must be demonstrated by clinical trials that are often time-consuming and expensive, and potentially important drugs are thereby delayed in coming to the public.

Critics of the drug industry point to other problems in drug regulation and in the pharmaceutical industry as a whole. For example, there are the problems of look-alike drugs and the use of brand names as opposed to generic drugs.[56] It is argued that a great deal of the attention in drug research is directed toward finding combinations of drugs that can be marketed under a brand name or in reproducing findings of already proven drugs so that they can be marketed with a different brand name. The brand-name drugs are invariably more expensive than generic drugs, and critics argue that the licensing of brand names actually aids the pharmaceutical industry by promoting the sale of higher-priced drugs. They also argue that drugs are sold and prescribed without adequate dissemination of information about the possible side effects of the drugs. Some states have intervened to reduce the problem of generic drug costs. These states now allow pharmacists to substitute a generic drug for a brand-name drug unless the physician specifically forbids such substitution. Many drugstores attempt to make their customers aware of this opportunity, so unless physicians believe that the generic drug would not be effective (some would argue for other, less noble reasons as well), citizens can get generic drugs.

A major attempt to modify drug regulations was made in 1979 in a Senate bill proposed by Senator Edward Kennedy. Among the most important issues in the proposed legislation was the shortening of the review periods required before marketing new drugs, especially so-called breakthrough drugs that offer great promise for serious illnesses and seem greatly superior to existing drugs. The proposed legislation also mandated that more information on drugs be disseminated to physicians and patients so that more informed decisions could be made about the drugs' use, and it attempted to limit certain drug-company promotion practices. Through skilled political management, the bill passed the Senate easily but did not pass the House of Representatives. Nevertheless, the legislation represents some possible directions for future drug regulation.

Associated with drug regulation in the FDA has been food regulation, especially the prohibition of carcinogenic substances in food. The Delaney Amendment requires the FDA to remove from the market foods containing any substance that "induces" cancer in human beings or animals. An issue developed over this amendment during the late 1970s in regard to the attempt to ban the sale of the artificial sweetener saccharin. In April 1977 studies in Canada showed that large amounts of saccharin tended to produce bladder cancer. Under the Delaney Amendment (passed in 1958), the FDA was then required to propose a ban on saccharin. The ban would have removed saccharin from the market as a general food additive but would have allowed its sale as an over-the-counter drug with a warning label. The proposed regulations aroused the interest of diabetics, the food and soft-drink industries, and weight watchers, among others. The outcry was sufficient to cause Congress to pass a bill in 1977 delaying for eighteen months the removal of saccharin from the market, requiring the labeling of items containing saccharin, and demanding more testing of the effects of saccharin, both as a carcinogen and as an aid in weight control.

The studies during the eighteen-month period did not provide any conclusive evidence on the safety of saccharin, but they did point to possible changes in the regulation of possibly carcinogenic or otherwise harmful substances. The reports of the National Academy of Science recommended that the government, instead of prohibiting all such substances, establish categories of risk with attached regulations ranging from complete prohibition to warning labels to no action at all. It suggested also that such decisions take into consideration the possible benefits from the continued sale of the substance. Because many believed that saccharin was highly beneficial for some people and was only a low risk, they suggested that it be allowed to remain on sale. These risk-benefit or cost-benefit considerations are a common aid to decision making (see chapter 14) in the public sector, although they are perhaps less valid when applied to risks of the occurrence of a disease such as cancer. For whatever reasons, Congress reauthorized the continuing sale of saccharin.

Another issue related to the regulation of pharmaceuticals is the regulation of tobacco, especially cigarettes. The Surgeon General determined some years ago that smoking cigarettes is harmful and required warning labels on packages and forbade advertising on electronic media. Since that time, state and local governments have imposed bans on smoking in public places. The Surgeon General and the FDA also have developed evidence on the thousands of deaths caused by smoking. In congressional hearings in 1994 the FDA presented evidence on the addictive nature of nicotine and began movements to strengthen the regulations on the sale, advertising, and use of cigarettes. In particular, if it declared nicotine to be a drug, the FDA could regulate cigarettes as the delivery system for that drug.

Cigarettes and their regulation also figure prominently in the discussion of financing health care. Several of the plans for national health insurance (see pp. 264–70) depend on an increased tax on cigarettes for at least part of the financing. For example, under the Clinton plan, taxes on cigarettes would have increased to $1 per pack, while the health-reform package developed by the House Ways and Means Committee would add an additional 45 cents to the existing 24-cent tax. Such a tax increase might in essence function like a regulation if it encouraged people to stop smoking, but that too would convey a benefit by reducing the estimated $65 billion spent on diseases caused by smoking.

Summary

Regulation is a common and pervasive form of public intervention in the health-care industry in the United States. It is not without controversy, and almost all forms of regulation have been under active review and reconsideration. Many regulations were replaced by competitive mechanisms using market forces to produce desired changes in the health-service industry during the Reagan and Bush administrations. The Clinton administration is by no means as negative about public intervention, but more regulations may be replaced. Even with the increasing public concern over health care in the 1990s, some conservatives want to reduce further public attempts to control this industry while liberals seek to maintain and expand regulations.

The Pursuit of National Health Insurance

The United States is the only Western industrialized nation without a significant program of national health insurance or direct health-service delivery by the public sector. As we have seen, this does not mean that the government has no role in medical care. In fact, approximately *14 percent* of the American people now depend on the federal government for their health care, and many more receive most or all of their care from emergency rooms in municipal hospitals. What the absence of national health insurance does mean is that citizens who do not fit into the particular categories eligible for public insurance—for example, the aged, veterans, the medically indigent —must rely on private health care or the often substandard and usually slow care available through emergency rooms in public hospitals. With rising medical expenses, the ever-present possibility of catastrophic illnesses with equally catastrophic economic consequences, and the declining availability of health insurance as an employee benefit, there have been increasing pressures to extend the public role in medicine to the entire population.

The idea of a national health insurance program for the United States goes back at least to the Truman administration. Indeed, Theodore Roosevelt, aware of health-care programs in European nations, had proposed something like a national health program at the beginning of the twentieth century. When President Truman proposed a comprehensive national health insurance program in 1945 as a part of the Social Security program, it met with severe opposition from the American Medical Association and conservative business organizations, who called the plan "socialized medicine." The AMA spent millions of dollars in its campaign against national health insurance. The adoption of Medicare in 1965 represented a partial success for those who wanted a national health insurance program, but pressures continued for a plan that would insure the entire population.

Interestingly, public opinion about health care has also changed. Although the AMA's arguments against socialized medicine were persuasive in the 1940s and 1950s, by 1973 a majority of Americans polled favored some system of public health insurance. By the 1990s as many as two-thirds of respondents in polls said they favored national health insurance of some sort.[57] The political importance of health care as an issue was highlighted in a 1991 senatorial election in Pennsylvania in which a relatively unknown Democrat (Harris Wofford), campaigning heavily on the issue of national health care, soundly defeated a popular ex-governor and ex-U.S. attorney general (Richard Thornburgh). Democrats quickly saw this as a possible avenue to the White House in 1992, and Bill Clinton seized this policy as a centerpiece of his campaign.

One major difficulty in the drive for some sort of national health insurance in the 1990s is that several alternative plans are available. Some plans have the backing of powerful interests in the medical establishment (a plan has even been proposed by the AMA),[58] some have the backing of the Republicans in Congress and others are proposed by Democrats in Congress, and still others by health advocacy groups. The Clinton administration began an active discussion of national health insurance, but its plan was but one among many. The political problem, therefore, will be to get enough coalescence around any one plan to have it adopted and then implemented successfully.[59] We now look at several broad alternative approaches to health insurance[60] and then look more specifically at several of the plans under active consideration.

"Play or Pay"

One approach to national health insurance is commonly referred to as "play or pay."[61] The idea is that all employers would have to provide at least a minimum of health insurance for their employees ("play") or contribute to a public insurance program that would cover their employees and everyone else not covered by private health insurance ("pay"). Most plans call for a payroll tax of 7 or 8 percent for companies that do not provide health benefits. These plans also depend to a great extent on the actions of the private sector, but they do include a public insurance program (usually an expanded Medicare program) to provide a safety net for the unemployed. A program like this is already in place in Hawaii; a more extensive program has been tried in Massachusetts, but it encountered substantial financial difficulties when the economy in that state sustained a number of serious reverses.[62]

The play-or-pay system largely would preserve the existing insurance system, although probably with more extensive regulation. It would also preserve the existing, fee-for-service medical-care system, again perhaps with greater regulation of costs. In addition, it would allow companies to provide better benefits to their employees than the minimums mandated under the law, although those benefits might be treated as taxable income for the recipients. The principal difficulty with this plan is that many small employers argue that health insurance costs would force them out of business, much as many small employers are being forced in the 1990s to drop medical coverage of their employees because of the costs.

The reform plan proposed by the American Medical Association contains most elements of the play-or-pay system and would require all employers, over time, to provide medical care to their employees. Combined with this fundamental change in the status quo would be reform of existing public programs to ensure greater equality of coverage (Medicaid) and greater financial soundness (Medicare). Further, the plan would impose several cost-cutting ideas, such as limitation of malpractice claims. While this proposal is to some degree self-serving on the part of the medical-care profession, it does demonstrate how pervasive the concern about access and cost issues in medical care is in the United States.

Canadian-Style Comprehensive Coverage

The most extreme proposal for public medical care would adopt something like the plan currently in operation in Canada—generally referred to as the "single-payer" system.[63] This program would change the medical industry in the United States rather fundamentally and would place the public sector, not private providers (doctors and hospitals), in the driver's seat in medicine. The simplest proposal of this type would extend Medicare, with its deductibles and copayments, to cover the entire population. Other plans involve all legal residents being issued cards that they would present to providers, with the providers receiving their reimbursement from government. Fees would either be set or maximum reimbursements established, with doctors and hospitals able to charge more if the patient was willing (and able) to pay.

Critics argue that this program would mean large tax increases and would put existing health insurance providers out of business in favor of large public bureaucracies. Further, the critics claim that the experience of Canada is that health-care innovation has been slower, and that there is often a waiting list for elective procedures. Advocates of the Canadian system, in contrast, argue that the claims of waiting lists and slower introduction of new technologies are exaggerated and have had little real impact on the quality of care. Indeed, they assert that Americans are receiving too many needless tests and treatments because that is the only way that doctors earn money in a fee-for-service environment. Further, advocates argue that some costs may be necessary for the better served under the old system if a more equitable system of medical care is to be introduced.

The Bush Administration

The Bush administration offered a plan for national health-care reform toward the end of its time in office, in part as a means of preventing the Democrats from capturing this issue entirely. There actually were several plans broached by the White House and its allies, all quite minimal and depending largely on the private sector to provide most of the coverage and on reduction of medical costs to make insurance plans affordable for individuals and small businesses.[64] The most basic proposal coming from the administration was a simple refundable tax credit to assist individuals who purchased private insurance.[65]

A more complete plan favored by some in the Bush administration was labeled "managed competition."[66] This plan would have had people who work for firms sufficiently large to provide cost-effective medical insurance to continue to receive insurance as they have in the past. But these large companies would receive tax writeoffs equal to only 80 percent of the average current cost of providing similar medical care in the country and would therefore be forced to pressure medical providers (doctors and hospitals) to give preferential rates if the providers wanted the large volume of business coming from the company. "Preferred provider plans" such as this are already in place for insurers such as Blue Cross-Blue Shield, and this plan would have extended that to most private insurance.

The remainder of the population, whether employed or not, would receive health insurance from newly created agencies called "public sponsors." Individuals would be offered several prepaid plans (HMOs) and perhaps a conventional insurance plan, but the assumption is that the insurance plans would cost more and that difference would have to be paid by the insured. This would mean that most people would choose to be covered through HMOs. These HMOs would have a great deal of market power, like the insurers for large firms, and could bargain with providers for the lowest rates. This market power would stabilize or even reduce the costs of medical care in the United States.

This plan would provide medical insurance for all Americans and should help control the costs of medical care. It also would provide citizens with some choices, although the choices might be only among different versions of the same type of coverage—the HMO. This program would, however, separate the population into several different groups for purposes of medical care (although certainly not as badly as the present system does). If the quality of medical care offered by HMOs is as good as that offered by fee-for-service providers, then this would make little difference. There might well be some inconvenience in receiving care from HMOs, but for many people that might be compensated for simply by having any form of health insurance.

The Clinton Administration Plan and Alternatives

The Clinton administration placed health-care reform at the top of its domestic agenda when it took office in January 1993. Almost immediately, Hillary Rodham Clinton began a series of meetings with "stakeholders" and ordinary citizens to collect ideas for the reform. The plan that she and the administration proposed was a complex one, depending on "alliances" of health-care providers. Very much as HMOs have done for years, these alliances would supply all the health-care needs for their members for a set annual fee, although fee-for-service plans also would be available. According to the provisions of the Clinton plan, those fees would be fixed at an average of $1,800 for an individual and $4,200 for families, below existing private insurance rates for much of the population. Individuals would also be required to pay deductibles and copayments for services on the fee-for-service plans. Businesses would be mandated to pay for their employees (up to 7.9 percent of their payrolls), with subsidies available for small business.

Universality was the central tenet of the Clinton proposals, and this was the issue over which the president said he would never compromise. Employer mandates were a central element of the universality, but also a focus of much criticism. For the unemployed or for people working for very small employers, there would be insurance paid for by the federal government, with the funds coming from cigarette taxes and perhaps other additional taxes. Employers could provide better insurance than the national minimums, but that might be treated as taxable income for the employee, or made not deductible as a business expense for the employer. The program therefore would tend to create much greater equality in access to medical care than is currently found in the United States. The program also had provisions for cost containment, initially through competitive incentives but later regulated prices, if necessary to reduce medical inflation to the general rate of inflation.[67]

As might be expected, the Clinton plan produced a good deal of criticism from various directions. A number of critics, even those who favored universality and mandates, regarded the plan as excessively complex and too heavily reliant on the alliances both to provide care and to minimize costs. These critics often advocated a single-payer plan such as that found in Canada. Other critics disagreed with the concept of universality, believing that it was too costly, and with imposing costs on employers to provide medical insurance. They sought to find some alternative like those proposed by the Bush administration that would rely more on voluntary efforts and the private sector. They also saw the Clinton plan as needing a huge and costly federal bureaucracy to administer it.

One of the principal alternatives to the Clinton plan was devised and championed by Senator Robert Dole (R-Kans.). This plan relied heavily on voluntary compliance and private insurance, and did not seek universal coverage of the population—the target was 91 or 92 percent of the population. The plan provided for subsidies for the less affluent for purchasing insurance, to be paid for by cost containment in Medicare and Medicaid. Further, this plan attempted to address the problem of people being locked into jobs by insurance by mandating portability of health insurance. There was also a "fail-safe" provision that would prevent the program from adding to the federal deficit. Although supported by a large number of Republican senators, Democratic control of Congress prevented this plan from making its way through the committee system.

Several other plans also emerged from Congress, including one from the Senate Labor and Human Resources Committee chaired by Senator Edward Kennedy (D-Mass.). This plan provided a number of alternative means for acquiring medical insurance, including private insurance, purchasing cooperatives at the state level, and participation in the existing Federal Employees Health Benefit Plan. This plan had many elements of "play or pay," with employers who do not provide insurance for their employees having to pay a substantial payroll tax. The plan also had a substantial tax on cigarettes to help fund the additional costs of the program.

The Senate Finance Committee chaired by Daniel Patrick Moynihan (D-N.Y.) prepared another plan for health insurance. This plan would be less universal than either of those advocated by the president or Senator Kennedy, with no employer mandates; participation in insurance-purchasing alliances would be voluntary. This plan counted on increasing the rate of coverage of the population gradually over seven years, with a national commission making policy recommendations to Congress if 95 percent of the population were not covered by 2002. The plan would be financed by an increased cigarette tax and by taxes on higher-priced private insurance plans.

The House Ways and Means Committee also authored a plan for national health insurance. This plan relied on the existing Medicare program (a new Part C) as a basis for providing health insurance to the currently uninsured and to Medicaid recipients, with most employees remaining on private insurance.[68] Thus, unlike the Clinton plan, it did not require the creation of a new federal bureaucracy but only the extension of an existing one. The bulk of insurance (80 percent) would still be private, provided by employers, with small employers eligible for subsidies of up to half the cost of insurance. Low-income insured workers would also be eligible for subsidies for their part of the premiums. This proposal also would have strong elements of cost control, with each state and the nation having a limit for health spending. The additional costs of the program would be financed by a gradual increase in the cigarette tax to 69 cents a pack and a tax on private insurance programs.

Finally, the House Education and Labor Committee developed its own plan for national health reform. This proposal had many of the same features of the Clinton plan but also contained expanded benefits and did not have the mandatory alliances. Instead there would be purchasing cooperatives formed at the state level, with employers with more than 1,000 employees allowed to opt out and create their own insurance plans. The financing of this program was rather similar to that in the Clinton plan, with an additional tax on the large employers that opt out of the basic plans.

After the various committees in both houses had acted, the majority leadership of both houses of Congress attempted to blend their several proposals into two plans. In the House of Representatives Congressman Richard Gephardt (D-Mo.) presented a plan that had many of the features of the Clinton proposal, most notably the demand for universal coverage and employer mandates to cover 80 percent of the cost of the average individual policy. It differed in the requirement for a range of options for all citizens and in providing subsidies to people with much higher incomes (as well as a number of other technical details).

In the Senate, Majority Leader George Mitchell (D-Me.) developed a plan that attempted to reconcile the basic intentions of the Clinton plan with criticisms of the plan. In the first place, the Mitchell plan dropped the goal of immediate universality and replaced it with a goal of 95 percent coverage by the year 2000. If that goal were not reached by voluntary means, then a system of mandates might be imposed by 2002. Most of the other features of the Mitchell plan were somewhat simplified versions of the Clinton plan.[69]

Summary

In the end, none of the proposals for reforming health care could be passed by Congress in 1994. As the debate wore on during the year, more questions than answers emerged about health care.[70] Many citizens and many politicians began to raise a wide range of questions about the consequences of the various proposals for reform. The politicians also worried about the impact on their political careers of voting for one or another proposal, especially just before mid-term elections. This fear was exacerbated by vast amounts of lobbying, especially by the insurance and health-care industries.[71] Further, it was impossible for liberals and conservatives to put aside their ideological differences to find a compromise that all could accept. For all sides, the pursuit of a perfect plan was the enemy of selecting an acceptable plan.

All the reform proposals faced insurmountable obstacles to their adoption, and perhaps even greater barriers to effective implementation. All the plans considered were complex. They grafted on top of an already complex system of medical-care provision one or another means of financing a program that could become universal. Universality was intended to address the problem of access. The plans all involved increases in the amount of money flowing through the public sector, although almost all were likely to reduce the total amount of money spent on medical care over what would have been required under the existing system. All the plans also involved imposing some costs on the private sector, although the degree of mandating contained in the plans varied substantially. These plans also all proposed to maintain choice for consumers, but many opponents of the Clinton plan and more comprehensive plans feared rationing and a decline in the quality of care available, especially for those with the resources to pay for high-quality care.[72]

Choosing among these alternative plans for health reform demonstrates a good deal about the politics of public policy in the United States. The conflict pits a number of special interests and their resources against the interests of the uninsured and even the general public, who might benefit from lower medical-care costs. Further, it demonstrates very clearly the conflict that can arise between the president and Congress over both the substance of policy and their relative power in the process. It also points out the degree of fragmentation that exists within the individual institutions, with a number of congressional committees drafting their own health reform plans.[73] Finally, this reform effort points to the importance of policy entrepreneurship. In this case several players—Hillary Rodham Clinton, Senator Dole, and Senator Moynihan—are all attempting to be successful entrepreneurs, but probably only one can succeed. And despite their skills, none may succeed.

The failure of comprehensive health-care reform did not end attempts at implementing some reforms. In particular, the federal government began to consider some regulatory reforms that could address some of the most egregious problems of the current health system. For example, there were proposals to require health insurers to cover illnesses clients have at the time they acquire insurance (preexisting conditions), and to make insurance portable when people change jobs.[74] Some thought is also being given to extending the federal employees' health plan to more Americans, and many Americans ask why they cannot have health coverage as good as that of the people who voted down reform.[75]

With the failure of the federal government to generate meaningful reforms, there are still some attempts at changing health care. One is a series of incremental reforms from the federal level.[76] Also, the individual states have also returned to making innovations in health care for their citizens and are again serving as the laboratories for a variety of reforms.[77] Already, twenty states have begun to experiment with the idea of alliances for small businesses and individuals to purchase insurance at rates lower than they could obtain individually. Other states (Washington and Oregon) have attempted to mandate that employers provide, and pay half the cost of, health insurance for full-time workers, but they are currently blocked by federal regulations from doing so. While all these efforts are encouraging, they run the risk of creating a patchwork of laws and regulations that may make it more difficult for companies to do business, and that may give some states competitive advantages over others.

Conclusions

Changing and reforming existing policy is always difficult, and health care is perhaps a particularly difficult policy field in which to produce change. A number of powerful interests—doctors, hospitals, pharmaceutical companies, and the like—have a direct interest in the area. Further, as issues of universal coverage arise, a range of business interests become concerned about the costs that may be imposed on them. Citizens are also concerned that by attempting to provide better medical care for the entire population, government may undermine the existing high-quality medical care available to the most fortunate segments of the society.

Although restoring or encouraging competition in the medical-care industry is appealing to many in the United States as a solution to the problems we have identified in the health care industry, there may be difficulties in implementing this concept. The health care industry differs from other industries in important ways that reduce the utility of competition as a remedy for its problems. In particular, the control that professionals exercise in determining the amount and kind of care consumed by patients makes usual competitive mechanisms less applicable. Those characteristics of the industry may, in turn, require a stronger role for the public sector if effective control over costs, quality, and access is to be attained.

First, very little information on the price or quality of medical care is available to the consumer. Prices for health services are rarely advertised; frequently the consumer does not even consider them. In fact, in a perverse way, consumers often choose a higher-priced rather than a lower-priced service in the belief that the more expensive service will be superior. And, beyond hearsay, little information is available to patients about the quality of services provided by individual physicians or hospitals. The public sector has been intervening to try to make more information available, but it is still difficult for the average consumer to make choices.

In addition, the provision of health care is, in many ways, a monopoly or cartel. Entry into the marketplace for potential suppliers is limited by licensing requirements and further controlled by the professions themselves, which limit the number of places available in medical schools. Thus, unlike other industries, the health-care field makes it difficult for competition to develop among suppliers. One possible means of promoting competition would be to break down the monopoly held by the medical profession by giving nurse practitioners and other paraprofessionals a greater opportunity to practice. The medical profession rather vigorously resists such changes. Hospitals do compete increasingly for patients, however, and with that competition has come some greater attention to the quality of care.

Bringing about any significant reforms in the delivery of health services in the United States will be difficult because of the power of the professions and of large medical organizations such as hospitals. Their strongest incentives are in the direction of preserving the status quo, and with a monopoly over the technology of medicine they are in a position to control the actual delivery of service. It may well be that only a large-scale program such as national health insurance will be sufficient to break the hold the professions have on medical care and provide better and more equitable medicine to most Americans. The widespread perception of crisis in medical care may make many Americans willing to accept very fundamental changes in the structure of the health-care industry. The defeat of health-care reform in 1994 has delayed that change, but it may yet be needed.

Notes

1. Calculated by Henry J. Aaron, "Health Care Financing," in *Setting Domestic Priorities: What Can Government Do?* ed. Henry J. Aaron and Charles L. Schultze (Washington, D.C.: Brookings Institution, 1992), 36.

2. The evidence is that most states have not replaced the health money they lost from block grants. See George E. Peterson et al., *Block Grants* (Washington, D.C.: Urban Institute, 1984).

3. Penelope Lemov, "States and Medicaid: Ahead of the Feds," *Governing* 6 (July 1993): 27–28.

4. Judi Hasson and Jessica Lee, "Poll: 43% Back Clinton Health Plan," *USA Today*, 30 June 1994.

5. Adam Clymer, "House Bill Asks 8.4% Payroll Tax for Canadian-Style Health Plan," *New York Times*, 28 January 1994.

6. Deane Neubauer, "Hawaii: The Health State," in *Health Policy Reform in the United States: Innovations from the States,* ed. Howard Leichter (Armonk, N.Y.: M.E. Sharpe, 1992); Camille Asccuaga, "Universal Health Care in Massachusetts: Lessons for the Future," in Leichter, *Health Policy Reform.*

7. Robin Turner, "Health Care in Minnesota: Model for U.S. or Novelty?" *New York Times,* 9 October 1993.

8. World Health Organization, *World Health Statistics Annual* (Geneva: WHO, annual).

9. "The Public Decides on Health Care Reform," *Public Perspective* 5 (September/October 1994): 23–28.

10. These are primarily the working poor employed in jobs without health-care benefits and not eligible for Medicaid as they would be if they were on welfare.

11. Henry J. Aaron, *Serious and Unstable Condition: Financing America's Health Care* (Washington, D.C.: Brookings Institution, 1991), 47–57.

12. Ibid., 45–47.

13. Robert Pear, "Tough Decision on Health Care If Employers Won't Pay the Bill," *New York Times,* 9 July 1994.

14. *New York Times,* 11 July 1994.

15. Peter Townsend, ed., *Inequalities in Health: The Black Report* (London: Penguin, 1988).

16. Steven Greenhouse, "The States' Stakes in Clinton's Health Plan," *New York Times,* 10 October 1993.

17. American Medical Association, *Physician Characteristics and Distribution in the U.S.* (Chicago: AMA, annual).

18. Rural areas tend to have a number of hospital beds but very low occupancy rates, thereby driving up costs.

19. Nicholas Eberstadt, "Why Are So Many American Babies Dying?" *American Enterprise* 2 (September 1991): 37–45. This finding, of course, gives comfort to conservatives, who stress individual responsibility and minimize the need for government intervention in the medical marketplace.

20. Aaron, *Serious and Unstable Condition,* 8–37.

21. The U.S. population is approximately 11 times as large as that of Canada, while we have approximately 100 times as many MRI units.

22. Spencer Rich, "Hospital Administration Costs Put at 25%," *Washington Post,* 6 August 1993.

23. John K. Inglehart, "Health Policy Report: Managed Competition," *New England Journal of Medicine* 328 (22 April 1993): 1208–12; Joshua M. Wiener and Laura Hixon Illston, "Health Care Reform: Six Questions for President Clinton," *Brookings Review* 11 (Spring 1993): 22–25.

24. Aaron, *Serious and Unstable Condition,* 45–47.

25. Julie Kosterlitz, "Wanted: GPs," *National Journal,* 5 September 1992.

26. Susan Hosek et al., *The Study of Preferred Provider Organizations* (Santa Monica, Calif.: Rand Corporation, 1990).

27. Paul B. Ginsburg et al., "Update: Medicare Physician Payment Reform," *Health Affairs* 9 (Spring 1990): 178–88.

28. Sandra Christenses and Scott Harrison, *Physician Payment Reform under Medicare* (Washington, D.C.: Congressional Budget Office, 1990).

29. Health Insurance Association of America, *Source Book on Health Insurance* (Washington, D.C.: The Association, 1993).

30. Garrett Hardin and John Baden, *Managing the Commons* (San Francisco: W.H. Freeman, 1977).

31. This approach has not been popular with a number of groups, including the Children's Defense Fund, which has been closely associated with Hillary Rodham Clinton. See Timothy Egan, "Oregon Health Plan Stalled by Politics," *New York Times*, 17 March 1993.

32. Susan Ferriss, "Plan in Oregon Would Expand Health Coverage to Poor Citizens," *Pittsburgh Post-Gazette*, 20 December 1991.

33. Susan Feigenbaum, "Denying Access to Life-Saving Technologies: Budgetary Implications of a Moral Dilemma," *Regulation* 16, no. 4 (1994): 74–79.

34. Thomas J. Marzen and Louis W. Sullivan, "ADA Analyses of the Oregon Health Care Plan," *Issues in Law & Medicine* 9 (1994): 397–424.

35. On the latter point, see Ivan Illich, *Medical Nemesis* (New York: Pantheon, 1976).

36. The same questions arise concerning such developments in medical technology as artifical hearts. See "One Miracle, Many Doubts," *Time*, 10 December 1984, 10ff.

37. Henry R. Glick, *The Right to Die* (New York: Columbia University Press, 1994).

38. Karen Davis, "Equal Treatment and Unequal Benefits," *Milbank Memorial Fund Quarterly*, Fall 1975, 449–88.

39. "Tougher Standards for Medigap Insurance," *Aging* 362 (1991): 44–45.

40. Advisory Council on Social Security, *Report on Medicare Projections by the Health Technical Panel* (Washington, D.C.: Government Printing Office, 1991).

41. Frank J. Thompson, *Health Policy and the Bureaucracy* (Cambridge, Mass.: MIT Press, 1981), 153–54.

42. Julie Kosterlitz, "Health Rip-Offs," *National Journal*, 20 June 1992.

43. Louise B. Russell and Carrie Lynn Manning, "The Effect of Prospective Payment on Medicare Expenditures," *New England Journal of Medicine*, 16 February 1989, 439–44.

44. Jeffrey A. Buck and Mark S. Kamlet, "Problems with Expanding Medicaid for the Uninsured," *Journal of Health Politics, Policy and Law* 18 (1993): 1–25.

45. Paul Jesilow and Gilbert Geis, "Fraud by Physicians Against Medicaid," *Journal of the American Medical Association* 266 (18 December 1991): 3318–22.

46. Leslie G. Aronovitz, *Medicaid: A Program Highly Vulnerable to Fraud*, GAO/T-HEHS-94-106 (Washington, D.C.: General Accounting Office, 25 February 1994).

47. Karen Davis et al., *Health Care Cost Containment* (Baltimore: Johns Hopkins University Press, 1990), 222ff.

48. Patricia Baumann, "The Formulation and Evolution of Health Maintenance Organization Policy, 1970–73," *Social Science and Medicine,* 1976,
129–42.

49. This conformed to the general tendency of the Reagan and Bush administrations to use market and quasi-market devices as means of reducing the costs
of government.

50. Elisabeth Rosenthal, "Doctors Who Once Spurned HMOs Now Often
Find Systems' Doors Shut," *New York Times,* 25 June 1994.

51. These are but two of a range of high-technology devices now common
in hospitals. Even when a patient does not use these devices, he or she will pay a
portion of the cost because it is amortized in room rates.

52. Linda E. Demkovich, "When Medicare Tears Up the Blank Check, Who
Will Lend Hospitals Capital?" *National Journal,* 21 January 1984, 113–16.

53. Donald A. Redelmeier and Victor A. Fuchs, "Hospital Expenditures in
the United States and Canada," *New England Journal of Medicine* 328 (18
March 1993): 772–78.

54. Penelope Lemov, "Curbing the Cost of Defensive Medicine," *Governing*
7 (March 1994): 12; Brian McCormick, "Study: Defensive Medicine Costs
Nearly $10 Billion," *American Medical News* 35 (15 February 1993): 4.

55. Peter S. Arno and Karyn L. Feiden, *Against The Odds: The Story of
AIDS Drug Development, Politics and Profits* (New York: HarperCollins, 1992).

56. "Drug Companies: Golden Pills," *The Economist,* 20 March 1993,
73–74.

57. "The Public Decides on Health Care Reform," *The Public Perspective* 5
(September/October 1994): 23–28.

58. Laura Buterbaugh, "In the Shadow of Healthcare Reform: AMA Puts
Own Stamp on the Debate," *Medical World News* 34 (1993): 22–23.

59. James S. Todd, "Finding the Common Ground: The Path to Health System Reform," *Vital Speeches* 60 (1994): 178–81.

60. Julie Kosterlitz, "A Sick System," *National Journal,* 15 February 1992.

61. Urban Institute, *Balancing Access, Costs, and Politics* (Washington,
D.C.: Urban Institute Press, 1991).

62. Larry Stevens, "States Test Medicaid Reforms," *Business and Health* 12
(August 1994): 51–52.

63. Jim McDermott, "Evaluating Health System Reform: The Case for a
Single-Payer Approach," *Journal of the American Medical Association* 271 (9
March 1994): 782–84.

64. Susan G. Garland, "Bush's Health Care Rx: A Diluted Dose of Market
Forces," *Business Week,* 3 February 1992, 26–27.

65. "Bush Hikes Health Budget: Proposes Tax-based Insurance Plan," *Medical World News* 33 (February 1992): 8.

66. Daniel S. Greenberg, "Washington Perspective—George Bush: Health
Care Reformer," *Lancet* 339 (22 February 1992): 482–83.

67. Arnold S. Relman, "Controlling Costs by 'Managed Competition'
—Would It Work," *New England Journal of Medicine* 328 (14 January 1993):
133–35.

68. Robert Pear, "Bill Passed by Panel Would Open Medicare to Millions of Uninsured People," *New York Times,* 1 July 1994.

69. Richard E. Cohen, "Now Comes the Real Test of Leadership," *National Journal,* 9 July 1994, 1638.

70. "The Health Care Battle: Open Fire," *The Economist,* 13 August 1994, 24.

71. Katharine Q. Seelye, "Lobbyists Are the Loudest in the Health Care Debate," *New York Times,* 16 August 1994.

72. The degree of choice actually existing in the current medical-care system appeared to have been exaggerated by the opponents of reform. See Robin Toner, "Ills of Health System Outlive Debate on Care," *New York Times,* 2 October 1994.

73. Richard E. Cohen, "Into the Swamp," *National Journal,* 19 March 1994.

74. Adam Clymer, "With Health Overhaul Dead, A Search for Minor Repairs," *New York Times,* 28 August 1994.

75. Robert Pear, "Health Care Debate to Shift to Federal Employees' Plan," *New York Times,* 7 September 1994.

76. Clymer, "With Health Overhaul Dead, Search for Minor Repairs."

77. Robert Pear, "States Again Try Health Changes as Congress Fails," *New York Times,* 16 September 1994.

10. Income Maintenance: Social Security and Welfare

The United States has frequently been described as a welfare state "laggard" because its levels of expenditures on social policies are low compared with those of other industrialized nations and because it has not adopted certain public programs (e.g., child benefits and sickness insurance) that are common in other countries.[1] Although this is true, the gap between the United States and other Western democracies has narrowed as American expenditures for social programs increased dramatically during the 1960s and 1970s and program services and expenditures in almost all countries were reduced in the 1980s. The increased level of expenditures reflected both new programs, especially during the Johnson administration's war on poverty, and increasing expenditures for established programs, particularly Social Security. U.S. social programs, broadly defined, in 1993 cost almost $700 billion and provided services to millions of clients. These social expenditures now account for approximately one-third of all federal expenditures; social expenditures are approximately 40 percent of total public expenditures.

The Reagan administration (1981-89) reduced the rate at which social expenditures expanded at the federal level. The amount spent on social programs in 1988 was at least as great as when that administration took office, although the amount spent was approximately 10 to 12 percent less than would have been spent under pre-1981 laws.[2] The gradual erosion of spending for social benefits continued during the Bush administration, with social spending less as a percentage of total federal spending in 1992 than before 1985. President Clinton placed welfare reform on the agenda during his presidential campaign and pressed Congress for reforms after his election. Nevertheless, despite the visibility of the welfare program (Aid to Families with Dependent Children, or AFDC), it is a relatively small proportion of total social spending, much less of total public spending, and a reformed program almost certainly would be more expensive than the existing program.[3]

Despite their apparent vulnerability to political pressures, some characteristics of social programs, especially social insurance programs such as

Social Security, make it difficult to cut them and even produce some demands for increases. Too many people (and/or their aging parents) depend on social insurance programs for politicians to be anxious to cut these programs. Pressures to preserve and enhance the programs are especially evident as the recession of the early 1990s eases but does not vanish, and as the population continues to age. Social programs are likely to remain the major battleground for forces of the political right and left in the United States.

What are these social programs that cost so much and touch the lives of so many citizens? Leaving aside programs such as public housing, education (see chapter 11), and health care (see chapter 9), all of which have obvious social importance, we are left with a broad array of programs that themselves provide a broad range of services and benefits. The largest programs, in terms of costs and number of beneficiaries, are social insurance programs, such as Social Security (old-age and disability pensions), unemployment, and workmen's compensation (see table 10.1). Also significant in terms of expenditures are means-tested benefits such as Aid to Families with Dependent Children, food stamps, and Supplemental Security Income. These programs are available only to individuals who can demonstrate that their earnings fall below the level of need designated by the program. Finally, there are the personal social services directed toward improving the quality of life for individuals through services such as counseling, adoption, foster care, and rehabilitation. These three major kinds of social programs address different social needs and usually benefit different clients. Likewise, each has its own particular programmatic and political problems, which we address in this chapter.

Social Insurance

The largest single federal program of any kind is Social Security. Although generally thought of as providing pensions for retired workers, the program actually offers other protections to its clients. It provides benefits, for example, for the survivors of workers who die before retirement. Thus the program provides benefits for children of a deceased worker until they reach the age of eighteen, if they are not employed. The program also offers disability protection so that if a worker becomes incapable of earning a living, he or she and any dependents can receive benefits. Finally, Medicare is linked with Social Security for financing purposes, as discussed in chapter 9. In addition to Social Security, two other significant social insurance programs exist in the United States. One, unemployment insurance, is managed by the states with a federal subsidy. The other, workmen's compensation, is managed by the states with employers bearing the major financial burden for the program. This program is the American equivalent of industrial accident insurance common in other industrialized countries.

TABLE 10.1

COSTS OF INCOME MAINTENANCE PROGRAMS

(IN MILLIONS OF DOLLARS)

	1960	1970	1980	1990	1991	Percentage increase
Social Security	$11,032	$29,686	$117,118	$244,100	$264,100	2,301
Unemployment	2,830	3,819	18,327	18,100	28,500	907
Public aid	3,609	4,864	20,001	32,762	36,800	919
Food stamps	0	577	9,083	23,400	24,100	3,177[a]
Public housing	177	702	7,209	16,300	20,100	10,356
Other	6,591	19,660	73,151	48,760	49,770	745
Total	$24,239	$59,308	$244,709	$383,422	$432,370	1,647
Percentage of public expenditure	18.0	19.8	27.6	31.9	32.0	—

a. From 1970.

TABLE 10.2

SOCIAL INSURANCE RECIPIENTS, 1993

Program	Number
Social Security	
Retired workers and families	29,600,000
Disabled workers and families	5,200,000
Survivors	7,400,000
Railroad retirement	
Workers	548,000
Survivors	268,000
Unemployment insurance	10,075,000
Workers' compensation	2,210,000 (est.)
Total	55,301,000

SOURCE: Social Security Administration, Social Security Bulletin, *Annual Statistical Supplement, 1994.*

Table 10.2 provides information on the recipients of social insurance benefits. By far the largest number of recipients were retired workers, although significant numbers of citizens received benefits under other social insurance programs. Likewise, the largest share of social insurance goes to retired persons, although the highest average benefit paid was for the unemployed, followed closely by disabled workers. Many social changes are responsible for the growing number of social insurance recipients. Because the average age of Americans is increasing, more people in the United States are eligible for retirement benefits. Slow economic growth during much of the 1980s and early 1990s increased the number of people eligible for unemployment benefits, although insured workers are eligible for this program for only a limited time. Social welfare programs are all entitlement programs, meaning that citizens who have paid for their social insurance cannot be denied benefits once they meet the criteria for eligibility for those benefits.

We must understand several important characteristics of social insurance programs, especially Social Security, if we are to comprehend the programs and the political debates that often surround them. First, social insurance programs do relatively little, given the volume of expenditures, to redistribute income across economic classes.[4] Instead, they tend to redistribute income across time and across generations. Unlike a private annuity, in which an individual pays in money that accumulates in a personal account, Social Security is not an actuarially sound insurance program. Social Security is a direct transfer program that taxes working people and their employers and pays out that money to program beneficiaries. The major purpose of Social Security is to distribute income across time; workers and their employers pay into the fund while employed, thereby reducing their income at that time, but receive benefits when they retire or if they become disabled; also, surviving members of the immediate family receive benefits if the worker dies.

Second, despite the absence of actuarial soundness, these programs are conceived as social insurance rather than government giveaway programs. Citizens believe that they are purchasing an insurance policy when they pay their payroll taxes during their working life. Defining the programs as social insurance has been crucial in legitimating them, as many citizens would not have been willing to accept a public pension to which they had not contributed; they would think it was charity. Further, most congressmen in 1935 (when the programs were enacted) would not have been willing to vote for the programs if they had not been defined as insurance. The insurance element is also important because of the contractual arrangement between the citizen and the government. More than any other public program, Social Security is an entitlement program; citizens believe themselves entitled to benefits and believe they have a legal and moral claim to receive those benefits in large part because they contributed throughout a working lifetime.

The insurance nature of these programs also helps explain their financing. Social Security is financed by payroll contributions, paid equally by employers and employees.[5] These payroll taxes are paid, not on all earnings, but on only the first $60,600 (in 1994) of earnings each year; the health insurance component is now paid on all earnings. Rates of tax and the threshold at which individuals stop paying social insurance taxes are expected to increase during the rest of the 1990s in order to pay for the rising costs of the program. Thus, instead of being a general tax, Social Security "contributions" as shown in table 10.3 are limited in much the same way that the premiums for a private insurance policy are fixed, although not all workers will pay the same amount for social insurance if they earn below the threshold. Because it was envisioned as an insurance program and not a vehicle for redistributive social policy, the Social Security tax has been a flat-rate tax rather than one that progressively increases, like the income tax has. Finally, Social Security is an earmarked tax: all the money collected is devoted to Social Security benefits, and only Social Security taxes are available for financing the benefits.[6] The restrictiveness of the financial system makes the tax, and the program in general, more palatable to many citizens, but it also severely constrains the financial base for the program. At various times there have been discussions of the Social Security system "going bankrupt," but given the political importance of the program, it is unlikely that Congress would allow that to happen.

TABLE 10.3

INCREASING RATES OF SOCIAL SECURITY TAXATION

	Tax rate		On earnings	Maximum
	OASDI[a]	HI[b]	to ($)	tax ($)
1960	3.00	n.a.	4,800	144
1965	3.625	.35	4,800	174
1970	4.20	.60	7,800	374
1975	4.95	.90	14,100	825
1980	5.08	1.05	25,900	1,588
1985	5.70	1.35	39,600	2,792
1988	6.06	1.45	45,000	3,380
1990	6.20	1.45	51,300	n.a.
1991	6.20	1.45	53,400	n.a.
1992	6.20	1.45	54,300	n.a.
1993	6.20	1.45	57,600	n.a.
1994	6.20	1.45	60,600	n.a.

a. Old Age, Survivors, and Disability Insurance.
b. Health Insurance (Medicare).

Another important element of the Social Security system is that it includes almost all working people. In 1994 about 90 percent of all employed Americans were covered by the program. This figure includes a large number of self-employed individuals, who pay a self-employment tax instead of having their contributions matched by an employer. The principal groups now excluded from the program are federal government employees hired before 1984, employees of many state and local governments, and some farm workers. These exclusions are made for reasons of administrative convenience or because of the constitutional inability of the federal government to levy a tax on a state or local government, but many employers who could avoid the system opt into it to provide protection for their employees. Despite the exclusions, Social Security is a national program and perhaps more than any other program unites all citizens as participants in a single government program.

Finally, the benefits of the program are only partially related to earnings.[7] Those who pay more into the program during their working lifetime receive greater benefits when they retire, although those at the bottom of the income ladder receive a larger rate of return on their contributions, and have a higher replacement of their earnings on retirement, than do those with higher earnings (see table 10.4). Social Security is not intended to be a wel-

TABLE 10.4

REPLACEMENT RATIOS OF EARNINGS IN SOCIAL SECURITY
BY INCOME GROUPS
(IN PERCENTAGES)

	Monthly earnings					
	$100	$500	$1000	$1387	$1800	$2033
Worker alone (aged 65+)	167	74	60	51	44	41
Worker with spouse (aged 65+)	250	112	80	77	66	62

fare program; at the same time it is slightly redistributive in that it attempts to ensure that those at the bottom of the earnings ladder have something approximating an adequate retirement income, although it is difficult to argue that anyone living entirely on Social Security, even at the full benefit level, really receives enough money to live comfortably. The average worker under Social Security receives only about 60 percent of preretirement income.

The redistributive element of Social Security has been increased by the increasing taxation of benefits paid to more affluent recipients. For most of its history, the pensions paid to retired Americans have not been taxable, regardless of the person's income. Beginning in 1984, however, 50 percent of Social Security became taxable for recipients with taxable incomes and tax-free interest income over $25,000 (individual) or $32,000 (couple).[8]

In 1993 the Clinton administration made 85 percent of the benefits taxable for recipients with those income levels. What this means is that for the approximately 20 percent of pensioners with substantial private incomes (from private pensions, investments, or whatever), the real value of Social Security benefits has been reduced substantially.

Problems in Social Security

Although the Social Security program is widely accepted by, and generally very popular with, the public, a number of problems with the program should be considered. These problems are generally policy issues that arise when the program is considered for renewal or modification. These policy problems, of course, have political ramifications and affect the way in which the program is treated in Congress and by the president. They also reflect the difficulties encountered in adjusting a program that has been successful but is being affected by social and demographic changes.[9]

THE RETIREMENT TEST

One policy problem is the retirement test—the penalty imposed on recipients of Social Security who wish to supplement their benefits by working. As the program is currently managed, if a recipient earns a certain amount of money (excluding income from private retirement funds or investments), a penalty is imposed on the benefits paid to him or her. In 1994 a recipient of Social Security up to the age of sixty-four could earn $8,040 a year but would lose $1 in benefits for every $2 earned over that amount. From age sixty-five to seventy, a worker earning over $11,060 a year would lose $1 for every $3 earned; over seventy, earnings are unlimited.[10] For the person younger than sixty-five, there is, in effect, a 50 percent tax on earnings over the income allowed, a tax rate higher than that now imposed on any individual paying the federal income tax.

There are several good reasons for removing, or at least relaxing, this retirement test. First, if the program is conceived of as social insurance rather than a means-tested benefit, then recipients should receive their benefits as a matter of right, much as would the recipient of a private annuity. The imposition of the retirement test in many ways gives the lie to the conception of Social Security as purely a social insurance program. Additionally, the imposition of the retirement test may make the program more expensive and more of a donation from the young to the old. As it becomes unrewarding for retirees to work, they will stop working and cease paying Social Security taxes, whereas if they continued to work they could, in some ways, pay their own benefits through taxation. For example, an average male worker who defers retirement to age seventy loses $17,600 from the net value of his Social Security contributions; a high-wage male worker loses $47,200.[11] This means that those who are working—in other words, the younger generations—must bear a higher tax cost for the program than would otherwise be necessary. This problem becomes especially troubling as the population ages and there are fewer active workers to pay for retirees.

Finally, there are humane reasons for eliminating or modifying the retirement test. With the increase in life expectancy of American citizens, many individuals are capable of continuing to work after the usual retirement age. In a society that frequently defines an individual's worth on the basis of his or her work, retirement and the inability to work without paying a penalty on that work may impose severe psychological as well as economic burdens on the retiree. More flexible or unlimited earnings would allow Social Security recipients to participate in the labor market, perhaps not to the extent they did previously, and would permit phasing out employment rather than a sudden and often traumatic retirement.

On the other side of the argument, we must realize that allowing retirees to continue working would have significant effects on other potential employees, especially those just entering the labor market. Every retiree who continues to work means one less job for a young person. And as unemployment among the young (and not so young) is already a significant public problem, the needs of the elderly must be balanced against the needs of younger people. Additionally, allowing the retiree to continue working and still receive benefits amounts to a direct transfer of income from the young to the old, based simply on age rather than on participation in the labor market. This may be a short-term problem; the economy may soon need the skills and abilities of workers who might otherwise retire under the Social Security system.

FIXED RETIREMENT AGE

Related to the problem of the retirement test is the question of a fixed retirement age. Under existing laws, the standard retirement age is sixty-five. After this age, individuals receive little additional benefit for working under the Social Security system, although they have to continue to pay Social Security taxes. In addition, if individuals choose to retire before reaching sixty-five, even if they have been paying into the system for years, their benefits are reduced. These rules provide a great incentive for workers to retire at the official age, and under this system all individuals are expected to retire at that age regardless of health or financial situation.

Good reasons can be found for both raising and lowering the retirement age. Some are based on reasons of cost containment in a system that is facing severe financial problems, and others are based on humane considerations. By raising the retirement age, the total costs of the program will be reduced because people will not be living on the program as long. When Social Security was adopted in 1935, only about half the male population could expect to live to age sixty-five, and those who reached that age could expect to live about twelve years. By 1990, however, over 72 percent of the male population lived to age sixty-five and would live, on average, fifteen years on Social Security. By 2010, 78 percent will live to age sixty-five and would be on the program for sixteen years.[12] Women live even longer, on average, than men and can expect to be on Social Security even longer. Thus there are more retirees and each retiree costs more, and total program costs are increased. In addition, the health status, the nature of work, and the educational levels of workers have all been improving. As we approach the twenty-first century, the average retiree will be in better health, have a relatively nonstrenuous and more intellectually challenging job, and may simply not want to retire. Finally, the absence of private pension plans for some workers may mean that they cannot maintain their lifestyles if they retire, encouraging them to continue to work.

On the other side of the argument are some reasons to lower the retirement age. Many people who have retirement incomes in addition to Social Security may want to retire while they are still in good health and capable of enjoying more years of leisure.[13] And at the systemic level, the lowering of the retirement age may create additional job openings for unemployed youths. In addition, the availability of a flexible retirement age may make it easier to modernize the nation's workforce. Workers with obsolete skills may move to Social Security more readily, and as a consequence some human costs of modernization and economic change may be reduced.

Clearly, some policies for determining benefits and appropriate retirement ages will have to be retained, but there are good reasons for making this determination more flexible and for balancing a number of needs. This flexibility could benefit individuals as well as the economy and society as a whole. Nevertheless, care would need to be taken that this flexibility took into account the needs and wishes of workers as well as administrative convenience and the financial problems of government.

THE TREATMENT OF WOMEN AND FAMILIES

A continuing issue is the treatment of women under the Social Security system. The system was designed in an era when the vast majority of women were housewives who did not work outside the home and who remained married to the same men for their entire lives. Those characteristics would hardly describe the average woman in the United States today, and as a consequence some aspects of the treatment of women under Social Security now appear outdated and blatantly discriminatory. Further, there are problems in the way other members of a family are treated and the protection they are (or are not) afforded in the system.

Several aspects of Social Security substantiate these claims of unfairness. For example, if a woman is married to a covered employee for fewer than *ten years* (twenty years until the 1977 amendments were added), a divorce takes all the husband's benefits away from her, and for Social Security purposes it is as if they had never been married. And, as we have noted, the benefits an individual receives are roughly based on contributions, so even if a woman returns to work or begins to work after the divorce, she will find it difficult to accumulate sufficient credits to earn a significant retirement benefit.

Also, if both husband and wife work, as is now true for many if not most married households in the United States, the pair receive little additional Social Security benefit. This is true even though they may pay twice as much in Social Security contributions as a couple with only one covered worker. Benefits are based on each partner's individual work record, and there is no spousal benefit unless one worker would receive more from a spousal benefit than from her or his own work record. Therefore, on average, the replacement rate for a one-worker couple at the average earnings level is 61 percent; for two-earner couples the replacement rate is 44 percent. The penalty at high rates of income is even more severe.[14]

An even broader question arises as to whether a woman, or a man, who chooses not to work outside the home should not in fact receive some Social Security protection based on his or her contributions to the household and to society through this work in the home. The idea of a "homemaker's credit" in Social Security has been advanced so that these individuals would have their own protection as part of Social Security. This protection may be especially important for disability insurance, for if the homemaker should become disabled, especially with children still in the home, this would impose additional financial burdens on the rest of the family. Other family members would have to do work he or she had once performed in the home, or pay to have it done. With the current financial pressures on Social Security, however, there is little likelihood of homemakers' benefits being expanded; if anything, the treatment of women under Social Security may be even less generous. For example, the Reagan administration reduced extra spouses' benefits and surviving spouses' benefits over the course of its years in office. The major beneficiaries of these spouses' benefits are women.

THE DISABILITY TEST

In addition to providing benefits in retirement or if a breadwinner in a family dies, Social Security also protects families if that breadwinner is unable to work because of sickness or injury. One important issue that arises under the disability insurance program is the "substantial gainful employment" test. The test, as administered, is rather harsh and requires that a person be totally disabled before he or she can receive benefits.[15] The individual must be disqualified from any "substantial gainful employment" if such employment is available in the geographical area of the potential beneficiary and if that applicant has the requisite skills. These standards are much more stringent than those applied in private disability programs, which require only the inability to engage in one's customary occupation, or for other public programs, such as the Black Lung program or veterans' programs. At present, well under 50 percent of all applicants for disability receive benefits. In addition, the Social Security Amendments of 1980 mandated frequent reexaminations of the eligibility of claimants under the program, with the result that significant numbers of people have been removed from the program.[16] Also, there has been a movement to tighten eligibility for people with substance-abuse problems. These programs to reduce eligibility even further often have occurred because of problems with implementation, especially lack of adequate staff.[17]

The stringency of the disability test requires workers who have any disability to absent themselves from the workforce almost entirely and thereby attempt to receive disability benefits. A situation may well arise in which an individual is too unhealthy to earn an adequate income but too healthy to receive benefits under the existing disability program. For both social and financial reasons, it would appear beneficial to have a more graduated disability test to assist those who have a partial disability but who wish to continue to be as productive in the labor market as they can. A person could be assigned a percentage disability and compensated accordingly. Such a test is already in use in the Veterans Administration, and it would seem possible to implement a similar arrangement for civilian disability benefits.

As noted, worker's compensation is another accident and disability program in the United States, although it is managed by the states rather than the federal government (except for the program covering federal employees). The disability tests employed in this program vary markedly from state to state, but in general are less stringent than the Social Security test.[18] Further, there are provisions for permanent partial disability payments that enable a person to continue working in some occupation even if not able to work in his or her original occupation. Worker's compensation programs now cover almost 90 percent of the American workforce but provide very different levels of benefit in the several states.[19]

Social Security and the Economy

Social Security is also believed to affect the economy of the United States. The most commonly cited effect is the reduction of individual savings and the consequent reduction in the amount of capital available for investment, compared with the situation if there were no public insurance program. Because individuals know that their retirement will be at least partly financed by Social Security, they do not save as much during their working lives as they might otherwise. Further, because Social Security as it is currently managed does not itself accumulate large reserves to pay future benefits but tends to be a direct intergenerational transfer program, there is less capital accumulation in the U.S. economy than there might otherwise be. Estimates of the magnitude of savings lost as a result of the Social Security program vary widely; they ranged from $3.6 billion to $38 billion in 1969.[20] Most experts agree that there has been some reduction in savings as a result of Social Security, but most now think that the disincentive effects are less than many conservative critics of the program have argued.[21]

The second major effect of Social Security on the economy is the lessened participation of older workers in the labor force. As noted, the retirement test and the fixing of a standard retirement age tend to provide disincentives for potential workers over sixty-five to continue working. As with the economic effect of reduced savings, it is difficult to estimate the magnitude of this effect on total growth and productivity, but several empirical studies have documented its existence. Also, as the number of young workers entering the labor market decreases, the skills of the older workers will become increasingly valuable to the economy.

Financing Social Security

We now come to the most frequently discussed question concerning Social Security: how can the program be financed? Periodically since the 1960s, there have been reports that Social Security was going bankrupt, raising the specter that many elderly people would be left with no income from their contributions. In 1984 President Reagan said that he did not believe that those currently making contributions to the system would ever receive that much back in benefits.[22] Many citizens came to believe that negative prognosis, and by the mid-1980s less than half of all Americans expressed confidence in Social Security. The lack of confidence was especially noticeable among the young. Given the entitlement nature of the program, such dire outcomes are extremely unlikely. Indeed, at other times the Social Security system has run large surpluses that politicians have sought to use to balance an otherwise unbalanced federal budget.[23] But the Social Security system as a program financed entirely by payroll taxes may be in difficulty, and the trust fund created to back the program may be in danger of being exhausted by the middle of the twenty-first century as the number of retirees increases relative to the number of workers.[24] Younger workers may be called on to finance the program with ever higher payroll taxes but may be reluctant to do so if they fear that they will not receive the benefits themselves.

There are several reasons for the financial difficulties of the Social Security program. The most obvious problem is the increasing number of aging Americans, a trend that began in the 1960s and is projected to continue if the birthrate continues to be low. In 1960 only 9 percent of the American population was over sixty-five. By 1990 that figure had increased to almost 13 percent, and it is expected to increase to almost 20 percent by 2025. Phrased differently, in 1984 each Social Security beneficiary was supported by the taxes of approximately three active workers. By 2030, it is estimated that each beneficiary will be supported by only 2.3 workers, and by 2050, by less than 2.2 active workers.[25] This obviously implies either an increasing burden on active workers or a modification of the existing financial structure of the program.

Another factor increasing the difficulties in financing Social Security has been the indexing of benefits to match increases in prices and wages. Under existing arrangements, the initial benefit levels paid retirees are adjusted annually to reflect changes in the average wages paid in the economy. In addition, in every twelve-month period during which prices increase more than 3 percent, benefits are adjusted so that retirees have approximately constant purchasing power from their pensions.

This indexing of benefits (a cost-of-living adjustment, or COLA as it is sometimes called) is an obvious target for those seeking to control the costs of social programs. As Social Security faced one more crisis in 1983, legislation was passed that imposed a one-time delay of six months in the COLA. Another suggestion, by a group of economists at the usually moderate to liberal Brookings Institution, would be to eliminate the COLA in a year in which inflation was less than 5 percent; if inflation was greater than 5 percent, the correction would be the rate of inflation less 5 percent. Another suggestion would have the COLA pegged several percentage points lower than the rate of inflation.[26] All these suggestions tend to encounter opposition from the growing and increasingly active lobbying organizations for the elderly.

The reasons for attacking the indexing of benefits as a means of reducing some of the financial problems in Social Security are twofold. First, it is a relatively simple change to make. Second, it has the potential to save significant amounts of money. For example, it is estimated that the six-month COLA delay in the 1983 legislation saved $40 billion from fiscal 1983 to 1988. Similarly, pegging the COLA rate at two percentage points below the rate of inflation would have saved approximately $53 billion from 1984 to 1989. But such measures may well be serious hardships on some of the elderly. One study has estimated that a COLA three percentage points below inflation would put over a million elderly below the official poverty line within several years; many people wonder why the federal budget and the Social Security system have to be made solvent on the backs of the elderly.[27] President Reagan, who was openly skeptical about the future of Social Security, agreed in July 1984 that even if inflation fell below the 3 percent figure, the COLA adjustment would still be made. Congress rapidly agreed with the president (especially given that there was an election soon), and there is every reason to expect future administrations to continue to index Social Security.

With the financial pressures on Social Security, there is a question whether the system can afford to continue financing itself entirely through payroll taxes. There are also questions about the payroll tax, perhaps the most important being that the tax is basically regressive, exacting a higher percentage tax from low-paid workers than from the more affluent. This regressive character of the tax is the result of the threshold above which individuals earning additional income do not pay additional tax. In 1994 individuals paid a payroll tax of 7.65 percent on the first $60,600 of covered employment for a maximum tax of $4,636; after that amount, they paid no more taxes for the old age, survivors, or disability programs.[28] The health insurance component is, however, paid on all wage income and is therefore a proportional tax. Thus, everyone who earns the threshold amount or less paid the same 7.65 percent of their income, while some earning $100,000 paid less than 5 percent of their income as Social Security taxes.

In addition, the Social Security tax is applied only to salaries and wages, not to earnings from dividends or interest. Because the system is conceptualized as providing insurance and not as providing benefits directly proportional to earnings, these disparities are justified; once you have paid your annual "premium" on the insurance policy, there is no need to pay more. The payroll tax for Social Security is regressive in another way as well. Most economists argue that workers actually bear the burden of the employers' contributions (the same 7.65 percent of salaries and wages up to the threshold) to Social Security. Employers count their contributions as a part of the costs of employing a worker and reduce wages accordingly.[29]

The payroll tax also has the disadvantage of being more visible than consumption taxes.[30] They see the amount of money deducted from each paycheck for Social Security, and they have some idea of how much money they are paying into the system. This visibility in turn means that the level of payroll taxation may be limited by real or potential taxpayer resistance. Although the tax is visible by counting it as well as the personal income tax, the total tax "bite" on wages is less obvious than if there were one large tax on income that was used for social benefits as well as the general purposes of government.

The earmarked payroll tax does have one advantage that some people believe is worth retaining. Because the receipts from this tax are relatively limited, politicians are prevented from using the Social Security system for political gain. That is, as general tax revenues (the income tax primarily) are not used to finance the system, it is difficult for a president or Congress to increase rates of benefits just before an election to attempt to win votes from the elderly. The COLA adjustment of benefits, however, may have some of the same effects because changes in benefits tend to go into effect shortly before election time in November. Further, the earmarked tax makes the system appear to most citizens to be a contributory insurance program instead of a welfare program.

Several proposals have been made to alleviate some of the financial problems of Social Security. One would be to remove the financing of Medicare from the payroll tax and finance that program through general revenues. This would provide Social Security with more money while retaining the existing rates of payroll taxation; in 1994, 1.45 percent of the 7.65 percent paid in payroll taxation was used to finance Medicare. Another mechanism, already mentioned, is to change the COLA adjustment and timing, although in a period of high inflation such a change might work a considerable hardship on the elderly. We have also mentioned that raising the retirement age, or at least making it more flexible, is another possible solution to the costs of Social Security, as would be a reduction of some of the welfare-like benefits attached to the program (e.g., spouses' benefits). One such minor benefit—the burial allowance—has in some cases already been eliminated.

These proposals represent rather minor tinkering with the program, but more significant modifications have been proposed. One would be to make the program truly comprehensive so that it would include all workers; new federal government employees are now in the system, but state and local government employees can still opt out. Expanding membership in the program would provide a larger financial base of white-collar workers who earn better-than-average incomes. This might also have certain psychological benefits: it would point out that all citizens are part of the same Social Security system.

Finally, others have suggested that we change the entire basis of Social Security financing from payroll contributions to general revenues, either through the income tax or through a value-added tax (VAT) like the one commonly used in Europe.[31] The VAT is a tax levied on businesses at each stage of the production process, based on the value that the business added to the raw materials it used to create the product it sells. The VAT has the advantage of being virtually invisible, its costs reflected only in the price of a product. It also has the advantage of being somewhat less regressive than the payroll tax, especially if some commodities (food, prescription drugs, etc.) are not taxed. The invisibility of the VAT would be an advantage for those managing the Social Security system, although many citizens might not regard it as such. The VAT would allow the income of the Social Security system to expand with less restraint than the present system of finances.

Social Security finance is likely to remain an important policy issue for years. The average age of the population continues to increase, and the costs of the program keep growing. In fact, these costs will probably increase more rapidly than will the yield from the payroll tax. Unfortunately for the managers of the program, the form of finance has become entrenched, and it may be difficult to modify without changing the insurance concept of the system and perhaps thereby reducing the general support for the program.

It has also been suggested that Social Security benefits should be counted as taxable income. The 1983 amendments to the Social Security Act permitted the taxation of benefits received by retirees with incomes at the higher end of the scale: $25,000 for individuals, $32,000 for a couple. Given that many of the elderly have very little income anyway (fewer than 10 percent were subject to the tax in 1984), and already find it difficult to exist on Social Security, such a program could produce substantial hardship if it was extended lower down the income ladder. But the passage of any provision to tax benefits indicates the perceived crisis in Social Security financing, and would in effect make Social Security a means-tested program.

Social Security is a large, complex, and expensive program. As a result, several important policy issues exist concerning its effects on citizens and on the economy. What is more fundamental, however, is that the program will persist, albeit in modified form. Some way must be found to finance the program so it will provide an adequate or at least minimal income for pensioners without bankrupting the working-age population. Likewise, there are increasing demands that we remove some of the rigidities and discrimination from the system and make it more humane and responsive. The system, in all probability, will continue to be a major success story in public policy, but one that will remain on the policymaking agenda.

Means-Tested Programs

The second major kind of social program is the means-tested program. To qualify for benefits under such a program an individual must satisfy a means test, or more accurately an absence-of-means test. Individuals cannot earn more than a specified amount or have any major assets if they are to qualify for a means-tested program. Rather obviously, then, these programs benefit groups of people, defined by economic criteria, that are generally neither the most influential in society nor the easiest to mobilize politically. Also, the means testing involved in the program tends to stigmatize and to some extent degrade individuals who must apply for the benefits. These programs are not entitlements in the strict sense of the term, although political and judicial actions have tended to make them more matters of right than in the past.[32]

These programs are regarded as handouts or giveaways by many citizens, who also describe recipients of such benefits as "lazy welfare cheaters" and sing songs about "welfare Cadillacs." President Reagan once referred to AFDC recipients as "welfare queens." Polls of Americans find that although they definitely want the AFDC system reformed, they are willing to spend to improve the system and do not want punitive restrictions implemented (see table 10.5). More intellectual critics of the programs blame them for social disintegration, family breakups, and rising rates of urban crime.[33] Racial issues are also involved in the management of means-tested benefits, for although the majority of welfare recipients are white, a disproportionate share of blacks and Hispanics receive welfare benefits. These means-tested benefits—Aid to Families with Dependent Children (AFDC), food stamps, Supplemental Security Income, and a variety of other programs—provide the only means of livelihood for many citizens and raise several important social, political, and economic issues.

TABLE 10.5
ATTITUDE TOWARD THE WELFARE SYSTEM

1. *Is welfare in need of reform?*	Fundamental reform	81%
	Minor reform	16%
	No answer	3%
2. *Would you pay more taxes*	Yes	68%
for a system that would get	No	27%
people off welfare?	No opinion	5%

3. *Do you agree with the following welfare reforms?* (% yes):

Take money from paychecks and tax refunds of fathers who refuse to make child support payments.	95
Require all able-bodied people on welfare to work or learn a job or skill.	92
Spend money to provide free day care to allow poor mothers to work or take classes.	90
Reduce welfare with a system of guaranteed public jobs.	74
End increases in welfare payments to women who give birth to children while on welfare.	42
Cut the amount of money given to all people on welfare.	25
Require women to get a job and get off welfare within two years; if they can't take care of their children at that time, give them to an orphanage.	17
Eliminate all welfare payments entirely.	7

SOURCES: Questions 1 and 2, *USA Today*, 22 April 1994. Question 3, Yankel-ovich poll, reported in *Time*, 20 June 1994.

AFDC, or Welfare

The largest means-tested program, and the one that generates the most political controversy, is AFDC, or welfare. This program benefited more than 14 million Americans, including approximately 10 million children, in 1993. The program cost the federal government over $11 billion, or less than 1 percent of all its expenditures and less than 5 percent of the federal deficit that year. AFDC takes a larger share of state governments' expenditures, especially as the welfare rolls increased substantially during the early 1990s.[34] It is an expensive program, although perhaps not so expensive as some believe, and because the program provides benefits on the basis of need rather

TABLE 10.6

CHANGES IN THE POVERTY RATE, 1960–91

(IN PERCENTAGES)

	1960	*1970*	*1975*	*1980*	*1985*	*1988*	*1991*
Total	22.2	12.6	12.3	13.0	14.0	13.0	14.2
Blacks	55.1	33.5	31.3	32.5	31.3	31.3	32.7
Children[a]	n.a.	14.9	16.8	17.9	20.1	19.0	21.1
Female-headed households	n.a.	38.1	38.1	36.5	40.2	32.1	34.8
Over 65 years of age	n.a.	24.5	24.5	15.7	14.1	11.4	11.9

SOURCE: U.S. Bureau of the Census, *Current Population Reports,* Series P-60, annual.

a. Fifteen and younger.

TABLE 10.7

POVERTY RATES USING ALTERNATIVE DEFINITIONS

OF POVERTY, 1987

(IN PERCENTAGES)

	Cash only	*Cash plus food and housing benefits*		*Cash plus food, housing, and medical benefits*	
		a	*b*	*a*	*b*
Total	13.0	12.0	12.4	8.5	11.0
Female-headed households	38.3	32.8	34.2	21.6	30.9
Elderly	12.2	10.2	10.7	2.1	6.4

SOURCE: Patricia Ruggles, *Drawing the Line: Alternative Poverty Measures and their Implications for Public Policy* (Washington, D.C.: Urban Institute Press, 1990), table 7.2.

a. Benefits valued according to prices in market.

b. Benefits valued according to income beneficiaries willing to give up to receive benefits. Given that noncash benefits are not available for any use, they tend to be considered less valuable than a cash benefit.

than contributions, it is a controversial program. It is especially interesting that the controversy over AFDC arose in the 1960s and 1970s rather than in the 1930s when it was adopted. The program was adopted as a part of the package that produced Social Security, but at that time the major controversy was over Social Security and not AFDC.[35] It was assumed that AFDC would be used by a relatively small number of widows with children, rather than by women who were remarried, divorced, or separated. Social Security has now become an widely accepted part of American life, while AFDC is perceived as a problem by the taxpayers who fund the program, as well as by recipients of the benefits. Changing family patterns, with a very large number of women working in the economy, also play a part in the low status of AFDC recipients.

In general, to qualify for AFDC a woman must have children and virtually no income, and there must be no one living in the household who is capable of providing support for the children. Actually, some males also qualify for AFDC; an increasing number qualify for assistance under the Family Support Act (see p. 302–3).

In 1988 fewer than 15 percent of the recipients were widows, wives of disabled men, or unemployed, those for whom the program was intended. Most AFDC recipients are now in fatherless families, with approximately half of those being families in which the parents were never married and the other half being separated and divorced mothers.

AFDC, although a national program, is administered by states and localities. Despite several attempts at reform and "nationalization" of the program, its administration is still decentralized. The federal government provides a small subsidy to the states for the program, with the remainder of the benefit coming from state and local funds. The benefits are not uniform across the nation and vary widely. In January 1992 the highest monthly benefit for a family of three was $924 in Alaska. If we leave aside Alaska and its extremely high cost of living, the highest payment was $680 in Connecticut. The lowest AFDC payment for a family of three was $120 in Mississippi; the average across the nation was $395 per month. None of the levels of benefits is particularly munificent, and substantial differences exist, even taking into account differences in the cost of living in the various localities. In addition, a number of states undertook to reduce their levels of AFDC benefits during the fiscal problems of the early 1980s. In some instances this meant just failing to increase benefits in line with inflation (see table 10.8), while in others it meant real cuts in program benefits.

In addition to general benefit cuts, states have begun to use AFDC payments to regulate the behavior of recipients.[36] The image of the "welfare mother" having illegitimate children in order to qualify for benefits is one that gives supporters of the program difficulties when they attempt to im-

TABLE 10.8

STATE ADJUSTMENTS IN AFDC PAYMENTS, 1991–92

Dollar amounts reduced	*Real benefits reduced*		*Real benefits unchanged*	*Real benefits increased*
California	Arkansas	Nebraska	Florida	Alaska
District of	Colorado	New Hampshire		Alabama
Columbia	Connecticut	New Jersey		Arizona
Maryland	Delaware	North Carolina		Hawaii
Michigan	Georgia	North Dakota		Kansas
Tennessee	Idaho	Ohio		Montana
Vermont	Illinois	Pennsylvania		Nevada
	Indiana	Rhode Island		New Mexico
	Iowa	South Carolina		New York
	Kentucky	Texas		Oregon
	Louisiana	Utah		South Dakota
	Maine	Virginia		
	Massachusetts	Washington		
	Minnesota	West Virginia		
	Mississippi	Wisconsin		
	Missouri	Wyoming		

SOURCE: Isaac Shapiro et al., *The States and the Poor* (Washington, D.C.: Center on Budget and Policy Priorities, 1991), 8.

prove funding and benefits. Indeed, several states have reacted against this popular image by refusing to continue to increase payments for mothers on AFDC who have additional children, with one state actually reducing benefits if there is an additional child.[37] Likewise, at least one state has acted to eliminate general assistance payments that had been paid to individuals not eligible for AFDC, and others have reduced the size and duration of the payments. Other states offer lower AFDC benefits to recipients who have just moved in from out of state.

These regulations have been joined by a number of other regulations on the behavior of AFDC recipients. For example, several states are beginning to reduce benefits if the children of AFDC recipients do not attend school regularly. Other regulations include reducing or eliminating benefits for teenage recipients who do not attend school regularly. Other states have enacted provisions that cut off AFDC payments to teenaged mothers who do not live with a parent or legal guardian. In a more general move, some states are beginning to require all welfare recipients to be fingerprinted to help reduce fraud.[38]

The AFDC program is not without problems (see below), but some of those problems have been exaggerated in the popular mind. First, as shown earlier, AFDC is not a big spending program; it actually costs the federal government relatively little. Further, once on welfare, most people do not spend their lifetime on the program. In 1994 over one-third of AFDC recipients had been on the program one year or less, and over 78 percent had been on it for five years or less. The median time on the program is twenty-two months. Also, almost as many whites as African Americans are on AFDC. Finally, as might be expected from the transitional nature of the program, divorce and separation, rather than having a child without benefit of marriage, accounted for the most beneficiaries.

Problems with AFDC

As mentioned, both taxpayers and the recipients of AFDC see numerous problems in the program. Naturally, the problems seen by the two groups are rarely the same, although to some extent they may be different ways of saying the same thing about certain aspects of the program.

MEANS TESTING

Programs that require recipients to prove that they are indigent create problems for the recipients, who become stigmatized, especially in a society that places a high value on success and income as symbols of personal worth. Most recipients of AFDC are relatively powerless anyway, and the stigma attached to being on programs such as AFDC tends to lessen their feelings of self-worth and power, which in turn may help to perpetuate the problems that caused them to go on AFDC in the first place. Unfortunately, the program as designed tends to perpetuate indigence rather than allow people to work their way out of poverty.

PUNISHMENT FOR WORKING

As part of the means testing of the program, individuals who attempt to work their way out of poverty are severely penalized. An individual can work no more than 100 hours per month, no matter what rate of pay is received. After a certain amount is earned each year (the sum varies by state), the AFDC recipient is required to return $2 in benefits for every $3 earned. This is in effect a tax higher than any income tax rate in the regular income tax system. Rather obviously, such a high rate of "tax" on earnings provides little incentive for individuals to work their way out of poverty. And given the relatively poor job skills of the typical AFDC recipient, along with the obvious problems of working when there are small children at home, the program presents a strong disincentive even to try to find work. Thus, once people go on AFDC, they find it difficult to get off, and the system perpetuates itself and poverty. In addition, because other benefits, such as food stamps and Medicaid, may be tied to receiving AFDC, going out to take a job may mean the loss of a great deal more than the AFDC check. Finally, if an individual on "welfare" takes a job and then leaves that job, it may take several weeks or months to get back on the program, with the associated difficulties in supporting a family during that time. The reforms of the AFDC program undertaken in 1988 addressed some of these problems, but states have been rather slow to implement many of the provisions, so staying on the program may still be more "profitable" than trying to work.

FAMILY STRUCTURE

The AFDC program also has severe effects on family structure. As noted, under most circumstances a woman with children cannot receive benefits if an able-bodied male lives in the home. This means that the traditional family, the virtues of which are stressed by politicians such as Bill Clinton and Dan Quayle, usually is not eligible for AFDC. This requirement makes it more difficult for a woman on AFDC to work, since she must either care for the children herself or find suitable day-care facilities. It may also have a deleterious effect on children, who grow up in a fatherless household. Especially for male children, such an arrangement has been shown to produce difficulties in adjustment in later life. These problems in the program are becoming less unusual, as single-parent families become more common in the United States. Growing up in a single-parent home may be less stigmatizing than it once was, but the social adjustment problems may remain. Still, with more women now working outside the home, the image of the welfare mother staying home and not working is more negative than ever.[39]

COSTS AND BENEFITS

Depending on whom you ask, the benefits of AFDC are either too high or too low. Those concerned about the costs of the program argue that the generous benefits encourage people to stay on welfare rather than find a job, and they simply do not want to pay taxes so that other people can refuse to work. On the other side of the argument, most recipients of AFDC benefits would point out that even the highest monthly state benefit of $924 is hardly sufficient for a life of leisure and that the average benefit across the country is only $395. The recipients and their supporters also would argue that in fact the benefits are too low to provide a decent living for the recipients and their children. These children inherit poverty along with the substandard housing, low-quality education, family disruption, and poor diet commonly associated with AFDC households.

At least in the 1990s, those favoring stringent controls on welfare spending are winning. A number of states in 1991 undertook to control, or even reduce, the size of the benefits offered under AFDC (see table 10.8, p. 299). The most stringent cuts were in California, which reduced the maximum payment and tightened eligibility requirements. It also reduced payments to new residents of the state to the level of the state from which they came; California would no longer be a "welfare magnet."[40] The general stringency of state government finances, and the backlash of many of the working poor and recently unemployed against recipients of public assistance, mean that cuts in these programs are likely to continue for some time. Indeed, these are only more visible examples of a long-term erosion of the value of AFDC payments. One study by the Congressional Research Service found that the average purchasing power of the maximum welfare payments across all states declined 42 percent from 1970 to 1991.[41] The program may appear expansive, but its recipients have become progressively more impoverished.

THE FAMILY SUPPORT ACT

The problems inherent in the AFDC program have not gone unnoticed by lawmakers, and one reaction was the Family Support Act of 1988.[42] This act, associated especially with Senator Daniel Patrick Moynihan (D-N.Y.), addresses a number of important issues in the structure of AFDC. It attempts to break the "cycle of poverty" that has led to several generations of family members following one another as recipients of AFDC. Among the provisions of the act are these:

1. *Greater help for families with two parents.* The act requires the states to amend their AFDC programs to provide at least six months' benefits per year (AFDC-UP) to families with both parents unemployed.
2. *Improved child-support enforcement.* This is intended to reduce the number of children requiring assistance from AFDC, as well as to have some impact on strengthening parental responsibility toward children.
3. *Job training.* States are mandated to provide enhanced job training and child-care services so that AFDC recipients will be able to get and keep reasonable jobs in the economy.[43]
4. *Enhanced Medicare benefits.* People who leave welfare for work will not automatically lose medical insurance, a major impediment to leaving AFDC, given that a declining number of jobs for which most people leaving welfare are qualified have health benefits.[44]

The Family Support Act certainly has not been a cureall for the problems of the AFDC program, nor has it eliminated poverty in the United States. Further, the requirements for implementation by the states have produced substantial variations in the generosity of the benefits and the speed of their adoption.[45] Still, the adoption of this program is a recognition of the changes that may be necessary to cope with the problems inherent in the basic system of providing financial support for the indigent in the United States.

Alternatives to AFDC

With all the problems associated with AFDC, even after the adoption of the Family Support Act, why is the program maintained? Perhaps because of inertia and general resistance to reform, especially for social programs that have few real supporters among the public. It can also be argued that although they may oppose the program in principle, conservatives have been major obstacles to change because the existing, rather punitive program is a means of regulating the poor and ensuring that their lives are so impoverished that they want to get off AFDC. There are alternatives to the existing program, some of which have been seriously proposed in the United States and some of which are in operation in Europe. These alternative programs might provide benefits for poor citizens without the stigma or the administrative complexity of the existing program.

FAMILY ALLOWANCES

One alternative, in operation in virtually all other democratic, industrialized societies, is the family allowance.[46] Under this program, families are given a monthly benefit check from the government, usually based on the number of children. For the more affluent, this simply becomes additional taxable income, while for the poor it may be a major source of income. But the most important aspect of the program is that it includes everyone, or at least all households with children. The stigma of receiving government benefits is therefore removed, and the program is substantially easier to administer than AFDC. The level of benefit for each child would have to be sufficient to match the current level of AFDC benefit, which would mean that a great deal of money would have to pass through the public sector as taxes and expenditures, but the effects would perhaps justify that decision, given the current negative consequences of the AFDC program.

THE NEGATIVE INCOME TAX

A second alternative to the existing AFDC program is the negative income tax.[47] Under such an arrangement, a minimal level of income would be determined, based on family size. Each family would then file its tax statement, with those earning below the established minimal level receiving a rebate or subsidy, while those above that minimal level would pay taxes much as usual. Such a program would establish a guaranteed annual income for all citizens and would be administratively simpler than AFDC. The recipients themselves would provide a good deal of the information necessary to calculate benefits, instead of having to rely on numerous state and local welfare offices. In addition, this program would establish equality in benefits across the United States, with perhaps some adjustments for different costs of living in different parts of the country. The negative income tax, as it is usually conceptualized, also would make it somewhat easier to work one's way out of poverty because it imposes only one-third or one-half reduction of benefits for any money earned, so even the working poor would benefit from the program.

The negative income tax was seriously proposed for the United States. Interestingly, President Nixon's 1969 proposal for a family assistance plan was much like a negative income tax.[48] If this program had been enacted, it would certainly have been the most sweeping reform of the welfare system ever made and would have meant a guaranteed annual income for all citizens. The program was not adopted by Congress, however. A coalition of liberals, who thought its benefits were too meager, and conservatives, who were ideologically opposed to the concept of a guaranteed minimum income, defeated the bill. In addition, social workers and other professionals believed that their jobs were threatened by a program that placed the major burden of proving eligibility on the individual citizen.

Although the program was not adopted in its entirety, there have been some movements toward a negative income tax in the United States. Several minor provisions of the Family Support Act provide for refundable tax credits that do not affect AFDC payments, and they therefore constitute a step toward a negative income tax. Also, the earned income tax credit operates through the tax system to benefit low-income taxpayers with at least one child in the family. The ideas behind this program (introduced in 1975) were to offset the effects of the Social Security tax on low-income individuals and to encourage people to work rather than take AFDC. This program now provides benefits (reduced taxes or in some cases direct cash transfers) to over 3 million American families.

WORKFARE

Most radical alternatives to AFDC have relatively little chance of being implemented in the United States. One more modest, and conservative, proposal was partially implemented by the Reagan administration, is already implemented in several states, and is a significant component of the proposed Clinton reforms.[49] This is referred to as "workfare."[50] The idea here is that citizens receiving welfare benefits should be made to work for the benefits. This typically means that the participants have to work enough hours to "earn" their benefits if paid at the minimum wage; they also receive a small allowance to cover the costs of going to work. This usually means working in some sort of public-service capacity (e.g., picking up trash in the parks). Such a program, while emphasizing the traditional work ethic, may further stigmatize AFDC recipients and is based on a preconception of malingering by the recipients. To the extent that it may be a substitute for real public-service jobs it may have the effect of substituting pay at well below the minimum wage for at least the minimum wage. In addition, implementing "workfare" actually would tend to increase costs, as the costs of finding jobs and administering the program would increase, and the participants would have to be paid a daily expense allowance.[51] Again, the provisions of the Family Support Act go some distance in providing greater opportunities for welfare recipients to work their way off the program.

CHILD SUPPORT

Although the popular image of the AFDC recipient is a woman who has a child out of wedlock, in reality almost half of AFDC recipients go on the program because of divorce or separation. These women are left with children to support and often lack significant job skills and work experience. Even in cases in which the legal divorce or separation decree awards child support to the mother and children, many men do not pay this support regularly, if at all. Several studies have found that a large percentage of the children whose families receive AFDC have fathers who are not paying child support.

The federal government has now undertaken to enforce child support, especially in cases in which the mother otherwise would be receiving benefits such as AFDC and food stamps. The Family Support Act of 1988 requires states to establish enforcement plans, and in 1994 employers were required to deduct child-support payments from the wages of fathers not in compliance with the law. This approach to the problem of poor children is not without its difficulties.[52] First, the delinquent fathers must be identified and located. Further, a federal study has found that these fathers tend to be relatively poor themselves, with 29 percent below the poverty line, and there may be little income to extract from them.[53] Still, states have adopted increasingly vigorous programs of enforcement and now are able to collect 80 percent of in-state support.[54] Some go so far as to confiscate the property as well as garnishee the wages of fathers who violate support orders.[55]

FULL EMPLOYMENT

Perhaps the simplest means of eliminating many of the problems of AFDC is to guarantee citizens jobs rather than social benefits. The federal government has been involved in a number of programs for job training and subsidized employment, the most prominent being the Comprehensive Employment and Training Act (CETA) in the 1970s and early 1980s.[56] The purpose of CETA was to enable people to acquire job skills by working with local private contractors and then to subsidize the employment of those trainees for several years. After that time, they were expected to have improved their productivity sufficiently to be able to earn a decent wage in the labor market. Although CETA continued in operation until 1981, it was severely criticized on several grounds—using inefficient and corrupt prime contractors, for example, and training people to do nonexistent jobs. Some critics charge that the CETA program placed too many trainees in the public rather than the private sector. Critics say this swelled the size of local government employment and created problems when the trainees' eligibility for CETA expired after the local governments had become dependent on their relatively cheap labor.

The combination of the recession and the continuing pressures to find an answer to problems of poverty and welfare led to the Bush administration's placing renewed emphasis on jobs and job training. The president announced Job Training 2000 as part of his economic program for the reelection campaign in 1992. As it was announced initially, the details were far from clear, but the idea that jobs were superior on almost all counts to welfare was firmly stated. The difficulty the president faced, as would any other welfare reformer, was the shortage of good jobs in the American economy even for workers with well-developed skills and ample job experience—assets that most welfare recipients lack.

The Clinton administration is continuing to place a significant emphasis on the development of jobs as perhaps the best means for addressing social problems. Robert Reich as Secretary of Labor has been both an academic and practitioner analyst of changing employment patterns in the world and the need for the U.S. economy to adjust to the globalized economy.[57] The welfare reforms proposed by the Clinton administration (see below) have a pronounced emphasis on work as a solution to the problem of welfare, but do not rely entirely on the private sector to develop those jobs. The federal government already has a number of job programs in place, but these have multiple, and often competing, goals, and their effects are not as positive as they might be.[58] The emphasis of these programs is on education and training, and many are targeted for young people. These programs may be beneficial in the long run, but in the short run they do not appear to be addressing the needs of many poor citizens, who often remain on welfare.

THE WAR ON POVERTY

Another attempt at a comprehensive solution to the problems of AFDC was the Johnson administration's war on poverty. During the administration of John F. Kennedy, poverty was "rediscovered" in the United States and became a popular political issue, especially among liberals. With President Kennedy's death, Lyndon Johnson used his formidable political talents and the memory of John Kennedy to create a series of legislative proposals to attempt to break the cycle of poverty, which, as we have seen, tends to be perpetuated by most existing social programs. The war on poverty differed from other social programs of the time in that it was less directed toward the short-term amelioration of deprivations than toward changing longstanding patterns and conditions of the very poor.[59] War-on-poverty programs did more than just hand out money, although they certainly did a good deal of that, by attempting to attack the cultural and social conditions associated with poverty. The programs also sought to involve the poor in the design and implementation of the programs more directly than had the more paternalistic programs common at the time.

The umbrella organization for the programs of the war on poverty was the Office of Economic Opportunity, created as a separate agency outside the Department of Health, Education, and Welfare. It was feared that the bureaucratic nature of HEW, and its commitment to social insurance programs as the mechanism for solving social problems, would hinder the activism envisioned for the war on poverty, and consequently an independent organization was established.

One of the aims of the war on poverty was to attack poverty by educating the children of the poor to a level at which they could compete successfully in school and in the economy. One of the most popular programs for children was Head Start, which attempted to prepare poor children to compete with other children when they entered school. The program tried to provide the skills that middle-class children generally have when they enter kindergarten but that children from economically deprived households frequently lack. Despite the popularity of Head Start, its demonstrable effects were rather modest. Children who participated in the program were indeed better prepared to enter kindergarten than children who had not been in the program, but their "head start" rapidly vanished. Without continuing extra assistance, after several years the Head Start children were not significantly different from children who had not participated.[60] Of course, depending on one's point of view, this could be an argument that the program had failed or that it needed more follow-up after the children reached elementary school. The war on poverty also provided programs such as the Neighborhood Youth Corps and the Job Corps to attempt to prepare somewhat older young people for jobs, or at least to provide temporary employment in public-service jobs. Additionally, a college work-study program was initiated to try to make it more possible for students from low-income families to attend college, a program that has been expanded and continues after the demise of the war on poverty.

For adults, the war on poverty initiated a variety of programs primarily intended to provide employment or to prepare people from poor households for productive employment. These programs commonly involved cooperation between the federal government and either state and local governments or private businesses. In addition to the employment-related projects, many of the smaller programs provided counseling, loans for small businesses, family planning, and a whole range of other social services. In general, the war on poverty provided something for almost everyone who needed and wanted work or help.

By the early 1980s most of the programs of the war on poverty had been dismantled, reduced, or modified. What happened? Several events reduced the emphasis that government originally placed on the programs. One was the escalation of the Vietnam war to the point that it diverted both attention and money from domestic programs, especially those lacking a solid political base and an institutionalized bureaucracy. Also, the goals of the war on poverty were so lofty, and perhaps so unrealistic, that it was easy for critics to point out that the programs had not been successful and to question the reasons for continuing to fund them. Further, the ever-increasing wealth that had fueled many public programs began to become less certain, and governments began to face real fiscal problems.[61]

Still, it would be difficult to argue that many of the programs of the war on poverty were really seriously tried. So many programs were started that some were funded only as pilot programs and others, such as Head Start, may have lacked the funds necessary to pursue their goals through to a successful conclusion. Further, to argue that even a large array of programs intended to change generations of poverty and deprivation could actually work miracles in a few years is unrealistic, and hence the "trial" given the programs may not have been a fair trial at all. Finally, with the election of Richard Nixon as president in 1968 the political climate that had spawned the programs changed, and since the impetus for the programs had so clearly been presidential, Congress had few strong advocates to defend the war-on-poverty programs.

But were the programs of the war on poverty, and the whole war itself, a massive failure or at best a noble experiment? As pointed out, it may be that instead of failing, they were never really tried. These programs did represent a major departure from the traditional means of attempting to solve, or at least ameliorate, the problems of poverty in the United States, and their impact may actually be more enduring than short-term evaluations indicate. Certainly the need to address the problems of poverty in the midst of affluence remains as pressing in the 1990s as it was in 1965 when the programs were initiated.

Whether the change is to come through better jobs in the private sector or through public programs, at least 30 million Americans are living beneath the official poverty line and are still waiting to be brought into the economic mainstream of American life. The loss of many well-paid industrial jobs increases the separation of American society into two groups—one affluent and the other increasingly deprived (relatively if not absolutely).

THE CLINTON PROPOSALS

President Clinton campaigned vigorously for welfare reform and began to push for the adoption of his plan during 1994. The plan his administration proposed would produce some substantial changes in AFDC and would effectively end the program as it has been known in the past. In the first place, welfare payments would be limited to two years for anyone who could physically work. Second, after that two years, receiving benefits would be contingent on preparing for a job in the private sector, unless the welfare recipient had a child under one year of age. The plan would not automatically deny benefits to intact families, as the existing AFDC program generally does. In addition, the program attempts to use regulatory mechanisms to enforce child-support payments by fathers, including efforts to establish paternity and denying occupational and driving licenses to fathers who do not support children.[62] Finally, there would be some money for educational efforts to reduce teen pregnancy.

The adoption of the Clinton plan faces a number of obstacles. First, it will be more expensive than the existing AFDC program, at least in the short run. The job-training provisions and subsidies for work would add a good deal to the expense of the program. This is especially true if governments become employers of last resort when the private sector does not provide jobs; one calculation is that the additional costs would be $6 billion.[63] If, however, the recipients do eventually get jobs with which they can support themselves and their families, the costs may be reduced over the long haul.

There is also a question whether there can be sufficient jobs created for all the potential workers. To match the average welfare payment across the United States these jobs would have to pay only $2.27 per hour, well below the minimum wage.[64] Unless health-care reform (see chapter 9) is also adopted, however, these jobs would have to provide benefits to compensate for the loss of Medicaid. Also, there would have to be some benefits for child care, or most of the income for a working mother would go to care for the children. Even if an AFDC recipient should get a job at the minimum wage ($4.25 per hour) and work full-time, the income would still be well below the poverty line, and there would still be the problem of lost benefits and the costs of going to work every day. With the declining number of low-skill jobs (over 46 percent of AFDC recipients have less than a high school education) in the economy, it is not clear whether this part of the plan can work.

There is also the question whether this program is really the best thing for welfare recipients, especially the children. There is some evidence that children do better—in school, socially, and ultimately economically—when they have at least one parent at home regularly to care for and nurture them.[65] This point has been stressed by conservatives such as former Vice-President Quayle, but also has been recognized by more liberal child advocacy groups. The emphasis on work in the Clinton plan, and most other plans for reform, is appealing to most Americans for ideological and financial reasons, but in the long run may actually exacerbate the cycle of dependency that the reforms are intended to break. While AFDC has some negative consequences for family life, going more strongly to the workfare model may have even more negative consequences on children.

Finally, simple politics will be a barrier to the enactment of welfare reform. Although there is widespread agreement that the welfare system needs to be reformed, there is no agreement on what direction those reforms should take. Conservatives see welfare and other social benefits as ultimately destructive to the will of people to work and want to control spending on social programs further. Liberals are not always as willing as many in the American public to impose a work requirement on welfare recipients and may want a more generous program than might be possible under existing financial circumstances.[66] It may simply be impossible to find common ground between these two factions, both of whom want to produce significant change from the status quo.

Other Means-Tested Programs

Although AFDC is the most common topic of discussion when the issue of means-tested benefits arises, a number of other benefits are available to less-privileged citizens. For example, food stamps are generally available to people on welfare as well as to working people whose income falls below certain limits. This program requires the participants to purchase the stamps at a discount and then use them to buy food and certain other necessities. Unlike most social programs, food stamps cannot be used legally other than for food, so that some of the common complaints against "welfare"—the misuse of the funds for alcohol, gambling, and so on—can be controlled. Further, this program helps create more demand for American agricultural products, so it could gain support from those interests as well as from the interests that support social assistance.

Supplemental Security Income is another important means tested program. As of 1992 it provided benefits to 5.6 million people. The largest number of these recipients qualify by falling into the categories of aged, blind, and/or disabled. These were the categories in earlier state assistance programs, but in 1974 these programs were federalized, thus removing them from the (then) weaker financial position of the states. These benefits have been indexed since the time they were federalized so that the assistance now offered to these groups is probably substantially superior to what it would have been if the program had remained at the state level.

The Persistence of Poverty in the United States

We began our discussion of agenda setting with a discussion of the impact of Michael Harrington's *The Other America* on the development of a poverty program in the United States.[67] Despite the attention brought to the problem and programs such as the war on poverty, the problem of poverty continues. In fact, poverty in the mid-1990s is nearly as great a problem as it was in the mid-1960s, when the war on poverty was beginning. Poverty had been declining during the 1960s and 1970s, but it began to increase again in the early 1990s. Further, the poverty rate is not uniform across the population, with female-headed households, blacks and native Americans, and children being particularly likely to live in poverty. Over 21 percent of all children under the age of eighteen now live under the official poverty line; 45.6 percent of all black children and over 41 percent of Native American children lived in poverty in 1991. Both of these rates of poverty have increased since the 1970s. In contrast, the poverty rate for the elderly has improved substantially over the decades since poverty became an issue; that poverty rate is now less than half what it was in 1970, despite a growing elderly population.

In general, the social policies of the Reagan and Bush administrations seem to have forced more people to live in poverty than would have been true under the continuation of the social policies existing earlier. A number of other factors, such as the slowing of economic growth and changing demographics, may have had some impact on the increasing poverty rate,[68] but public policy has been an important element. The Clinton administration is returning to some of the social activism of previous Democratic administrations, although in a somewhat more restrained manner. The emphasis for the most part has been on developing more jobs and getting people ready to take those jobs rather than on direct grants to improve the situation of the poor.

There may, however, need to be more than just jobs if poverty is to be eliminated. As pointed out earlier, a minimum-wage job will not pull a family of three or four above the poverty line, and in most areas will not do so for an individual.[69] Given that many if not most of the family units involved have a single wage earner (usually female), there is little possibility of combining incomes to bring the family above the poverty line. There may be a need to link social benefits—food stamps, energy assistance, Medicaid —with work more carefully than in the past. This is a part of welfare reform efforts, but it may need to be extended to families already working rather than receiving welfare.[70]

Poverty is a symbolic issue, but it is also a matter of careful counting.[71] How do we know who is poor and who is not? The official definition of poverty for 1992 was a family of four living on an income of $13,190 or less; adjustments are made for family size, urban versus rural areas, and so on. This definition does not include as income all noncash public benefits, such as food stamps, Medicare or Medicaid, and housing subsidies. Because of the availability of those benefits and the relationship of poverty status for eligibility for other public programs, conservative economists during the Reagan and Bush years argued for a change in the definition of poverty.[72] Such a change in the definition would have shown that many fewer people were in poverty (see table 10.7, p. 297) and would thereby have benefited an administration that consistently argued that its policies had not harmed the poor. In addition, such a change in definition might have the effect of a "reverse Harrington"; if the problem can be defined out of existence, it becomes much easier to eliminate it from the public agenda. The Clinton administration and Congress are also concerned about the definition of poverty and its current level. They have chosen, however, to address the problem indirectly—through employment programs and welfare reform—rather than directly.

The Homeless

In addition to the increasing number of people living in poverty in the United States, an increasing number of people are homeless. Often the homeless are not included in the official poverty figures because they are not caught in the statistical nets used to calculate those figures. Instead, they live on the margins of society, often without government benefits of any sort, sleeping in shelters or on the streets, and eating in soup kitchens. Were it not for their visibility in many urban areas, the homeless might not really be counted as a part of the society at all.

The reasons for homelessness are numerous. Government policies have reduced the number of subsidized low-income housing units available and have forced many people—including families—onto the streets.[73] Further, changes in mental health laws requiring minimal possible restraint led to the release of many patients from institutions to poorly prepared community mental health programs, and some of those patients have since found their way to the streets.[74] Increases in chemical dependency have also made their contributions to homelessness in the United States. Finally, the declining number of jobs at which a person with a low level of education can earn a wage sufficient to support a family, or even an individual, has had an impact on homelessness.

For whatever reason, there is now a significant social policy problem that is not being addressed effectively. The federal government has little or no policy for coping with the issue of homelessness. The only federal program of any consequence is the McKinney Act, authorizing several kinds of emergency assistance such as housing, food, health care, and drug and alcohol treatment. The federal government appropriated $4.2 billion from 1987 to 1993, with most of this amount being spent through state and local governments.[75] Although this appears to be a significant amount of money, it is rather meager compared with the magnitude of the need, and the program does not address the fundamental causes of the social problem.[76] More homeless persons now are being assisted by private organizations than by governments at any level. This emphasis on the private sector corresponds well with the emphasis on volunteerism during both the Reagan and Bush administrations, but it has done little to solve the underlying problems. Private assistance may undergo further strains as a continuing economic slowdown reduces many people's capacity to give, and the persistence of the problem erodes the public's compassion.[77]

There is little evidence that approaches to homelessness have been altered significantly after a return to a Democratic administration. This is in part because of an absence of a clear policy solution to a multidimensional problem. People are homeless for a variety of reasons, so addressing the problem will require an equally broad and probably expensive strategy. Further, many of those reasons, such as addiction and mental illness, may be difficult for public policies to "solve" through conventional policy instruments. The Clinton administration appears to have a number of other domestic policy priorities—such as health and welfare reform—and may rely on state and local governments, and especially the private charitable sector, to address the problem of homelessness.

Personal Social Services

The final category of social service programs delivered by the public sector receives less attention than either Social Security or AFDC, largely because these programs cost much less and deliver benefits that do not depend on either age or income. The term "personal social services" applies to a range of services, such as adoption, foster care, suicide prevention, counseling, and the like, that are definitely not for the poor alone. In fact, some services, such as adoption, are used primarily by middle-class families. Eligibility for most personal social services is determined by citizenship or by definition of need based on attributes other than lack of income, rather than by means testing. Again, unlike many other social services, personal social services

—adoptions, for example—are viewed positively and carry no stigma. Even for services that are not so positively regarded (e.g., suicide prevention or alcoholism counseling), there is greater sympathy for the client or victim than for the poor person who must accept AFDC benefits.

Personal social services, perhaps more than even AFDC, are dominated by professional social workers. As a consequence, these programs can appear formidable to a poorly educated potential client. It may, in fact, be virtually impossible for the poor or the poorly educated to use these programs effectively. This, in turn, may mean that additional economic benefits may have to be provided when more personal counseling might have been sufficient. Then, in terms of policy analysis, there may be a situation in which too much of one service (AFDC or other means-tested benefits) is being provided as a substitute for a less expensive, and ultimately superior, service.

Private Social Programs

Finally, we should point out that although most Americans tend to think about social programs as benefits provided directly by government, a large number of social benefits are conferred by the private sector, usually with the indirect support of government. Take, for example, pensions. We discussed earlier the very large and important program for public pensions provided through the Social Security Administration. There are also a huge number of private pensions—some 61.8 million workers in 1991 had pension rights through their employers, and millions of others had purchased private annuities or contributed to individual retirement accounts. Even many ordinary workers have pension rights through their employers, through their unions, or through their own savings and investments.

The federal government supports these private social benefits in at least two ways. First, an employee can deduct from his or her taxable income most contributions made to these programs, and the contributions made by the employer are not taxable until the employee begins to receive the pension. In addition, the federal government now supervises and guarantees pensions through the Pension Benefit Guaranty Corporation, much as it does bank deposits through the Federal Deposit Insurance Corporation. Given that the majority of recipients of these private programs are members of the middle class, these supports amount to a major social benefit for that segment of the population. Much the same pattern of economic distribution holds true for federal support for private medical insurance, disability insurance, and owner-occupied housing through the tax system.

Conclusion

The disjuncture between the poor and the nonpoor is not evident in Social

Security, but it is in almost all other elements of social policy in the United States—and in most other countries as well.[78] Especially in the United States, this dual pattern makes the politics of social policy very difficult for reformers. The political struggle quickly is translated into a conflict of "us versus them," or between the "haves" and the "have nots." This struggle is exacerbated when the economy is not growing and any benefits granted the poor are perceived as directly reducing the standard of living of the middle classes.

The social services are composed of a large number of rather diverse programs. What holds them together is an overriding concern with individual needs and conditions, some economic and some personal. The programs that have been tried and that are still in operation represent attempts on the part of government to improve the conditions of its citizens, although the programs in operation by no means represent entirely satisfactory solutions to the problems. Many of the programs are as unpopular with their clients as they are with the taxpayers who fund them. This chapter has pointed to some ways of modifying existing programs, as well as some more sweeping changes in program structure that may benefit both government and program clients. The problems will not go away; if anything, the 1980s and 1990s have brought increasing demands for services, especially for the elderly and the homeless. What must be found is a means of providing adequate benefits through a humane mechanism that will not bankrupt the taxpayers. This is no easy task, but it is one that policymakers must address.

The emerging international market and its effects on wages, earnings, and employment will place even greater pressures on social policy in the United States. One of the enduring problems of social policy in the United States likely to be exacerbated by internationalization is the number of people who work and work full-time but who still earn wages that keep them in poverty. Further, if average real wages continue to fall as they have, then the amount of money available to fund retirement benefits will also decrease, and financial pressures on Social Security will increase. After at least a decade of neglect, it may be time for some serious analysis and reform of social policy.

Notes

1. See Harold Wilensky, *The Welfare State and Equality* (Berkeley: University of California Press, 1975), 32–36. For a different view, see Theodore R. Marmor, Jerry L. Mashaw, and Philip L. Harvey, *America's Misunderstood Welfare State* (New York: Basic Books, 1990).

2. For one analysis, see Fred Englander and John Kane, "Reagan's Welfare Reforms: Were the Program Savings Realized?" *Policy Studies Review* 11

(1992): 3–23.

3. In 1991 welfare was 10.2 percent of federal social expenditure and 4.7 percent of total federal expenditure. It was 11.4 percent of total social expenditure and 4.8 percent of total public expenditure.

4. Donald O. Parsons and Douglas R. Munro, "Intergenerational Transfers in Social Security," in *The Crisis in Social Security*, ed. Michael J. Boskin (San Francisco: Institute for Contemporary Studies, 1977), 65–86.

5. Self-employed persons pay a rate equal to the combined sum of contributions of employers and employees.

6. This separation of pensions and other social insurance benefits from general taxation is unusual in the rest of the world. See Margaret S. Gordon, *Social Security Policies in Industrial Countries: A Comparative Analysis* (Cambridge, England: Cambridge University Press, 1990).

7. Michael D. Hurd and John B. Shoven, "The Distributional Impact of Social Security," in *Pensions, Labor and Individual Choice*, ed. David Wise (Chicago: University of Chicago Press, 1985).

8. The actual determination of taxability is somewhat more complicated. See David Pattison and David E. Harrington, "Proposals to Modify the Taxation of Social Security Benefits: Options and Distributional Effects," *Social Security Bulletin* 56 (Summer 1993): 3–13.

9. This program, like so many, has been "path dependent," and its initial formulation has largely determined its development. See Ellen Immergut, *Health Policy* (Cambridge, England: Cambridge University Press, 1991).

10. Joseph Bondar, "Beneficiaries Affected by the Annual Earnings Test, 1989," *Social Security Bulletin* 56 (Spring 1993): 20–34.

11. C. Eugene Steurle and Jon M. Bakija, *Retooling Social Security for the 21st Century* (Washington, D.C.: Urban Institute Press, 1994), 220.

12. Social Security Agency, Office of the Actuary, *Life Tables for the United States Social Security Area, 1900–2080* (Baltimore, Md.: SSA, 1992).

13. There has been a tendency for people to retire earlier, especially for the more affluent who have retirement incomes in addition to Social Security.

14. Steuerle and Bakija, *Retooling Social Security for the 21st Century*, 97.

15. Deborah Stone, *The Disabled State* (Philadelphia: Temple University Press, 1985).

16. Bernadyne Weatherford, "The Disability Insurance Program: An Administrative Attack on the Welfare State," in *The Attack on the Welfare State*, ed. Anthony Champagne and Edward J. Harpham (Prospect Heights, Ill.: Waveland Press, 1984).

17. General Accounting Office, *Social Security Disability: SSA Needs to Improve Continuing Disability Review Program*, GAO/HRD-93-109 (Washington, D.C.: GAO, July 1993).

18. "Workers' Compensation," *Social Security Bulletin* 56 (Winter 1993): 28–31.

19. The maximum payment in Connecticut is $737 per week, while that in Georgia is $225 per week.

20. For a review, see George F. Break, "The Economic Effects of Social Se-

curity Financing," in *Social Security Financing,* ed. Felicity Skidmore (Cambridge, Mass.: MIT Press, 1981), 45–80.

21. For a detailed analysis, see Henry J. Aaron, Barry P. Bosworth, and Gary Burtless, *Can America Afford to Grow Old? Paying for Social Security* (Washington, D.C.: Brookings Institution, 1989), 55–75.

22. Practical politics prevented President Reagan from doing anything to reduce Social Security benefits. See Paul E. Peterson and Mark Rom, "Lower Taxes, More Spending, and Budget Deficits," in *The Reagan Legacy,* ed. Charles O. Jones (Chatham, N.J.: Chatham House, 1988), 224–25.

23. Jonathan Rauch, "False Security," *National Journal,* 14 February 1987, 362–65.

24. Aaron, Bosworth, and Burtless, *Can America Afford to Grow Old?*

25. U.S. Board of Trustees of the Federal Old-Age, Survivors and Disability Insurance Trust Funds, *Annual Report, 1993* (Washington, D.C.: Government Printing Office, 1993).

26. Linda E. Demkovich, "Budget Cutters Think the Unthinkable—Social Security Cuts Would Stem Red Ink," *National Journal,* 23 June 1984.

27. Ibid.

28. As noted, the health insurance component of the payroll tax (1.45 percent) is applied to all income.

29. Break, "Economic Effects of Social Security Financing."

30. See B. Guy Peters, *The Politics of Taxation* (Oxford: Blackwell, 1992).

31. Charles E. McClure, "VAT versus the Payroll Tax," in Skidmore, *Social Security Financing.*

32. R. Shep Melnick, *Between the Lines* (Washington, D.C.: Brookings Institution, 1994).

33. Most of these critics are on the political right, e.g., Charles Murray, *Losing Ground* (New York: Basic Books, 1984) and his "Stop Favoring Welfare Mothers," *New York Times,* 16 January 1992; and Lawrence M. Mead, *The New Politics of Poverty* (New York: Basic Books, 1992). There are, however, critics on the left, for example, David T. Ellwood, *Poor Support: Poverty and the American Family* (New York: Basic Books, 1988); Frances Fox Piven and Richard Cloward, *Regulating the Poor,* 2d ed. (New York: Vintage Books, 1993).

34. Penelope Lemov, "Putting Welfare on the Clock," *Governing,* November 1993, 29–30.

35. Edwin W. Witte, *The Development of the Social Security Act* (Madison: University of Wisconsin Press, 1962), 5–39.

36. Julie Kosterlitz, "Behavior Modification," *National Journal,* 1 February 1992, 271–75.

37. Ibid.

38. Kevin Sack, "Fingerprinting Allowed in Welfare Fraud Fight," *New York Times,* 9 July 1994.

39. Julie Kosterlitz, "Reworking Welfare," *National Journal,* 26 September 1992.

40. Paul E. Peterson and Mark E. Rom, *Welfare Magnets: A New Case for a National Standard* (Washington, D.C.: Brookings Institution, 1990).

41. Cited in Isaac Shapiro et al., *The States and the Poor* (Washington, D.C.: Center on Budget and Policy Priorities, December 1991), 8.

42. Michael Wiseman, "Research and Policy: A Symposium on the Family Support Act of 1988," *Journal of Policy Analysis and Management* 10 (1991): 588–89.

43. Kay E. Sherwood and David A. Long, "JOBS Implementation in an Uncertain Environment," *Public Welfare* 49 (1991): 17–27.

44. This problem will, of course, be rectified if the Clinton plan, or any other plan, for universal health insurance is passed.

45. Sherwood and Long, "JOBS Implementation in an Uncertain Environment," 17–27.

46. Sheila Kammerman and Alfred Kahn, "Universalism and Testing in Family Policy: New Perspectives on an Old Debate," *Social Work* 32 (1987): 277–80.

47. Hermione Parker, *Instead of the Dole: An Enquiry into the Integration of Tax and Benefit Systems* (London: Routledge, 1989).

48. M. Kenneth Bowler, *The Nixon Guaranteed Income Proposal: Substance and Process in Policy Change* (Cambridge, Mass.: Ballinger, 1974).

49. For different views, see Lawrence J. Mead, "The New Politics of New Poverty," *Public Interest* 103 (Spring 1991): 3–20; Richard A. Cloward and Frances Fox Piven, "The Fraud of Workfare," *Nation* 256 (24 May 1993): 693–96.

50. General Accounting Office, *Workfare Programs*, GAO-PEMD-84-2 (Washington, D.C.: General Accounting Office, 2 April 1984).

51. Richard P. Nathan, *Turning Promises into Performance: The Management Challenge of Implementing Workfare* (New York: Columbia University Press, 1993).

52. Irwin Garfinkel, Sara S. McLanahan, and Philip K. Robins, *Child Support and Child Well-Being* (Washington, D.C.: Urban Institute Press, 1994).

53. General Accounting Office, *Child Support Assurance: Effects of Applying State Guidelines to Determine Fathers' Payments*, GAO/HRD-93-26 (Washington, D.C.: GAO, January 1993).

54. Nadine Cohodas, "Child Support: No More Pretty Please," *Governing*, October 1993, 20–21.

55. Mimi Hall, "Child Support: States Pay If Parents Don't," *USA Today*, 28 March 1994.

56. For a general discussion of employment policy, see Margaret Weir, *Politics and Jobs* (Princeton: Princeton University Press, 1992).

57. Robert B. Reich, *The Work of Nations: Preparing for 21st Century Capitalism* (New York: Knopf, 1991).

58. General Accounting Office, *Multiple Employment Training Programs: Conflicting Requirements Hamper Delivery of Services*, GAO/HEHS-94-78 (Washington, D.C.: GAO, January 1994).

59. Sar A. Levitan, *The Great Society's Poor Law: A New Approach to Poverty* (Baltimore: Johns Hopkins University Press, 1969).

60. Some later research, however, is finding some latent effects of Head

Start, much like the the "sleeper effects" described in chapter 7. See William Celis III, "Study Suggests Head Start Helps beyond School," *New York Times,* 20 April 1993.

61. Richard Rose and B. Guy Peters, *Can Government Go Bankrupt?* (New York: Basic Books, 1978).

62. At least one state has already done so. See "In Maine, No Child Support, No Driving," *New York Times,* 28 June 1994.

63. Jason DeParle, "Clinton Plan Seeking Welfare Costing $6 Billion a Year," *New York Times,* 10 March 1994.

64. Calculated at a 40-hour week for 50 weeks per year.

65. Rochelle L. Stanfield, "Valuing the Family," *National Journal,* 4 July 1992, 1562–66.

66. Lawrence M. Mead, *The New Politics of Poverty: The Nonworking Poor in America* (New York: Basic Books, 1992).

67. For a more recent view, see Michael Harrington, *The New American Poverty* (New York: Holt, Rinehart and Winston, 1984).

68. Paul Starobin, "Unequal Shares," *National Journal,* 11 September 1993, 2176–79.

69. Sar Levitan, Frank Gallo, and Isaac Shapiro, *Working but Poor: America's Contradiction,* rev. ed. (Baltimore: Johns Hopkins University Press, 1993).

70. Ibid., 99–125.

71. Patricia Ruggles, *Drawing the Line: Alternative Poverty Measures and Their Implications for Public Policy* (Washington, D.C.: Urban Institute Press, 1990).

72. John L. Palmer, Timothy Smeeding, and Barbara Boyle Torrey, eds., *The Vulnerable* (Washington, D.C.: Urban Institute Press, 1988).

73. Marybeth Shinn and Colleen Gillespie, "The Roles of Housing and Poverty in the Origins of Homelessness," *American Behavioral Scientist* 37 (1994): 505–21.

74. Ann Braden Johnson, *Out of Bedlam: The Truth about Deinstitutionalization* (New York: Basic Books, 1990).

75. General Accounting Office, *Homelessness: McKinney Act Programs Provide Assistance but Are Not Designed to Be the Solution,* GAO/RCED-94-37 (Washington, D.C.: GAO, May 1994).

76. Ibid.

77. Peter Steinfels, "Apathy Is Seen toward Agony of Homeless," *New York Times,* 20 January 1992.

78. Martin Rein and Lee Rainwater, *Public-Private Interplay in Social Service Provision* (Armonk, N.Y.: M.E. Sharpe, 1988).

11. Educational Policy in the United States

Education traditionally has had a central position in American public policies. Although the United States as a nation has been slow to adopt other social programs—pensions, unemployment insurance, national health insurance, and the like—we have always been among the world leaders in public education. It is true that most public involvement in education has been at the state and local levels and that the federal government has become directly involved in elementary and secondary education only relatively recently. In the 1990s, however, the federal government has become a major actor in educational policy at all levels and exerts its influence through direct expenditures as well as through a variety of indirect instruments. Also, in the 1990s the adequacy of American education has come into question, as American students perform at or near the bottom of international standardized tests, and poor education has become identified as a major problem in American economic competitiveness.[1]

The public role in education began very early in the United States, with the State of New York adopting free public education in 1834. Education later was made compulsory in all states until a student reached a certain age (this provision was temporarily revoked in some southern states as a means of avoiding racial integration). Even in the early years of the Republic the federal government had some role in education. The Northwest Ordinance of 1787, in planning the organization of the Northwest Territories of the United States, divided the land into townships and the townships into sections. One of the sixteen sections in every township was to be set aside for supporting free common education. Following that, in 1862 Congress passed the Morrill Act, granting land and a continuing appropriation of federal funds to establish and maintain in each state a college dedicated to teaching "agriculture and mechanical arts." From this act grew the system of land-grant colleges that has produced such major educational institutions as Cornell, Texas A&M, and the Universities of Wisconsin, Illinois, and Minnesota. The research and extension activities of these institutions have been important for the expansion of American agricultural productivity in addition to their broader educational activities.

In the 1990s the federal government has a large-scale involvement in education.[2] In 1992 the federal government spent $61.4 billion on education. This appears to be a huge amount of money, but education is actually a smaller percentage (4.4) of total federal spending than it had been in 1980 (5.8 percent). In addition to the amount of money being spent, a wide variety of federal organizations provide assistance for education. In 1992 all cabinet departments except one (Commerce) had some involvement with education, as did a variety of federal agencies such as the National Science Foundation, the National Aeronautics and Space Agency, and the Agency for International Development.

There have been several important tendencies in American education and educational policy. First, the emphasis on education is indicative of the general attitude the United States has taken toward social mobility and social change, the belief that education is important because it gives people "chances not checks."[3] The prevailing American ethos is that government should attempt to create equal opportunity through education rather than equal outcomes through social expenditure programs. Individuals who have the ability are presumed to be able to better their circumstances through education and to succeed no matter what their social or economic backgrounds may have been. It is perhaps important to note here that, despite the evils of segregation, blacks in the South prior to *Brown* v. *Board of Education* were given access to public schools and public educational opportunities through the Ph.D. degree. One cannot realistically argue that the opportunities were at all equal, but education was more easily available to blacks than might be expected, given their social status in those states. The norms of educational opportunity appeared to cover even social groups that were systematically discriminated against.

Related to the role of education in social mobility is the importance of American public schools for social integration and assimilation. The United States has absorbed a huge number of immigrants, 8 million of whom arrived in the first decade of the twentieth century alone. The institution that was most important in bringing those new arrivals into the mainstream of American life was the public school system. This was certainly true for adults who learned English and civics in "Americanism" classes in the evenings. Also important in this regard is that the public schools in the United States traditionally taught all the children living in the community. Only a very few wealthy families sent their children to private schools; everyone else in the community went to the same school, often all the way through their elementary and secondary years.[4] The tradition of comprehensive schools that provided a variety of educational opportunities, from college preparatory through vocational, was important in reinforcing the ideology of a classless society and in at least promoting social homogeneity, if not achieving it.

The 1980s and 1990s also have been period of large-scale immigration to the United States, and the public schools continue to play a role in assimilating the children of millions of new Americans. But the social and economic realities of the 1980s and 1990s appear to have broken down some of the homogenizing impact of the public schools, and education has become increasingly segregated, ethnically and economically.[5] To some degree this lack of homogenization has been by choice, as "multiculturalism" has become one of the rallying cries for those who want a more diverse society and a more diverse educational system to support that society.[6] Deciding just how to manage increasing diversity of the society and still meet the educational needs of all segments of the society is one of the major questions now facing American education.

Despite the centrality of public education at the elementary and secondary levels, there has never been a state monopoly on education. Existing alongside the public schools were religious schools (almost 10 percent of the elementary students in the United States in 1994 attended parochial schools) and other private schools. This diversity is especially evident in postsecondary education, with 22 percent of all college students attending private institutions.[7] Almost anyone can open a school, provided it meets the standards set by government or other accrediting bodies. If anything, the diversity of options for students in American education has been increasing over the past several decades. The sense that the public schools are not doing an adequate job of education has spawned a variety of new educational providers, ranging from very strict schools concentrating on the "Three Rs" to unstructured attempts to promote greater creativity and free exploration of ideas.

Finally, the emphasis in governance has always been on local and parental control in American education. Of all the major social functions of government, education is the one clearly retaining the greatest degree of local control and local funding. In fact, the largest single category of public employment in the United States is made up of public school teachers employed by local governments. And the control that government exercises over education is often local. There are 14,741 local school boards in the United States, as well as 22,000 counties and cities that frequently have a substantial role to play in providing public education. Despite all those opportunities for local political action, there have been pressures for even greater local control and parental involvement. These pressures have come from white suburbanites, inner-city minority parents, and ideologues, all of whom believe that the public schools should be doing things differently.

Although the local school has traditionally been a positive symbol of local government and the community, there are now a number of doubts about education and pressures for change. These problems are to some degree reflected in the evaluation Americans give their schools. When asked to grade schools, respondents to national polls have tended to give their own community schools a grade of C, while they give schools nationally a very low C—barely passing (table 11.1). It should be noted, however, that parents with children in public schools have substantially higher evaluations of public schools than do people with no children in school or with children in private schools. The negative feelings about public schools are reinforced by numerous findings that American students do not do as well on standardized tests as do students in Western Europe, Korea, or Japan. The perceived problems, and the proposed reforms to deal with the problems, are discussed later in this chapter.

TABLE 11.1
PUBLIC'S GRADES FOR PUBLIC EDUCATION,
1974–93

	School in own community	Schools nationally		School in own community	Schools nationally
1974	2.63	—	1984	2.36	2.09
1975	2.38	—	1985	2.39	2.14
1976	2.38	—	1986	2.36	2.13
1977	2.33	—	1987	2.44	2.18
1978	2.21	—	1988	2.40	2.10
1979	2.21	—	1989	2.35	2.02
1980	2.26	—	1990	2.44	2.11
1981	2.20	1.94	1991	2.47	2.08
1982	2.24	2.01	1992	2.41	2.01
1983	2.12	1.91	1993	2.37	2.05

SOURCE: *Phi Delta Kappan,* annual.
NOTE: 4.0 = A; 3.0 = B; 2.0 = C; 1.0 = D; <1.0 = F.

The Federal Government's Role in Education

It does not make a great deal of sense to discuss the public role in education, as most education is public, but it is important to describe the role of the federal government. The involvement of the federal government in education has been controversial, and it was thought that the Reagan administration might further reduce federal involvement. Reagan's first secretary of education, Terrel Bell, came into office pledging to dismantle the then newly created Department of Education. But the need for improved education and educational funding became more apparent as the four years of the first Reagan administration progressed, and not only was the Department of Education saved, but some new initiatives for improving American education were launched under its sponsorship.

President Reagan's second secretary of education, William Bennett, appeared to reverse the initial direction of the administration and launched a federal effort to improve what he considered to be the deplorable state of American education. That campaign was based on one individual's view of good education—largely a highly structured curriculum stressing basic skills and the canon of Western civilization.[8] The campaign was carried on more with rhetoric than resources, but it did point to the importance of national educational policy in a postindustrial and highly competitive world. By most objective indicators, however, the quality of education did not improve under Bennett's leadership.

The Bush Administration

George Bush campaigned in 1988 as the "education president." That campaign pledge was vague, and the first several years of his administration provided little clarification for its meaning. He promoted several spending programs for magnet schools and rewards for schools that improved student achievement, but until 1991 very little happened with education policy. The issue of education remained an important one nationally, and the apparent ineffectiveness of President Bush's first appointee as secretary of education produced a relatively early change at that position. The immense federal budget deficit and the generally conservative nature of the Bush administration did not permit any substantial federal financial involvement in education during the first half of the administration, despite pleas from state and local officials for assistance. The Bush administration advocated better education for the United States at every possibility but did relatively little to provide local school districts with additional resources to meet those educational goals.

In 1991 President Bush unveiled a plan in an attempt to meet his campaign pledges on education. An ambitious plan, entitled *America 2000: An Education Strategy,* was unveiled by the president and his then new secretary of education, Lamar Alexander. This plan had four major elements:

1. *National testing.* Unlike competency testing (see pp. 340-41), the national tests proposed were to be diagnostic and public. This would

enable communities to judge how well their local schools were doing and exert political pressure for better education. The scores on the tests (in principle voluntary) could also be used by prospective employers, thereby pressing both students and schools to do better.

2. *New schools.* The federal government would fund 535 new schools (one for each congressman and senator) that would serve as models of what could be done with public education. Federal funding was to be supplemented by funds from business so that the new schools could "break the mold" of existing educational programs.

3. *Improving teachers.* "America 2000" included several recommendations for improving the quality of the teachers in America's schools. These included merit pay and alternative means of certifying competency for teaching, especially in subjects such as mathematics and science.

4. *Choice.* Consistent with the market-oriented philosophy of many Republicans, President Bush proposed that more of a market in education be created, so parents would have more opportunity to choose and schools would feel more pressure to perform. This is one of many ideas about promoting choice in education (see pp. 337–40).

The Clinton Administration

Education, unlike health reform and welfare reform, was not a central element of President Clinton's campaign for office. But he and his administration have not ignored the need for addressing the educational needs of the society. For the first year of Clinton's administration, education policy had three principal concerns. One was the role of education in economic competitiveness and in sustaining the place of the United States in the world economy. A second concern was the role of education in coping with the social and economic disparities that exist within the United States. Finally, the administration was concerned with early childhood education and sought to increase funding for programs such as Head Start.[9]

Several major pieces of legislation are indicative of the Clinton administration's approach to education issues.[10] One of the first is Goals 2000, a linear descendant of the Bush administration's education efforts. This is a broad-scale reform act promoting state and local level efforts for improving American education and making it equal to that in other industrialized democracies. The administration also advocated the School-to-Work Opportunities Act, intended to strengthen the vocational and technical education available to students who do not go on to college. Finally, the administration has advocated the reauthorization of the 1965 Elementary and Secondary Education Act, the major source ($10 billion) of federal support for education.

The School-to-Work Opportunities Act is a major program for the Clinton administration. This program is an attempt to coordinate the activities of the Department of Education and the Department of Labor to enable those students who do not get a college degree (almost three-quarters of the total) to prepare themselves for good jobs. As well as being an educational program, this act is an attempt to cope with the global competitiveness problem. Implementation of this program will not be easy. It is to be implemented by state and local governments and will require cooperation between two bureaucracies that have not always seen eye to eye on how best to meet the education and training needs of the society.[11]

Local Financing and the Federal Role

We should discuss one aspect of local control in education because it contributes to the need for federal involvement. This is the funding of public education through the local property tax, the traditional means of financing education, which in the 1980s presented two significant problems. One is that property tax revenues have not generally kept pace with inflation (table 11.2). The administration of the property tax involves assessing the value of property and applying a rate of tax to the assessed value. In an inflationary period, assessments may not reflect the real value of the property, and certainly not the costs of goods and services, unless revaluation is done very frequently. Thus, many local school boards find that their funding is no longer adequate. The second problem is that even if there were no inflation, the tax base available to some school districts would be markedly different from that available to others. To provide the same quality of education, parents living in poorer districts would have to tax themselves at higher rates than would those living in more affluent areas. This is an extremely regressive way to finance a basic public service, as the poor have to pay a higher rate of tax to provide the same level of education.

The usual result of this pattern of funding is that the education provided to poorer children is not as good as that provided to wealthier students.[12] Thus, it is argued that the local property tax is an inequitable means of financing education and that some alternative, such as federal or state general revenues, should be used to equalize access to education. The federal contribution to educational funding has been declining slightly over the recent past (table 11.3), and although the states have taken up some of the slack, localities still must bear the major responsibility for funding education. As discussed later, the court system has already begun to bring about some changes in school finance in the direction of greater equality and greater state funding, but the inadequacy of local taxation remains an important reason for federal involvement in education.

TABLE 11.2

PROPERTY TAX REVENUES OF LOCAL GOVERNMENTS, 1960–91

(IN MILLIONS OF DOLLARS)

	Current	Real[a]	Percentage of total revenues
1960	15,798	17,851	47.8
1970	32,963	28,367	40.7
1975	50,040	31,061	34.2
1980	65,607	26,594	28.2
1985	99,772	32,825	28.2
1988	127,191	35,909	25.3
1990	149,765	38,116	29.2
1991	161,706	39,180	26.7

a. Converted to constant (1967) prices using consumer price index.

TABLE 11.3

SOURCES OF EDUCATIONAL FUNDING

(IN PERCENTAGES)

	1970	1980	1985	1990
Federal government	10.7	11.4	8.6	8.2
State governments	31.5	38.8	38.8	37.2
Local governments	32.1	26.1	25.6	27.1
All other	25.7	23.6	27.0	27.4

SOURCE: U.S. National Center for Educational Statistics, *Digest of Education Statistics*, annual.

Higher Education

It has traditionally been more acceptable for the federal government to be involved with higher education, perhaps because the students are almost adults and are assumed to have formed their basic value systems before the central government could influence them, or perhaps simply because of the higher per student expense. At any rate, the federal government began somewhat earlier to assist institutions of higher education than elementary schools. During the Lincoln administration the federal government initiated the land-grant college system that continues to receive substantial federal support, especially for its agricultural extension activities. The federal government also runs or supports several institutions of higher education of its own—the service academies, Gallaudet College (for the deaf), and Howard University. In addition to the direct funding of almost eighty colleges and universities, the federal government provides substantial indirect support for almost every college and university in the United States.

The major form of indirect federal subsidy for colleges and universities comes through the funding of individual students. These funding programs obviously benefit students directly, but without the federal funds many students could not attend college and many colleges might have to close. A variety of federal programs have aided students. The largest has been the GI Bill, enabling veterans of World War II, Korea, and, to a lesser extent, Vietnam to attend college with the government paying virtually all the costs. For nonveterans, one of the largest programs of student aid was also justified as a defense program—the National Defense Education Act. Passed in 1958, just after the Soviet Union launched *Sputnik I,* this act was intended to help the United States catch up in science, although students in the social sciences and foreign languages benefited as well. Federal assistance reached beyond defense-related concerns during the 1960s and 1970s. The college work-study program was adopted as part of the war on poverty but was moved from the Office of Economic Opportunity to the Office of Education and began to benefit a wider range of students. Likewise, the Education Amendments of 1972 instituted something approaching a minimum income for college students. The Basic Educational Opportunity Grant (or Pell grants), the centerpiece of the program, gave students $1,800 minus what the student's family could be expected to contribute, a figure later increased slightly to account for inflation. While this was not much money if the student wanted to attend Harvard or Yale, it provided the means to attend at least some institution of higher education. In the 1990s Pell grants have been subject to considerably stricter eligibility requirements and lower levels of funding for each student.

The federal government also assists students by guaranteeing student loans (Stafford loans) and even providing some student loans for very-low-income students (Perkins loans). The guaranteed loans are particularly important because they allow government to leverage a great deal of private money for students in higher education with minimal direct federal outlays. The federal government agrees to guarantee a private lending institution that the money the institution lends a student will be repaid even if the student reneges—as many have reneged. In turn, the money is offered to the student at a lower interest rate than would otherwise be available, and repayment does not have to begin until after the student leaves higher education. The failure of many students to repay their loans and the fraudulent use of the loans by some trade schools (whose students are also eligible for loans) have brought this program into question, but it remains a major source of funding for students in higher education; some 5.5 million received some benefit from the guaranteed loan program in 1993, with an average loan of $2,960.

All the above-mentioned programs benefit primarily students entering college just out of high school. One federal program benefits more mature students. The provisions of the income tax code that provide student deductions if students go to school to maintain or improve their job skills support a variety of trade and technical schools as well as academic institutions. Although the university never sees the money, this program stimulates attendance, especially among a segment of the population that might not otherwise attend college. There have been calls to extend the deductibility of college fees to the parents of college students, in addition to the other tax expenditures for education, amounting to $3.8 billion in 1990. That plea has not been successful. In the first place, it would be an expensive benefit going to middle-class parents in a time of tight budgets; second, it would seem to contradict the thrust of tax reform in the 1980s (see pp. 228-31) toward a simpler tax system with fewer "loopholes."

Finally, the federal government supports higher education in other ways—for example, by providing aid for facilities through the Higher Education Facilities Act of 1963 and for dormitories through the Department of Housing and Urban Development. Federal research money (almost $10.5 billion in 1988) helps institutions of higher education meet both direct and indirect costs and offers specialized grant programs for such fields as public service and urban studies. In short, the federal government is central to the maintenance of American higher education. But the large amounts of federal money invested in higher education give the federal government a substantial amount of control over the policies of the universities. This has been manifested primarily through controls over the hiring of women and members of minority groups as faculty members. In the *Grove City College* case,[13] however, the Supreme Court diminished the influence of the federal government to some degree in ensuring greater equality in higher education programs. Before that decision, if a college was found to be discriminating, all its federal money could be withdrawn. In its 1984 ruling the Court found that only money directly supporting the activity in which the discrimination occurred could be withdrawn. So, for example, if discrimination was found in the programs covered by Title IX (athletics and student activities), the government could not withdraw money from student support or from federal research grants.

Given the generally conservative policies of the Bush administration, that discrimination was not pursued vigorously either by the Department of Education or the Department of Justice. In fact, one member of the administration argued against scholarships being given on the basis of race to needy students even in private institutions, although he was forced to recant that position. Later the administration offered a more moderate plan to eliminate most race-specific scholarship aid.[14] This has to some extent been modified by the Clinton administration with a more vigorous program of affirmative action and attempts to improve the status of minority populations.

Since 1980, federal funding for higher education students has not fared well. The Reagan administration cut back on federal support for higher education. The base level of the Pell grant was cut by $80 and income restrictions were tightened. This resulted in approximately 100,000 fewer Pell grant recipients in 1983 than in 1981. There was also a drop of some 460,000 in the number of new guaranteed student loans. There were reductions in federal funding of social science and humanities research through cuts in the budgets of the National Science Foundation and the National Endowment for the Humanities. Clearly the policy of the Reagan administration was that higher education is primarily a state and local government function, if government is to be involved at all, and that the federal government should be only minimally involved.

The Bush administration reversed that basic policy thrust of lower federal support only slightly. The general commitment of the Bush administration to education was manifested in a somewhat more supportive attitude and increased funding for programs such as the National Science Foundation. Education was argued to have been a central priority in the Bush administration, although the flow of federal funds was only slightly improved over that in the Reagan administration.[15]

The Clinton administration has reversed that trend somewhat, but has had to face severe budget restraints as well as attempt to fund a variety of other policy priorities such as welfare and health reform. The Clinton budget has allocated more money to education including funds for the National Service Corps, "Americorps."

Elementary and Secondary Education

The role of the federal government in secondary and elementary education has been less significant historically and is less significant today than its involvement in higher education. Nevertheless, there is definitely a federal role in precollegiate education. Other than the planning provisions of the Northwest Ordinance, the first involvement of the federal government in elementary and secondary education resulted from the passage of the Smith-Hughes Act (1917), which made funds available for vocational education. In the 1930s surplus commodities and money were provided to school districts for hot lunch programs, with those programs expanded during the war on poverty to include breakfasts for children from poor families. Then the Lanham

Act of 1940 made federal funds available to schools in "federally impacted areas," which was understood to mean areas with large numbers of government employees and especially areas in which tax-exempt government properties reduced the tax base used to fund education. In 1958 the National Defense Education Act authorized funds to improve science, mathematics, and foreign language teaching in the elementary and secondary schools as well as at the college level.

The major involvement of the federal government in elementary and secondary education currently is through the Elementary and Secondary Education Act of 1965. This act was the culmination of efforts of a number of education and labor groups to secure more extensive federal funding for education.[16] The legislation was passed along with a number of other social and educational programs during the Johnson administration, and like so much of that legislation, it could not have been passed without the substantial legislative skills of Lyndon Johnson and the memory of John Kennedy. But before it could become law, legislators had to remove the barriers that had blocked previous attempts at federal aid to education.

One of these barriers was the general belief that education should be controlled locally. The federal aid that had already been given to schools had been peripheral to the principal teaching functions of the schools—the exception being the National Defense Education Act—in the belief that such aid could not influence what was taught in the classroom. The Elementary and Secondary Education Act (ESEA) involved direct, general subsidies for education, and it was feared that this would influence what was taught. But as the federal government became increasingly involved in many aspects of education and social life through other mechanisms, such as the courts, this fear of federal control diminished.

Another issue that arose with respect to federal subsidies to education was the question of funds for parochial schools. Such aid involved constitutional questions about the separation of church and state. Most Protestant groups opposed aid to parochial schools as a violation of that separation, while Catholic groups opposed any aid program that did not provide assistance to parochial schools. ESEA funds eventually went to parochial as well as public schools, although the money could not be spent for teaching religious subjects. The legislation specified that the money was to go to the students, not to the schools, which helped defuse any significant criticism based on separation of church and state.

Federal aid to education also encountered opposition before the 1965 act because of the possibility that the money might be used by segregated school systems in the South. The passage of the Civil Rights Act of 1964 had already prohibited the use of federal funds in any program that discriminated on the basis of race. This provision meant that this issue was largely decided by the time the 1965 legislation was considered. On the other side, southern school systems had been afraid that federal subsidies would be used to enforce desegregation, using a carrot instead of a stick. Nevertheless, these school systems were already under pressure from the courts to desegregate, and so the acceptance of ESEA money was to be a minor additional step toward their eventual desegregation.

The 1965 ESEA legislation was passed as a component of the war on poverty, but as implemented it provided assistance to almost all school districts in the United States. Only 5 percent of all school districts in the country received no ESEA money.[17] The legislation provided funds for hiring teachers' aides, stocking libraries, purchasing audiovisual materials, and developing compensatory programs. The basic intention of the program was to enable students from poor families to perform better in school and to learn to compete more effectively in the labor market.

Federal funds from ESEA were allocated to the states according to a formula, as is true of a number of federal programs. The formula adopted for ESEA in 1965 allocated each state federal funds equal to one-half of its annual per pupil educational expenditure multiplied by the number of low-income children. These funds were to be used for remedial programs (Title I) and to purchase materials, but the principal policymaking and programming were to come from the federal government rather than from the local school boards. The 1965 formula aided the high-income states more than the low-income states, as it was based on the amount of money already being spent. This formula quickly came under attack and was amended in 1967 to provide greater assistance to the poorer states. Under the 1967 formula a state could receive half of its own per pupil expenditures or half of the national mean per pupil expenditure, whichever was higher. Also, the definition of low-income students was eased so that school districts could claim more students and receive more federal funding. These 1967 amendments had the effect of equalizing funding between richer and poorer states and of producing rapid increases in ESEA expenditures.

During the Nixon administration the categorical nature of the funds allocated through ESEA came under severe attack, as a part of the "new federalism."[18] Efforts to convert ESEA funding into another of the block grants that characterized that administration's approach to federal grants did not succeed, however, and the federal government retained nominal control over the ways in which money was to be spent. What did change was the formula for computing aid. In 1974 a new formula was adopted that put both rich and poor states at a disadvantage, as measured by their per pupil expenditures. It narrowed the range of allowable per pupil grant funds from 80 to 120 percent of the national mean. In other words, the very wealthy states could claim only 120 percent of the national average per low-income pupil when computing aid, while the very poor states could claim only 80 percent of the national average (not the national average). And instead of receiving 50 percent of the per pupil figure, the states could receive only 40 percent. These changes reduced the amount a state would probably receive from ESEA funding, although amendments to the legislation did specify that no state would receive less than 85 percent of what it had received under the previous formula.

As with so many public programs, implementation was crucial to the success of the ESEA programs. And in many ways ESEA represents a classic example of a program being modified through implementation. The U.S. Office of Education, which was charged with implementing ESEA, was quite passive in ensuring the attainment of the stated goal of the program: the equalization of educational opportunity for economically deprived children. The tendency of those who implemented the program at state and local levels was to pork-barrel the funds and spread them around among all school districts, regardless of the concentration of low-income students. As a result, wealthier suburban school districts used ESEA funds to purchase expensive "frills," while many inner-city and rural school districts still lacked basic materials and programs that might compensate for the backgrounds of the pupils.[19] This initial failure in implementation resulted in part from the close ties between the U.S. Office of Education and local school districts and in part from the misinterpretation of the intention of Congress, which had established the program, not as general assistance to education, but strictly as a compensatory program. With some changes in the Office of Education and greater concern about the use of the funds, the implementation of ESEA has been improved, although a number of questions remain about the ways in which the funds are being used. The Title I money, or that portion of the program that is most directly compensatory, is now targeted more clearly on the poorer districts, but the money available under other provisions of the act is still widely distributed and used by much wealthier schools and school districts to supplement their programs.

The Reagan administration returned federal aid to education to a more compensatory focus through a reauthorization of ESEA in the Education Consolidation and Improvement Act (ECIA) of 1981. The act supports compensatory education for deprived students in virtually all school districts but, unlike the bulk of ESEA funding, is concentrated in school districts with the most poor children. This act also supports education for the handicapped, adult education, and aid for school districts heavily impacted by federal installations with large numbers of children to be educated. ECIA now accounts for about 80 percent of federal aid to elementary and secondary education, with the remainder primarily in a block grant to state and local governments for educational purposes.

In addition to the impact of the federal government on education through its spending programs, it also has a substantial impact through numerous regulations and mandates. Among the most important of the legal mandates is the Education for All Handicapped Children Act of 1975, which mandated that all handicapped or "exceptional" students be educated in a manner suitable to their special needs. This legislation was intended primarily to assist children with learning disabilities and physical handicaps in receiving education through the public schools. The meaning of the act, however, has been extended to include educationally gifted children, so school districts are now required to provide a variety of special programs for a variety of different students. Bilingual education has also been mandated in same circumstances for minority students. All these programs add to the costs of providing public education, but impose most of the costs on state and local governments.

Has all this federal aid to education and regulation of education really improved the quality of American education? There is some evidence that ESEA Title I reading programs have been successful in raising the reading levels of low-income students.[20] Further, to the extent that additional funding can aid education in any number of ways, some of which are difficult to quantify, these programs have certainly produced benefits. It is ironic, however, that in spite of all the federal money directed at improving the quality of education ($7 billion in 1984), the issue of the quality of American education is as prominent in the 1990s as at any time since the launching of *Sputnik I* in 1957. As was true then, many of the issues concern education in science, mathematics, and engineering. The difference is that in the 1990s the perceived need is to improve competitiveness against the Japanese and West Europeans rather than to protect the country against a perceived Soviet military threat. In the new competition, there is a strong sense that education is failing and that the American workforce is decreasingly capable of competing. Some of the blame for these failures is placed on families that do not nurture students sufficiently, some on the students themselves, but a great deal of the blame is directed at the public schools.

Issues of Educational Policy

Even with the victory of advocates of federal funding for elementary and secondary education, a number of problems remain in public education, and some new ones are arising. In general, the public schools and their teachers have lost some of the respect with which they were traditionally regarded, and educational policy has been the subject of more heated discussion than was true during most of our history. In fact, it is not uncommon for politicians or analysts in the 1990s to charge that the public schools have failed and to call for significant change. President Bush's program for improving the schools was but one statement of this sentiment. Some would counter this argument by pointing out that it is perhaps not so much that the schools have failed but that too much has been demanded of them and that the schools cannot be expected to solve all of society's problems. These analysts would argue that the resources and tasks given the schools have not been equal and that too much has been expected for too little money. Several specific issues illustrate both sides of this argument, but what may be most important is that education, which has been regarded as one of the great success stories of American public policy, is no longer considered quite so successful.

Quality of Education

One common complaint against the schools that has continued since the 1950s is that "Johnny can't read"—that is, that the schools are failing in their fundamental task of teaching basic skills such as reading, writing, and computation. In addition to reading, this criticism has extended to such progressive teaching techniques as the "new math." Substantial evidence that would appear to support this point includes the continuing decline of SAT scores since the 1960s (table 11.4). It should be noted, however, that an increasing proportion of high school students were taking the SATs in the early 1980s, so the reduction in scores simply may reflect to some degree the number of students not intending to go to college but being required to take the test solely to judge the quality of their education. Test scores in the early 1980s did show a modest upward turn after almost two decades of steady decline. The scores then remained virtually constant before dipping again in the early 1990s. That fall coincided with continuing concerns about the competitiveness of the American economy and its workforce, and it produced yet another round of complaints about education.

The complaint about the schools' failure to teach basic skills can be contrasted to the complaints of another group of critics who regard the existing educational system as excessively rigid and stultifying. These critics believe that public schools destroy the innate creativity of children; they would prefer more "open" education with fewer rigid requirements and greater emphasis on creativity and expression. Other critics believe that the existing public schools are excessively rigid in teaching a single class or racial perception of the world, instead of providing a broader perspective on the human experience. They demand a broader curriculum, or perhaps different schools for minority children. Quality in education, therefore, is not a self-evident attribute but may have definite class and racial components and may include creativity as well as the ability to solve math problems.

Even if the school systems were doing a good job for the majority of

TABLE 11.4

AVERAGE SAT SCORES, 1967–93

	Verbal	*Mathematics*
1967	466	492
1970	460	488
1975	434	472
1980	424	466
1985	431	475
1986	431	475
1987	430	476
1988	428	476
1989	427	476
1990	424	476
1991	422	474
1992	423	476
1993	424	476

students, they still might not be doing a good job for disadvantaged students. Those students have a number of special needs that are not met through many conventional classrooms. Title I of the Elementary and Secondary Education Act has sought to meet those needs, but its widespread distribution and uncertainty about methodologies has limited its success.[21] When ESEA was reauthorized in 1994 there were a number of suggestions for making the program more effective at producing change for poor students. Unfortunately for those goals, it will be difficult to keep this act from distributing funds as widely as it has in the past, given the tendency of the U.S. Congress to convert any legislation possible into "pork barrel" programs.

Vouchers and "Choice"

Although the various complaints about education sometimes seem worlds apart, they have in common a desire to modify the education offered through the public schools. One way to respond to these complaints is to decentralize the school system. This is in the tradition of local control over education but merely alters the definition of what the appropriate local area is. In New York City the conflict between parents in Ocean Hill-Brownsville and the city's public schools represented one of the most explosive events of this movement. Later, Chicago decentralized a good deal of its school system to the individual school level, giving parents a great deal of direct managerial authority over teachers and curriculum. This experiment has been judged by many to be a success, but for most problems in public education decentralization may not be the answer.[22]

Related to the idea of decentralization of public schools is the possibility of choice among schools within a school system. In almost any school system some schools have the reputation, and perhaps the reality, of being better than others. These schools are often in middle-class neighborhoods, with parents who place pressure on the school board, principal, and teachers for high-quality education. Some school systems also use magnet (specialized or selective) schools to promote educational quality and achieve racial integration. One solution to general problems of quality in education is to allow any student in a public school system to attend any school in the system. This proposal would create something approaching the market system implied in voucher plans (see below) but would keep the funds in the public schools.

A more common policy option proposed to the problem of quality education is the use of educational vouchers.[23] The voucher plan would give each parent a "check" equal to some amount of money but good only for education. The parents could spend that voucher either in the public schools, where it would pay the entire cost of the child's education, or at a school where the voucher might not cover the entire cost and the parents would have to spend some of their own money. Under the voucher plan, parents would have significantly greater control over the education their children would receive: they could choose an open school, a fundamental school stressing basic skills and discipline, a religiously oriented school, or any other school that met state standards. One voucher or choice program implemented in Milwaukee was specifically targeted for low-income students and did not require additional parental funds.[24]

The idea of educational vouchers has been around for several decades but received a large boost from the work of John Chubb and Terry Moe published by the Brookings Institution.[25] These scholars argued that the fundamental problem with public education was organizational; schools and school systems were too bureaucratic to provide good education. They believed that the only way to remedy that problem was to create competition and choice for parents and students. Although Chubb and Moe argued that vouchers would not be necessary, they came to be considered a part of the proposed reforms. The Bush administration's advocacy of choice in education placed voucher plans at the center of the debate over improving American education.

Although the voucher plan is appealing as a means of improving choice in education and thereby improving education, a number of questions have been raised.[26] Perhaps the most fundamental question about the voucher plan is whether it would increase stratification in education; one of the fundamental virtues and goals of American education, after all, has been its attempt to promote social homogeneity and integration. If a voucher plan did not cover the full price of a child's education, many low-income parents would not be able to make up the difference between the value of the voucher and the tuition of private schools, especially the better private schools. The voucher plan might subsidize middle-class parents and not improve the quality of education for the poor, who need that improvement the most—plans like that in Milwaukee are an obvious exception. In fact, the voucher plan might well undo the racial integration that resulted from years of effort and policymaking. All these questions are reinforced by the Coleman Report and numerous other studies of education pointing out that the home background of children is crucial to educational success.[27] A voucher plan would tend to benefit children who would probably succeed anyway, and it might divert funds from schools and children who need the most help.

Also, although educational vouchers could be used only for schools that met established state standards, there are still questions about the propriety of spending public money for education over which the state has no control and about the possibility that the voucher system might actually lower the quality of education. It is not entirely clear where the capital—both human and physical—required to implement this reform of the education system would come from. As a consequence, a full-scale voucher plan might result in the formation of a number of small and inadequate schools, none of them providing the quality of education that could be offered by large, comprehensive public schools. It may be that education is a service that is not amenable to market logic and competition.

The idea of the voucher plan is justified by the market ideology. Some analysts think that the introduction of competition into the education marketplace will improve the quality of education by increasing the choices available to consumers and placing competitive pressures for improvement on existing public schools. For this education marketplace to function effectively, however, the consumer must have access to information about the "product" being produced. This may be difficult if a number of new schools are started in response to a voucher plan. After all, even in established systems of public and private education, it is difficult to assess quality, especially because much of the difference in educational success of students is accounted for by family backgrounds, and much of the effect of education may not be evident until far in the future.

Related to the voucher plan have been schemes to provide "tuition tax credits" for parents sending their children to private schools. These credits were actively supported by the Reagan administration as a means of providing better education and education in line with the "cultural and moral values" of the parents, and the proposals surfaced several times in the Bush administration. The credits would provide tax credits of 50 percent of tuition paid to a private school (up to some maximum amount). The political arguments, and educational arguments, for tuition tax credits are similar to those for vouchers. They would promote greater pluralism in education and allow parents greater choice. In addition, as many minority students have been shown to perform better in private (especially Roman Catholic) schools, such a program could be of substantial benefit to minorities.

Those opposed to tuition tax credits, such as the National Education Association, the Parent Teachers Association, and the American Federation of Teachers, argue that these tax credits will only undermine public education and create a two-class educational system. Even though some minority students seem to do better in private schools, their parents must still have the means of paying anything over the $500 (or other amount) of the tax credit, so the students who benefit will be middle-class students, who may not need the benefit. Finally, programs such as this, which would tend to benefit parochial and other religiously based schools, raise the continuing question of the separation of church and state in education.

Thus, while few educators or policy analysts would claim that education is currently what most citizens want it to be, it is not entirely clear that a voucher plan, or other plans promoting choice, would improve it all that much. The benefits of the voucher plan may be as much psychological as real: it would appear to offer parents more choices and to allow them greater control over their children's education. Nevertheless, the effects on the general quality of education may be difficult to provide or discern. This is especially true if one effect of the programs is to siphon significant amounts of money away from public education and into private schools. For most students, the effect of "choice" will be less money for their public schools to spend and likely poorer-quality education.

Competency Testing

Another means of approaching issues of educational quality is competency testing.[28] This plan is intended to address the claim that students are being promoted who have not mastered the material required at each grade level, that they are being promoted simply to get them through the school system, and that students who cannot read and write are graduating from high school. Competency testing would require a student to pass a test on basic educational skills—reading, writing, and computation—before being awarded a high school diploma. This program is intended to ensure that at least minimal standards of quality are enforced. Advocates of competency testing also argue that it would provide more incentives for students to learn and teachers to teach.

Although many leaders of minority communities have argued that the public schools do not adequately prepare minority students, they have not been supporters of competency testing. The program has been attacked as racist because a disproportionate share of the students who fail the tests in states where such programs are in operation (most notably in Florida) are nonwhite. These competency tests, now being challenged in the courts, are claimed to be biased against nonwhites because the tests employ standard English and are based on values and concepts derived from white middle-class culture and thinking. The tests are, at best, a minimal demonstration of educational quality. The poor scores on the tests are, however, indicative of the concern over the poor quality of education being offered some students.

The federal government has been an advocate of various forms of competency testing for the public schools. It has supported the National Assessment of Educational Progress, a test given to students in the fourth, eighth, and eleventh grades, for twenty years.[29] In addition, the Bush administration's proposals for improving education made in 1991 were based heavily on the efficacy of standardized testing and something close to a national curriculum. These proposed tests would not prevent a student from graduating from high school, but they could be used to compare student performance so that, in essence, poor performers might as well not have graduated in the eyes of prospective employers. These tests are also intended to provide parents and taxpayers with a measure of the effectiveness of their schools that can be used to generate political pressures on poorly performing school systems.

Testing Teacher Competence

In addition to testing the quality of the product of the schools—the students—a number of reformers in education have argued that the producers—the teachers—should also be tested. The tradition in education had been that once a teacher graduated from a school of education, he or she would be given a certificate, usually renewable after additional course work, and he or she would soon receive tenure and could then teach for life. Numerous parents and education experts thought that the traditional system was insufficient to guarantee that teachers could indeed educate students effectively. A policy of testing teacher competence is widely supported by the public (85 percent in one poll), and some form of competency testing for teachers has been adopted in forty-four of the fifty states.

Initial scores on the teachers' tests appeared to justify the arguments from the critics of the existing educational system. In several southern states only about half the teachers who took a test passed it the first time. As the testing became more general across the United States, the failure rate dropped significantly, and testing has become a standard part of the certification process for new teachers. Even though it is now widely used, there are still a number of complaints about the use of testing. First, just as for pupil competency testing, it is argued that the tests are discriminatory; indeed, a much higher proportion of nonwhites fail the test than do whites. Also, teachers' unions argue that the test—especially if given to established classroom teachers—does not adequately measure all the things a teacher must do to be effective. Finally, testing is seen as just one more hurdle that can keep teachers out of the classroom where they are needed.

Competency testing in itself certainly cannot guarantee a supply of good teachers in the United States. There are other problems. One is low teacher salaries, a problem that the Reagan administration identified as a major part of its efforts to improve education. Another problem is the declining interest in teaching among young women, who once were the major source of talent in elementary and secondary education but now have numerous other, more lucrative, careers open to them. Another problem is the working conditions found in many schools, especially problems of discipline and personal safety.[30] Finally, teachers no longer command the respect that they traditionally had in American society, and many of the psychic rewards of teaching are gone for much of the teaching profession. Unless the public schools can attract enough qualified and dedicated teachers, all the other reforms in educational policy may be of little avail.

The Separation of Church and State

The First Amendment to the Constitution of the United States forbids the establishment of a religion and ensures the free exercise of religion. In public education, these two clauses have caused a number of controversies about education and government's role in education. The two clauses may, in fact, be interpreted as being in conflict. For example, if schools require a prayer, this is deemed an establishment of religion (*Engle* v. *Vitale*, 370 U.S. 421 1962). Conversely, prohibiting prayer is seen by some as a limitation on the free exercise of religion.

Issues of church and state in education arise over two areas. The first is school prayer. Since 1962, when the Supreme Court outlawed official school prayer, there have been attempts on the part of religious groups to have prayer returned to the schools, either through a constitutional amendment permitting prayer or through mechanisms such as silent meditation and voluntary attendance at prayers. The issue of prayer in school resurfaced in 1984 when a Reagan administration proposal directed at improving the quality of American education contained a provision allowing local school boards to permit a moment of silent meditation at the beginning of the school day; this was presumed to promote discipline as well as moral education. When individual states attempted to impose such plans, they were struck down by the Supreme Court (*Wallace* v. *Jaffree*, 472 U.S. 38). In 1990 the Court did permit religious groups formed by students to use school facilities for their meetings after school hours, and this may be an opening wedge for greater use of the public schools for religious exercises.

If the Supreme Court followed the election returns, the justices would be likely to side with former Presidents Reagan and Bush and their fundamentalist supporters on the issue of school prayer. Large majorities of the American population are in favor of permitting prayer in schools. As with many other issues, elite groups tend to be more sensitive to the civil liberties issues involved in school prayer, and attempts at passing a school-prayer amendment in Congress have been unsuccessful. The usual tactic has been to block consideration of the issue by procedural mechanisms rather than by a vote that would make it clear to constituents how their congressmen felt about school prayer.

The second area of controversy concerning the separation of church and state is public support for religious schools. In deciding this issue, the Supreme Court has been forced to make a number of difficult decisions, but over the years it has tended to allow greater public support for religious education. For example, in 1930 the Court upheld the right of states to provide textbooks to children in parochial schools on the same basis as books are provided to students in public schools.[31] In 1947 the Court upheld bus transportation for parochial school students at public expense. Both rulings were upheld on the grounds that these expenditures benefited the students, not the church.[32]

In contrast, in 1971 the Court struck down a Pennsylvania law that had the state pay part of parochial school teachers' salaries, arguing that this was of direct benefit to the church and created excessive entanglement between church and state.[33] The Court has also permitted states to provide teachers for exceptional students in parochial schools, but not on the premises of these schools. In a somewhat contradictory fashion, the Court in 1976 upheld general grants of public money to church-affiliated colleges.[34] Most recently, the Court has ruled that the State of New York violated the separation principle by creating a school district that served only the disabled children of a Hasidic Jewish sect that did not want its children to attend public schools.[35]

The reasoning behind all these decisions may appear tortuous, but three principles stand out. The first principle is that aid to students and their families is more acceptable than aid to institutions. Second, institutions of higher education are permitted more entanglement between church and state than are elementary and secondary schools. Finally, the public sector should not have to spend additional money on education because of the special religious demands of a group, but neither should it impose additional financial burdens on the religious groups.

Unionization and Management

The image of the American "schoolmarm" is ingrained in the popular mind. Leaving aside any sexist stereotypes about all elementary and secondary school teachers being female, the point here is that the image of the school-teacher has been a positive one—the image of a person dedicated to education and to students, even in the face of adverse circumstances. The teacher and the school were considered integral parts of the American community.

The image of the teacher is now changing, partly because of increasing unionization and a growing number of teachers' strikes.[36] No longer the representatives of culture and learning in small towns, teachers are now more likely to be employed by large school districts and to be members of an organization that bargains collectively for improved wages and benefits. One of the two major teachers' organizations is the American Federation of Teachers (AFT), affiliated with the AFL-CIO. This organization is clearly a union and has been quite willing to employ the strike weapon in its dealings with school districts. The second major teachers' organization, the National Education Association (NEA), is a professional organization, but its local chapters operate as collective bargaining units. The NEA has been more reluctant to use the strike to gain its ends, although certainly a number of its local chapters have struck. As of 1993 approximately 73 percent of the teachers in the United States were members of these organizations or local teachers' unions. In almost any year there will be several hundred strikes by public school teachers. The sight of teachers picketing and of children out of school until October and even November has changed the once positive image of the teacher. As local government budgets are squeezed in the 1990s, there will be demands for more students in each classroom and less money for raises, and striking teachers may become an even more common phenomenon.

In addition to forcing parents to make arrangements for their children during strikes, the increasing labor unrest in education has more important consequences. We have mentioned that many Americans believe that the quality of American education is not as high as it should be. The sight of educators on strike tends to erode the public image of education even further. Of course, those who favor the more militant actions by teachers quite rightly point out that good teachers will not work for the salaries they are sometimes offered and that fewer good students will be attracted into careers in teaching. But there are still important problems of symbolism and public image when teachers go on the picket line.

Equalization of Resources

As mentioned earlier in this chapter, most public education is financed by local property taxes, and this basis of finance can produce substantial inequities in education. Local school districts with poor resource bases must either tax their poorer constituents more heavily or, more commonly, provide inferior education to the district's children.[37] Further, given that poorer school districts frequently have concentrations of minority-group families, this form of education finance also affects racial and cultural integration and the perceived fairness of government. These inequalities in educational opportunity may, in turn, perpetuate racial differences in economic and social opportunities.

Reliance on the local property tax to finance public schools has been challenged successfully in the courts. In two early cases the courts have entered this policy area, but they have not provided any definite answers to the questions involved. In *Serrano* v. *Priest* (1971), the California Supreme Court ruled that the great disparity between richer and poorer school districts in the Los Angeles area violated provisions of both the state and the federal constitutions. In particular, this disparity constituted a denial of equal protection for the residents of the poorer district. The court did not, however, make any direct recommendations on how this disparity could be ameliorated to meet constitutional standards. One common assumption was that the state might have either to take over educational finance entirely or to alter the formula for distributing state equalization payments.

In a similar case, *San Antonio School District* v. *Rodriguez* (1973), the U.S. Supreme Court ruled that the differences between two school districts in Texas were not so great as to constitute a violation of the equal protection clause. The Court did not say how much of a difference would constitute such a violation. This decision left the constitutionality of the continuation of these disparities between school districts up in the air, but the problems of local school districts' attempting to provide decent education with low taxable property remain quite tangible.[38]

In the 1990s the answer to the enduring questions came when the Texas state courts decided that the existing system of school finance violated the state constitution's requirements for "an efficient system for the general diffusion of knowledge." The Texas Supreme Court ordered Texas to find some means of redressing the differences among the 1,044 school districts in the state.[39] Those school districts have massive disparities: the 5 percent of the richest school districts spend $11,801 per pupil, while the poorest 5 percent spend $3,190 per pupil.[40] The state legislature first opted for regional tax sharing, but the voters rejected this amendment to the state constitution in a referendum.[41] The final plan called for wealthier school districts to transfer some of their taxable property to poorer districts so that those poorer districts could provide a better education for their pupils.[42]

The question was settled in Texas through the courts, but this is a general problem for all fifty states. Some states have begun to address questions of equality of funding for education without the direct intervention of the courts. The most important example is Michigan, which has decided to substitute a 2 percent sales tax and a tripling of the cigarette tax for the property tax as the source for educational finance. Voters were given the choice of this option or an increase in the state income tax and chose the consumption taxes.[43] The courts did not mandate this change, but it did follow several embarrassing events, such as the closing of a school district in northern Michigan several months before the scheduled end of the term due to a lack of funds. This revenue source is statewide and will be divided according to the relative needs of the school districts.

The states have a variety of mechanisms for equalizing the access to funding, and ESEA money can also be used for that purpose.[44] One state, Kentucky, which historically had one of the most unequal and least effective school systems in the country, attacked this problem directly and centralized the funding of schools, with a great deal of success.[45] Disparities in funding and quality persist across the country, however, and many children continue to receive substandard education because of the state, county, or neighborhood in which their parents happen to live. As a part of its "Goals 2000: Educate America Act," the Clinton administration hopes to provide some equalization funding for poorer districts.[46]

The school district in which a student lives may affect the quality of his or her education, but the state in which that school district operates may also make a difference. There are pronounced variations in the level of funding for public education by state (table 11.5); a student in New York has 176 percent more spent for his or her education than does a student in Mississippi. There are also substantial variations in the average salaries offered to teachers in different states; the highest average salary (in Connecticut) is nearly twice the average salary in South Dakota. The relatively poor states of the South and upper Midwest do the worst in terms of support for public education, while the industrial states of the Northeast tend to do the best.

These data illustrate that there is no national policy or national standard for education, and a child's life chances may depend on where he or she grows up. The differences in actual educational outcomes, however, may not be as disparate as the amounts of money being spent. Some states with very low levels of per pupil expenditures, such as Iowa, South Dakota, and Utah, actually have very good results on standardized tests such as the SAT.[47] In fact, there is actually a slight negative statistical relationship between the amount of money spent per pupil and scores on the SAT.[48] Part of this success may be attributed to relatively homogeneous populations in these states, while some of the observed outcomes may be a function of the smaller schools in rural America and the closer personal attention the pupils receive in those settings. Further, students in small rural schools do not have to cope

TABLE 11.5

INEQUALITIES IN EDUCATIONAL FUNDING

Per pupil expenditures, 1989–90
National average = $4,960

High		Low	
Alaska	$8,374	Utah	$2,730
New York	8,062	Idaho	3,078
New Jersey	7,991	Mississippi	3,096
Connecticut	7,604	Alabama	3,327
Rhode Island	6,248	Arkansas	3,485

Average annual teacher salaries, 1990–91
National average = $32,977

High		Low	
Connecticut	$43,808	South Dakota	$22,376
Alaska	43,435	North Dakota	23,574
New York	42,080	Arkansas	23,611
California	39,598	Mississippi	24,366
New Jersey	38,411	Idaho	24,485

SOURCE: Tax Foundation, *Facts and Figures on Government Finance, 1993* (Washington, D.C.: Tax Foundation, 1994), 316–17.

with as much crime and social disruption as is found in urban areas, where more money is spent.

Desegregation and Busing

Finally, we come to desegregation and busing. The important educational question here is whether the school system can be expected to solve all of society's problems or whether it should concentrate more narrowly on education. This question is frequently raised with respect to desegregation, particularly in regard to busing. The argument is that little is being done to change the underlying causes of segregation, especially segregated housing, and that the only institution in society that works under such stringent requirements for desegregation is the public school system. Frequently busing affects popular support for public education. The decline of public education after desegregation becomes a self-fulfilling prophecy as white parents either remove their children from the integrated school and send them to a private school or move their families out of the affected area. The latter move is probably more destructive because it erodes the financial basis of the schools.

The Bush administration began to remove some federal pressure for desegregation from school districts in 1992 when it joined with a Georgia district to seek release from court-directed desegregation. The courts in general have become less active in forcing desegregation, and the Clinton administration has embarked on no particular activism in behalf of the Department of Justice or the Department of Education for new efforts at desegregation.

On the other side of the argument is the central importance of education in the formation of the values and attitudes of students. Desegregation appears to benefit black children by improving not only the quality of their education but also their self-image. It may also be important in reducing the social isolation of white children from black children. Social integration has traditionally been one purpose of American public education, and it may be important for the society to continue to pursue that goal through desegregation. After years of fighting for an end to segregation, somewhat paradoxically some minority groups now have come to favor a resegregation of students. The advocates of separate minority schools argue that the curriculum of most public schools does not reflect the interests or needs of their community and that students can learn better without racial tensions and when taught by teachers from their own race. This resegregation may be occurring de facto, especially in northern cities, as residential patterns become increasingly segregated.[49]

The new and old issues surrounding desegregation can be, and have been, debated at length, but the issue of busing has been so emotionally charged that rational discourse is frequently impossible. The connection between educational quality and racial equality is an important one for the society that must be pursued within both policy domains.[50] Some argue that education is too central to the formation of the social fabric of the United States to be allowed to become isolated from other social concerns. But education also may be too important in a highly technological society to be compromised in any way in an attempt to solve other social problems, and it may be that too many social responsibilities are being placed on schools and their teachers. How this debate is resolved may say a great deal about the future of American society and the American economy.

Conclusion

Education has been and remains a central concern of American public policy. While traditionally the concern of state and local governments, it has become increasingly influenced by federal policy, in part because of education's close connection to other goals, such as economic growth. But while education has been an important and highly respected public function, it is currently under attack. The quality of education, the competence of school personnel, and the place of education in social change are all topics of vital concern to many Americans. Several policy instruments have been proposed to attempt to rectify the perceived difficulties in these areas, the most commonly discussed being the voucher plan, but few statements on educational policy have gained wide public acceptance.

This debate over education policy is in part a result of the absence of a widely accepted theory of causation in education. Unlike health or science policy, educational policy is a subject about which reasonable people often disagree radically. Voucher plans are intended in part to allow people to make individual choices concerning education without having to pay too great an economic price. The role of government as the funding agent for these programs, however, may require greater attention to the real benefits of certain forms of education and a decision about just how far the use of vouchers can be allowed to extend. This is a task for rational policy analysts who recognize that such an analysis must be subjected to serious political and social scrutiny. This is especially true because education is an issue about which almost everyone has an opinion; and because the students involved are the children of those people, there will be controversy.

Notes

1. Catherine S. Mangold, "Students Make Strides but Fall Short of Goals," *New York Times,* 18 August 1994.

2. National Center for Education Statistics, *Digest of Education Statistics* (Washington, D.C.: Government Printing Office, 1992).

3. Richard Hofferbert, "Race, Space and the American Policy Paradox," paper presented at 1980 Conference of the Southern Political Science Association.

4. In areas in which parochial schools were important, these schools also tended to draw from a wide range of social classes, if not religions.

5. Karen De Witt, "Nation's Schools Learn a Fourth R: Resegregation," *New York Times,* 19 January 1992.

6. For diverse views on this topic, see Gerald Graff, *Beyond the Culture Wars: How Teaching the Conflicts Can Revitalize American Education* (New York: Norton, 1992); Russell Jacoby, *Dogmatic Wisdom: How the Culture Wars Divert Education and Distract America* (New York: Doubleday, 1994).

7. U.S. Bureau of the Census, *Statistical Abstract of the United States, 1994* (Washington, D.C.: Government Printing Office, 1994).

8. See his *Our Country and Our Children: Improving America's Schools and Affirming Our Common Culture* (New York: Touchstone, 1988). There have been a number of books advocating such a traditional curriculum for American schools, including Allan Bloom, *The Closing of the American Mind* (New York: Touchstone, 1987).

9. Jeffrey L. Katz, "Head Start Reauthorization," *Congressional Quarterly Weekly Report* 52 (18 June 1994): 1653–55.

10. Rochelle L. Stanfield, "Standard Bearer," *National Journal,* 2 July 1994, 1566–70.

11. Rochelle L. Stanfield, "Team Players," *National Journal,* 13 November 1993, 2723–27.

12. Jonathan Kozol, *Savage Inequalities: Children in America's Schools* (New York: Crown, 1991).

13. *Grove City College* v. *Bell,* 465 U.S. 555 (1984).

14. Scott Jashik, "Secretary Seeks Ban on Grants Reserved for Specific Groups," *Chronicle of Higher Education* 38 (11 December 1991): A1, A26.

15. Rochelle L. Stanfield, "We Have a Tradition of Not Learning," *National Journal,* 7 September 1991, 2156–57.

16. Norman C. Thomas, *Educational Policy in National Politics* (New York: David McKay, 1975).

17. The figure is now roughly 8 percent.

18. Michael D. Reagan, *The New Federalism* (New York: Oxford University Press, 1972).

19. Jerome T. Murphy, "Title I of ESEA: The Politics of Implementing Federal Educational Reform," *Harvard Education Review,* 1971, 35–63.

20. *Title I of ESEA: Is It Helping Poor Children?* (Washington, D.C.: NAACP Legal Defense Fund, 1969).

21. Rochelle L. Stanfield, "Making the Grade?" *National Journal,* 17 April 1993.

22. Robert Guskind, "Rethinking Reform," *National Journal,* 25 May 1991, 1235–39.

23. Myron Lieberman, *Privatization and Educational Choice* (New York: St. Martin's, 1989).

24. John Witte, "The Milwaukee Parental Choice Program Third Year Report," *LaFollette Policy Report* 6 (1994): 6–7.

25. John E. Chubb and Terry M. Moe, *Politics, Markets and America's Schools* (Washington, D.C.: Brookings Institution, 1990).

26. Jeffrey R. Henig, *Rethinking School Choice: Limits of the Market Metaphor* (Princeton: Princeton University Press, 1994).

27. James S. Coleman, *Equality of Educational Opportunity* (Washington, D.C.: Government Printing Office, 1966). Since that time, Coleman has modified his view to be substantially less supportive of busing.

28. D.M. Lewis, "Certifying Functional Literacy: Competency and the Implications for Due Process and Equal Educational Opportunity," *Journal of Law and Education* (1979): 145–83. Also, Chubb and Moe, *Politics, Markets and America's Schools,* 197–98.

29. John L. Palmer and Isabel V. Sawhill, eds., *The Reagan Record* (Washington, D.C.: Urban Institute Press, 1984), 364–65.

30. Jessica Portner, "Educators Keeping Eye on Measures Designed to Combat Youth Violence," *Education Week* 13 (9 February 1994): 21.

31. *Cochran* v. *Board of Education,* 281 U.S. 370 (1930).

32. *Everson* v. *Board of Education,* 330 U.S. 1 (1947).

33. *Lemon* v. *Kurzman,* 403 U.S. 602 (1971).

34. *Roemer* v. *Maryland,* 426 U.S. 736 (1976).

35. *Board of Education of the Kiryas Joel Village School District* v. *Grumet* 114 U.S. 2481 (1994).

36. See, for example, Lonnie Harp, "Michigan Bill Penalizes Teachers for Job Actions," *Education Weekly* 13 (27 April 1994): 9.

37. Stephen M. Barro, *Countering Inequity in School Finance,* vol. 3, *Federal Policy Options for Improving the Education of Low-Income Students* (Santa Monica: Rand Corporation, 1994).

38. Another equity funding case is being contested in Alabama: *Alabama Coalition for Equity, Inc.* v. *Guy Hunt.*

39. *Edgewood* v. *Kirby,* 804 S.W.2D 491 (Tex. 1991).

40. Sam Howe Verhovek, "Texas to Hold Referendum on School-Aid Shift to Poor," *New York Times,* 16 February 1993.

41. Lonnie Harp, "Texas Voters Reject Finance Plan: Consolidation Called Last Resort," *Education Week* 12 (12 May 1993): 1, 16.

42. Lonnie Harp, "Texas Finance Ruling Angers Both Rich, Poor Districts," *Education Week* 13 (12 January 1994): 18.

43. William Schneider, "Voters Get an Offer They Can't Refuse," *National Journal,* 26 March 1994, 754.

44. Rochelle L. Stanfield, "Equity and Excellence," *National Journal,* 23 November 1991, 3860–64.

45. Reagan Walker, "Blueprint for State's New School System Advances in Kentucky," *Education Week* 9 (7 March 1990): 1, 21.

46. Rochelle L. Stanfield, "Learning Curve," *National Journal,* 3 July 1993, 1688–91.

47. Dirk Johnson, "Study Says Small Schools Are Key to Learning," *New York Times,* 21 September 1994.

48. The Spearman rank-order correlation is −0.26. This finding is to some degree confounded by the different percentages of students taking the SAT in different states. Many of the high-scoring states had a small percentage of students taking the SAT.

49. De Witt, "Nation's Schools Learn a Fourth *R.*"

50. Rochelle L. Stanfield, "Reform by the Book," *National Journal,* 4 December 1994, 2885–87.

12. Energy and the Environment

As we prepare to enter the twenty-first century, the people of the United States face two significant problems that affect the relationship between our economy and the physical world. One is a demand for energy that has become virtually insatiable and is much higher per capita than that of almost any industrialized economy. The other policy problem is the need to manage the effluents of an industrialized society and to preserve the natural environment. These two policy areas are discussed together here, in part because they interact in several crucial ways.

First, the high consumption of energy, especially the use of fossil fuels, produces huge quantities of pollution, and the periodic shortage and high prices of petroleum and natural gas place pressures on industries to burn cheaper coal, with the cost being even higher levels of pollution. Even the transportation of fossil fuels, especially oil, presents several well-known and politically visible threats to the environment. Failure to address the energy problem with nontraditional sources will almost certainly exacerbate the environmental problem.

In addition, some regulations issued by the Environmental Protection Agency (EPA) to reduce pollution (e.g., emission controls on automobiles) have tended to require using more energy than would otherwise be used. Both energy and environmental issues also have a large technical and scientific element, and governments have required the development of new technologies to meet their environmental demands. Ultimately, however, changes in human behavior—including such simple things as energy conservation and recycling—may be more important than technological change in producing improvements in the environment.

Both energy and environmental policy are also closely linked with the continuing concerns about the American economy. Uncertainty about energy supplies, including those arising from frequent political instability in the Persian Gulf, and rising energy prices make investment decisions more difficult for businesses and contribute to inflation. Likewise, critics charge that strict environmental controls make economic development projects more expensive or in some cases impossible. Still, if the economy picks up, all the more pollution will be produced.

Finally, both energy and environmental policies increasingly are linked to global concerns. Pollution is no longer a national question about clean water and clean air. It has taken on a pronounced international dimension with concerns about global warming, ozone depletion, transborder pollution, and decreasing biological diversity.[1] Also, energy is an international concern, not only because the United States imports so much of its energy needs, but also because the immense demand of the United States and other industrialized countries tends to increase the price and to lower availability for the developing countries. This chapter examines energy and environmental problems, the responses of governments to these problems, and some possible alternative policies.

Energy: Problems and Policies

Energy is a crucial component of the American way of life. We are accustomed to using, and squandering, energy to a degree unimaginable even in other industrialized societies. The large American automobile, now a dying if not extinct species, was a symbol of that attitude toward energy usage, as is the single person driving an automobile to work each day. The United States uses over 24 percent of all the energy used in the world. This country uses 90 percent more energy per capita than does Sweden, although it uses slightly less per capita than does Canada. (Both countries have standards of living similar to that of the United States.)[2] While energy usage is related to industrialization and higher standards of living, the United States uses much more than is required to maintain the comfortable standard of living to which most citizens have been accustomed.

Until the 1970s, energy was not perceived as a problem for the United States. The embargo by the Organization of Petroleum Exporting Countries (OPEC) on export of oil to the United States in 1973 demonstrated the dependence of the United States on imported oil.[3] The rapidly escalating price of oil that resulted from OPEC's price-fixing and restricted production, and then a second embargo, emphasized even more the dependence of the United States on foreign oil to supplement relatively large quantities of domestic oil, natural gas, and coal. On the basis of the experiences of the 1970s, it is clear that we need seriously to examine the energy policies of the United States and probably to alter some of those policies. That policy lesson does not appear to have been learned, however, and the cheaper oil of the 1980s and 1990s has produced more relaxed attitudes toward energy use. These relaxed attitudes continued even after the scares produced during the Iran-Iraq war and later the Gulf war. In addition, the policies of the Reagan and (especially) Bush administrations stressed exploration and exploitation rather than conservation as the best way to eliminate energy difficulties.

Energy Sources

In spite of the importance of foreign petroleum and the American love affair with the automobile, petroleum is not the only source of energy used in the United States, and other available sources of energy could be more highly developed. Oil is, however, the major energy source for the United States, accounting for 43 percent of all energy consumed, a percentage that has fluctuated little in the past decade. Approximately 43 percent of the oil the United States consumes is imported. A little simple arithmetic reveals that approximately 18.5 percent of the total U.S. energy supply is imported oil.[4] Again, the total amount of oil we import has been increasing as domestic supplies have become more difficult (and expensive) to extract and as demand has continued to increase. This has produced political pressures to open exploration in more environmentally fragile parts of the United States, such as the Alaska Wildlife Refuge and off the Florida coast.

This reliance on imported oil produces a number of problems for the United States. First, it makes energy supplies for the United States extremely uncertain and places the American economy in the position of a hostage to foreign powers. Second, the money we pay for foreign oil goes outside the United States and is difficult to match with exports. The U.S. negative balance of payments of the 1970s and the 1980s has continued in the 1990s, and this has negative consequences for the domestic economy (see chapter 8). Over 11 percent of U.S. imports are energy, without which the balance-of-payments deficit would be approximately half what it actually is.[5] Finally, oil is a finite resource, and proven world reserves of oil are sufficient only for a limited number of years at current rates of consumption. This means that eventually the American economy will have to convert to some other form of energy, and continued reliance on foreign oil may only delay the hard economic, social, and technological choices we will have to make when this particular energy resource is depleted.

Natural Gas

The United States has been more blessed with natural gas than with petroleum. Currently, almost all natural gas used in the United States comes from domestic sources. Natural gas is also a limited resource, however, with something between thirty-five and sixty years' worth of proven reserves available at current and predicted rates of consumption.[6] Therefore, natural gas does not constitute a long-term alternative for the United States. In addition, natural gas is so valuable for its industrial uses—in the fabrication of plastics and synthetic fibers, for example—that it may be inefficient to use it to heat buildings and cook meals.

Alternatives to domestically produced natural gas include importing gas in liquid form from Algeria or the former Soviet Union. These sources would extend the availability of natural gas supplies but would present the same political and economic problems that imported oil presents. In addition, the technology involved in transporting liquid natural gas is still being developed fully, and massive explosions can occur if great care is not exercised. Given the environmental difficulties already encountered with oil spills, the development of a new technology that may produce even greater difficulties simply to preserve an energy supply for a relatively short period may not be politically acceptable.

Coal

America's most abundant energy resource is coal. The United States has enough coal to last approximately 200 years, and it exports substantial quantities of coal to Japan and to parts of Europe. In addition to supplying relatively cheap energy, coal can be used as a raw material for industrial purposes, as is natural gas. If coal usage were developed more fully, the demand for natural gas and petroleum might be reduced. Coal has several disadvantages as an energy resource, however. First, there is the environmental problem. Coal does not burn as cleanly as does oil or natural gas, and a good deal of American coal is rather high in sulfur. When this coal is burned, it forms sulfur dioxide (SO_2), which then combines with water to form sulfuric acid (H_2SO_4). This is a major source of the "acid rain" that threatens forests and wildlife in the northern United States and Canada. Also, the extraction of coal presents other environmental difficulties, since much coal is most efficiently extracted by strip mining. This method may deeply scar the landscape and render the land unusable for years. Improved methods for reclaiming strip-mined land have been developed, but the recovery of the land still takes time and money, and the original natural landscape is lost forever.[7] But mining coal by building tunnels presents huge health and safety problems for the miners.[8]

In addition to the environmental problems, no technology yet exists for using coal to power automobiles or trucks. The "synfuels" project that was one component of President Carter's energy plan was intended to find a way to extract a liquid fuel from coal ("gassification"), but at present no such technology exists at a reasonable price.[9] Thus, coal can be used to generate electricity and heat, but not for transportation, which accounts for 26 percent of the energy used in the United States. The development of other technologies (e.g., improved storage batteries and better electric cars) may help, but at present the usefulness of coal for transportation is limited, and transportation is a major use of energy in the United States.

Finally, there are massive logistical problems in using coal as a major energy source. Coal is more difficult to transport than petroleum or natural gas, which are readily movable through pipelines. At present, American railroads do not have sufficient rolling stock or suitable roadbeds to manage major increased shipments of coal, and a good deal of the coal is located a substantial distance from the points of principal energy demand. There may be increased use of water transportation, especially if the Tennessee-Tombigbee waterway is ever completed, but even that possibility will require investment in boats or barges to make the use of coal a more practical option than it is at present.

Nuclear Power

As of 1992, the United States had 111 nuclear power plants that produced approximately 8 percent of the total energy used in this country and almost 22 percent of all electricity. For several states two-thirds of electrical power comes from nuclear power. At one time it was believed that nuclear power would meet future energy needs as, particularly with fast breeder reactors, the supply of energy appeared almost endless. But after the near-disaster at the Three Mile Island nuclear plant, and the real disaster at Chernobyl in the former Soviet Union, the possibility of a nuclear future appears less likely. In part this is true because, without the breeder reactor and its potential dangers, the United States must deal with the limited supply of fissionable uranium. More important, safety and environmental problems, and the problems of disposing of nuclear waste, have called the feasibility of nuclear power into question for the public as well as for many experts.[10]

The Three Mile Island and Chernobyl incidents pointed to the possibility that nuclear power plants might present health and safety hazards for citizens living near them and possibly even for people living hundreds of miles away. It would be difficult to estimate the extent of damage to the health of citizens if the "China syndrome" had occurred and the reactor core had melted. If a nuclear power plant has no incidents of this sort, the additional radioactivity in its vicinity is indeed negligible, but there is the possibility—although advocates of the technology argue that it is remote—of a serious accident. The accident at Chernobyl produced at least 330 deaths during the first four years after it occurred, and there are estimates of up to a half million additional deaths as a result of this one nuclear accident.[11] The American nuclear industry points to the inadequate design of the Soviet reactor and the ever safer designs available in the United States, but many Americans see only the atomic horrors produced in Ukraine.

357

Even if there were no danger of accidents, the environmental and health problems associated with nuclear waste disposal would present difficulties. Some nuclear wastes lose their radioactivity very slowly: the half-life, or the time required for half the nuclear activity to be exhausted, of plutonium-239 (one of the by-products of nuclear reactors) is 24,000 years. This means that government must find a means of disposing of these wastes so as to prevent contamination of the environment. There are proposals for burying these wastes, but almost no one wants the facilities near their home. Government must also find a means to prevent terrorists from gaining control of the radioactive material, because it would constitute a powerful instrument for blackmail. The disposal of nuclear wastes presents environmental problems and potential problems in guarding large areas against possible terrorist attacks and thefts.

Finally, the construction of nuclear power plants has been so slow that many electrical utilities have become frustrated and abandoned the projects. Because of the dangers of accidents and contamination, the requirements for inspection and reinspection of the plants as they are built have slowed the construction of the plants significantly, as have the lawsuits filed by opponents of nuclear power. Operating costs of nuclear power plants will certainly be less than those of fossil-fuel plants, but the initial capital investment and the relatively short operating life of nuclear plants have caused many private utilities to cancel plans to build these facilities. These problems put much of the burden for energy production back on to fossil fuels, with their associated pollution and finite global supply.

The regulatory difficulties of coping with nuclear power in the United States are indicated by the long controversy over the Seabrook nuclear plant in New Hampshire.[12] The Public Service Company of New Hampshire originally announced plans to build twin reactors at Seabrook in 1972. A series of legal disputes and demonstrations, as well as rising costs, caused the cancellation of one of the reactors in 1984, even after $800 million had been spent on it. Construction of Unit 1 was completed in July 1986. The Chernobyl accident in 1986 led the surrounding states and their utility companies to withdraw their cooperation in building the plant. After investing $2.1 billion in Seabrook without generating a single kilowatt, Public Service of New Hampshire filed for bankruptcy protection in 1988. After intervention by the Reagan administration, the Nuclear Regulatory Commission (NRC) permitted testing of the plant beginning in June 1989, and on 1 March 1990, the NRC granted an operating license to the new owner, Northeast Utilities.[13] While this scenario represents an extreme case, it is little wonder that all nuclear power plants ordered since 1974 have been cancelled.[14]

Other Energy Sources in Use

Several other energy sources are currently being used in the United States, although none accounts for a significant percentage of total energy capacity. These include hydroelectric power, wood, and some solar and geothermal power. To date, with the exception of hydroelectric power, these have not offered much hope for rapid development, although a great deal is promised for solar power, and geothermal power (power produced with the heat from natural sources in the earth) is apparently successful in Iceland and parts of

Europe. Wood is perhaps our oldest power source, and it is an energy source that is renewable. But the constraints on the amount of wood available, its cost, and the pollution problems it presents limit its usefulness, in spite of a growing number of Franklin stoves and wood-burning furnaces in the northern United States.

Unconventional Energy Sources

As the problem of America's energy future has become more apparent to citizens, politicians, and scientists, a number of alternatives to fossil fuels and nuclear power have been explored. The search has been for energy sources that are renewable, clean, safe, and compatible with the American lifestyle. Of the four criteria, the last has appeared least important as some understanding of the uniqueness of that life-style has begun to penetrate our collective consciousness. At present, there appear to be five major possible alternative energy sources, two of which are variations on existing power sources. These two variations are the extraction of oil from the shale found in Colorado and Wyoming, and nuclear fusion (rather than fission). The oil-shale technology, if developed, would have an immense environmental impact, much like that of strip-mined coal. Further, the extraction process for shale oil would produce a number of undesirable effluents in an area that is both beautiful and environmentally fragile. In addition, the extraction of oil from shale would require huge amounts of water in an area already short of water. And all this is for a relatively small amount of oil, compared with current levels of consumption.

The technology of fusion power is still in the beginning stages despite significant research and development expenditures. The idea of this power source is to approximate, in a laboratory or power station, the processes that produce the energy of the sun. This will require temperatures of tens of millions of degrees and the technology to create and then contain a superheated "plasma" of charged particles.[15] Claims of "cold fusion" being achieved in the late 1980s generated a huge wave of optimism, but further investigations found the claims at best highly suspect, so fusion still appears to require incredibly high temperatures. In other words, fusion will require massive technological developments, but it might someday produce cheap and virtually limitless supplies of energy, with much less radioactivity than is caused by nuclear fission. European researchers were able, in late 1991, actually to produce some limited amounts of power using a fusion technique, and American researchers also have produced a brief sustained fusion.[16]

Limited amounts of solar power are also in use in the United States, heating some houses and businesses and heating water for home use. But the use of solar power to produce electricity for mass distribution ("big solar") will require technological breakthroughs as well as answers to some environmental questions. Although we theoretically have a limitless source of solar power, many areas of the United States may not receive the amount of sunlight they need when they need it most. For example, northern cities need energy most during the winter, for heating, but they receive little sunlight then; one possible use for solar power, however, may be to take care of peak-loading from airconditioning in the summer. Also, the photovoltaic cell—the means of converting sunlight into electrical energy—is at present underdeveloped and inefficient. Thus, to make sufficient quantities of electricity with "big solar" projects will require large land areas devoted to solar panels, and some environmentalists may regard this as just another form of pollution. Solar-powered automobiles have also been developed, with engineering contests now existing for these vehicles. None of the winners, however, appears likely to be available in automobile showrooms at any time in the near future.

There has also been a great deal of discussion about using wind power to generate electricity. The windmill, which used to dominate rural landscapes, is to many people now the symbol of the energy future. Again, like solar power, wind power is already in use in small and decentralized ways, but the unreliability of the source and the mental vision of thousands of windmills dotting the American plains and coasts have reduced the attractiveness of this alternative.[17] Possibly, with better means of storing electricity, wind power will become a practical means of meeting at least some of America's future energy requirements.

Finally, there is the possibility of using the agricultural productivity of the United States as a means of addressing energy needs. Gasohol, a combination of gasoline and methyl (wood) alcohol produced from plants, is already sold in some areas of the United States as a fuel for automobiles. The same plant material used for gasohol could be converted into methane gas and used in the same manner as natural gas to heat homes. There are also a number of options for using the substantial forest reserves of the United States, and the by-products of timber production, as alternative energy resources.

The production of energy from biomass has several advantages. One is that it is renewable. Use of rapidly growing plants—or agricultural by-products such as cornstalks—would have less impact on the environment than some other energy sources. The methane gas that is one usable product of the biomass process, however, has been demonstrated to be at least as much a culprit in the "greenhouse effect" as carbon dioxide. In addition, massive amounts of land would have to be cultivated to produce the necessary quantitites of organic material. This means of energy production has the decided advantage for Americans of producing a product that, unlike solar, wind, or fusion power, can be burned in automobiles. Of course, more efficient electric automobiles and storage batteries may be developed, but gasohol or even pure methanol already can be burned in a modified internal combustion engine. The technology for burning methane gas in automobiles is also being developed. Thus, biomass production may serve the American lifestyle better than other alternative forms of energy production. At present, price is a major barrier to the production of significant quantities of methanol; the price of alcohol has been higher than the price of gasoline. With higher and uncertain petroleum prices and increased methanol production, however, methanol may become a more competitive energy source.

Policy Options

Broadly speaking, there are two ways of addressing the energy problems of the United States. One is conservation, or discouraging energy consumption by citizens and industry. Conservation was the principal approach of the Carter administration to the energy problem. For example, orders specified the range of temperatures in public buildings, and there were tax incentives for insulation and other energy-saving modifications for homes. But more than anything else, the issue of conservation was highlighted by controversies over deregulation of oil and natural gas prices, especially for so-called new oil and gas. The idea was that any gas and oil discovered after the passage of the legislation would be priced at a rate determined by the market, rather than at the controlled price of domestic oil and gas, which was then below world prices. This would allow the price of oil and gas to rise, thereby encouraging conservation. But it would also mean huge "windfall" profits for oil and gas companies. To attempt to make the impacts of decontrol more equitable across the society, a windfall profits tax on oil companies was part of the Carter energy package.

Another important aspect of the Carter approach to energy problems was the Synthetic Fuels Corporation, intended to develop substitutes for petroleum from coal and other resources. As noted earlier, this research has yet to bear fruits that are economically feasible, but there have been some significant advances. Finally, there was to be a stockpile of petroleum—the Strategic Petroleum Reserve—that would delay the effects of any future oil embargoes on the United States. The mere mention by President Bush that this reserve could be used, for example, served to stabilize petroleum prices during the Gulf war.

The Reagan administration's approach to energy was more market and production oriented. During his 1980 campaign, candidate Reagan stressed the need for the market to deal with energy problems and condemned the Department of Energy as a "wasteful bureaucracy."[18] Reagan's first administration assumed that price deregulation would encourage the market to produce more energy and that price increases would make some energy sources (e.g., oil in old wells) profitable to exploit. Also, the administration—with the special attention of Interior Secretary James Watt—sought, largely unsuccessfully, to exploit energy resources on public lands, such as the Alaska lands "locked up" under the Carter administration. There was some leasing of federal lands for coal mining—some 16,000 acres in the Powder River Basin of Montana and Wyoming, for example—but the favorable prices offered to private coal companies when the coal market was glutted was condemned as poor resource management and a national "fire sale." This sale was especially vulnerable to criticism because of the environmental sensitivity of the area leased. The stable and even declining price of petroleum on the international market, however, has made the planned exploitation of shale oils in equally sensitive areas of the West less attractive, and that development has been slowed.

The price of oil had other effects on national energy policy in the 1980s. First, it made the development of the Strategic Petroleum Reserve more feasible; by January 1984 it had reached 360 million barrels (almost a month's supply), which was a 300 percent increase over what was available in 1980. Further, as shale oils became less attractive, so too did synthetic fuels, and the Synthetic Fuels Corporation had a difficult time maintaining any interest in the private sector.[19] President Reagan was successful in 1984 in having Congress rescind funding for the Synthetic Fuels Corporation.[20] Stable energy prices also made the continued deregulation of oil and natural gas feasible; the Reagan administration pushed for complete deregulation, including the abrogation of existing pipeline contracts calling for the delivery of natural gas at a certain price. This policy was, however, far from successful and created a number of market inefficiencies and local pricing difficulties.[21]

In summary, during the Reagan administration energy policy was not a major concern. Energy prices were relatively stable, and the international market had plentiful oil. Also, energy consumption in the United States declined; existing supplies and sources were more than adequate, and the market-oriented strategies of the administration were largely successful. Not surprisingly, the Bush administration continued a similar approach to energy policy. This should not be surprising given the apparent successes of the Reagan administration and the close links of the new president to oil interests in his home state of Texas.

In general, President Bush pursued a policy of finding and exploiting new fossil-fuel resources. In his National Energy Strategy announced in early 1991, however, President Bush offered a somewhat more diversified approach to energy policy. He advocated increasing domestic oil production to 3.8 million barrels a day but also called for a research and development program on alternative energy sources such as biomass and solar power.[22] Nevertheless, many critics, even some in the business community, argued that the president did not place adequate emphasis on energy conservation.[23]

The Clinton administration has yet to make any major initiatives in energy policy. Coming to office at a time of relatively plentiful energy and bringing a host of other agenda items with him, President Clinton has invested little political capital in energy issues. Secretary of Energy Hazel R. O'Leary has been a very visible figure, but not because of any bold initiatives in new policy. Instead, she has received high marks from the public and from Washington insiders for her opening of numerous files on U.S. atomic testing during the height of the Cold War. These files pointed to a number of severe abuses by government, and she has set out to try to compensate the victims of some of the most egregious of those abuses.[24]

It once was popular to talk about the energy "crisis" in the United States, and indeed in the 1970s a crisis seemed to loom as prices soared and supplies dwindled. Those fears now appear exaggerated because energy is not an immediate problem. Yet there is reason to believe that this halcyon period may be only a short respite from an ongoing energy problem. Supplies of fossil fuels in the world are finite. The ending of the immediate problems in energy therefore provides a false sense of security and prevents the search for viable long-term energy sources. This is especially true in view of the fact that many citizens are suspicious of technological solutions (e.g., nuclear power) to energy problems. Further, the continuing dependence of the United States on foreign oil may make the economy and society hostage to forces over which we have no control. It may require yet another energy "crisis" for citizens and government to be willing to return to the active consideration of alternative energy futures for the United States.

One of the best presentations of the policy options facing the United States with respect to energy is Amory Lovins's discussion of "hard" versus "soft" energy paths.[25] Although there have been numerous criticisms of the apocalyptic conclusions reached by Lovins, his analysis of the alternative routes is important. The hard route is said to continue to increase energy consumption as fast or faster than national economic growth and to rely on fossil fuels, especially coal, or on nuclear power to supply that energy. This option is both production oriented and centralized in its use of large-scale energy production and distribution, primarily through existing electrical utilities. The soft route, in contrast, would allow energy use to grow less rapidly than national economic growth and would stress conservation. The soft route would also stress decentralized production of energy, with each family or small community having its own power source, usually of a renewable variety.

Lovins's analysis is important for several reasons. First, economic growth is often linked with energy consumption. In fact, the usual assumption has been that these two are inextricably linked, but they need not be in Lovins's decentralized vision of the future. Second, he stresses the connection between environmental issues (he is an environmental activist) and energy issues, as we have been doing here. Finally, he stresses the links between political decision making, political structures, and energy sources. He fears the centralization that might occur in politics as a result of large-scale use of nuclear power, with the attendant need to protect waste storage sites and even the power plants themselves.

The energy "crisis" implies a need to change our lifestyle so as to conserve energy, to live more frugally and with different forms of energy, or to locate additional sources of petroleum, natural gas, and uranium. Or all three. There are few clear answers to the problems posed for the country by its expanding need for energy and the eventual exhaustion of our traditional sources. Americans tend to believe that technological solutions can be found to the problems that face the country, but the application of technology has yet to make a significant dent in the continuing problems of energy.

Also, it is important to discuss the political and social effects of the energy crisis and not just its technical aspects. As mentioned, the choices made about energy supplies may well be so basic that they affect the manner in which governments function, or in more extreme versions they may affect the level of government that citizens regard as most important. In a future characterized by highly decentralized energy, a centralized federal government may be less important than the community government. The community, as opposed to the large urban area, may become the appropriate unit of social organization. Like so many other policy areas, energy policy may be too important to be left to the experts; there must be active citizen understanding and involvement to shape humane as well as technologically feasible politics.

Environmental Policies

Just as Harriet Beecher Stowe's *Uncle Tom's Cabin* is alleged to have helped initiate the Civil War and as Michael Harrington's *The Other America* is said to have helped initiate the war on poverty, so it is sometimes said that Rachel Carson's *Silent Spring* helped launch the environmental movement in the United States. Her description of the horror of a spring without the usual sounds of life associated with that time of the year helped make citizens and policymakers understand the possible effects of the pollutants—especially insecticides—being poured into the air and water of the United States. This is no small problem. Even after several decades of increased environmental awareness, tons of pollutants are still dumped into the air and water or stored in rusting barrels to poison the land for years. It is difficult to determine the amount of disease and the number of deaths that result from this pollution or to estimate the amount of property damage it causes, but the damage produced in each of these categories could be substantial. That economic damage, however, may be minimal compared to the human and aesthetic damage produced by uncontrolled pollution.

America does have multiple pollution problems. Further, we have found that these problems are not confined to our own air and water but that they are global. Scientific research published during the 1980s pointed to a gradual warming trend in the earth's atmosphere—the "greenhouse effect" —that could alter climates and even produce massive coastal flooding if the polar ice caps were to melt. This warming appears to be largely the product of carbon dioxide being put into the atmosphere by burning fossil fuels.[26] Other scientists have pointed to the destruction of ozone in the earth's atmosphere that will permit more ultraviolet radiation to reach the surface and increase the risk of skin cancers. Much of this atmospheric change is a result of the release of chlorinated fluorocarbons (CFCs) into the atmosphere from aerosol cans, refrigeration units, and numerous industrial applications. Still other scientists have pointed to the destruction of the tropical rain forests that supply not only much of the world's oxygen but also a large number of as yet undiscovered useful plants.[27] Also, the United States exports acid rain to Canada and imports water and air pollution from Mexico and Canada. It no longer appears sufficient to address environmental problems within the context of a single country; concerted international action and policies are needed.

Within the context of the United States, environmental problems have been addressed through a variety of statutes now enforced by the Environmental Protection Agency (EPA). Few people question the desirability of a clean environment, but some would like to see that value balanced more carefully with other, equally important values, such as economic growth, jobs, and controlling inflation. The slowdown of the American economy in the late 1980s and early 1990s led many citizens to question whether the nation can afford such stringent controls on pollution, especially when many U.S. jobs are going to countries with much less stringent environmental controls on manufacturers. It is also argued that environmental controls have contributed to the inflation that has plagued the American economy by making some commodities, such as automobiles, more expensive than they would otherwise be. Great progress has been made in environmental policy, but the challenges have changed to some extent, and the connections with energy policy and economic policy have become even clearer.

The Politics of Pollution

It would be difficult in the 1990s to find a group that actively favors environmental degradation. Instead, the politics of pollution is generally phrased in terms of what are acceptable tradeoffs between environmental values and other values. There is sufficient public concern about the environment that it would be almost impossible to make wholesale retreats from existing environmental programs. For example, in 1990, 71 percent of the respondents to a national poll said they would support environmental protection laws regardless of the costs, while only 21 percent disagreed with that proposition. This unequivocal support for environmental protection is up from less than 50 percent in the early 1980s.[28] At the same time, individuals want to preserve their jobs and firms want to preserve their industries and are willing to sacrifice at least part of the environment toward those ends.

One contemporary example would be the continuing conflict between logging interests and environmentalists in the Pacific Northwest over the spotted owl. Environmentalists want to save old-growth forests to protect that endangered species, while loggers see primarily the loss of their livelihoods if the owl is saved.[29] Both sides have powerful reasons to support their positions, and the resolution will affect the long-term tradeoff between the values of the environment and the economy. Other emerging conflicts between the environment and the economy will require careful decision making by government.

Some tradeoffs have to be made. As the U.S. economy slowed during the 1980s, some of the blame for the slowdown was placed on more stringent environmental controls in the United States than in other countries. Similarly, a portion of inflation was blamed on regulations of all kinds, including environmental regulations; the cost of the average American automobile increased by several hundred dollars because of environmental controls.[30] These same environmental controls made the automobile somewhat less energy efficient, so in this case energy conservation and environmental concerns constituted another tradeoff. A similar energy versus environment tradeoff can be seen in coal mining. The cheapest means of mining coal, strip mining, is extremely destructive to the environment. Further, potential petroleum reserves have been found in environmentally sensitive areas in Alaska and along the Florida coast. Even if all Americans are to some degree in favor of a clean environment, it will be difficult to find much agreement on how individual tradeoffs among values will be made.

Stakeholders in the environmental arena are obvious. Industry is a major actor, for many environmental regulations restrict the activities of businesses. Local governments are also the objects of environmental controls, for much water pollution is produced by poorly treated sewerage coming from local government sources, and federal and state governments have imposed expensive mandates on local governments requiring them to clean up water supplies. Again, most of the interests affected by pollution legislation have not opposed the legislation as much on ideological grounds as on technical grounds, arguing that many of the regulations are technologically infeasible or are so expensive that enforcing them would make the cost of doing business prohibitive.[31] Local governments in particular have argued that they simply do not have the money to comply.

On the other side of the debate are the environmental interest groups, such as the Sierra Club, the National Wildlife Federation, and the Friends of the Earth. A few of these organizations—most notably the Sierra Club—have been in existence for years, but the majority are products of the environmental mobilization of the late 1960s and 1970s. In the 1990s there are approximately 9 million members of national environmental groups, with more members of local organizations.[32] Yet there are disagreements among members of these groups as to the tactics they want to follow and their willingness to make tradeoffs with other values, such as economic growth. Some environmental groups have become increasingly confrontational, placing large spikes in trees to make them dangerous to cut with power saws, and harassing hunters and the wearers of fur coats. Environmentalists no longer fit the image of the mild-mannered bird watcher; some are militant advocates of their political and moral positions.

Finally, government itself is an active participant in environmental politics. The major actor in government is the Environmental Protection Agency (EPA), organized in 1970 to take the lead in environmental regulation for the federal government. Given its mission and the time at which it was formed, many employees of the EPA were, and are, committed environmentalists. This commitment put them into conflict with political appointees of the Reagan administration who did not share those values. Before the scandals that caused her ouster, Anne Burford Gorsuch had numerous conflicts with employees of the EPA who did not accept her values and thought she was too much in league with industry. Given the commitment to environmental politics by Vice-President Al Gore,[33] among others in the Clinton administration, there has been a return to a stronger commitment to environmental protection.[34]

The EPA is not the only federal agency with environmental concerns; one enumeration found almost thirty federal organizations to have some environmental regulatory responsibilities. Some, such as the Department of the Interior, which manages federal lands, have a substantial impact on federal policies but may have their own ideologies, which are not purely environmental. The Forest Service in the Department of Agriculture, for example, tends to regard forests as crops rather than natural assets, and therefore it seeks to generate revenue by harvesting them. The Department of Defense also has massive environmental responsibilities, including cleaning up large-scale pollution on military bases.[35] The large number of agencies involved in the environment has meant some lack of coordination, but consequent attempts to coordinate and to produce greater uniformity in regulation have enjoyed little success because of the diverse interests in this policy community.[36]

Making environmental policy is in part a technical exercise. There are a huge number of complex technical questions about the nature of environmental problems and about the feasibility of solutions offered for problems. Making environmental policy is also an ideological exercise on the part of many of those involved, especially the environmental groups. Most fundamentally, making environmental policy means finding tradeoffs among environmental values, technical feasibility, and economic growth that can satisfy the multiple constituencies involved in this policy area.

Given the complex tradeoffs involved in this policy area, there has been increased interest in risk-based decision making. The logic of this approach is that rather than focus on absolute prohibitions against all hazards, government decision making should focus on the most dangerous pollutants and then seek to reduce those hazards to levels deemed to be "safe."[37] Further, this approach calls for balancing the costs and benefits of the production of potentially dangerous substances. Of course, this approach offends committed defenders of the environment who would prefer to retain the traditional regulatory regimens.[38] The Environmental Protection Agency has also been attempting to tailor its regulatory interventions more closely to the characteristics of particular industries.[39]

The Legislation

Except for some older pieces of legislation, environmental legislation was passed in the 1960s and 1970s. Most of this legislation had built into it specific guidelines so that authorization would expire after a certain number of years. There have been reauthorizations of these acts, each with some variations on the original legislation. Even among those very committed to environmental protection, there is some interest in developing alternatives to direct regulation as a means of reducing pollution. There is the need to build policy regimens that produce greater compliance, less impact on economic performance, and lower administrative costs. We now discuss each area of legislation and the enforcement of environmental policy, as well as the alternatives proposed to the existing system of regulation.

WATER POLLUTION

Federal interest in water pollution goes back to the Refuse Act of 1899, which was intended to prevent the dumping of refuse in navigable waters and was enforced by the Army Corps of Engineers. This legislation provided the principal federal means of attacking water pollution until more stringent legislation was passed in the 1970s. The Water Pollution Control Act of 1956 was another piece of relatively early federal legislation. This act allowed interested parties around a polluted body of water to call a conference concerning that pollution. The recommendations of the conference would be passed on to enforcement officials in the states involved. If the states did not act within six months, the federal government (through the Department of the Interior) could intervene and seek an injunction to stop the polluting. Although there were possibilities of more stringent enforcement through the court system, only one injunction was issued during the fifteen years the 1956 law was in effect. But by making federal matching funds available for the construction of sewage treatment facilities, the act did encourage cities and towns to clean up their water.

The early legislation on water pollution having proved ineffective, the federal government took a major step forward in 1965 with the Water Quality Act. This act relied on the states, as had the 1956 act, but made the first steps toward establishing criteria for water quality. Each state submitted to the Department of Health, Education, and Welfare (after 1970 to the Environmental Protection Agency) standards for water quality. These standards were to be in measurable quantities (e.g., the number of bacteria per unit of water). After HEW or the EPA approved these quality standards, they were to be translated into specific effluent standards (e.g., an industry would release only so many tons of pollutants each month). It was then anticipated that the states would enforce these standards; if they did not, the secretary of HEW was given the authority to enforce the standards approved by the state within that state's boundaries.

The state basis of the Water Quality Act proved to be its undoing. States were competing with one another to attract industries, and states that adopted more stringent water-quality standards might scare industries away. Thus, water-quality standards tended to converge on the lowest common denominator. Even then, states rarely if ever enforced their standards. Also, the federal government did little to encourage more vigorous enforcement by the states, and nothing to enforce the standards themselves. It became clear that the states had little incentive to enforce pollution standards and clean up their water, and as a consequence more effective national standards would be required.

Those national standards were developed through the 1972 Clean Water Act (CWA). Technically amendments to the Water Pollution Control Act, this legislation established national goals, with 1983 established as the deadline for all streams to be safe for fish and for human swimming, and a date in 1985 designated for all harmful discharges into navigable streams to cease. That goal had to be abandoned after a flood of lawsuits and an enumeration of the costs persuaded government that it was too optimistic. Still, the requirements said that all private concerns were to adopt the "best practicable technology" by 1977 and the "best available technology" by 1983. Standards for public sewage treatment were less demanding, with all wastes to receive some treatment by 1977 and with the "best practicable technology" standard applied by 1983 continued as the policy guidelines.[40] As the regulatory regime developed, risk assessment became a more important tool for analysis.

This legislation established a nationwide discharge permit system, enabling the Environmental Protection Agency to specify the amount of effluents that could be released and monitor compliance with the technology requirements. As noted, this legislation set nationwide standards, although a good deal of the implementation was done at the state level. States could not use low water-quality standards as a means of competing for industry, but their implementation of the standards continued to differ substantially.

President Reagan vetoed the reauthorization of the CWA in 1986, arguing that compliance was too expensive for industry and local governments. Congress overrode the veto, with the perhaps unexpected support of many industrial organizations. Industry appeared to accept the existing set of standards as a reasonable compromise between what they might want and what more militant environmentalists might want.[41] As a part of the general pattern of devolution of authority in the federal system, the Reagan administration placed greater reliance on the states.[42] Further amendments and rewriting during the Clinton administration have strengthened some aspects of the legislation but have also weakened some important regulations (e.g., on control of chlorine).[43]

Also, in 1986 amendments were added to the Safe Drinking Water Act that added 86 contaminants to the list of substances prohibited from public drinking water. This act was originally passed in 1974 and, like a good deal of all environmental legislation, had faced implementation difficulties because of its reliance on state and local governments, as well as suits by citizens as a means of bringing problems to the attention of the EPA. Despite the enforcement problems, and the problems of vagueness in the legislation itself, there has been progress in cleaning up the water in the United States (see table 12.1).

AIR POLLUTION

Air pollution did not become a matter of federal concern as early as water pollution did, perhaps because of the lack of a clear constitutional peg on which to hang any attempt at enforcement. Federal control over navigable streams provided such a legal peg for water-pollution legislation. In addition, the effects of air pollution failed to produce much public attention, even though twenty people died during severe air pollution in Donora, Penn-

TABLE 12.1

IMPROVEMENTS IN WATER QUALITY (PERCENTAGE OF TESTED
WATERSHEDS EXCEEDING PERMISSIBLE STANDARDS)

	1975	1980	1985	1989
Coliform bacteria	36	31	38	20
Dissolved oxygen	5	5	3	3
Phosphorus	5	4	3	3
Lead	n.a.	5	<1	<1

SOURCE: U.S. Bureau of the Census, *Statistical Abstract of the United States* (annual).

sylvania, in 1948 and even though an obvious smog problem plagued the Los Angeles area as early as the 1950s.

The first federal legislation against air pollution was the Clean Air Act of 1963. This legislation was similar to the 1956 Water Pollution Act in that it relied on conferences, voluntary compliance, and possible HEW enforcement. Only once during the seven years in which the act was in effect did HEW attempt to force a firm to cease polluting. Also, in 1965 the act was amended to authorize the secretary of HEW to set standards for automobile emissions, using measurable standards like those of the Water Pollution Control Act Amendments of 1972.

The Clean Air Act was significantly amended in 1970, and the EPA was directed to establish ambient ("surrounding") air-quality standards. There were to be two sets of standards, primary and secondary. Primary standards were those necessary to protect public health and were to be attained by 1975. Secondary standards, those necessary to protect vegetation, paint, buildings, and so forth, were to be attained within "a reasonable time." Also, the EPA was given the authority to establish emission standards for certain new plants, such as cement and sulfuric acid factories and electrical generating stations fired by fossil fuels ("point sources"), which had greater than average potential for significant air pollution. The 1977 amendments to the Clean Air Act required developing state plans for controlling new point sources of pollution and for higher standards of protection for certain areas (e.g., parks) within a state.

The Clean Air Act amendments also have addressed emissions from automobiles, which continue to constitute the principal air-pollution problem for most American cities. The 1970 standards superseded the weak hydrocarbon standards and carbon monoxide standards obtained in the 1965 Motor Vehicle Air Pollution Control Act. The 1970 amendments mandated a

90 percent reduction in the level of hydrocarbons and carbon monoxide emissions by 1975, with similar reductions in oxides of nitrogen to be achieved by 1976. Although the standards set by the amendments were tough, a variety of factors slowed their implementation. Primarily, the technology for achieving these reductions was difficult and expensive to develop, and some of it, such as the catalytic converter, had side effects that were perhaps as dangerous as the emissions they were designed to eliminate. In addition, many pollution controls reduced gasoline mileage, and increasing energy shortages brought the conflict between environmental concerns and energy problems to the attention of citizens and policymakers alike. This began to place a great deal of unwelcome pressure on automobile manufacturers to create more fuel-efficient and cleaner-running automobiles. After some delays, those standards have been largely met. The success of one round of "technology forcing" standards has produced demands for even greater reductions in automobile emissions. These demands from environmentalists, and the countervailing resistance from industry, caused changes in air-pollution legislation to stall from 1977 to 1990. Despite the stagnant legislative scene, the quality of air in the United States has been improving, in large part a function of the old legislation (table 12.2).

The legislative impasse over air-pollution legislation was broken in 1990 with a major set of amendments to the Clean Air Act. These amendments addressed some of the traditional concerns over air quality within the United States, but also began to address larger global issues such as the greenhouse effect and acid rain. The provisions of the amendments included the following:

1. Protection of the ozone layer by banning use of CFCs in aerosol sprays and regulation of their use as refrigerants.
2. Plans to reduce acid rain by halving emissions of sulfur dioxide and oxides of nitrogen. Environmental requirements on fossil-fuel power plants were strengthened considerably.
3. Further emission requirements on automobiles and requirements for oil companies to create cleaner-burning fuels.[44]
4. Increased restriction on "toxic air pollutants." The EPA was given the power to control emissions of over 200 substances from a variety of sources, ranging from coke and steel mills to dry cleaners, and to demand installation of new technologies to limit or eliminate emissions.

The 1990 amendments to the Clean Air Act depended largely on traditional "command and control" regulation. These regulations were not well received in the Bush administration which, in addition to being led by the

TABLE 12.2

IMPROVEMENTS IN AIR QUALITY

(MILLION METRIC TONS EMITTED)

	1970	1980	1985	1988	1991
Particulates	19.0	9.1	7.9	7.9	7.4
Sulfur oxides	28.4	23.8	21.7	21.5	20.7
Nitrogen oxides	19.0	23.6	19.4	19.7	18.8
Carbon monoxide	123.8	100.0	83.1	75.5	62.1
Lead	199.1	66.0	18.3	5.9	5.0

SOURCE: U.S. Environmental Protection Agency, *National Air Quality and Emission Trends Report*, annual.

"environmental president," sought to maximize use of market mechanisms to solve social and economic problems. The Environmental Protection Agency, in contrast, received something of a new lease on life with this legislation and with the 1990 Pollution Control Act was capable of exerting greater pressures to clean up America's air.

In line with the general movement of environmental controls away from strict hierarchical regulatory regimens, there is an increasing emphasis on negotiation and accomodation in air-pollution policy. For example, in late 1994 the Environmental Protection Agency negotiated an agreement with ten northeastern states to reduce air pollution from factories (especially electrical power plants).[45] This followed a similar agreement (among twelve states) to reduce significantly the amount of air pollution coming from automobiles. The outcomes of these negotiations are not all that either industry or environmentalists would have wanted, but the bargaining that surrounded these pacts has produced agreements that all affected interests, including the states that will implement the agreements, can live with.

GENERAL ENVIRONMENTAL LEGISLATION

In addition to the legislation addressing specific kinds of pollution, the National Environmental Policy Act (NEPA) of 1970 established guidelines for environmental controls for projects involving the federal government. The principal component of this legislation was the Environmental Impact Statement, which was required for any federally funded project that might have an effect on environmental quality. Before a project can be approved, the Environmental Impact Statement must be filed, detailing the environmental impact of the project, its potential negative consequences, and possible alternatives. These statements must be prepared well in advance of the proposed starting date of the project to allow citizen participation and review; they are then filed with the Council on Environmental Quality in the Executive Office of the President.

The NEPA also allows citizens to challenge a project on environmental grounds, and over 400 court cases were filed during the first five years that the legislation was in effect. The legislation requires that environmental considerations be taken into account when a project is planned, but does not indicate the weight that is to be attached to these considerations compared with other costs and benefits of the project. This ambiguity in the legislation has been the source of many court cases and has made decisions difficult for the judge involved. In the case of the Alaska pipeline, court challenges required special legislation to allow the project to continue in the face of determined opposition by conservation groups. That case also pointed to the increasing conflict between energy needs and environmental protection. Similar conflicts are emerging over proposals to open the Alaska National Wildlife Refuge to oil exploration.

Toxic Waste

Toxic wastes are one of the by-products of a society that has become dependent on synthetic products for its way of life. The usual estimate of the volume of hazardous waste in the United States, used by the EPA, is that around 250 million tons are created each year—one ton per citizen in the United States.[46] Only about 10 percent of this waste is disposed of safely.[47] In addition to the hazard itself, the problem with hazardous wastes is that they tend to be persistent; chemicals have to be stored for years or even centuries and have to be kept away from people and their water and food supplies. Such storage is expensive, and before there was a full understanding of the dangers of these wastes, or proper regulation, industries disposed of these wastes in a very haphazard manner, thus endangering many citizens.

The issue of hazardous wastes first came to widespread attention in 1977 when the Love Canal dump near Buffalo, New York, spilled wastes into a nearby residential neighborhood. Eventually several hundred residents had to be moved out of their homes; most have never returned. Hazardous wastes again came to widespread attention in 1982 when it was found that the town of Times Beach, Missouri, had been contaminated with the extremely toxic chemical dioxin. The town had to be evacuated. Although these have been the most obvious manifestations of the toxic waste problem, there are approximately 30,000 toxic waste dumps across the United States, and several thousand of them pose serious threats to the health of citizens. It is estimated that up to $50 billion would be required to clean up existing waste dumps and dispose of all the chemicals stored in them in an environmentally safe manner.

The federal government adopted two major pieces of legislation to address the problem of toxic wastes. The first was the Resource Conservation and Recovery Act (RCRA) of 1976, which was reauthorized in 1980. This act required the Environmental Protection Agency to determine what chemicals were hazardous and the appropriate means of disposing of them and to establish a system of permits to ensure that hazardous chemicals were indeed disposed of properly. Because of the technical complexity of the task, and the low priority attached to the exercise during the Carter administration, the necessary regulations were not promulgated until 1980. The regulations were attacked by industry as being too stringent and by environmentalists as being too lenient. By the time President Carter was ready to leave office, toxic waste issues were beginning to be assigned a high priority in the EPA.

When the Reagan administration came into office in 1981, it began almost immediately to attack the "regulatory excess" that it believed to be characteristic of the RCRA. Specifically, using the authority of the Paperwork Reduction Act and an executive order promoting deregulation, the Office of Management and Budget sought to dismantle some of the reporting and permit regulations of the RCRA. The OMB also cut funding for the enforcement of RCRA by almost 25 percent.[48] The attempts by the Reagan administration, under the leadership of the then head of the Environmental Protection Agency, Anne Burford Gorsuch, met strong opposition from environmental groups and some congressmen, and the EPA did not achieve the degree of deregulation desired. When scandals within the EPA forced Gorsuch from office, the new EPA administrator, William Ruckelshaus, began to restore some teeth to a law that had become almost unenforced. Under the Bush administration the "Quayle Commission," established to review and eliminate regulations, tended toward weakening the provisions of the RCRA.

The second major program for dealing with toxic wastes is the Superfund. This is a program for cleaning up hazardous waste sites, with the funds for the program coming from a tax on oil and chemical companies. The program, as proposed by the Carter administration, contained regulations requiring industry to clean up its own sites, as well as providing funds to clean up particularly hazardous sites. The program was finally adopted just before the Reagan administration came into office, with substantially weaker penalties for industries violating the act than had been proposed, but the act did provide a means of addressing some of the worst hazardous waste sites in the United States.

The Reagan administration quickly moved away from the regulatory strategy and rapid timetable of the Carter administration and toward "negotiated settlements" between the industries and the Office of Waste Programs

Enforcement in the EPA. There was a great deal of emphasis during this time on having industries clean up their own sites and on avoiding conflict with industries. Members of Congress grew increasingly impatient with what they regarded as a slowing of the planned cleanup schedule and a change in the intended mechanisms for achieving cleanups. They investigated the Superfund for alleged mismanagement and removed its head from office.

The EPA under Ruckelshaus soon began to pursue cleaning up dumps more actively. Even with that increased activity, a tiny fraction of the 1,000 "priority" hazardous sites have been cleaned up. This slowness is in part a function of the costs. It cost on average over $21 million to clean up one site in the late 1980s, and those costs were escalating rapidly.[49] Against that level of need, Congress appropriated $9 billion over five years.

Both the RCRA and the Superfund are potentially important for addressing the problem of a massive amount of toxic waste threatening the environment. The implementation of these programs has been slowed by difficulties in writing the necessary regulations and by partisan and ideological opposition within the Reagan and Bush administrations. Also, somewhat paradoxically, the "strict liability" provisions of the legislation, which make the producers of toxic wastes responsible for it over its entire lifetime, have deterred enforcement. It is often cheaper for producers to take the risk of criminal prosecution and dispose of wastes illegally than to identify the wastes to the EPA and bear the costs of their safe disposal.[50] The delays and enforcement difficulties have only made the toxic waste problem more serious.

There is a need for a large-scale effort to identify existing waste sites, clean them, and devise regulatory mechanisms for the safe disposal of such wastes in the future. The government has a number of policy tools at its disposal for addressing these tasks, including prosecution, accommodation and negotiation, and direct federal action to remove the toxic materials.[51] All these approaches have some advantages and disadvantages for coping with problems arising from private-sector wastes. The problem is confounded by the large volume of toxic wastes generated by the federal government itself, especially the Department of Defense.[52] Toxic wastes will remain a serious environmental problem for the United States for decades to come.

Implementation of Environmental Controls

The principal organization charged with the implementation of environmental control legislation is the Environmental Protection Agency, organized in 1970 to administer the growing body of environmental legislation. It was conceived as an executive agency, responsible to the president but independent of any cabinet department. The agency was charged with implementing a variety of air, water, and toxic waste programs but in so doing encountered a number of difficulties, some of which were political, involving the relationship between the EPA and other federal agencies and the states. The EPA was given a rather broad set of responsibilities and a wide field of action that inevitably brought it into conflict with other federal and state agencies. When the EPA sought to flex its environmental muscles, it almost inevitably ran into conflicts with agencies that wanted to build dams, roadways, or waterways. It also ran into difficulties with the heads of private industries who believed that the standards imposed on them by the EPA were too stringent and lessened their ability to compete in the marketplace, especially the world market. The EPA was given an unenviable task to perform; and because it was made up mostly of people committed to the environmental movement, it set out to accomplish that task with some zeal. The difficulties it encountered were intensified because many of the projects it sought to stop were pet projects of some congressman or senator, and the agency's reputation on Capitol Hill was not the best.

The EPA was also given a difficult administrative task. Congress was relatively specific about the dates by which certain levels of pollution reduction were to be achieved. This gave the administration little latitude and little opportunity to bargain with polluting industries. Also, Congress, in attempting to specify so precisely the conditions for alleviating pollution, wrote into the legislation several contradictory paragraphs, which in turn created more implementation difficulties for the EPA. Finally, the strategy adopted for a good deal of the program—technology-forcing regulations—created substantial difficulties for implementors and industries seeking to comply with the legislation.[53] When standards were adopted to reduce air pollution by 1975 to 10 percent of what it was in 1970, the technology to produce that improvement in air quality simply did not exist. It was believed that passage of the legislation would result in the development of the technology, but the result was a delay in implementation rather than any technological breakthroughs. Certainly a number of improvements have been made, especially in the internal combustion engine, as a result of this legislation, but the major innovations anticipated have not materialized.

One major implementation problem associated with environmental policies has been standard setting. We noted that such terms as "primary and secondary standards of air quality" and "best available technology" were not clearly defined in the legislation. Even if they had been, it would still have been necessary to convert those standards into permissible levels of emissions from individual sources of pollution (e.g., for each factory and municipal waste treatment facility). Overall goals for pollution reduction are relatively easy to establish, but great difficulty is encountered in translating those goals into workable and enforceable criteria. And the criteria developed must be applicable to polluters, not just to pollution, if any significant improvements in environmental quality are to be achieved. At times the difficulty of setting those standards has forced the EPA to adopt a "best practice" doctrine: if a plant is doing things like every other plant, then it must be doing things right. Also, the standard setters have been under pressure to accept more risk and not to be so strict about environmental controls for the sake of economic growth and competitiveness.[54]

The enforcement of established criteria has presented several interesting questions. First, should a mechanism exist for making tradeoffs between environmental protection and economic growth? For example, the Sierra Club succeeded in obtaining a court ruling that the air-pollution legislation did not allow any degradation of existing air quality, an interpretation resisted by the EPA. This ruling meant that people living in an area with very clean air—probably an area with little or no industry—might be forbidden to bring in any industry. A related question is how to allocate any proposed reductions in effluents among industries or other polluters. For example, should there be across-the-board percentage reductions with each polluter reducing pollution by 20 percent or whatever, or should attention be given both to the level of emissions and the technological feasibility of reducing pollution at each source? For some industries even minor reductions in effluents might be very difficult to attain, while others might be able virtually to eliminate their effluents with only a limited investment. How should these considerations be taken into account?

Second, although environmental protection legislation is filled with legal weapons to force compliance from polluters, including the authority to close down an offending industry, in reality the enforcement of the legislation has been much less draconian. Politically, the EPA cannot afford to close an industry that provides a major source of employment, either nationally or in a single community. Thus, frequently the agency's hands are tied, and the level of compliance desired or mandated has not been achieved.

Finally, although the Environmental Protection Agency has been given a number of legal and administrative mechanisms for producing improved air and water quality, its hands are frequently tied by the complex systems for standard setting and implementation. State governments, for example, are essential in devising plans for reducing pollution, and local communities have to become involved in building new waste-treatment facilities. And the Environmental Protection Agency itself is not responsible for distributing matching federal funds for those treatment facilities, so instead of being distributed on the basis of the severity of the pollution being caused, the funds are allocated on a first-come, first-served basis. Consequently, instead of developing definitive standards and practices, the enforcement of environmental legislation is frequently only a by-product of compromise, negotiation, and bargaining.[55] This characteristc does not, of course, distinguish environmental policy from most other policy, but it does run counter to some of the rhetoric about the Environmental Protection Agency's "running roughshod" over the interests of industries and local communities.

Alternatives to Regulation

As we have been demonstrating, the principal means of addressing environmental problems has been through direct regulation—the mandating of certain actions or the attainment of certain standards—enforced through legal penalties or possible closings. It has been argued that a more efficient means of producing improvements in the environment would be to impose effluent charges or taxes.[56] In other words, instead of telling an industry it could emit only a certain number of tons of effluents each year, government would allow it to emit as much as it desired. The polluter would, however, have to pay for the amount of pollution discharged, and the greater the quantity, the higher would be the costs. And possibly some means of graduating the charges could be devised so that the greater the volume of effluents, the higher the rate of payment.

The presumed advantage of effluent charges is that they would allow more efficient industries to pollute, while less efficient industries would either have to close down or improve their environmental standards. The more efficient industries could afford to pay the effluent tax and still make a profit, while less efficient industries could not. This market-oriented solution to the pollution problem would be compatible with economic growth and efficiency.[57] It is argued that it would be a definite improvement over direct regulation as a means of forcing the tradeoff between those competing values, and it would give most industries a real incentive to improve their environmental performance.

Another component of the market-oriented approach to environmental regulation is to make permits to pollute tradeable. The 1990 amendments to the Clean Air Act permit utility firms to trade rights to pollute, particularly in sulfur dioxide. The initial allocation of these allowances was related roughly to the amount of pollution the firms emitted in 1987. These amendments require the firms to begin to reduce their total emissions by 1995, with the choice for each firm being to invest in pollution-control devices or buy pollution rights from other utilities that are reducing their emissions.[58] Again the assumption is that this mechanism will produce an efficient allocation of resources as well as reduced pollution.

Effluent taxation also has been criticized. It is regarded by some critics as a mechanism for buying the right to pollute, even to kill. To those critics the value of a clean environment is greater than the value of economic growth in almost any circumstance, and they cannot accept the idea of balancing the two. In addition, enforcing a pollution tax might be even more difficult than enforcing existing regulatory standards. Effluents would have to be monitored almost continuously to determine the total amount of discharge, whereas under the present regulatory system more infrequent monitoring often is sufficient, as is less exact measurement.

The air and water of the United States are much cleaner in the 1990s than they were before the passage of the environmental legislation. Fish are returning to streams that were once biologically dead, and cities such as Pittsburgh, once constantly shrouded in smoke and grit, now can be seen from a distance. Despite these successes, the EPA and its legislation have come under a great deal of criticism. The agency has been attacked from both sides—for being insensitive to the needs of industry and for being too soft on polluters. And questions about the role of the EPA are likely to become even more important as scarce resources and slow economic growth raise the average citizen's concern about national priorities. The Reagan administration began early to question the efficacy of many standards and to soften environmental regulations, especially on automobile-caused pollution. This was intended to assist the depressed automobile industry and allow American automobiles to compete with imported automobiles, at least on price.

Decisions in one policy area impinge on many other areas. Environmental policy cannot be discussed apart from energy policy or from policies concerning economic growth. But the institutions of government frequently do not provide mechanisms for rectifying these conflicts of values. Each policy area is treated separately, has its own constellation of interests and professional standards, and seeks to maximize the returns from political activities for the participants in the policymaking. As both national resources and government resources dwindle, however, decisions by "subgovernments" may be a luxury we can no longer afford.

The 1990s may be the decade during which some important questions about the relationship between Americans and their physical environment are decided. We as a nation must decide how much value to attach to a clean and relatively unspoiled environment, compared with the value we attach to the mastery of that environment through energy exploration and economic growth. Although renewable energy resources and some shifting of attitudes about the desirability of economic growth may soften these hard choices, there must still be choices. These choices will arise with respect to specific issues, such as the opening of more Alaskan lands to energy exploration or how to manage the oil shale of the West. They may also arise over specific issues such as the disposal of increasing quantities of toxic industrial wastes and the need to develop cleaner means of producing the goods to which we have become accustomed. Also, Americans will be asked what they personally will give up for a cleaner environment. Are styrofoam cups worth the emission of CFCs into the environment and the swelling of solid-waste dumps? Are we willing to spend an hour or so every week recycling materials to prevent pollution and conserve energy? The summation of the individual choices, along with the regulatory choices made by government, will say a good deal about the quality of life in the United States for years to come.

Notes

1. Constance Mungall and Digby J. McLaren, eds., *Planet under Stress: The Challenge of Global Change* (New York: Oxford University Press, 1990).

2. Statistical Office of the United Nations, *Yearbook of World Energy Statistics 1990* (New York: United Nations, 1993).

3. Robin C. Landon and Michael W. Klass, *OPEC: Policy Implications for the United States* (New York: Praeger, 1980).

4. U.S. Department of Energy, *Annual Energy Review 1993* (Washington, D.C.: U.S. Department of Energy, 1994).

5. International Monetary Fund, *Balance of Payments Statistics* (Washington, D.C.: International Monetary Fund, monthly).

6. There may well be more natural gas available, but relatively low prices have deterred exploration. See Mark Fischetti, "There's Gas in Them There Hills," *Technology Review* 96 (1993): 16–18.

7. James M. McElfish and Ann E. Beier, *Environmental Regulation of Coal Mining* (Washington, D.C.: Environmental Law Institute, 1990).

8. Barbara E. Smith, *Digging Our Own Graves: Coal Miners and the Struggle over Black Lung Disease* (Philadelphia: Temple University Press, 1987).

9. Processes of this type have existed for some time, but are not economically feasible at anything like current energy prices.

10. Felicity Barringer, "Four Years Later, Soviets Reveal Wider Scope to Chernobyl Horror," *New York Times*, 28 April 1990; David Marples, *The Social Impact of the Chernobyl Disaster* (New York: St. Martin's, 1988).

11. John L. Campbell, *Collapse of an Industry: Nuclear Power and the Contradictions of U.S. Policy* (Ithaca, N.Y.: Cornell University Press, 1988).

12. Henry F. Bedford, *Seabrook Station: Citizen Politics and Nuclear Power* (Amherst: University of Massachusetts Press, 1990).

13. Matthew. L. Wald, "License Is Granted to Nuclear Plant in New Hampshire," *New York Times*, 2 March 1990.

14. Bedford, *Seabrook Station*.

15. Rodman D. Griffin, "Nuclear Fusion," *CQ Researcher* 3 (22 January 1993): 51–64.

16. Michael Kenward, "Fusion Becomes a Hot Bet for the Future," *New Scientist* 132 (16 November 1991): 10–11.

17. Todd Wilkinson, "Gone With the Wind," *Backpacker* 20 (September 1992): 11.

18. *New York Times,* 2 March 1980.

19. Michael M. Crow and Gregory Hager, "Political versus Economic Risk Deduction and the Failure of U.S. Synthetic Fuel Development Efforts," *Policy Studies Review* 5 (1985): 145–52.

20. Regina S. Axelrod, "Energy Policy: Changing the Rules of the Game," in *Environmental Policy in the 1980s: Reagan's New Agenda,* ed. Norman J. Vig and Michael E. Kraft (Washington, D.C.: CQ Press, 1984).

21. Henry G. Broadman, "Natural Gas Deregulation: The Need for Further Reform," *Journal of Policy Analysis and Management* 5 (1986): 496–516.

22. "Briefing on Energy Policy," *Weekly Compilation of Presidential Documents* 27 (25 February 1991): 188–90.

23. "Wimping Out on Energy," *Business Week,* 25 February 1991, 30–34.

24. Eugene Feingold, "Finding Trust in Government," *Nation's Health* 24 (May 1994): 2;"DOE's Growing Fallout," *Environmental Action* 26 (Spring 1994): 6.

25. Amory B. Lovins, *Soft Energy Paths: Toward a Durable Peace* (New York: Harper & Row, 1979); L. Hunter Lovins, Amory B. Lovins, and Seth Zuckerman, *Energy Unbound* (San Francisco: Sierra Books, 1986).

26. See Stephen H. Schneider, *Global Warming: Are We Entering the Greenhouse Century?* (New York: Vintage, 1989); National Academy of Sciences, *Our Earth, Our Future, Our Changing Global Environment* (Washington, D.C.: National Academy Press, 1990).

27. The journal *Diversity* is a good source of information about the resources existing in these settings.

28. Riley E. Dunlap, "Trends in Public Opinion toward Environmental Issues, 1965–1990," *Society and Natural Resources* 4 (1991): 285–312.

29. Margaret E. Kriz, "Jobs vs. Owls," *National Journal* (30 November 1993): 2913–16.

30. Murray Weidenbaum, "Return of the 'R' Word: The Regulatory Assault on the Economy," *Policy Review* 59 (1992): 40–43.

31. For example, the Safe Drinking Water Act requires monitoring for 83 substances, although a number have never been found in any public water supply. See Margaret E. Kriz, "Cleaner Than Clean?" *National Journal,* 23 April 1994, 946–49.

32. Christopher J. Bosso, "After the Movement: Environmental Activism in the 1990s," in *Environmental Policy in the 1990s,* ed. Norman J. Vig and Michael E. Kraft (Washington, D.C.: CQ Press, 1994).

33. Vice-President Gore's book on environmental politics became a part of the presidential campaign in 1992. See Al Gore, *Earth in the Balance: Ecology and the Human Spirit* (Boston: Houghton Mifflin, 1992).

34. Margaret Kriz, "That Was the Week That Was," *National Journal,* 2 February 1994, 393.

35. General Accounting Office, "Federal Facilities: Issues Involved in Cleaning Up Hazardous Wastes," GAO/T-RCED-92-82 (Washington, D.C.: GAO, 28 July 1992).

36. This has been described as "bureaucratic pluralism," even by some

within the EPA. See Walter A. Rosenbaum, "Into the 1990s at EPA," in Vig and Kraft, *Environmental Policy in the 1990s.*

37. Richard N.L. Andrews, "Risk-Based Decisionmaking," in *Environmental Policy in the 1990s.*

38. Donald T. Hornstein, "Reclaiming Environmental Law: A Normative Critique of Comparative Risk Analysis," *Columbia Law Review* 29 (1992): 562–633.

39. Margaret Kriz, "The Greening of Environmental Regulation," *National Journal,* 18 June 1994, 1464–67.

40. For a review of developments, see Debra S. Knopman and Richard A. Smith, "Twenty Years of the Clean Water Act," *Environment* 35 (1993): 17–20, 34–41.

41. "Oil Officials Fear Stricter Water Act Provisions from New Congress," *Oilgram News* 74, no. 218 (1986): 2.

42. James P. Lester, "New Federalism and Environmental Policy," *Publius* 16 (1986): 149–65.

43. Margaret E. Kriz, "Clashing over Chlorine," *National Journal,* 19 March 1994, 659–61.

44. Margaret Kriz, "Clean Machines," *National Journal,* 16 November 1991, 2789–94.

45. James C. McKinley, Jr., "Ten States Agree on a Program for Air Quality," *New York Times,* 2 October 1994.

46. Mark Crawford, "Hazardous Waste: Where to Put It?" *Science* 235 (9 January 1987): 156.

47. Peter A.A. Berle, "Toxic Tornado," *Audubon* 87 (1985): 4.

48. Steven Cohen, "Federal Hazardous Waste Programs" in Vig and Kraft, *Environmental Policy in the 1980s.*

49. Environmental Protection Agency, *A Preliminary Analysis of the Public Costs of Environmental Protection, 1981–2000* (Washington, D.C.: EPA, May 1990).

50. Zachary A. Smith, *The Environmental Policy Paradox* (Englewood Cliffs, N.J.: Prentice Hall, 1991), 179–86.

51. Thomas W. Church and Robert T. Nakamura, *Cleaning Up the Mess: Implementation Strategies in Superfund* (Washington, D.C.: Brookings Institution, 1993).

52. *Superfund: Backlog of Unevaluated Federal Facilities Slows Cleanup Efforts,* GAO/RCED-93-119 (Washington, D.C.: General Accounting Office, July 1993).

53. Charles O. Jones, "Speculative Augmentation in Federal Air Pollution Policymaking," *Journal of Politics* 42 (1975): 438–64.

54. Graeme Browning, "Taking Some Risks," *National Journal,* 1 June 1991, 1279–82.

55. Some analysts have argued that there may be *insufficient* negotiation in the enforcement of environmental legislation, and that better compliance could be achieved through bargaining rather than conventional regulatory enforcement. See Eugene Bardach and Robert Kagan, *Going by the Book* (Philadelphia:

Temple University Press, 1983).

56. A. Myrick Freeman, "Economics, Incentives and Environmental Regulation," in Vig and Kraft, *Environmental Policy in the 1990s.*

57. Barnaby J. Feder, "Sold: $21 Million of Air Pollution," *New York Times,* 30 March 1993.

58. Margaret Kriz, "Emission Control," *National Journal,* 3 July 1993, 1696–1701.

13. Protective Policies: Defense and Law Enforcement

The Constitution of the United States lists "to provide for the common defense" as the second purpose of the government of the United States. Going back to Lexington and Concord and the Minutemen, military defense has been a visible and sometimes extremely expensive function in a country favoring small government and few government employees.[1] Not all threats to peace and order are foreign, and from the beginning policing and law enforcement have been a major government function. This activity has been largely a state and local function but, like education, has seen a growing involvement by the federal government. Some of that involvement has been purely financial, but increasingly the federal government is directly concerned with the enforcement of laws.

This chapter examines both these functions of government. Interestingly one (defense) appears to be of less concern to the average citizen, while the other (law enforcement) is of growing concern. Indeed, in a growing number of surveys during the 1990s crime and personal safety were listed by citizens as the most pressing problem of government (see table 13.1). These two policy areas have some obvious similarities (e.g., the use of force in the name of the public), but also have some more subtle similarities (e.g., potential threats to civil liberties). There are also some obvious and important differences between the policy areas we explore here.

Defense Policy

The task of providing for the common defense is now a much more complex and expensive task than it was when an effective military force could be raised by each man in the community taking down the rifle from over the fireplace. Military spending accounted for 25 percent of federal spending in 1994, down from 35 percent in 1980. In 1992 military spending was 5.2 percent of gross national product; thus, $5.20 out of every $100 in the economy went for military defense. This figure was down from 6.5 percent of GNP in 1985. In some parts of the United States, such as Norfolk,

TABLE 13.1

MOST IMPORTANT ISSUES FOR AMERICANS

(IN PERCENTAGES, UP TO THREE MENTIONS RECORDED)

	November 1991	August 1992	January 1993	September 1993	January 1994
Unemployment	23	27	22	20	18
Economy (general)	32	37	35	26	14
Drugs	10	6	6	6	9
Health care	6	12	18	28	20
Crime	6	7	9	16	37

SOURCE: *Gallup Poll Monthly,* September 1992, 11; January 1994, 43.

Virginia, and Southern California, defense (whether the military or civilian defense contractors) is a major component of the local economy.

Defense policy has become even more controversial after the apparent end of the Cold War and the short Gulf war. The demands placed on the defense establishment now involve greater complexity and planning for greater uncertainty than when the adversary was clear and the types of weapons needed, at least for deterrence, were largely agreed upon. Further, many Americans expected a "peace dividend" from the end of the Cold War, but government leaders have not been as anxious to dismantle the military establishment as were their more optimistic citizens. Even military leaders, however, accept the necessity of reducing defense expenditures in the present political and financial climate; therefore, defense expenditures were expected to decrease by about $40 billion by 1995. If the federal budget declines at the projected rate, this will reduce defense spending to "only" about 20 percent of federal spending.

Nevertheless, the current budget projections also call for an *actual* increase in defense spending in the late 1990s as a number of weapons systems still under contract begin to be delivered, with the obvious question whether those weapons are still necessary. Also, the shift from nuclear deterrence to conventional warfare and peacekeeping may make defense more expensive. A missile can sit in a silo for some time with minimal maintenance costs, but soldiers and sailors have to be paid every month and fed every day. Deciding on defense policy has never been easy, but it is likely to be even more difficult because most of the rules have changed in a very short period of time and there is little certainty about the future.

The Environment of Defense Policy

A number of factors condition the manner in which defense policy is made and the likely outcomes of the policy process. Unlike many other policy areas, influences on defense policy are to a great extent beyond the control of officials in government making the decisions. In part because of the uncertainty involved in making defense policy, there may be greater perceptual differences among individuals involved in the process than is true for other policy areas.[2] For example, the degree of threat that any decision maker perceives in the international environment will affect his or her willingness to allocate resources to defense. These perceptual differences may be exacerbated now that the clear threat of the Soviet Union has largely ended and the United States must make policies to contend with the possibility of smaller-scale, but still dangerous, armed conflicts around the world.

These smaller-scale conflicts also raise questions whether the role of the United States should be that of a global policeman or merely one more nation in the international community, albeit the only remaining superpower.[3] Further, if the United States is to act as the international policeman, should it do so alone or in concert with international organizations such as the United Nations and the Organization of American States? An even more basic question is whether the national interests of the United States are served by using its military forces for these peacekeeping and relief functions around the world, no matter how desirable those tasks may be on humanitarian grounds.

ADVERSARIES AND POTENTIAL ADVERSARIES

The fundamental factor that shaped the formulation of defense policy was the international climate and the relationship between the United States and the Soviet Union. Almost as soon as the two superpowers ceased being allies after World War II, they became adversaries on a global scale. Early stages of that adversarial relationship included the Berlin blockade and the Korean war, which were followed by the U-2 incident, the Cuban missile crisis, Vietnam, and Afghanistan, not to mention hundreds of minor incidents.[4] None of these incidents involved direct conflicts between troops of the two superpowers, although conflicts between the troops of one superpower and those of allies or surrogates of the other occurred several times. The degree of hostility expressed between the United States and the Soviet Union varied, however; there were periods of détente breaking the Cold War and some important negotiated agreements (e.g., the nuclear test ban treaty and the SALT agreements) that lessened tensions, at least for a while.

In addition to conventional conflicts, there was a nuclear arms race with each country developing massive stockpiles of nuclear weapons, capable of destroying the world several times over. Nuclear weapons have not been used since World War II, and there were several successful attempts to reduce their numbers (or at least reduce their rate of growth) even during the peak Cold War years. Still, the remaining stockpiles of these weapons represent a crucial factor that defense policymakers must always take into account, especially now that the former Soviet Union has disintegrated into a number of smaller states. Several of the new states retain large stockpiles of weapons and have national ambitions that may lead them to rattle the nuclear saber, if not actually use the weapons.[5] Russian President Boris Yeltsin has made a proposal to reduce stockpiles in Russia and the United States severely, and President Clinton has accepted an accelerated reduction of atomic stockpiles, despite continuing instability in the world.

Although the world was very dangerous during the Cold War and the stockpiling of nuclear weapons by the two superpowers, it may be more dangerous now that "peace" has broken out. Instead of there being one Soviet Union with nuclear weapons, a number of the former Soviet republics now have weapons on their soil. The leaders of the largest republic, Russia, have said that the weapons are no longer aimed at the United States, but it is not clear where they are aimed. The Gulf war also pointed to the presence of nuclear, chemical, and biological weapons in a number of countries and the apparent willingness of those countries to use force to attain their political and economic goals. Some of these potential adversaries, such as North Korea, still appear to be fighting the Cold War; others, such as Iraq, are pursuing more nationalistic or economic goals.

Although many of these potential adversaries are small and relatively weak militarily, they are widely dispersed around the globe, and the American defense establishment must decide how quickly, and in how many simultaneous situations, it must be prepared to respond.[6] Further, those planners must decide how much force both we and our potential adversaries can bring to bear in these potential conflicts. There is the danger that the U.S. military has been so attuned to large-scale international conflicts that it will not be capable of coping effectively with the seemingly more mundane low-level conflicts that seem more probable in the 1990s. The "bottom-up review" of defense policy in 1994 was premised on the possibility of several smaller conflicts, such as the Gulf war.[7] This question became realistic in the fall of 1994 when there was a potential confrontation with Iraq at the same time that troops were in Haiti.

ALLIES

The United States also has friends in the world, although its allies do not always agree with the United States on defense and foreign policy issues. The most important alliance for the United States has been the North Atlantic Treaty Organization (NATO), which has linked nations in Europe and

North America for their mutual defense since the late 1940s. NATO has been responsible for the defense of western Europe and the North Atlantic, and the United States commits by far the largest share of personnel and material to the alliance.[8] The Soviet Union also had allies, and its equivalent to NATO was the Warsaw Pact. The United States also has important defense agreements with Japan, South Korea, Israel, and Australia.

The events of the late 1980s made many people—defense analysts and ordinary citizens alike—question the continuation of NATO, at least in its traditional format. The Warsaw Pact has disintegrated, and there is little likelihood of an invasion of western Europe. Further, economic problems at home and the continuing economic and political integration of western Europe mean that there is less need for a large American military presence in Europe; almost all the divisions stationed in Germany since the end of World War II have come home. Similarly, the United States was willing to give up major military bases in the Philippines, in the belief that they will be much less valuable in a world without direct East-West confrontations.

Although these alliances are apparently now less valuable, the experience of the Gulf war pointed out that Western nations, and even some former adversaries from the Warsaw Pact, could band together to confront a perceived common threat. The existence of the UN stamp of approval on their actions in the Persian Gulf made the alliance more viable, but there is some sense that the United States has friends around the world that can be counted on in many military situations. The alliances may be ad hoc arrangements rather than continuing treaty commitments, but there will still be ways of generating collective action to maintain international security. Further, economic and social issues (including human rights) may well become more important in defining security arrangements in the future, so the United States needs to learn to adjust its own thinking about how to make and maintain international alliances.[9]

Technology

The technology of modern warfare has advanced far beyond what was available even during the Vietnam conflict twenty-five years ago. Nuclear armaments are a major part of the technological change, but systems for delivering weapons have improved even more rapidly. In the 1950s it took hours for a plane to fly from the former Soviet Union to the United States; a missile can now make a comparable journey in fifteen minutes, and a missile launched from a submarine offshore could arrive in a few minutes. There even are plans for war in space; "killer satellites" and orbiting weapons were part of President Reagan's Strategic Defense Initiative ("Star Wars").[10] The technology of conventional warfare also has advanced and now includes laser-guided weapons, infrared night-vision scopes, stealth airplanes, computers, and anti-missile defenses that featured prominently during the Gulf war. There is also discussion of a whole new generation of weapons, for example, the potential for laser weapons, that would have been science fiction a few years ago.

The advance of weapons technology has several implications for defense policy. One is that defense is now a constant activity; there is no longer any time to raise an army and then go to war. A standing army historically is something of an anathema to many Americans, but in the 1990s the U.S. military numbers approximately 2 million uniformed personnel plus almost 1 million civilian employees in the Department of Defense. The technology for modern war is now widely dispersed, so many smaller countries can bring sophisticated weapons to the battlefield. The need to master modern technology to be effective implies that the "citizen soldier" model of the past is increasingly less viable.

Another feature of the increased technological component of modern warfare is cost. This is in part a function of having to maintain a large standing military establishment, but it goes beyond that. One new air force B-1 or B-2 bomber costs almost $1 billion; one army tank costs approximately $10 million, and one proposed new carrier for the navy could be several billion dollars.[11] Therefore, any discussion of improving the technical quality of American military forces must be conducted within the context of very high costs. Indeed, as the need to control public spending is combined with the declining threat from the former Soviet Union, new strategies of weapons procurement may be devised to keep American forces well armed, but as inexpensively as possible.[12] One of the most important strategies will be the modernization of existing weapons instead of the development of whole new systems.

Public Opinion

Finally, American defense policy is made in a relatively open political arena and is definitely influenced by public opinion. As is true for many public issues, public opinion about defense is ambiguous. There are few committed advocates of unilateral disarmament in the United States, even after the apparent end of the Soviet threat, and virtually all politicians advocate a strong defense for the United States. Nevertheless, there are a sufficient number of questions about program costs, about whether many of the high-technology weapons purchased actually contribute that much to the security of the United States, and about the manner in which the military power of the United States should be used (e.g., in the Caribbean, Central America, or other parts of the Third World). All these questions are political as well as technical military issues and will be fought out in Congress and the media as well as in the Pentagon.

Nuclear weapons constitute an even greater public opinion problem. A significant portion of the population, although favoring a strong defense for the United States, was opposed to the nuclear arms race between the United States and the Soviet Union. The public generally applauded the negotiated freezes on nuclear weapons and the reduction in the numbers of such weapons stockpiled by both sides. There is virtual unanimity on one point: the United States should never be the first country to use nuclear weapons in a conflict. This is true whether the conflict is one among superpowers or more limited conflicts such as the Gulf war.

With the negotiated reduction in nuclear forces in the United States and the former Soviet Union, the issue of nuclear weapons did not vanish. The one remaining superpower, and the successor states to the former one, possess substantial stocks of nuclear weapons, as well as the means to deliver those weapons. Further, despite the existence of the nuclear nonproliferation treaty, and the efforts of the United Nations to enforce that treaty, nuclear weapons appear to be spreading around the globe, potentially to terrorist groups as well as legitimate governments.[13] The threat of nuclear weapons will be something that the United States must live with for the foreseeable future. Simple agreement among Americans that the weapons are an immense danger will not eliminate the fact of their existence.

U.S. Force Configurations

Table 13.2 lists the strategic weapon holdings of the United States, Russia, and China. This listing is subject to extremely rapid change. With the end of the Cold War and the dismantling of the (former) Soviet Union, much of this vast arsenal appears to be dinosaurs left from an earlier age. Pledges from Boris Yeltsin, leader of the Russian federation, and from then President Bush to dismantle much of the strategic forces meant that these weapons were fol-

TABLE 13.2

NUCLEAR WARHEADS IN POSSESSION OF UNITED STATES
AND MAJOR POTENTIAL ADVERSARIES

Deliverable by	*United States*	*Russia*	*China*
Bombers	2,900	1,374	150
ICBMs	2,000	6,178	110
Submarine-launched missiles	3,520	2,600	24

SOURCE: International Institute of Strategic Studies, *The Military Balance, 1993–94* (London: Brassey's, 1994).

lowing the path of intermediate-range weapons in Europe and would be destroyed. Both the United States and Russia will retain some nuclear arsenal, but neither will be of the magnitude, or the threat, that has characterized them for several decades. In particular, most of the missiles will be fitted with a single warhead, rather than the multiple warheads now on many missiles. In the downsizing, the United States is likely to hold on to its submarine-launched weapons most dearly, and to be more willing to trade away other parts of its "triad."[14] As promising as these developments are, the uncertainty about whose "finger is on the button," and indeed how many buttons there are, in the former Soviet Union makes the world still a dangerous place and makes maintaining some nuclear deterrent an important part of American defense policy.

The balance in nonstrategic forces in the world is less easy to define. Table 13.3 gives the balance of conventional forces between the United States, Russia, and China. The countries formed out of the former Soviet Union have a very large military force, but the own fragmentation among and within these new countries may make those forces less dangerous than they might otherwise be. Still, the actual force levels of the United States are smaller than those of some other countries. In any conflict with those countries, it is hoped that the superior technical capabilities of some American weapons, as well as superiority in the number of attack aircraft, will level the balance.

TABLE 13.3

CONVENTIONAL LAND FORCES OF UNITED STATES
AND MAJOR POTENTIAL ADVERSARIES

	United States	Russia	China
Personnel	768,000	1,000,000	2,300,000+
Main battle tanks	15,300	25,000	13,700
Artillery	6,000	24,000+	14,500+

SOURCE: International Institute of Strategic Studies, *The Military Balance 1993–94* (London: Brassey's, 1994).

Table 13.4 shows the balance of naval forces between the United States and its potential adversaries. The United States has fewer surface ships and far fewer general-purpose submarines than Russia. The numerical superiority of the former Soviet Union may in fact underestimate the strength of the U.S. Navy, given the capabilities contained in one attack-carrier battle

TABLE 13.4

NAVAL FORCES OF UNITED STATES AND MAJOR
POTENTIAL ADVERSARIES

	United States	*Russia*	*China*
Submarines	108	200	46
Carriers	12	3	0
Other major surface vessels	155	167	56[a]

SOURCE: International Institute of Strategic Studies, *The Military Balance,
1993–94* (London: Brassey's, 1994).
   a. Excludes numerous patrol craft.

group. In addition, superior detection equipment and satellite tracking make
submarines of other countries relatively less effective. Thus, despite reduction in naval construction, and the far-flung missions that the U.S. Navy
must serve, on balance the edge seems to go to the naval forces of the United
States.

   If nothing else, this toting up of personnel and weapons systems demonstrates the huge destructive potential that can be unleashed in a few mo-
ments by a number of countries in the world. Such great power carries with
it great responsibility and the need for effective strategic doctrines to prevent
the use of nuclear weapons, or, one hopes, any weapons. The doctrines of a
bipolar world (e.g., mutually assured destruction) are no longer valid, yet
because of that there is perhaps less security than existed even during the
height of the Cold War.

Problems of Defense Policy

Maintaining the defenses of the United States presents several significant
policy problems, none of which can be solved readily. One of these is how to
manage nuclear strategy in a multipolar world. Others are more specific
problems, such as the interaction of specific defense issues (e.g., the acquisition of weapons and manpower) with either fundamental features of the
economic system or fundamental American values. These problems have
grown more complex as the uncertainty about the military future of the
United States makes choices more difficult and more risky.

Military Procurement

The first major defense problem is the problem of acquiring new weapons systems.[15] In a modern, high-technology military force, new weapons are not bought "off the shelf" but represent years or even decades of research and development. This in turn presents several problems for the military managers who seek to acquire the weapons. One problem is attempting to predict years in advance just what sort of weapons will be required to secure American national security. For example, during the Reagan years a great deal of money was funneled into the Strategic Defense Initiative.[16] Given changes in the strategic environment, that program now appears to be of limited utility.

Another problem for procurement officials is deciding what form of competition to demand among potential suppliers of the weapons. One option is to have possible competitors develop full-scale, operating systems and then test those weapons against each other. The other option is to settle on one or a limited number of vendors for the weapons system very early in the development process and then work with the contractor to develop the weapon. Although the former option corresponds to the usual ideas about bidding for contracts and getting the most "bang for the buck" from the Department of Defense's money, it may ultimately produce more expensive and less effective weapons. If a firm must develop fully operational weapons in order to compete for a program, it may choose simply not to compete; hence many potentially useful ideas (especially from smaller firms) will be lost. Second, if this kind of competition is carried out, then any firm competing for government contracts may have to amortize its failures across winning contracts in order to make a profit, and consequently the costs of weapons systems as a group will increase. The other option would be to sell the weapons to other countries, a strategy that came back to haunt several countries, including the United States, during the Gulf war and that may not be the best strategy of reducing the level of military tension in the world.

But awarding contracts for major weapons systems on the basis of only prototypes and engineering projections may produce numerous disappointments and cost overruns. Despite screening by skilled military and civilian personnel in the Department of Defense, good ideas on the drawing board may not work when they are brought to full-scale production and deployment. There are a number of examples in recent weapons systems; the Sergeant York (DIVAD) antiaircraft cannon, the Bradley fighting vehicle, the C-17 aircraft, and several missile systems, for example, have not performed as expected.[17] Even if the manufacturer is capable of making the system work as promised, there may be large cost overruns; the delivered price of the C-5A was several times the projected price.

Given that most contracts for weapons are "cost plus" and virtually guarantee the manufacturer a profit, manufacturers have a strong incentive to bid low on projects and allow costs to escalate later. The Department of Defense has instituted controls to try to prevent the most flagrant violations of this contracting system, but it is difficult to control genuine cases of cost underestimation when a project is well into production. If a workable product can be attained, it will almost certainly be better to go ahead with the project and permit cost overruns rather than begin again at the beginning.

Another problem arising from the procurement process is that a manufacturer awarded a contract for a particular weapons system becomes the "sole source" for that system and for the parts that go along with it. This allows firms to charge exorbitant prices for spare parts and tools; simple wrenches costing a dollar or less have been billed to the Department of Defense for several thousand dollars. Some of these apparent excesses were more media events than real cost problems, and curbs have been instituted to stop some of the greatest abuses, but the underlying problem in weapons procurement remains.

The division among the armed services may also produce problems in procuring weapons, or at least may make weapons cost more than they should. Again, there are two options. One would be to attempt to force the services to use the same weapons, if at all possible; the other would be to allow the services to acquire systems more suited to their individual needs. For example, both the air force and the navy fly airplanes that perform similar missions; why can they not use the same planes? In addition to the long-standing rivalries between the services, there may be a danger that weapons resulting from an integrated procurement process would be neither fish nor fowl. For example, the weight added to a plane to make it strong enough to make carrier landings for the navy may make it less suitable as an air-superiority interceptor for the air force.

Yet procurement of a number of different weapons may produce higher costs, for the research and development costs of each can be amortized across fewer units of production. In addition, the budgetary process of the United States presents problems for weapons procurement. Unlike the large majority of countries, the United States has an annual defense budget, and there is a possibility (and some real examples) that an ongoing weapons system may lose its funding. This, of course, presents problems for both contractors and the military. To date, proposals for a multiyear procurement process have been adopted only in part because Congress wishes to maintain its control over the public purse.[18]

The continuing fiscal crisis of the federal government and the winding down of the Cold War have introduced other budget problems into the procurement process. Procurement plans as of early 1992 were to continue to develop prototypes of new weapons systems and to test these prototypes, but not to produce the systems in any quantity.[19] The idea was that the armed forces could remain technologically modern, yet do so at limited expense. If there were an outbreak of hostilities, then the weapons systems could go into production. On the one hand, this approach to procurement appears to violate some of the assumptions about contemporary military preparedness mentioned earlier, in which speed of response is an essential element. On the other hand, this may be the only way to maintain the technological edge demonstrated during the Gulf war while reducing the amount of money spent on the military.

Thus the process of equipping a modern army is a difficult one, and it is made more difficult by the budgeting process and budget problems of the United States. It is made even more difficult by the close ties between the Department of Defense and their defense contractors—the military-industrial complex, or the fifth branch of the armed forces—that may make an independent evaluation of some proposed weapons systems difficult to obtain. These problems are harder to solve because Congress demands to preserve its budgetary powers and the defense establishment needs the cooperation and capabilities of contractors; given the importance of hardware and technology for the modern military, however, significant attention must continue to be given to these questions.

Updating the Strategic Deterrent

Much of the strategic deterrent force of the United States is aging; in some cases, it may be obsolete. The B-52 bomber entered service in the 1950s and, despite updates and modifications, is a very old weapon. The Minuteman missile is by no means obsolete but was vulnerable to a Soviet first strike. These problems with existing weapons led to the development of three new weapons systems—the B-1 and B-2 bombers and the MX missile—all of which have been at the center of controversy.

The B-1 bomber was designed as a supersonic penetrating intercontinental bomber that can fly to the target and return, depending on speed and electronic countermeasures for its survival. After several prototypes were built and tested, the Carter administration canceled the project in 1977, arguing that bombers may not be as efficient as cruise missiles and that the development of the "stealth" technology, which would make an airplane less visible to radar, would make the B-1 obsolete quickly. This decision caused a great deal of negative reaction in the military—especially in the air force —and was reversed by the Reagan administration, which called for a force of 100 B-1 bombers. The continuing problems with the prototypes of the B-1, and the rapid development of stealth technology incorporated into the B-2, led to the end of the B-1. Now B-2 production may be stopped after only twenty planes, a victim of the end of the Cold War and tight Pentagon budgets.

Updating the U.S. missile fleet presents an even more difficult problem. The MX was designed to reduce the vulnerability of Minuteman missiles, as well as to upgrade the accuracy and number of warheads in the U.S. nuclear arsenal. While existing Minuteman III missiles have three independent warheads, the MX could carry ten. The most important controversy about the MX was the original "racetrack" deployment strategy of the Carter administration. The idea was to put each of the (then) 200 MX missiles on a transporter, which would move around an oval "racetrack" containing twenty-six hardened launch sites; it was assumed that the Soviets (or any other power) would not know where the missiles were at any time and could not destroy them without using at least 5,200 warheads (200 missiles times 26 sites). The Reagan administration rejected this proposal, in part because of strong opposition from the western states (sites probably would have been in Utah and Nevada), where thousands of acres would have been needed for the racetracks, and in part because the administration thought there were means—with spy satellites, for example—by which the Soviets would indeed know where the missiles were.

The Reagan administration decided to proceed with the production of 100 MX missiles and appointed a bipartisan Commission on Strategic Alternatives (the Scowcroft Commission) to make suggestions for basing the MX. This commission also recommended the development of a new, small, and highly mobile missile that could be fired from a mobile launcher and therefore moved almost anywhere, much as cruise missiles can be. This suggestion soon came to be known as the "Midgetman" missile. The Midgetman would have only a single, rather small warhead, but given its relatively low cost and its relative invulnerability, it could present a serious deterrent, especially given the destructive capacity of even a small warhead. This missile has not been purchased, despite plans for up to 600, and only 50 MXs have been purchased.

While all these advances in weapons technology were once of tremendous importance for the defense of the United States, their importance is not now clear. Are they really necessary for the threats that may be posed by smaller nuclear powers, or will these weapons and a host of other strategic weapons become merely quaint relics of the past? Already the long journeys of Trident submarines have an element of the Flying Dutchman about them,[20] and in late 1991 the B-52s that had been on constant alert since the 1950s stood down. Again, there is need for a thorough and careful examination of just what we are buying for the military of the 1990s.

The All-Volunteer Military

During the Vietnam war, the use of conscription to provide manpower for the armed forces became increasingly unpopular in the United States. Therefore, in 1975 the draft was phased out and replaced by an all-volunteer force. While this was politically desirable, that policy decision presents several problems for the armed forces in the 1990s.[21] These problems will be reduced but by no means eliminated by the "build-down" of forces now being implemented.

The most obvious problem is that the military must now compete directly with civilian employers for the same pool of young people, instead of being able to train young people in the military for a short time and perhaps induce some of them to remain in the service. Given the risks associated with serving in the military, it is not surprising that there have been difficulties at times in filling enlistment quotas. There are special difficulties in attracting educated and skilled personnel to the armed forces, for these are the people whose services are in demand in the civilian labor market. Thus, for much of its history, the all-volunteer force has been plagued by stories of low-quality recruits.

This diminished during the recession of the early 1980s and again in the 1990s, when any job seemed attractive, and there were long queues of potential enlistees waiting to enter the armed forces. But the quality problem may well resurface as the economy recovers. The military has lessened its demand for young men somewhat by using women in jobs formerly filled by males (although still not in combat positions) and by using civilians in jobs once filled by uniformed personnel. There is still a problem, however, in attracting enough highly skilled personnel to a military increasingly dominated by technical weapons systems. There seems to be an increasing disparity between the skills required to function effectively in a modern armed force and the personnel generally available to the military, although performance of the all-volunteer forces and the reserves in the Gulf war allayed these fears somewhat.

Associated with the general problem of attracting personnel is the problem of compensating them. An obvious means of attracting and retaining people in any job is to pay them adequately; this is especially true for the military, given the dangers and hardships associated with serving in the armed forces. Unfortunately, military pay is generally not competitive with private-sector pay, even when the value of allowances and benefits is included in the comparison. Military pay is much better than it was before the introduction of an all-volunteer military, but it is not yet capable of attracting as many of the best personnel in the labor market as the armed forces require. With the end of the Cold War, patriotism and defending the United States also have been less effective motives in recruitment. Nevertheless, military pay has become more expensive in the aggregate and now accounts for a larger percentage of the defense budget than it did before the all-volunteer force. An increased reliance on reserve forces has helped reduce the financial burden somewhat, but adequate compensation for military employment is likely to remain an issue.

Associated with the general problem of pay for military personnel is the especially difficult problem of retaining people whom the armed forces have trained. For example, someone who trains as a pilot in the air force is frequently able to command twice his military pay working for a private airline. Even skilled enlisted personnel, such as machinists and radar operators, have found that the private sector offers them a much greater economic reward than continuing in the military would offer. The economic slowdown of the early 1990s made military employment appear more attractive, but that was only a short-term phenomenon. As military pay failed to keep pace with wages in the private sector, many military personnel found themselves in a difficult economic position.[22] The retirement option available to military personnel (full retirement benefits after thirty years) may make staying in the service more desirable, but the loss of crucial skilled personnel continues, and there are some pressures to make military retirement less generous. For example, one of the principal recommendations of President Reagan's private survey of government costs was to make military retirement much more like retirement programs in the private sector.

Finally, there are philosophical and constitutional questions about the development of an all-volunteer military. Given historical patterns and perhaps continuing discrimination in the labor market, an all-volunteer force may be composed increasingly of members of minority groups. This may be seen as imposing an excessive cost of national defense on these groups. More generally, the traditional ideal of the U.S. military has been that of the "citizen soldier"; traditionally we have rejected the idea of a professional standing army. The policy of an all-volunteer force makes it more likely that we will have a professional military force and that we will not have large numbers of young Americans serving for a time in the armed forces.

This pattern of recruitment, in turn, may make the military more of a group apart from the rest of society and may make it less amenable to civilian control. Thus, paradoxically, although we may need a professional military to be able to handle the highly sophisticated weapons in the contemporary arsenal, we may lose some control over those weapons and their potential for massive destruction. In addition, the end of the Cold War, and the sense that the military is not really that necessary, may (again, paradoxically) make the military a more distinctive element of the society. There is little evidence to support a claim that a "warrior caste" has developed in the United States, but the current personnel system of the armed forces may make that development more possible than it would be with conscription.

Other Personnel Issues

The military of the United States cannot be isolated from the social issues that influence life in the country as a whole. In particular, how to integrate women into the armed forces and how to deal with homosexuality have become important concerns for the military. Women have been involved unofficially in the military for the entire history of the United States[23] but have been a part of the military officially only since 1942. For most of this involvement, women have been assigned to support roles, including clerical duties, nursing, and a variety of other activities far removed from actual fighting. Further, men and women have been kept apart; for example, women were not allowed to serve on ships in the navy.

During the late 1980s and early 1990s the military began to allow women into more positions. The navy began to allow women on some ships and then extended that to include all ships except submarines. The air force began to allow women to train for combat positions, and the army permitted women to serve in all positions except front-line combat positions. If the United States does engage in any armed conflicts in the future, it is clear that women will be involved more directly than in the past and that there will almost certainly be more women casualties than ever before.

The issue of the rights of homosexuals to serve in the armed forces has been even more controversial than the integration of women into combat. During his presidential campaign, President Clinton promised to give homosexuals full rights to serve, but once in office he was faced with strong pressures from within the military and public opinion to modify that stance. The suggested compromise position was referred to as "Don't ask, don't tell," meaning that recruiters would not inquire about sexual preference and recruits would not volunteer that information. Sexual orientation would not in itself be a cause for release from the armed forces. The criteria for dismissal instead would be involvement in homosexual acts and causing disruptive incidents.[24]

This compromise position satisfied neither side in the dispute.[25] Members of the homosexual community believed that the president had reneged on his promise. These advocates believed that this compromise position still did not accord homosexuals the same rights to military service as those of the heterosexual community. Opponents of the compromise in the military services and in Congress believed that this decision gave too much to a group they believed would undermine military discipline and reduce the effectiveness of the armed forces. In addition, the courts have become involved and have issued a number of rulings, most of which have tended to increase the rights of homosexuals to serve in the military. For example, a ruling in 1994 reinstated a homosexual officer who had been dismissed earlier for publicly stating that he was homosexual.[26]

Conventional Forces and Strategies

With all the concern about nuclear weapons and nuclear disarmament, it is easy to forget that the most likely use of force by the United States is with conventional forces. These forces were used twice under the Reagan administration—once in Lebanon and once in Grenada—and three times during the Bush administration—in Panama, in the Gulf war, and in Somalia. The Clinton administration decided to use military forces to deal with the problem of Haiti. In addition, the navy has been used frequently to "show the flag" in the Caribbean, the Mediterranean, and the Persian Gulf. While these activities were taking place, American troops remained on duty in western Europe, South Korea, Okinawa, Guantanamo Bay in Cuba, and several other places around the globe. The ability of the United States to respond to threats to its national interests around the world with conventional forces is an important element in defense planning.

One of the important elements in the ability of the United States to project its presence around the world is the Rapid Deployment Force. This is a force of troops ready to be deployed by air on very short notice. Materials have been positioned in places around the world so that troops can be supplied during the time that might be required to have seaborne supplies delivered to them. The Carter and then the Reagan administration positioned supplies for up to six divisions (a program called POMCUS) in western Europe and the Persian Gulf region; in the event of a confrontation, troops can be flown in without the need to air-lift heavy equipment and munitions. Both these programs are designed to make the U.S. armed forces more flexible and mobile.

Technology plays a major role in flexibility and mobility. For example, the deployment of the M-I tank during the Gulf war showed it to be extremely reliable, fast, and effective despite its technological sophistication. The problem then becomes acquiring enough of these weapons to meet the needs of the armed forces. But what are those needs? What should the armed forces be preparing for? The current doctrine is that the armed forces should be preparing for one-and-a-half wars; that is, the armed forces should be preparing for one major and one minor conflict to occur at any one time.[27] Even that level of conflict might strain the available resources, especially if the conflicts involved the logistical problems of the Gulf war and did not include a convenient friendly power such as Saudi Arabia.

Planning to meet contingencies with conventional forces is important not only for the ability to project the forces of the United States necessary to implement national policy. It is also important because a strong conventional force would make the use of weapons of mass destruction, meaning primarily theater nuclear weapons, less likely. Plans still exist for the use of such weapons in the event of apparent defeat by conventional forces; once the use of those weapons begins, it will be difficult to contain their escalation. The problem of escalation has largely been eliminated in Europe but would definitely be present when dealing with smaller powers and might also result in use of chemical and biological weapons. Thus, the availability of nuclear weapons makes conventional forces that much more important.

Having an effective conventional deterrent also depends on the readiness of those forces to fight when needed. There is some fear among military leaders, as well as military analysts, that reductions in military spending will reduce the capacity of the military to meet the demands that may be placed on it. There is the fear that American defense forces have become "hollow" and might not have sufficient readiness if there were another crisis on the order of the Gulf war.[28] Given the numerous crises around the world, such as Bosnia, Rwanda, and numerous places in the former Soviet Union, those fears may be more than academic even if the role of the United States is only that of peacekeeper.[29]

Defense and/or Jobs

As the Cold War has virtually ended and many if not most Americans are ready for a significant cut in the defense budget, we find that cutting back is not as simple as it appears. In part the economic prosperity of the United States is built on its military-industrial complex, and reducing defense expenditures means reducing employment. This is true for the men and women in the armed services and for employees in defense industries. As of 1992, approximately 1.3 million people were employed in defense industries.[30] While the defense establishment will not shrink to nothing, or anything close to it, the likely cuts will mean a loss of employment for a large number of people.

Economically, the end of the Cold War arrived at a difficult time for the United States. Unemployment is already high in many areas without soldiers returning to the domestic labor force or workers in aircraft factories or tank factories being laid off. Defense cuts have had a major impact on the politics of the defense budget. Most congressmen are in favor of reducing the budget in principle but are much less interested when it has a direct impact on their districts. In an interesting Freudian slip, Senator Dianne Feinstein (D-Calif.) once argued that the B-2 bomber did not deliver a "big enough payroll." Thus, to a great extent, defense spending has been reconceptualized not as a program to protect the country but as a means of providing jobs and a (thinly) disguised industrial policy.[31] Also, the United States is a successful exporter of arms when it wants to be, so promoting defense industries may be a means of addressing some of our balance-of-payments problems.

In addition to the general economic problems that this loss of employment creates, it may have other costs. For the military, it may mean the loss of a great deal of talent, especially in the officer corps and in career non-enlisted personnel, which could be important for any future military activities of the United States. For the individuals, many of whom joined the all-volunteer military (see pp. 399-401) in the hope of a career, it may mean a huge adjustment of life plans and career prospects. Even for military personnel who can remain in the service, reductions will mean very slow promotions[32] and probably some career frustration. Finally, for the already frayed U.S. budget, this force reduction will mean a huge amount of money for separation payments.

Another strategy for the armed forces is to find new tasks on which to employ its capabilities to ensure continued employment for its personnel and continued funding from Congress. The most obvious opportunity for the use of the military is in the "war" on drugs. It is obvious that the rhetoric of the issue is already suited to the use of the military, and some of the missions in the war may also be. There are, however, questions concerning the desirability of military involvement in this policy area. For example, do Americans want the military to be seen as occupier of its own country, especially in the inner cities where the drug problem is most obvious and most violent? Also, do we want to use American military might to attack the problem in other countries, especially those of Latin America which have many unpleasant memories of previous U.S. military expeditions? Finally, is the military really capable of doing the police work necessary to be effective in drug control? As right as this involvement may be for supporting the military budget, it may be wrong for a variety of other reasons.

Making defense policy is exceedingly difficult. It involves planning for an uncertain future that contains adversaries whose strength and strategies are not readily predictable. It also involves allies whose commitments to a common purpose and a common set of policies are uncertain. Defense policy also involves making prospective decisions about weapons that may take years or even decades to develop and that may not perform as well as (or perhaps even better than) intended. Finally, defense involves huge costs that may be politically unpopular even when the public strongly supports a strong military posture for the United States. Defense policymaking is a series of gigantic gambles about the future, gambles that most of those involved hope never actually have to be taken.

Defense policy was the subject of intense and sustained political debate during the Reagan administration. Although Ronald Reagan came into office promising to modernize and strengthen America's armed forces, and won reelection stressing the same themes, his ambitious program of military procurement and expansion came into conflict with the increasing federal deficit. After Reagan left office some programs were delayed, while others have been scaled down and a few eliminated. President Bush's use of the military in the highly successful Gulf war renewed its confidence and its sense of mission. But that may not be enough to save the military budget in an era of declining resources and declining threat. The Clinton administration came to office seeking to cut defense further, but has found both conventional military and more novel humanitarian tasks for the armed forces to perform.

Law Enforcement

Defense involves the use of force, or the threat of the use of force, outside the borders of the United States. Law enforcement involves the legitimate use of coercion within the borders of the country. Most of the policies we have talked about (taxation is a notable exception) confer benefits on citizens. Law enforcement tends to be directed at penalizing certain citizens and at the same time providing significant benefits to other citizens. This traditionally has been a concern of state and local governments in the United States, but as with most other policy areas, the federal government has come to play a larger role. This is true in terms of financial support for the subnational governments, as well as its role in the direct provision of police protection to the American population.

The role of the federal government in police protection is not entirely new. Indeed, the first organization formed in the federal government—the U.S. Coast Guard—was established primarily to catch smugglers. Countless western movies and television programs have portrayed the role of the U.S. marshal as the principal peace officer in the territories of the American West before they gained statehood. In less dramatic settings federal marshals have been responsible for the implementation of the orders of federal courts since they were created in the early nineteenth century. The military has also served this function in our history, especially when there was a threat of major violence or civil disorder. One of the most notable recent examples was when President Eisenhower called in federal troops to prevent violence when Central High School in Little Rock, Arkansas, was integrated in 1957.

Perhaps the most familiar law enforcement organization in the federal government is the Federal Bureau of Investigation (FBI). A component of the Department of Justice, this organization is responsible for enforcing a number of federal laws (e.g., kidnapping and bank robbery). During the Cold War the FBI also had major responsibilities for detecting and catching foreign agents. That function continues, albeit against the agents of different countries and especially in protection against terrorism. The FBI gained a reputation for efficiency and incorruptibility during the many years in which J. Edgar Hoover was its director.[33] The reputation of the bureau has declined somewhat, but it is still a very effective law enforcement organization.

In addition to the FBI, the Coast Guard, and federal marshals, a number of other law enforcement bodies exist in the federal government. The Secret Service in the Department of the Treasury is responsible for protecting the safety of the president and the vice-president and for catching counterfeiters of U.S. currency. Also within Treasury, the Bureau of Alcohol, Tobacco, and Firearms (BATF) is responsible for enforcing a variety of federal taxes and other laws having to do with the three commodities in its title.[34] The Drug Enforcement Administration (DEA) enforces federal laws concerning selling and possessing illegal drugs. Postal inspectors are responsible for enforcing laws concerning the use of the mails for fraudulent or other illegal purposes. The Customs Bureau is responsible for enforcing laws about imports into the United States, including some aspects of drug laws and the protection of endangered species. Finally, the Immigration and Naturalization Service and the Border Patrol are responsible for enforcing immigration laws. This is a rather long list of organizations for a government presumably having a minimal role in law enforcement.

The role of the federal government in law enforcement is predicated on several of the powers given to it in the Constitution. One of these is the power to tax, with the role of the BATF and Customs being based largely on that very basic power. Many of the powers of the FBI come from the powers of the federal government to deal with issues that transcend state borders. For example, kidnapping became a federal concern after the kidnapping of the Lindbergh baby and the interstate pursuit of the criminal. The federal government also used its powers in interstate commerce to regulate the sale and distribution of certain drugs, with the DEA obviously deriving most of its powers from that source. Finally, the federal government obviously has the power to protect its own officials and the value of its currency, and that gives the Secret Service its source of constitutional justification.

Federal Support to State and Local Governments

In addition to providing police protection directly, the federal government supplies some support for state and local governments that bear the major burden of policing. The kind and amount of this support have tended to vary across time, but there is some ongoing support for this important activity coming from Washington. Fighting crime is not generally a controversial issue, so politicians usually can safely spend for this function even when there are pressures to reduce the size of the federal budget.

John DiIulio has argued that there have been two federal "wars on crime," with a third being initiated in the 1990s.[35] He (and the founders of the programs) argued that the first was the war on poverty (pp. 306–9), which included programs that were an attack on the root causes of crime as well as poverty. This war was also fought with a number of more direct weapons to attack crime, such as the Omnibus Crime Control and Safe Streets Act of 1968. This act provided a substantial amount of federal funding for local governments through the Law Enforcement Assistance Administration (LEAA), greater funding than the entire Department of Justice budget by 1968.

The second federal "war on crime" was more of a direct attack on crime and criminals. This war occurred during the Reagan administration and was spearheaded by the Comprehensive Crime Control Act of 1984 and the Anti-Drug Abuse Act of 1988. The LEAA was phased out and with it much of the federal support for local law enforcement (other than for antidrug programs). This war tended to focus on providing stiffer sentences for perpetrators of federal crimes and especially on the linkage between illegal drugs and other crimes.

The third "war" against crime contains some elements of the strategy of the two previous ones.[36] Like DiIulio's first war, it provides a good deal of money for local law enforcement—presumably 100,000 more police will be on the streets because of the 1994 Crime Control Bill. That bill also contains a strong element of crime prevention and social policy. Like the second war, this third war focuses on federal crimes and federal law enforcement and provides for new death penalties for sixty federal crimes. Given public fears of crime in 1994, there was little question that the federal government should be taking an active role in fighting crime; the policy question was what form that assault should take.

Issues in Law Enforcement Policy

As in most policy areas, there are a number of enduring issues in law enforcement policy. These help illustrate the complexity of this area. It is sometimes easy to think that given that government has been in the business of enforcing laws and policing for any number of years, the issues and approaches to the issues would be well established. This is not true, in part because this policy involves the intersection of a number of issues and interactions with a number of other policy areas.

THE CAUSES OF CRIME

The first and most fundamental issue is defining the root causes of crime. On the one hand, there is the belief that crime results from the failure of society to enforce its values on people who do not share those values. The advocates of this position then believe that the best and perhaps only way to address problems of crime is to ensure that convicted criminals receive swift, sure, and harsh punishment.[37] Further, there is the belief that current programs of parole and pardon put criminals back on the streets too quickly. For example, there has been a move in several states and at the federal level to have a "three strikes and you're out" approach to sentencing.[38] That is, if an individual is convicted of three major crimes, then he or she must go to jail for life without the possibility of parole.

The contrary position is that crime results from social and economic problems, including problems in family structure. From this perspective, the best and most efficient means of dealing with crime is to address the socioeconomic issues.[39] It is argued that instead of punishing the criminal after he or she has already decided to commit a criminal act, the emphasis on the social roots of crime would help prevent crime. In addition to programs for improving socioeconomic conditions generally, advocates have stressed the need for programs that would help parents learn how to raise their children without the violence that seems to breed additional violence.[40] Even some police forces have begun to think of their role as dealing with "problems" instead of clearing up crime "incidents."[41]

The selection of one model or another of causation for crime involves a series of choices about how to spend public money. If the punishment route is selected, government will have to spend a great deal of money for police protection and prisons. This is often expensive—it costs approximately $60,000 per year to keep a prisoner in jail. This is close to double what it costs to send a student to an expensive private university for a year.[42] In contrast, focusing on the social roots of crime requires a good deal of expenditure on education, social services, family support, and similar programs. It also requires spending money on rehabilitative services for prisoners already in jail.

Neither policy choice is without its costs and benefits, and the choice involves fundamental value decisions. Some of these values will be expressed by professional policy analysts and policymakers. Like education, however, crime and punishment are issues about which the average American is also likely to have an opinion. These opinions can be seen in the responses to polls about the basic purpose of prisons (table 13.5). The American public has tended to think that criminals can be rehabilitated and deserve a second chance. The spate of violent crime in the 1990s has reversed that opinion dramatically, and now most Americans seek retribution rather than rehabilitation in the prison system. Likewise, states are passing legislation removing educational and recreational facilities from prisons, simply as a means of punishing prisoners as much as possible.[43]

GUN CONTROL

The problem that many citizens now identify as most important in their lives is violent crime. Probably the major instrument of that violence is the firearm. There are an estimated 60 million handguns in the United States, with millions of other firearms, including semiautomatic assault weapons, in the hands of private citizens. The Second Amendment to the Constitution gives citizens the "right to bear arms," although that right is phrased in the context of the need for a militia.[44] The advocates of gun control point to the

TABLE 13.5

ATTITUDES TOWARD PUNISHMENT AND REHABILITATION,
1971–93 (IN PERCENT)

"Is the primary task of prisons to punish criminals or re-
habilitate them?"

	1971	1976	1980	1989	1993
Punish	15	21	32	38	61
Rehabilitate	76	65	53	48	25

SOURCE: George Pettinico, "Crime and Punishment: America Changes Its
Mind," *Public Perspective,* September 1994, 30–31.

number of murders by handguns each year (approximately 12,000 in 1993,
or well over half the total number of murders[45]) to argue for their control,
especially the cheap "Saturday Night Specials" that are bought and used in
the heat of the moment. Critics of gun control argue that criminals will always find a way to get guns and that law-abiding citizens need some means
of protecting themselves, their families, and their property.

State and local governments have already begun to regulate the ownership and sale of firearms. Almost all large local governments require that
handguns be registered. Some also require a waiting period between application for purchase of a handgun and the delivery of the weapon. This is to allow the police time to check on the reliability of the purchaser. Further, the
federal government has regulated automatic weapons and other especially
dangerous weapons since the days of Prohibition and the fight against gang-
sters. More recently, the federal government began to regulate sales of weapons through the mails and then adopted the "Brady bill" in 1993; this bill
imposes a federal requirement for a five-day waiting period between application for a handgun and its delivery.[46]

It is clear that there is no absolute right for a citizen to own any kind of
gun he or she wants or to get a gun anytime he or she wants. The question,
then, is what sort of restrictions are permissible under the Constitution.
There is also a question of what sort of restrictions are politically possible.
The National Rifle Association (NRA) has developed into an active, well-
financed, and usually successful lobbying organization opposing gun control. The passage of the Brady bill was seen by some as a signal of the declining influence of the NRA.[47] That power appeared to wane even further
when the association was ultimately unsuccessful in preventing the ban on
assault weapons in the Clinton crime bill (see below).

Despite the lobbying of the NRA, gun control tends to be popular among the American population. In a poll taken in late 1993, 87 percent of Americans (and 79 percent of gun owners) favored the Brady bill. Seventy-seven percent of respondents (66 percent of gun owners) favored a ban on cheap handguns and 72 percent a ban on all handguns. The only question for which there was not majority support was an absolute ban on handguns, although 39 percent of respondents favored a measure of that sort.[48]

THE DEATH PENALTY

Related to the question of punishment of criminals is whether government should impose the ultimate sanction: the death penalty. If the general answer to that question is yes, then there is the subsidiary question of under what circumstances the death penalty should be imposed. Fourteen states now impose the death penalty. Some, such as Florida and Texas, do so vigorously, while in other states the penalty is rarely imposed even when it is passed on a convicted felon. The federal government also can impose the death penalty for certain federal crimes, and the 1994 crime bill increases dramatically the number of crimes for which that penalty can be applied. The increase in the use of the death penalty seems to suit most Americans: 72 percent of respondents favored the death penalty in a 1993 survey.[49]

The arguments around this issue are practical, constitutional, and moral.[50] The practical questions revolve around whether the death penalty is really an effective deterrent to violent crime. Advocates believe it is, although some of the states with the highest murder rates are also among those that impose the death penalty most readily. Advocates also argue that the death penalty is a certain deterrent to the criminal in question committing any more crimes. Opponents of the death penalty argue that it is not really a deterrent and that most of the acts for which the death penalty is imposed are not calculated choices by the perpetrators. Opponents further argue that the legal work required to have the penalty implemented is very often monumental and costs government more than might be spent in keeping the convicted criminal in jail for life.

The constitutional questions revolve around whether the Eighth Amendment to the Constitution, which outlaws "cruel and unusual punishment," in practice outlaws the death penalty. Supporters of the penalty argue that when this amendment was written, the death penalty was used, so it was not "unusual" under the amendment. They believe that this phrase referred more to practices such as torture. Opponents of the practice argue that the penalty is indeed cruel under contemporary interpretations of that word. For a period of time, the Supreme Court tended to side with the opponents and in effect outlawed the execution of prisoners.[51] The Court reversed its stand in 1977 and began to permit the use of the penalty.

A second constitutional question concerning the death penalty is whether the act as currently administered violates the equal protection clause of the Fourteenth Amendment. Opponents of capital punishment argue that African Americans and other minorities are much more likely to be put to death than whites are, even when they have committed roughly comparable crimes.[52] They also point to a pronounced economic bias in the imposition of the penalty, with poor defendants having difficulty in securing adequate legal counsel to prevent their being sentenced to death.[53] Supporters of the death penalty argue that there are more violent crimes per capita by members of minority groups and that the differential rate of executions may merely reflect an unfortunate social reality.

Finally, there is a moral question about the use of the power of the state to put people to death. Critics of the death penalty argue that imposing the penalty makes government and society little better than the criminals they are punishing. Critics further argue that the finality of the sentence encounters the risk of executing innocent people, who then have no meaningful recourse. As we discussed with decision theory (pp. 68–70), even if the probability is small that the decision to execute is incorrect, it will produce social costs that may be greater than any benefits created. Supporters of the death penalty recognize the severity of the punishment, and few if any take the imposition of the death penalty lightly. Nevertheless, they argue that individuals who commit extremely brutal crimes and crimes involving certain victims (children, for example) have forfeited their rights to live in a civilized society.

The debate over the death penalty continues. Supporters have received some comfort from the inclusion of a large number of new crimes punishable by the death penalty in the Clinton crime bill. In addition, the Supreme Court has reduced the capacity of convicts on death row to receive stays of their sentences.[54] Opponents of capital punishment also received some good news when Justice Harry Blackmun, near retirement, wrote a dissenting opinion saying that he would no longer take part in any decisions to execute prisoners. He had made this decision despite the fact that he had voted a number of times previously to permit states to execute prisoners.[55]

THE RIGHTS OF THE ACCUSED

In addition to protections against cruel and unusual punishment, the Bill of Rights gives a number of protections to the accused. For example, the accused are protected against self-incrimination (Fifth Amendment), they are assured a trial by a jury of their peers, and they are protected against unlawful search and seizure of their persons and property (Fourth Amendment). They are also guaranteed that the writ of habeas corpus be available to them so that they will know why they are being arrested and so that they cannot be held for long periods of time without some formal charge against them being filed. Finally, the accused have a right to legal counsel when they go to court (and now even before they do).

The above is an impressive list of protections. In fact, some critics believe that the list is too long and that the police are being "handcuffed" in their attempts to arrest and convict criminals. This feeling has become all the more pronounced over the past several decades as the courts have tended to interpret the rights of the accused more broadly and to require the police to be more careful in how they treat the accused. For example someone about to be arrested must now be advised of his or her legal rights, including the right to counsel.[56] Also, the courts have tended to interpret the protections against unreasonable search strictly, so the police must have sound reasons to receive a search warrant and even stronger justification if they search without first receiving a warrant. Still, in the media event that was the O.J. Simpson trial, the judge admitted some crucial evidence gathered before a search warrant was issued because it was discovered incidental to other, proper police activities.[57] All these protections for the accused have produced a number of cries that too many criminals are able to escape conviction on mere technicalities.

Defenders of the current restrictions on police behavior argue that civil liberties are more than "technicalities," they are fundamental to the nature of the American political system and the judicial process. They argue that if the police and prosecutors cannot make sustainable cases against defendants within these restrictions, they are not doing their jobs properly. Defenders of the restraints on police and prosecutorial behavior argue that the police now have a number of powerful scientific tools (e.g., DNA testing) that should enable them to produce convictions without having to use more suspect means of investigation. The defenders, however, would be willing to trade a few convictions in order to be sure that the fundamental civil liberties of all Americans were protected.

Going along with the question of perceived difficulties in prosecuting accused criminals is the question of pardon and parole. Frequent newspaper accounts relate paroled convicts committing major crimes, sometimes within days of having been released from prison. Yet the possibility of parole is often a motivating device for better behavior in prisons, in what could otherwise be extremely dangerous settings.[58] In addition, prisons in most states in the United States are filled to capacity—the United States has the highest rate of per capita incarceration of any industrial democracy. If there is no option for early release, then even more prisons will have to be built, with a further drain on state and local resources. As with most policy problems, there is no quick and easy answer.

The Clinton Crime Bill

Given the degree of public concern about crime, particularly violent crimes, the Clinton administration developed and advocated a major federal crime bill. The nature of the bill and the politics that surrounded it illustrate a number of points we have been making about the policy process. The first point has to do with the social and political construction of the issue of crime.[59] While the majority of the efforts and money in the bill were dedicated to direct law enforcement, the legislation also contained some recognition of the socioeconomic roots of crime. Approximately one-third of the expenditures in the original bill were to go for social and educational programs designed to prevent crime, especially among the young. These proposed expenditures permitted opponents of the bill to describe it as a social welfare program rather than a "tough" anticrime bill[60] and eventually to force some reductions in social spending.

A second point is that the crime bill was designed to provide state, and especially local, governments with large amounts of money for hiring additional police and a number of other purposes. Critics of the bill refer to these provisions as "pork barrel legislation" rather than an attempt to address the fundamental problems of crime.[61] The bill did require a distribution of spending, with a large proportion of spending—perhaps larger than might be justified by their relative rates of violent crime—going to rural and suburban communities rather than large central cities. That subsidy for their constituents did not stop conservative critics from arguing that the bill really was no more than a subsidy for the cities.

A third point about the Clinton bill was that it tended to offend a range of groups in the society. As it was finally written, the bill offended many members of minority groups, as well as the congressmen who represented them. One of the original drafts of the bill had contained a strong racial-justice provision that would have addressed the perceived disparities in sentencing, especially in the use of the death penalty, between white and nonwhite criminals.[62] The negotiations over the final version of the law deleted these provisions, and several potential supporters then abandoned the bill, although the leadership of the Black Caucus in Congress maintained its support. On the other side of the ideological spectrum, the National Rifle Association lobbied extremely hard against the bill because it contained provisions banning the sale of certain weapons, mostly semiautomatic assault rifles. As noted earlier, this once omnipotent interest group had recently lost a major battle over the Brady bill and felt it could not lose another.

A final point about the Clinton crime bill is that it illustrates the tendency of problems to float upward in a federal system, despite the Constitution's reserving powers to the states. The crime bill gives the federal government a role in a number of crimes, especially domestic violence, that previously had been almost the exclusive preserve of state and local governments. In part it was good politics for federal legislators to be seen as concerned about the rising crime rate, so they agreed to intervene. Further, the perception that the federal government has more resources than the other levels of government to "solve" these problems has tended to push the problems upward.

Given all these objections, the bill could not be passed as first proposed, and that failure illustrates another very important point about the process of legitimating public policies. Critics of the bill appeared to fix their attention on the one or two features they could not support, rather than on those they might have liked about the legislation. Adopting legislation almost invariably involves compromise, and the failure to compromise may be a major barrier to effective government action. This is perhaps especially true in the United States, given the inherent tendency of the system toward gridlock.[63] In the end, a compromise was forged and the bill was passed by Congress and signed by the president.

The bill that was passed still contained a mixture of punishment and prevention.[64] Of the $30.2 billion allocated over six years, the bulk of the money went to hiring local police officers ($8.8 billion), building prisons ($7.9 billion), the incarceration of criminal aliens ($1.8 billion), and other programs directed at catching and punishing criminals ($4.8 billion). After cuts, there was still $6.9 billion for prevention programs such as fighting violence against women ($1.6 billion), noncriminal "drug courts" ($1 billion), and recreation opportunities for inner-city children ($562 million).[65] The bill also had a number of regulatory features, the most important outlawing the sale of nineteen kinds of assault rifles and clips with over ten bullets, expanding the federal death penalty, and allowing adult treatment of thirteen year olds charged with major crimes.

Conclusion

We have been discussing the ways in which governments in the United States attempt to protect their citizens from "enemies, domestic and foreign." This is one of the defining duties of any government,[66] and it is one in which governments have been engaged since their inception. But the issues involved in this policy area have become more complex. First, in defense, there is no longer a clearly identifiable enemy against whom to plot strategy. Instead, the task is one of preparing for a wide range of threats to national security, including some for which the military is not particularly well adapted. Further, there are demands for the use of the military for a range of purposes that go well beyond conventional national defense and require the armed forces to fulfill virtually a social mission on the international scene. Finally, domestic social and political concerns have invaded the world of the armed forces and have required some rethinking of the values and mores of those armed forces.

Crime is an equally complex policy and political problem. It is perhaps even more complex than defense given that the United States attempts to combat crime while maintaining an open and free society. Police measures that might be effective in curtailing the growth of crime are simply not possible if the tradition of the open society is to be maintained. Even without the complications of civil liberties there would be other difficulties for a government attempting to solve a serious crime problem, not least of which is understanding the root causes of this social pathology and therefore the means of best addressing the problem.

Notes

1. For some sense of the ups and downs of defense employment (civilian and uniformed), see B. Guy Peters, "Public Employment in the United States," in *Public Employment in Western Democracies,* ed. Richard Rose et al. (Cambridge, England: Cambridge University Press, 1985).

2. See, for example, Robert K. Jervis, *Perception and Misperception in International Politics* (Princeton: Princeton University Press, 1976).

3. Joseph S. Nye, *Bound to Lead: The Changing Nature of American Power* (New York: Basic Books, 1992).

4. See, for example, James A. Nathan and James K. Oliver, *United States Foreign Policy and World Order,* 2d ed. (Boston: Little, Brown, 1981).

5. Dunbar Lockwood, "Purchasing Power," *Bulletin of the Atomic Scientists* 50 (March 1994): 10–12;"Former Soviet Republics Clear Way for Nunn-Lugar Monies," *Arms Control Today* 24 (1994): 28–29.

6. Patrick E. Tyler, "As Fear of a Big War Fades, Military Plans for Little Ones," *New York Times,* 3 February 1992.

7. David C. Morrison, "Bottoming Out?" *National Journal,* 17 September 1994, 2126–30.

8. Julian Critchley, *The North Atlantic Alliance and the Soviet Union in the 1980s* (London: Macmillan, 1982).

9. Robert L. Bernstein and Richard Dicker, "Human Rights First," *Foreign Policy* 94 (1994): 43–47; William Korey, *The Promises We Keep: Human Rights, the Helsinki Process and American Foreign Policy* (New York: St. Martin's, 1993).

10. For an analysis of this famous, or infamous, program, see Congressional Budget Office, *Analysis of the Costs of the Administration's Strategic Defense Initiative, 1985–89* (Washington, D.C.: Congressional Budget Office, May 1984).

11. Lawrence J. Korb, "The 1991 Defense Budget," in *Setting National Priorities: Policy for the Nineties* (Washington, D.C.: Brookings Institution, 1990). See also David C. Morrison, "How Many Carriers Are Enough," *National Jour-*

nal, 4 September 1993, 2162.

12. Gordon Adams, *The Politics of Defense Contracting: The Iron Triangle* (New Brunswick, N.J.: Transaction, 1981); "Mission Implausible," *U.S. News and World Report,* 14 October 1991, 24–31.

13. There were a number of reports in the summer of 1994 of plutonium from Russia being available for sale, potentially to terrorists.

14. Owen Cote, "The Trident and the Triad," *International Security Quarterly* 16 (1991): 117–36.

15. Pat Towell, "Pentagon Banking on Plans to Reinvent Procurement," *Congressional Quarterly Weekly Report* 52 (16 April 1994): 899–904; Lauren Holland, "Explaining Weapons Procurement: Matching Operational Performance and National Security Needs," *Armed Forces and Society* 19 (1993): 353–76.

16. The program has cost approximately $5 billion per year since the mid-1980s.

17. The General Accounting Office has done a number of evaluations of these and other poorly performing weapons systems, e.g., *More Effective Review of Proposed Inventory Buys Could Reduce Unneeded Procurement,* GAO/NSIAD-94-130 (Washington, D.C.: General Accounting Office, June 1994). See also Scott Shuger, "The Stealth Bomber Story You Haven't Heard," *Washington Monthly* 23 (January 1991): 1–2, 14–22.

18. Korb, "The 1991 Defense Budget," 136–38.

19. Eric Schmitt, "Military Proposes to End Production of Most New Arms," *New York Times,* 24 January 1992.

20. Eric Schmitt, "Run Silent, Run Deep, Beat Foes (Where?)," *New York Times,* 30 January 1992.

21. Martin Binkin, *America's Volunteer Military* (Washington, D.C.: Brookings Institution, 1984).

22. *New York Times,* 12 June 1994.

23. For example, Molly Pitcher played a partly real, partly mythical part in the Battle of Monmouth during the Revolutionary War.

24. Michael R. Gordon, "Pentagon Spells Out Rules for Ousting Homosexuals: Rights Group Vow a Fight," *New York Times,* 23 December 1993.

25. Tamar Lewin, "At Bases, Debate Rages over Impact of New Gay Policy," *New York Times,* 24 December 1993.

26. Jane Gross, "Navy Cannot Discharge Gay Officer, Court Rules," *New York Times,* 1 September 1994.

27. Tim Weiner, "Proposal Cuts Back on Some Weapons to Spend More on Personnel," *New York Times,* 8 February 1994.

28. William W. Kaufman, "'Hollow' Forces," *Brookings Review* 12 (1994): 24–29.

29. Eric Schmitt, "Military Making Less into More, but Some Say Readiness Suffers," *New York Times,* 5 July 1994.

30. Other estimates show substantially greater employment generated by defense purchases. These are rather conservative estimates from the Department of Labor.

31. James Kitfeld, "The New Partnership," *National Journal,* 6 August 1994.

32. David C. Morrison, "Painful Separation," *National Journal,* 3 March 1990, 768–73.

33. Mr. Hoover himself had a somewhat more complex career. See Anthony Summers, *Official and Confidential* (New York: Putnam, 1993).

34. This organization became very visible during the siege of the Branch Davidian compound in Waco, Texas, in 1993.

35. John DiIulio, "Crime," in *Setting Domestic Priorities: What Can Government Do?* ed. Henry J. Aaron and Charles L. Schultze (Washington, D.C.: Brookings Institution, 1992).

36. Ibid.

37. For a discussion of this controversy in the context of the Clinton crime bill, see W. John Moore, "Shooting in the Dark," *National Journal,* 12 February 1994, 358–63.

38. This phrase means that if a person is convicted of three felonies, he or she will be imprisoned for life without the possibility of parole. See "Crime in California: Three Strikes, You're Out," *The Economist* 330 (15 January 1994): 29–32; William Tucker, "Three Strikes and You're Dead," *American Spectator* 27 (March 1994): 22–26.

39. Committee on Ways and Means, U.S. House of Representatives, "Children and Families at Risk" (Washington, D.C.: Government Printing Office, January 1994).

40. This appears to be especially true for child and spousal abuse. See David J. Kolko, "Characteristics of Child Victims of Physical Abuse," *Journal of Interpersonal Violence* 7 (1992): 244–76; Cathy Spatz Widom, "Avoidance of Criminality in Abused and Neglected Children," *Psychiatry* 54 (1991): 162–74.

41. Herman Goldstein, *Problem-Oriented Policing* (New York: McGraw-Hill, 1990).

42. Some students seem to think that the two experiences are equally pleasant.

43. Most correctional officials oppose these changes, arguing that all they will do is make the prison population more restive and difficult to control.

44. The wording of the amendment is: "A well regulated Militia, being necessary to the security of a free State, the right of the people to keep and bear Arms, shall not be infringed."

45. Federal Bureau of Investigation, *Crime in the United States* (Washington, D.C.: Government Printing Office, annual).

46. The act was called the Brady bill after James Brady, President Reagan's press secretary, who was wounded severely in the attempted assassination of Reagan in 1981. After that, his wife, Sarah, became a vigorous advocate of gun control.

47. Peter H. Stone, "Under the Gun," *National Journal,* 5 June 1993, 1334–38; Holly Idelson and Paul Nyhan, "Gun Rights and Restrictions: The Territory Reconfigured," *Congressional Quarterly Weekly Report* 51 (24 April 1993): 1021–27.

48. "Gun Owners Don't Fit Stereotypes," *USA Today*/CNN/Gallup Poll, reported in *USA Today,* 30 December 1993.

49. George Pettinico, "Crime and Punishment: America Changes Its Mind," *Public Perspective* 5 (September/October 1994): 29.

50. Welsh S. White, *The Death Penalty in the Nineties: An Examination of the Modern System of Capital Punishment* (Ann Arbor: University of Michigan Press, 1991).

51. *Furman v. Georgia,* 408 U.S. 238 (1972).

52. Gregory D. Russell, *The Death Penalty and Racial Bias: Overturning Supreme Court Assumptions* (Westport, Conn.: Greenwood, 1994).

53. This may not be strictly a constitutional argument because the Constitution and its amendments do not mention economics as a forbidden category for differentiating among individuals.

54. Stephen Reinhardt, "The Supreme Court, the Death Penalty and the Harris Case," *Yale Law Journal* 102 (1992): 205–22.

55. Marcia Coyle, "Blackmun's Turnabout on the Death Penalty," *National Law Journal* 16 (7 March 1994): 39.

56. This is called "Mirandizing" an arrestee, after Ernesto Miranda, whose conviction was overturned because he was not told of his right to remain silent. *Miranda v. Arizona,* 384 U.S. 436 (1966).

57. Kenneth B. Noble, "Ruling Helps Prosecution of Simpson," *New York Times,* 20 September 1994.

58. Prisons are already dangerous enough. See Mark S. Fleisher, *Warehousing Violence* (Newbury Park, Calif.: Sage, 1989); George M. Anderson, "Prison Violence: Victims Behind Bars," *America* 159 (26 November 1988): 430–33.

59. See a discussion of this idea in chapter 3, pp. 46–47.

60. John W. Moore, "Shooting in the Dark," *National Journal,* 12 February 1994, 358–63.

61. Senator Alphonse D'Amato (R-N.Y.) went on the Senate floor singing a parody of "Old MacDonald Had a Farm" complaining about the "pork" in the legislation.

62. "Crime Control Issues," *Congressional Digest* 73 (June 1994): 169–70.

63. Morris P. Fiorina, "An Era of Divided Government," *Political Science Quarterly* 107 (1992): 387–410; Charles O. Jones, *The President in a Separated System* (Washington, D.C.: Brookings Institution, 1994).

64. Neil A. Lewis, "President Foresees Safer U.S.," *New York Times,* 27 August 1994.

65. Contained in this total is the "midnight basketball" provision that was so prominent in the negative comments about the bill. See Don Terry, "Basketball at Midnight: 'Hope' on a Summer Eve," *New York Times,* 19 August 1994.

66. See Richard Rose, "On the Priorities of Government," *European Journal of Political Research* 4 (1973): 247–89.

PART FOUR

Policy Analysis

INTRODUCTION

Now, after discussing the processes through which policies are adopted and some characteristics of certain policy areas, we must look at the means of evaluating policies. Methods of evaluation are of two disparate types. Although they are almost diametrically opposed, both means are central to understanding why some policies should be preferred over others.

The first approach to policy analysis is economic and quantitative. Although there are a number of such methods, cost-benefit analysis is the one most commonly used. This form of analysis attempts to reduce all the costs and benefits of a proposed project to a common economic measuring rod. By so doing, it gives the decision maker a relatively clear choice among the alternatives competing for the use of scarce resources. Using this approach, a project that produces the greatest net benefit for the society would be chosen over other options for funding.

The second approach to policy analysis is ethical. Whereas cost-benefit analysis applies strictly utilitarian standards to issues of policy choice, ethical analysis spreads the net of human values more broadly and seeks to apply other forms of valuation to the outcomes of the policy process. In addition to the economic good created by policy choices, other values, such as life, liberty, and equality, can be pursued through the policymaking process. Thus, ethical analysis may give very different, albeit much "softer," answers if applied to the same policy.

14. Cost-Benefit Analysis

Much of this book has been concerned with the process through which policies are adopted and with the characteristics of policies adopted in the United States. This chapter extends those interests by discussing the principal method of policy analysis used when making policy choices: cost-benefit analysis. Because governments operate with limited resources and limited ability to predict the future, they must employ some techniques to help them decide how to utilize those scarce resources. Cost-benefit analysis is the most commonly employed technique, other than the informal techniques arising from intuition and experience. The fundamental principle of cost-benefit analysis is that any project undertaken should produce a benefit for society greater than the cost of the project.[1] Second, when several projects promise to yield positive net benefits and when all cannot be undertaken because of limited resources, then the project that creates the greatest net benefit to the society should be selected. This technique is perhaps most applicable to capital projects, such as highways or dams, but it can also be applied to other public programs. In fact, cost-benefit analysis was required of all proposed regulations during the Reagan administration as a means of trying to curb the growth of government involvement in the economy.

There is obviously a decided utilitarian bias underlying cost-benefit analysis.[2] The costs and benefits of a project are all collapsed onto the single measuring rod of money, and those that create the greatest net benefit are deemed superior. This implies that the dominant value in society is economic wealth and, further, that more is always better. The dominance of wealth is presumed to be true even if rather perverse distributional consequences arise from the program. I discuss the philosophical and practical issues that arise with cost-benefit analysis later in the chapter. These implications may be sufficiently troubling, especially in a democratic political system, for some critics to argue for alternative means of evaluating policies. But cost-benefit analysis does have the advantage of reducing all the costs and benefits of public programs to that single dimension, whereas other forms of analysis may produce apparent confusion by lacking such a common dimension. With that single dimension, cost-benefit analysis can give an answer as to whether a project is desirable or not, while other methods tend to produce more ambiguous results.

Principles of Cost-Benefit Analysis

In the world of cost-benefit analysis, more is always better. Although it does have serious intellectual foundations, which we explore in a moment, the method is in many ways no more than a systematic framework within which to collect data concerning the merits and demerits of a public program. And it is not a new idea: the Army Corps of Engineers used the technique as early as 1900 to evaluate the merits of proposed improvements to rivers and harbors. The basic idea is to enumerate the positive features of a program and attach a monetary value to them, and at the same time to enumerate the negative features and attach a monetary value to those features. The net balance of costs and benefits will then determine if a program is economically feasible, although many other questions about its desirability may remain.

One principal idea underlying cost-benefit analysis comes from the tradition in welfare economics that has sought to develop an acceptable social welfare function, or a socially desirable means for making collective policy decisions.[3] That is, how can societies take the numerous and often conflicting views of their citizens and generate the policy choice that is the most acceptable to the society? One of the first welfare criteria of this sort was the Pareto principle, which argued that a policy move was optimal if no move away from it could be made to benefit someone without hurting someone else.[4] Stated another way, a Pareto optimal policy move would be one that benefits at least one person without hurting anyone. Clearly, in the real world of political decision making, moves of this kind are rare indeed, and politics is frequently about who gets what at the expense of whom.

A substitute welfare criterion was advanced by Nicholas Kaldor and John Hicks. They argued that a policy change was socially justified if the winners gained a sufficient amount to compensate the losers and still had something left for themselves.[5] This does not imply that those winners necessarily will compensate the losers, or that government could even identify the losers, but the idea is that the society as a whole is better off because of the overall increase in benefits. This welfare criterion obviously is a justification of the reliance of cost-benefit analysis on the production of the greatest net benefit possible. It can only be hoped that the benefits created will somehow find their way to the individuals who may have been harmed by the policy choice, but at least those benefits have been created. Intellectually, this approach has another problem. It requires aggregating utilities across a range of individuals, and that requires doing the nearly impossible by making interpersonal comparisons of utility.[6]

A second fundamental idea underlying cost-benefit analysis is that of the consumer's surplus.[7] Stated simply, this is the amount of money a consumer would be willing to pay for a given product, minus the amount he or she must actually pay. Consumers tend to value the first unit of a product or service they receive more highly than the second, and the second more than the third; the first quart of milk where there has been none is more valuable than the second. But the units of a product are not priced marginally; they are sold at an average price. This means that the utility of increased production will give consumers a surplus value from the production. Thus, any investment that reduces the cost of the product or service produces a benefit in savings that increases the consumer surplus. The investment by government in a new superhighway that reduces the cost to consumers of driving the same number of miles—in time, in gasoline, and in potential loss of life and property—creates a consumer surplus. And as the time, gasoline, and lives saved by the new highway may be used for other increased production, the actual savings represent a minimum definition of the improvement to society resulting from the construction of the new highway.

Also important in understanding cost-benefit analysis is the idea of opportunity costs: any resource used in one project cannot be used in another. For example, the concrete, steel, and labor used to build the superhighway cannot be used to build a new dam. Consequently, all projects must be evaluated against other possible projects to determine the most appropriate way to use resources—especially financial resources. Projects are also compared, implicitly if not explicitly, with taking no action and allowing the money to remain in the hands of individual citizens. Again, the basic idea of getting the most "bang for the buck" is important in understanding cost-benefit analysis.

When identifying and assessing costs and benefits, the analyst must also be concerned with the range of effects of the proposed program and at what point he or she disregards effects as being too remote for consideration.[8] For example, building a municipal waste incinerator in Detroit, Michigan, will have pronounced effects in Windsor, Ontario, Canada, that must be considered, even though that city is outside the United States. The prevailing air currents may mean that ash and acid from the incinerator also come down in Norway and Sweden, but those effects may be so minimal and so remote that they can be disregarded. Engaging in this form of analysis requires making judgments about what effects are sufficiently proximate and important to include as part of the calculations.

Finally, in evaluating costs and benefits, we must be concerned about the role of time. The costs and benefits of most projects do not occur at a single time but accrue over a number of years. If our superhighway is built, it will be serviceable for fifty years and will be financed over twenty years through government bonds. Policymakers must be certain that the long-term costs and benefits as well as the short-term consequences are positive. This, of course, requires some estimation of the nature of the future. We may estimate that our new superhighway will be useful for fifty years, but oil shortages may so reduce driving during that period that the real benefits will be much less than anticipated. Or, conversely, the value of gasoline may increase so much that the savings produced are more valuable than assumed at present. These kinds of assumptions must be built into the model of valuation for it to aid a decision maker.

In part because of the uncertainty over future costs and benefits, and in part because of the general principle that people prefer a dollar today to a dollar next year, the costs and benefits of projects must be converted to present values before useful cost and benefit calculations can be made. That is, the benefits that accrue to the society in the future have their value discounted and are consequently worth less than benefits produced in the first year of the project. Likewise, costs that occur in future years are lower than costs that occur in the first few years. Thus, cost-benefit analysis would appear to favor projects that have a quick payoff rather than greater long-term benefits but perhaps higher maintenance and operation costs. While there may be a good logical justification for these biases in the method, they do certainly influence the kinds of program that will be selected and that will have definite social implications, not least of all for future generations. Other forms of analytic aids for government decision makers, such as "decision trees" (see p. 69), include probabilities of outcomes as a means of coping with the uncertainties of the future, but cost-benefit analysis tends to rely on discounting future costs and benefits.

Doing Cost-Benefit Analysis

To understand the application of cost-benefit analysis better, we now work through the steps required to justify the construction of a new dam on the Nowhere River. This project is being proposed by the Army Corps of Engineers, and we have to determine whether or not it should be undertaken. We first have to decide if the project is feasible and acceptable on its own, and then if it is preferable to other projects that could be funded with the same resources. Again, this decision is being made first on economic grounds, and we may have to bring other forms of analysis and other criteria into the decision process at a later time.

Determining Costs and Benefits

One of the most important factors to consider when performing a cost-benefit analysis, especially of a public project, is that all costs and benefits should be enumerated. Thus, unlike projects that might be undertaken in the private sector, public projects require an explicit statement of the social, or external, costs and benefits. In the public sector, projects whose strictly economic potential may outweigh their costs may not be adopted because of the possibility of pollution or the loss of external benefits such as natural beauty. In fact, one of the principal logical justifications for the existence of the public sector is that it should take into account these external factors and attempt to correct them in ways not possible in the private sector.[9] Even with that social justification, however, the values of the costs and benefits are usually computed in economic terms just as if they were to accrue in the private market. This reliance on market logic for nonmarket decisions is one of the fundamental ironies in cost-benefit analysis.[10]

Thus, for our dam project, we can think of two lists of attributes (see table 14.1). On one side are the costs of the project, the main one being the economic cost of constructing the dam, which should reflect the market valuation of the opportunity costs of using the same resources for other purposes. Also, the dam will impose an economic cost by flooding the houses and farmland of present inhabitants of the area. But there are also social, or human, costs involved here, as these farms have been in the same families for generations, and the farmers have resisted the project from the beginning. Finally, there are further social costs in that the proposed dam will impound a river that currently has some recreational value for canoeists and is essentially an unspoiled natural area.

TABLE 14.1

COSTS AND BENEFITS OF DAM PROJECT

Costs	*Benefits*
Construction costs	Hydroelectric power
Flooded land	Flood control
Relocation of families	Irrigation
Loss of recreation	New recreational opportunities

On the other side of the ledger are the benefits of the program. First, the dam will provide hydroelectric power for the region. In so doing it will be a source of electric power that does not consume scarce fossil fuels and does not create the air pollution that would result from producing the same amount of electricity with fossil fuels. Also, the dam will help control the raging Nowhere River, which every spring overflows its banks and floods a number of towns, cities, and farms downstream from the proposed dam. In addition, the impounded water behind the dam will provide irrigation water for the remaining farmers, enabling them to grow more crops. Finally, although canoeists will lose some recreational benefits as a result of the building of the dam, citizens who enjoy power boating and water skiing will benefit from the large lake formed behind the dam. Thus, although this proposed dam does impose a number of costs on the society, it also provides a number of benefits in return. To proceed with this analysis, we must now begin to attach some quantifiable values to these costs and benefits in order to be able to make a decision as to the feasibility and desirability of the project.

Assigning Value

Assigning a real monetary value to all the costs and benefits of this mythical project would be difficult. For some costs and benefits the market directly provides a value. We know or can estimate accurately the costs of building the dam and the market value of the hydroelectric power it will produce. Although such costs are generally measurable through the market, the market may not fully measure the costs and benefits. For example, if our dam is to be built in a remote area with little more than subsistence agriculture, bringing in a large number of highly skilled and highly paid workers may distort prices and increase the costs of building the dam. Similarly, not only is the hydroelectric power salable but it may produce substantial secondary benefits (or perhaps costs) by stimulating industrialization in this rural and remote area. The experience of the Tennessee Valley Authority and its impact on the Tennessee Valley as a result of the development of cheap electric power illustrate this point rather nicely.[11] We cannot fully predict these secondary benefits, nor can we rely on them to make the project feasible, but they do frequently occur.

Some other costs and benefits of the project, although not directly measurable through the market, can be estimated in other ways. For example, we have to estimate the dam's recreational value to the people who will use the lake to water ski and its cost to those who will no longer be able to use the river for canoeing. We can do this by estimating the people's willingness to pay for their recreation.[12] Just how much time and money are they willing to invest to enjoy their recreation? Evidence for this calculation can be gained from surveys of recreation participants, or their actual behavior in renting equipment and travel to recreation sites. These calculations will help provide some measure of the economic value of the lake, or the free-flowing stream, to the population.

The creation of the dam and the lake behind it help illustrate another point about valuing costs and benefits. The lake will produce lakefront property, which tends to have higher values than does other nearby property, so something of the aesthetic value of the impoundment can be calculated. This is similar to estimating the value of clean air by looking at prices of similar housing in polluted and less polluted parts of a city.[13]

This means of valuation returns to the concept of the consumer's surplus. The first unit of a particular commodity is valued more highly than any subsequent units, so that as production is increased, each unit is marginally less valuable to the consumer. In our dam example, if there already have been a number of impoundments in the area, as there have been in the Tennessee Valley, then a new lake would have less value to recreation consumers, and they would be less willing to pay than if this were the first lake in an area with a large number of free-flowing streams. Likewise, one more hydroelectric power station in an area that already has cheap electrical power is less valuable than it would be in an economically backward area, and consequently citizens would be less willing to pay for that new power plant.

Finally, on some aspects of the project the market provides little or no guidance about valuation. For the farmers who are displaced by the project, we can place an economic cost on their land, their houses, and their moving costs. But we cannot readily assign an economic value to houses that are the ancestral homes of families and that are therefore more valuable psychologically than ordinary houses.[14] Similarly, there is some value in not disturbing a natural setting, simply because it is natural, and this is a difficult thing to which to assign an economic value. As a result, at times absolute prohibitions are built into legislation to prevent certain actions, so planners cannot depend entirely on net benefit ratios. The Environmental Protection Agency's guideline for preserving the habitats of endangered species, which resulted in the now notorious case of the snail darter in the Little Tennessee River and the more recent case of the delta smelt in California, is an example of the application of regulations to prevent some actions regardless of the relative economic costs and benefits.

The willingness-to-pay approach questions the people directly involved with the project about their valuation of costs and benefits. For some of those costs and benefits the population at large may be equally important as judges of the value. Federal regulators are now under congressional mandates to find ways to assess the value that the public assigns to the costs of environmental problems such as oil spills. These "contingent value" measurements by passive users are now being undertaken by survey methods. The first of these has been conducted by the National Oceanic and Atmospheric Administration and has so far gained broad support from environmental groups.[15] This method of valuation has, however, met general opposition by business concerns, with the probability that its use will eventually end up in the court system.[16]

It is fortunate that the dam we are building does not require any direct decisions about loss of life or injury to human beings. For projects that do—for example, building the superhighway as a means of saving lives—we come to perhaps the most difficult problem of valuation: estimating the value of a human life.[17] Although it is convenient to say that life is priceless, in practice decisions are made that deny some people their lives when that loss of life is preventable. If this is the case, then some subjective, if not objective, evaluation is being made of the worth of lives. One standard method of making such a judgment involves discounted future earnings. In this method the life of the individual is worth whatever the individual could have earned in the course of his or her working life, discounted to present value. Therefore, a highly paid corporate executive's life is worth more than a housewife's or a college professor's. This mechanism for evaluating lives clearly conforms to the basic market valuation, although it can be clearly disputed on humane grounds.

Another means of assessing the value of lives in performing a cost-benefit analysis uses the size of the awards to plaintiffs in legal cases of negligence or malpractice that resulted in loss of life. In other words, what do panels of citizens or judges consider a human life is worth? This constitutes another version of the market criterion, albeit one in which considerations of human suffering and "loss of companionship" have a greater (some would say too great because of the emotionalism involved) impact on the economic valuation.

Another means of assessing the value of a human life is somewhat similar to the "willingness to pay" criterion. In theory, individuals would be willing to pay almost anything to preserve their own lives and the lives of their loved ones. Nevertheless, individuals engage in risky behavior and risky occupations all the time, and when they do so, they make a subjective statement about the value of their life.[18] Because we know how much more likely it is for a coal miner to be killed at work than it is for a construction worker—either in the mines or as a result of black lung disease—we can estimate from any differences in wages how much these individuals would appear to value their lives. This method does, of course, imply a certain level of knowledge that individuals may not have, and it assumes that the collective bargaining process, through which wages of coal miners and construction workers are determined, accurately reflects both individual preferences and the market values of lives. It does, however, offer another feasible means of estimating the value of life, one that uses the assessment of individuals themselves rather than that of the market or the courts.

Discounting

We now return to the problem of time. The costs and benefits of a project do not all magically appear the year the project is completed, but typically are spread over a number of years. Table 14.2 shows the stream of benefits coming from the dam on the Nowhere River over a twenty-year period. This is the projected feasible lifetime of the project, as the Nowhere River carries a great deal of silt and the lake behind the dam is expected to fill with silt after that period. How do we assess these benefits and come up with a single number that we can compare with costs to determine the economic feasibility of the project?

TABLE 14.2

HYPOTHETICAL COSTS AND BENEFITS OF DAM PROJECT
FOR TWENTY YEARS

| | *Year* | | | | | | | | | | | | | | | | | | | |
	1	2	3	4	5	6	7	8	9	10	11	12	13	14	15	16	17	18	19	20
Costs	5	8	7	2	1	1	1	1	1	1	1	1	1	1	1	1	1	1	1	1
Benefits	0	0	0	3	4	5	5	5	5	5	5	5	5	5	5	4	4	4	3	2

To calculate such a figure, we must compute the present value of the future benefits. We have already decided on the time span of the project; the only task that remains is to determine the discount rate that should be applied to a public investment. And, as with the valuation of costs and benefits, disagreements may arise about what that rate should be.[19] One method is to use the opportunity costs of the use of these funds. Presumably any money used in a project in the public sector will be extracted from the private sector by some means such as taxation or borrowing, and consequently the rate of return these resources could earn if they were invested in private-sector projects is the appropriate rate of discount for public-sector projects. This is not always a practical solution, however, as rates of return differ for different kinds of investments, and investors apparently choose to put some money into each kind of investment. Is building a dam more like speculative mining investments, building a steel mill, or investing in an insured savings account? Which of the many possible rates of return should be selected?

Several other issues arise with respect to the selection of a discount rate. First, in discussing projects for which most benefits are to accrue in the future, there is an element of uncertainty. In our example we have assumed that the probable life span of the dam will be twenty years, but in reality the lake may fill up with silt in fifteen years. Consequently, it may be more prudent to select a discount rate higher than that in the market because we cannot be sure of the real occurrence or real value of the benefits. And because these benefits are expected to be further away in time, they are less certain; therefore, even higher rates of discount should be applied. Also, with inflation and the uncertainties about the development of new energy sources, we may need to be more conservative about discount rates.

Second, some argue that there should be a "social rate of discount" lower than that established by the market.[20] Such an arbitrarily set discount rate would be justified on the basis of the need for greater public investment and the need to provide a capital infrastructure for future generations. Further, as the size of the public sector is to some degree determined by the rate of discount, that rate should be set not by the market but by more conscious political choices concerning the appropriate level of public activity. But the economic counterargument is that, in the long term, the society will be better off if resources are allocated on the basis of their opportunity costs. If a public project is deemed infeasible because of the selection of a market-determined discount rate, then the resources that would have been used in that project are argued to produce greater social benefit in a project that is feasible under that rate of discount, regardless of whether the project is public or private. If there is no such project available, then the money would be better saved until such a project does materialize.

Finally, a question arises about intergenerational equity. What do we owe our posterity or, put the other way around, what has posterity ever done for us? If the discount rate is set lower than that determined by the market, then we will tend to undertake more projects that have an extended time value and that will benefit future generations. But we will also deprive the present generation of opportunities for consumption by using those resources as investment capital. This is as much a philosophical as a practical issue, but it is important for our understanding of alternative consequences arising from alternative choices of a rate of discount for public projects.

Using several discount rates, let us now work through the example of levels of benefit from the dam. Let us assume that the prime interest rate in the United States is approximately 8 percent. If we use this market-determined interest rate, the $100 in benefits produced after one year is worth

$$V = \$100/1.08 = \$92.59.$$

And $100 in benefits produced after two years would be worth

$$V = \$100/(1.08)^2 = \$85.73.$$

And $100 in benefits produced in the twentieth year of the project would be worth only $21.45 in present value. Thus, if we use this market rate of discount in evaluating a public project, the net benefit of that project at present value is positive. This project has a rather high cost during its early years, with the benefits occurring gradually over the twenty years. With a higher discount rate such a project is not feasible. If we use a discount rate of 18 percent, which would have seemed very reasonable in the late 1970s, then the net benefit of the dam at present value would be negative and the project would be economically infeasible.

Discounting is a means of reducing all costs and benefits of a project to their present value, based on the assumption that benefits created in the future are worth less than those created immediately. Philosophically or ideologically one might want a low discount rate to encourage public investment but object to the entire process of discounting. Should we simply not look to see if the stream of benefits created is greater than the total costs, no matter how and when they occur? This would, of course, be equivalent to a discount rate of zero. This point might be valid philosophically, but until the argument is accepted by economists, financiers, and government decision makers, public investment decisions will be made on the basis of present value and on the basis of interest rates that approximate the real value of the rate of return in the private sector.

Choosing among Projects

We have determined that our dam on the Nowhere River is feasible, given that a benevolent deity has provided us a discount rate of 8 percent for this project. But it is not yet time to break ground for the dam. We must first compare our project with the alternative projects for funding. Thus, the opportunity-cost question arises not only with respect to the single project being considered and the option of allowing the money to remain in private hands but also with regard to choices made among possible projects in the public sector.

We have said that the fundamental rule applied is to select the project that will produce the greatest total benefit to society. If we apply the Kaldor-Hicks criterion (p. 426), we see that this project is justified simply because it will create more benefits to spread around in the society and presumably compensate those who lost something because the project was built. Thus, in the simplest case, if we were to choose to undertake only a single project this year—perhaps because of limited manpower for supervision—we would choose Project D from table 14.3 simply because it creates the largest level of net benefit. By investing less money in Projects A and B we could have produced slightly more net benefit for society, but we are administratively constrained from making that decision and must choose only the one most productive investment.

More commonly, however, a particular resource—usually money—is limited, and with that limitation in mind, we have to choose one or more projects that will result in maximum benefits. Let us say that the ten projects listed in table 14.4 are all economically feasible and that we have been given a budget of $50 million for capital projects. Which projects should we select

TABLE 14.3

COSTS AND BENEFITS OF ALTERNATIVE PROJECTS
IN MILLIONS OF DOLLARS

Projects	Costs	Benefits	Net benefit
A	70	130	60
B	90	140	50
C	200	270	70
D	150	250	100

for funding? In such a situation, we should rank the projects according to the ratio of net benefits to initial costs (the costs that will be reflected in our capital budget) and then we should begin with the best projects, in terms of the ratio of benefits to initial costs, until the budget is exhausted. In this way, we will get the greatest benefit for the expenditure of our limited funds. And projects that we might have selected if we were choosing only a single project would not be selected under these conditions of resource constraint.

This problem of selecting among projects demonstrates the first of several problems that arise from the application of the basic rule of cost-benefit analysis. Given the budgetary process and the allocation of funds among agencies, we may produce a case of "multiorganizational suboptimization." This is a fancy way of saying that if our agency has been given $50 million, we will spend it, even if other agencies have projects that will produce

TABLE 14.4

CHOOSING A PACKAGE OF PROJECTS BY NET BENEFIT RATIO
(IN MILLIONS OF DOLLARS)

Project	Costs	Cumulative costs	Benefits	Net bene-fits	Net benefit ratio
A	2	2	12	10	5.0
B	4	6	20	16	4.0
C	10	16	40	30	3.0
D	10	26	35	25	2.5
E	8	34	28	20	2.5
F	16	50	51	35	2.2
G	2	52	6	4	2.0
H	15	67	42	27	1.8
I	10	77	26	16	1.6
J	18	95	45	27	1.5

greater benefits to society but do not have the funds in their budgets. Thus, if I had the money, I would continue to fund the projects listed in table 14.4, even though several of them have relatively low net-benefit ratios and even though there were better projects that other government bureaus wanted to fund. Of course, I would have been asked what benefits my proposed projects would produce when the capital budget was being considered, but because of political considerations, my budget is excessive for the benefits that could be produced from alternative uses of the money. This is not, of course, a flaw in the method; it is a flaw in the application of the method in complex and competitive government settings.

A not unrelated problem is that cost-benefit analysis places relatively little importance on efficiency or cost effectiveness. It looks primarily at total benefits rather than at the ratio of benefits to costs produced. It could be argued that this tends to favor the ax over the scalpel as a cutting tool. In other words, the method tends to favor large projects over small projects. This may be an inefficient use of resources and may also lock government into costly projects, whereas smaller projects might provide greater flexibility and greater future opportunities for innovation. Capital projects are inherently lumpy, so only projects of a certain size are feasible, but the concentration on total net benefits in cost-benefit analysis may exaggerate the problems of size and inflexibility.

We have now worked our way from the initial step of deciding what costs and benefits our project provides to deciding if it is the best project to undertake, given our limited resources and the competing uses of the money. At each stage we had to use a number of assumptions and approximations to reach a decision. The cost-benefit analysis does provide a "hard" answer as to whether or not we should undertake a project, but that answer should not go unquestioned. We now discuss some criticisms of cost-benefit analysis and some possible ways of building greater political and economic sophistication into the use of the method.

Extensions

We have so far been discussing a very basic approach to the method of cost-benefit analysis. There are, however, a number of extensions and modifications that are important for thinking about the utility of the method. First, other techniques, such as cost-effectiveness analysis, have many things in common with cost-benefit analysis but have their own particular perspectives on the analysis. For example, cost-effectiveness analysis does not require the assessment of the value of various outcomes to the extent required in cost-benefit analysis, but rather assumes that an outcome is desirable. Unlike cost-benefit analysis, this technique cannot tell the analyst whether an outcome is beneficial, only what it will cost to achieve a specified quantity of the outcome. Therefore, cost-effectiveness analysis tends to be used frequently in health policy and medicine, where curing a disease is a prima facie good; the question is how much will it cost.[21] Even then, however, some physicians do not like the concept of attaching a price to a cure and thinking about efficiency in medical care.[22]

Criticism and Modification

We have discussed some critical problems regarding cost-benefit analysis. Such things as the difficulty of assigning monetary values to nonmonetary outcomes, the choice of time ranges and discount rates, and the reliance on total net benefit as the criterion all introduce uncertainties about the usefulness of the outcome. We now discuss more basic problems that arise concerning the method itself and its relationship to the political process. Perhaps the most important is that some naive politicians and analysts might let the method make decisions for them, instead of using the information coming from the analysis as one element in their decision-making process. If the method is used naively and uncritically, its application can result in decisions that many people would deem socially undesirable. For example, all costs and benefits are counted as equal in the model, and even if they could be calculated accurately, some individuals would argue that the cost of death might be more important than other costs. Thus, we might wish to reduce deaths to the lowest possible level and then perhaps apply a cost-benefit analysis to other aspects of the project. We might use this "lexicographic preference" as a means of initially sorting projects, when a single dominant value such as life or the preservation of endangered species is involved. That is, we take only projects that "pass" the one crucial test and then subject those to cost-benefit analysis.

Perhaps the most socially questionable aspect of the cost-benefit analysis is that it gives little attention to the distributive questions involved in all policies.[23] All benefits and costs are counted equally in the method, regardless of who receives or bears them. A project that increased the wealth of a wealthy man by several million dollars and was financed by regressive taxation of $100,000 would be preferred in cost-benefit calculations to a project that produced a benefit of $900,000 for unemployed workers and was financed by progressive taxation of $200,000. This is an extreme example, but it does point to the distributional blindness of the method. Of course, advocates of the method justify it by saying that the society as a whole will be better off with the greatest increase in benefits, and presumably winners can later compensate losers. In reality, winners rarely if ever do so, and usually losers cannot be directly identified anyway. Redistributional goals may be included directly in the analysis by attaching some weight greater than one to positive changes in the salaries of low-income or unemployed persons, or redistributional objectives may be imposed on the analysis after the fact. But because government exists in part to attempt to redress some of the inequities produced in the marketplace, some attention must be given to redistributional goals when evaluating public projects.

Furthermore, the utilitarian and "econocratic" foundations of cost-benefit analysis may not be entirely suitable for a functioning political democracy.[24] In cost-benefit analysis, money alone is the measure of all things, and decisions made according to the method can be expected to be based on the economic rather than the political values involved. I discuss in chapter 15 some possible ethical alternatives that may be more suitable in a democracy. The difficulty is that these other criteria lack the apparent precision of cost-benefit analysis and lack its ability to provide a definitive answer to questions about the desirability of a policy intervention.

Finally, cost-benefit analysis has been referred to as "nonsense on stilts."[25] This means that there are so many assumptions involved in the calculations, and so many imponderables about the effects of future projects, that cost-benefit analysis is the functional equivalent of witchcraft in the public sector. Although these criticisms have been phrased in exaggerated language, to some degree they are well taken. It is difficult, if not impossible, to know the value of eliminating an externality, just as it is difficult to know just how much life, health, and snail darters are worth economically. Cost-benefit analysis can be used to avoid difficult political decisions and to abdicate responsibility to experts who can supply the "correct" answer. Of course, this fundamental abdication of political responsibility is indeed an "insidious poison in the body politick." Only when the results of analysis are integrated with other forms of analysis, such as ethical analysis, and are combined with sound political judgment can the "correct decisions" ever be made.

Notes

1. Edward C. Gramlich, *Benefit-Cost Analysis for Government Programs* (Englewood Cliffs, N.J.: Prentice Hall, 1981).

2. Steven Kelman, "Cost-Benefit Analysis: An Ethical Critique," *Regulation* (1981), 33–40.

3. Kenneth Arrow, *Social Choice and Individual Values* (New York: Wiley, 1963); Allan Feldman, *Welfare Economics and Social Choice Theory* (Boston: Martinus Nijhoff, 1986).

4. P. Hennipman, "Pareto Optimality: Value Judgment or Analytical Tool?" in *Relevance and Precision*, ed. J.S. Cramer, A. Heertje, and P. Venekamp (New York: North-Holland, 1976).

5. Nicholas Kaldor, "Welfare Propositions of Economics and Interpersonal

Comparisons of Utility," *Economic Journal* 49 (1939): 549–52; John R. Hicks, "The Valuation of the Social Income," *Economica* 7 (1940): 105–24.

6. Richard Posner, *The Economics of Justice* (Cambridge, Mass.: Harvard University Press, 1983).

7. E.J. Mishan, *Cost-Benefit Analysis,* exp. ed. (New York: Praeger, 1967), 24–54.

8. David Whittington and Duncan MacRae, Jr., "The Issue of Standing in Cost-Benefit Analysis," *Journal of Policy Analysis and Management* 5 (1986): 665–82.

9. E. J. Mishan, "The Post-War Literature on Externalities: An Interpretative Essay," *Journal of Economic Literature* 16 (1978): 1–28.

10. John Martin Gilroy, "The Ethical Poverty of Cost-Benefit Methods: Autonomy, Efficiency and Public Policy Choice," *Policy Sciences* 25 (1992): 83–102.

11. "The TVA—Hardy Survivor," *The Economist* 312 (1 July 1989): 22–23.

12. Edith Stokey and Richard Zeckhauser, *A Primer for Policy Analysis* (New York: Norton, 1978), 149–52.

13. This is referred to as a "hedonic price model" in which the contributions of intangibles to price are assessed. See Paul Portney, "Housing Prices, Health Effects and Valuing Reductions in the Risk of Death," *Journal of Environmental Economics and Management* 8 (1981): 72–78.

14. Robin Gregory, Donald McGregor, and Sarah Lichtenstein, "Assessing the Quality of Expressed Preference Measures of Value," *Journal of Economic Behavior and Organization* 17 (1992): 277–92.

15. Peter Passell, "Polls May Help Government Decide the Worth of Nature," *New York Times,* 6 September 1993. See also J.A. Hausman, *Contingent Valuation: A Critical Assessment* (Amsterdam: North-Holland, 1993).

16. Robert E. Niewijk, "Misleading Quantification: The Contingent Valuation of Environmental Quality," *Regulation* 17, no. 1 (1994): 60–71.

17. Steven E. Rhoads, ed., *Valuing Life: Public Policy Dilemmas* (Boulder, Colo.: Westview, 1980); W. Kip Viscusi, "Alternative Approaches to Valuing the Health Impact of Accidents: Liability Law and Prospective Evaluations," *Law and Contemporary Problems* 46 (1983): 49–68.

18. Jack Hirschleifer and David L. Shapiro, "The Treatment of Risk and Uncertainty," in *Public Expenditure and Policy Analysis,* 3d ed., ed. Robert H. Haveman and Julius Margolis (Boston: Houghton Mifflin, 1983), 145–66.

19. For a general discussion of the problems of discounting, see Robert E. Goodin, "Discounting Discounting," *Journal of Public Policy* 2 (1982): 53–71.

20. William J. Baumol, "On the Social Rate of Discount," *American Economic Review* 10 (1968): 788–802.

21. Ray Robinson, "Cost-Effectiveness Analysis," *British Medical Journal* 307 (25 September 1993): 793–95.

22. David M. Eddy, "Cost-Effectiveness Analysis: Will It Be Accepted?" *Journal of the American Medical Association* 268 (1992): 132–36.

23. Alphonse G. Holtmann, "Beyond Efficiency: Economists and Distribu-

tional Analysis," in *Policy Analysis and Economics: Developments, Tensions, Prospects,* ed. David L. Weimer (Boston: Kluwer, 1991).

24. Peter Self, *Econocrats and the Policy Process: The Politics and Philosophy of Cost-Benefit Analysis* (London: Macmillan, 1975).

25. Peter Self, "Nonsense on Stilts: Cost-Benefit Analysis and the Roskill Commission," *Political Quarterly* 10 (1970): 30–63; Kelman, "Cost-Benefit Analysis."

15. Ethical Analysis of Public Policy

All the mathematical and economic capabilities in the world and all the substantive knowledge of policy areas are of little consequence if we have no moral or ethical foundation on which to base our evaluation of policies. Most of the important questions concerning policy analysis have as much to do with the "should" questions as with the "can" questions. That is, most important policy decisions involve an assessment of what should be done by government as much as they involve the feasibility question of what government can do. The range of technical possibilities for action is frequently broader for policymakers than is the range of ethically justifiable possibilities for acting "in the public interest." But, unfortunately, many values that should affect policy decisions in the public sector conflict with one another. Analysts frequently confront choices among competing positive values, rather than clear-cut decisions about options that are either completely right or completely wrong.

In making almost all allocative decisions, policymakers must choose among worthy ends; they do not have the luxury of picking the only acceptable policy. Also, policymakers must choose among alternative means to reach the desired goals, and those means themselves may have substantial ethical implications. Finally, in attempting to make decisions on ethical grounds, decision makers are confronted with an overwhelming utilitarian bias in the discussion of public policy.[1] As noted in chapter 14 concerning cost-benefit analysis, the prevailing conception is that government should do what creates the greatest economic value for the society, rather than worry too much about the "softer" values we discuss in this chapter.

The basic concept behind utilitarianism—providing the greatest net benefit to society—is in the main admirable, but it can be used to justify actions that violate procedural norms as well as usual conceptions of fair distribution of the benefits of society. Further, this approach tends to reduce all considerations to economic ones, and a variety of other values may be equally important for determining the proper course of government action. This chapter presents several of the important ethical premises that constitute alternatives to utilitarianism and that can be used to guide policy decisions. It also discusses some of the difficulties of implementing these ethical and moral values in real public-sector decisions.

Fundamental Value Premises

Any number of premises have been used to justify policy decisions. These range from vague concepts such as "Americanism," "Aryan purity," "the principles of Marxism-Leninism," and that old standby, "the public interest," to well-articulated philosophical or religious principles. The main difficulty in ethical analysis of policy decisions is finding principles that can be consistently applied to a number of situations and that produce acceptable decisions in those situations.[2] Words such as "justice," "equity," and "good" are tossed about in debates over public policies in a rather cavalier fashion. The mature analyst must attempt to systematize his or her values and learn to apply them consistently to all kinds of issues. The analyst therefore must be a moral actor as well as a technician, or else will remain what Meltsner refers to as a "baby analyst" throughout his or her career.[3] As we pointed out when discussing the application of cost-benefit analysis (see chapter 14), values are involved throughout the policy process and are embedded in policy options and even in commonly used analytic methods. In order to understand what one wants, one must explicate and examine those values.

In this chapter I discuss five important nonutilitarian value premises for making policy decisions: preservation of life, preservation of individual autonomy, truthfulness, fairness, and desert. These values would probably be widely accepted by the public as important standards for assessing policies, and they have a wide range of applicability across policy issues. As I point out, however, these values cannot be applied unambiguously, and conflicts are embedded in each issue as well as across the several issues.

The Preservation of Life

The preservation of human life is one of the most fundamental values we could expect to see manifested in the policy process. The sanctity of life is, after all, a fundamental value of Judeo-Christian ethics and is embodied in all professional codes of ethics.[4] Despite the importance of preserving human life as an ethical criterion, a number of conflicts arise over its application in real-world decision situations. These are "tragic choices" because the resources available often do not permit everyone to be aided, and those not aided are condemned to die earlier than they might otherwise.[5]

One obvious conflict over the use of resources to save lives exists between identifiable lives and statistical lives. Here we are faced with the tendency of individuals to allocate resources differently if known lives of specific individuals are at stake from how they would evaluate them if some un-specified persons would be saved at some time in the future. If we know that certain individuals will die in the near future, we tend to provide them with the resources they need to save themselves, even though the same resources could save many more unidentified lives in the future if government allocated them differently.

In medical care this problem is manifested in the conflict between acute and preventive medicine. Preventive medicine is almost certainly the most cost-effective means of saving lives that could be lost as a result of cancer, circulatory diseases, or accidents, but it is difficult to identify the direct beneficiaries. Nevertheless, the victims of disease are clearly identifiable, have identifiable families, and consequently are more difficult to refuse care than the unknown statistical beneficiaries of preventive medicine. This pattern of decision making was referred to in chapter 3 as the "mountain-climber syndrome," in which we may spend thousands of dollars to save a stranded mountain climber, even though we could save many more lives by spending the same amount of money on highway accident prevention. It is virtually impossible to say no to stranded mountain climbers and their families, although if the appropriate ethical criterion is to save as many lives as possible, that is perhaps what we should do.

But even if all the lives at stake in a decision are identifiable, in some instances allocative decisions must be made. Table 15.1, although it concentrates on a relatively small number of individuals who are potential recipients of a liver transplant, points out the broader problem of being forced to choose among lives. Each individual in table 15.1 is worthy of receiving the lifesaving treatment simply because he or she is a human being. But because organs for transplants are scarce and because the demand for them far exceeds the supply, decisions must be made that will allow some people to live and force others to die. What criteria can be applied in making such a choice? One might be the conventional utilitarian criterion: the individuals who will contribute the most to the community (economically especially) should be allowed to live. Another criterion might be longevity: the youngest persons should be allowed to receive the treatment, thus saving the greatest number of person-years of life. Another criterion might be autonomy: individuals who have the greatest probability of returning to active and useful lives after treatment should receive the treatment. Another criterion might be whether the disease requiring the treatment is self-inflicted or not. For example, should chronic alcoholics be given the same preference for receiving a new liver as other patients? At least one state in the United States has ruled that Medicaid should not pay for such treatments for active alcoholics and drug abusers.[6]

TABLE 15.1

WHO SHALL LIVE AND WHO SHALL DIE?

Patient	Sex and age	Occupation	Home life	Medical stability	Civic activities and other considerations
A	M 55	Cardiac surgeon on the verge of a major new technique	Married, two adult children	Bad long-term prognosis, maybe 2 years	Philanthropist with very high net worth; rumors of unfaithfulness
B	F 38	Owner of successful designer shop	Widow, three children, ages 4, 8, and 13	Good	From out of state; excellent violinist in community orchestra
C	M 46	Medical technician	Married, six children, ages 8 to 14	Good	Union boss
D	M 29	Assembly-line worker	Single	Good	Retarded—mental age, 10 years; ward of the state
E	F 36	Well-known historian, college professor; Ph.D.	Divorced, custodian of one son, age 5, ex-husband alive	Fair prognosis, but odd case which would allow perfection of new surgical technique	Excessive eater, drinker, and smoker; very popular professor; other medical conditions
F	M 60	Ex-state senator; now retired	Widower	Good	Criminal record (extortion)
G	M 45	Vice-president of local bank	Happily married, three sons, ages 15 to 25	Good	Deacon of local church, member of Rotary Club

SOURCE: *Washington Post*, 22 March 1981.

A variety of other criteria could be used to justify one choice over another, but there is still a choice among real lives to be made. In addition, some even broader allocative questions arise from this example: How many transplant centers should be developed in American hospitals? Should there be sufficient capacity to help all the patients who might need this treatment, regardless of the cost and the underutilization of the facilities most of the time? Or should only enough centers be developed to meet average demands? Should individuals who can afford to pay be allowed to jump ahead of others in line to receive new organs if their payments can fund future surgeries for the less fortunate?

Even though the preservation of life may be an important or even dominant value for public policymaking, in many situations the definition of life itself is subject to debate. This is true legally as well as morally. The use of therapeutic abortion as a means of birth control presents one problem of this sort: determining when human life begins.[7] This issue has been fought in the court system and in the streets of many American cities and towns with no resolution that both sides of the issue can accept. Even here, the question is not always clear, as many abortion opponents would accept abortions in the case of rape or incest, and many abortion supporters would not accept the procedure as a means of determining the gender of children in a family. Issues concerning artificial means of prolonging life even when a person would be considered dead by many clinical criteria illustrate the problem of defining life at the other end of the life cycle.[8] Also, assisted suicide for the terminally ill has raised the possible contradiction of the value of preserving life and the value of preserving autonomy (see below).[9] Thus, while all policymakers and all citizens may agree on the importance of preserving human life, serious disagreements arise over just what constitutes a human life.

Finally, in some situations the government sanctions and encourages the taking of human lives. The most obvious example is war; others are capital punishment and, in some instances, the management of police response to threats to their own lives and safety. The question here, then, is what criteria we can use to justify the taking of some lives while we deplore and prohibit the taking of others?[10] Obvious criteria that we might apply are self-preservation and the protection of society against elements that could undermine it or take other lives. But to some degree there is a definite inconsistency in the arguments here, and government must justify placing higher values on some lives than on others. Again, the fundamental point is that although there may be broad agreement in society on the importance of preserving human lives as a goal of all public policies, this criterion is not obviously and unambiguously enforceable in all policy situations. We must have a detailed analysis of all such situations and some understanding of the particular application of the criterion in each of those varied situations.

The Preservation of Individual Autonomy

Another important value for public policy, especially in a democracy, is that the autonomy of each citizen to make decisions about his or her own life should be maximized. This principle underlies a considerable body of conservative political thought, which assumes that the interests of the individual are, everything else being equal, more important than those of the society as a whole.[11] It further assumes that individuals may at times select alternatives that many other people, and society as a whole acting through government, might deem unacceptable. Thus, child labor, sweatshops, and extremely long working hours with low wages were all justified at one time because they preserved the right of the individual to "choose" his or her own working conditions.[12] With such an extreme definition of individual autonomy, the public sector would be excluded from almost all forms of social and economic activity. But even using this extreme version of autonomy the state did intervene to protect individuals against fraud and breach of contract, and it did to some degree protect children and other less competent individuals more than it did adults, who presumably were able to make their own decisions. In addition, advocates of an enhanced role for the public sector have argued that the welfare state, by increasing the options available to citizens, especially less advantaged citizens, actually enhances individual freedom and autonomy.[13]

Several interesting questions arise in the public sector in regard to individual autonomy. One involves an extension of the above comments. What groups in society should the state attempt to protect, either against themselves or against those who would defraud them or otherwise infringe on their rights? Children have traditionally been protected—even against their own parents—because they have been assumed to be incapable of exercising full, autonomous choice.[14] The state has been empowered to operate *in loco parentis* to attempt to preserve the rights of children. Likewise, the state has protected mentally incompetent adults who cannot make rational, autonomous choices. Less justifiably by most criteria, the state has operated to limit the choices of welfare recipients (see pp. 296–300), unwed mothers, and individuals who, although they may have full mental capabilities, are stigmatized in some fashion by society and punished for making questionable choices in the past. Again, the question is, what criteria should be used to decide which groups the state should treat as its children?

The state may also intervene to protect the life of an individual who has made an autonomous decision to end his or her life. Legislation that makes suicide a crime and attempts to prevent individuals from purposely ending their lives indicates the apparent belief that the value of preserving life supersedes the value of preserving individual autonomy. In this hierarchy of values, the decision to end one's life is taken by definition to indicate that the individual needs the protection of the state. The same principle is apparently applied to individuals who have made it clear that they do not wish to be kept "alive" by artificial means when all hope of their recovery to a fully conscious and autonomous life is lost. In such an instance there are several conflicting values, and we return to the question of what actually constitutes a human life. The potentially conflicting principles of preserving life and preserving autonomy become even more confused here because an individual who once made an autonomous choice about how he or she would like to be treated may at the crucial time no longer be able to decide anything autonomously and may, in fact, never be able to do so again.

In less extreme instances, the state may also restrain the autonomy of an individual for the sake of protecting him or her. Consumer protection is an obvious example; government may disregard the traditional principle of *caveat emptor* and simply prohibit the sale of potentially harmful products in order to protect the citizen. On the one hand, the conservative, or any other person interested in preserving individual choice, would argue that such protections are harmful inasmuch as the paternalistic actions of government prevent citizens from being truly free actors. On the other hand, the complexity of the marketplace, the number of products offered for sale, and the absence of full information may prevent individuals from making meaningful judgments. As a consequence, government is justified in intervening, especially because many of the products banned would affect persons incapable of making their own informed choices—for example, children. At less of an extreme, governments require labeling and full disclosure of information so that citizens are able to make rational and informed autonomous decisions about the products they purchase.

At times government also forces citizens to consume certain goods and services because they are presumably for the citizens' own good. Two examples of these "merit goods" are automobile seat belts and motorcycle helmets.[15] Measures requiring people to use these have been supported by a number of safety organizations and by many citizens, but other citizens argue that they should be "free to be foolish," to make their own choices, and to assume certain risks.[16] As appealing as that argument sounds within a free society, there are also potential costs from risky decisions that extend beyond the individual who is willing to take the chance. Their families are potentially harmed, both emotionally and economically, by such risky behavior. The society as a whole may have a stake in the individual decision because public money may well have to pay for a long and expensive hospitalization from a preventable injury. Thus, as with all the ethical principles that can be applied to public decisions, there tend to be few absolutes and a great deal of balancing of ideas and ethical criteria when government must act to make policy.

Professional licensing and laws that control the licensing of drugs also have been criticized as unduly restricting the free choice of individuals. It is argued that individuals should have the right to select the form of treatment they would like, even if the medical establishment deems it quackery. So, for example, activists for AIDS victims have criticized the Food and Drug Administration in the United States for delaying approval of some drugs that may have potential for ameliorating the symptoms of AIDS and slowing the progress of the disease.[17] The criticisms have been particularly pointed because these drugs already are licensed and available in other industrialized countries. Similar arguments were made earlier about the failure of the FDA to approve laetrile as a drug for the treatment of cancer. In both cases, the individual is being denied the right to choose courses of treatment for a deadly disease. Of course, the counterargument from the FDA is that these restrictions are justified because they increase the probability that the individual will receive treatments that are known to have some beneficial effects.

Lying/Truthfulness

Most systems of ethics and morality prohibit lying.[18] People generally regard lying as wrong simply "because it is wrong." It can also be considered wrong because it allows one individual to deprive another of his or her autonomy. When one person lies to another, the liar deprives the other person of the ability to make rational and informed decisions. In some instances, telling "little white lies" may prevent awkward social situations, but perhaps more stringent criteria should be applied to justify lies told by government, especially in a democracy.

Lying to the public by public officials has been justified primarily as being in the public's own good. Political leaders who accept this paternalistic justification assume that public officials have more information and are unwilling to divulge it either for security reasons or because they believe that the information will only "confuse" citizens. They may therefore lie to the public to get average citizens to behave in ways that they—the public officials—prefer. Public officials also seem to believe that citizens would behave in the same way if they had all the information available to the political leader. Even if citizens would not behave as public officials want them to, officials think that they *should* behave in that manner, and the lie is therefore justified as a means of protecting the public from itself and its own irresponsibility or ignorance.

Such lying obviously limits the autonomy of the average citizen when making policy choices or evaluating the performance of those in office. Even white lies are questionable—the importance of autonomy in democratic political systems may demand much closer attention to honesty, even though the short-term consequences of telling the truth may not benefit incumbents.

In times of war officials may need to lie, or at a minimum withhold information, for security reasons or to maintain morale, but even that largely justifiable behavior will tend to undermine the legitimacy of a democratic system. In part, citizens may find it difficult to know when the lying has stopped, a problem that became very evident during the Cold War.

Other white lies told by officials to the public involve withholding information that might cause panic or other responses that are potentially very dangerous. For example, a public official may learn that a nuclear power plant has had a minor and apparently controllable accident that is not believed to endanger anyone. The official may withhold this information from the public in the belief that doing so will prevent a panic; a mass flight from the scene could cause more harm than the accident. But, as with other ethical situations, the decision to lie about one thing and not about others makes it difficult for the official (and government as a whole) to behave consistently. Perhaps the only standard that can be applied with any consistency in this case is the utilitarian criterion: the harm prevented by the lie must outweigh the ill effects caused by the lie. Determining this utilitarian balance is relatively easy when we are balancing the possible few deaths and limited property damage from a minor nuclear accident against probable widespread and violent panic. Continued lying, however, will eventually generate a public loss of trust in government and its officials, and the cost of such skepticism is difficult to calculate.[19]

A special category of lying is the withholding of information by public officials to protect their own careers. This is a problem for the "whistleblowers" who would expose deceit, as well as for the liars, and it happens in the private as well as the public sector.[20] Attempting to act ethically and responsibly has placed many individuals in difficult situations. For example, the man who blew the whistle on government cost overruns on the Lockheed C-5A airplane lost his job; so did the EPA official who exposed the agency's shortcomings under Rita Lavelle; and so did many other conscientious officials in less dramatic circumstances.[21] The problem caused when someone blows the whistle on a lie is especially difficult to analyze when the individual at fault does not lie directly but simply does nothing to expose errors made in government.

The whistleblower must go to some lengths in order to make the information about official lying known to the public and must accept substantial career risks. Because of these difficulties, policymakers may want to devise means to encourage whistleblowers and protect them against reprisals. The federal government in the United States and many state and local governments have devised programs to protect whistleblowers, but there are still substantial risks for the individual who chooses to act in what he or she considers a responsible manner. In conjunction with, or in the absence of, programs encouraging officials to divulge information, legislation such as the Freedom of Information Act can at least make it more difficult for government to suppress information.[22]

Thus, in addition to the general moral prohibition, lying carries a particular onus in the public sector because it can destroy individual citizens' ability to make appropriate and informed choices about their government. Although a lie may be told for good reasons (at least in the mind of the liar), it must be questioned unless it has extremely positive benefits and is not told just for the convenience of an individual official. The long-term consequences for government of even "justifiable" lying may be negative. Citizens who learn that government lies to them for good reasons may soon wonder if it will not lie to them for less noble reasons, and may find it difficult to believe the official interpretation of anything. In the United States, for example, the Vietnam war, Watergate, and "Irangate" created a sense of distrust toward government among an entire generation of citizens that manifests itself in somewhat general disaffection with government.

If strictures against lying are to some degree dependent on a desire to preserve the political community and a sense of trust within it, then somewhat different rules may apply in international politics. Although there is a concept of the international community of nations, the moral bonds within that community tend to be weaker than the bonds that exist within a single nation. Further, a political leader's paramount responsibilities are to his or her own citizens. Therefore, lying in international politics may be more acceptable; political leaders regularly face the problem of "dirty hands," which seems to be part of the job of being a political leader in an imperfect world.[23] That is, leaders may be forced to engage in activities that they know to be wrong in most circumstances, such as lying, in order to serve the (largely utilitarian) goals of protecting and preserving the interests of their own country.

Fairness

Fairness is a value to which citizens expect government to assign maximum importance. One standard justification for the existence of government is that it protects and enforces the civil and political rights of all individuals and does so with as much equality as possible. Further, it is argued (at least by liberals) that government has the legal and economic capacity to redress inequities in the distribution of goods and services that result from the operations of the marketplace.[24] Government, then, is charged with ensuring that citizens are treated fairly in the political system and perhaps in the economy and society.

But just what is "fair treatment of citizens"? In different schools of social and political thought the word "fair" has different meanings. To a conservative, for example, fairness means allowing individuals maximum opportunities to exercise their own abilities and to keep what they earn in the marketplace through those abilities. Some conservatives consider it fair that people who cannot provide for themselves should suffer, along with their families, although they disagree about how much suffering is acceptable.[25] Similarly, many conservatives do not consider it fair for government to take property from some citizens in order to benefit others; in this view, property as well as people has rights.[26]

The familiar Marxist doctrine of "from each according to his abilities to each according to his needs" implies a very different standard of fairness.[27] That statement implies that all members of the society, provided they are willing to contribute their abilities (however limited), are entitled to have their material needs satisfied. According to this standard of fairness, those with lower earning capacities need not suffer, although the doctrine does not imply a standard of absolute equality. There is, however, no uncontested definition of "needs," so this standard could be an open-ended entitlement for citizens were it to be accepted.

The standard of fairness applied in most contemporary welfare states is something of a mixture of the conservative and Marxist standards, although it generally lacks the intellectual underpinnings of either.[28] The mixed-economy welfare state that operates in industrialized societies usually allows productive citizens to retain most of their earnings and at the same time requires them to help build a floor of benefits under the less fortunate so that the less fortunate can maintain at least a minimal standard of living. Unlike the situation in the Marxist state, this redistribution of goods and services to the less fortunate from the more successful is conducted in the context of free and open politics.

As well as being concerned with fairness across classes and among individuals, governments increasingly must be concerned about fairness across generations. The current generation is custodian of the natural resources of the society and must make decisions about the use of those resources. Is it *fair* for the current generation to use such a large share of the proven reserves of resources such as oil, copper, chromium, and the like? Further, is it *fair* for this generation to incur a massive public (and private) debt that will impose burdens on, and restrain the opportunities of, future generations? What principles can be used to justify choices that have intergenerational consequences?[29] How can those principles be included in the analytic techniques used to make policy decisions?[30]

Can these operating principles of the contemporary welfare state—principles that arise largely from political accidents and a pragmatic evolution process—be systematized and developed on a more intellectual plane? One promising approach to such a systematic justification of the welfare state can be found in philosopher John Rawls's concept of justice in a society. In his essay "Justice as Fairness,"[31] Rawls develops two principles of justice for a society. The first is that "each person participating in a practice, or affected by it, has an equal right to the most extensive liberty compatible with like liberty of all." This is a restatement of the basic right of individuals to be involved in governmental decisions that affect them, a principle not incompatible with the cry "No taxation without representation!" This first principle of justice would place the burden of proof on anyone who would seek to limit participation in political life; it can therefore be seen as a safeguard for procedural democracy in contemporary societies. Thus, Rawls places a pronounced emphasis on the decision-making procedures employed when evaluating the fairness of those decisions and the fairness of the institutions of society. This may present great difficulties for the citizen and the analyst, however, if the decisions reached by participatory means conflict with more substantive conceptions of fairness.

The second principle of fairness advanced by Rawls is more substantive and also more problematic. Referred to as the "difference principle," it states that "social and economic inequalities are to be arranged so that they are both: (*a*) to the greatest benefit of the least advantaged; and (*b*) attached to offices and positions open to all under conditions of fair equality of opportunity."[32] This principle places the burden of proof on those who attempt to justify a system of inequalities. Inequalities can be seen as just only if all other possible arrangements would produce lowered expectations for the least-well-off group in society. To help a society that is striving for equality, citizens are asked to think of their own place in society as shrouded behind a "veil of ignorance," so it cannot be known to them in advance.[33] Would they be willing to gamble on being in the lowest segment of the society when they decide on a set of inequalities for the society? If they would not, then they have good reason to understand the need of the society to equalize the distribution of goods and services. Of course, it is impossible to apply the logic of the veil of ignorance within existing societies, but it is a useful concept for understanding the rational acceptance of redistributive government policies, and in justifying such policies politically.

Several interesting questions arise with respect to Rawls's difference principle. One is the place of natural endowments and individual differences in producing and justifying inequalities. Should individuals who have special natural abilities be allowed to benefit from them? This borders on the basic ethical principle of desert, or the degree to which any individual deserves what he or she receives in the world (see below). This question, then, is reminiscent of a Kurt Vonnegut story in *Player Piano*, in which individuals' particular talents are balanced by the "great handicapper."[34] Individuals who can run particularly fast, for instance, are required to wear heavy weights to slow them down, and those who have creative gifts are required to wear earphones through which come loud and discordant noises to distract them from thinking and using that creativity. Does Rawls regard such a homogeneous and ultimately dull society as desirable or fair? One would think not, but he does point out that natural endowments are desirable primarily because they can be used to assist those in the lowest segment of society. Thus, noblesse oblige is expected of those who possess natural talents.

Does the same expectation hold true for those whose endowments are economic rather than physical or intellectual? It would appear that in Rawls's view equality is a natural principle that can be justified by decision making that would occur behind the veil of ignorance, as well as by the cooperative instincts that Rawls believes are inherent in humans. Again, in his view, these economic endowments should exist only to the extent they can be used for the betterment of the lowest segments in society.

Quite naturally, critics point to what they consider the natural rights of individuals to retain their holdings,[35] and to the potential incentives for work and investment that are inherent in a system of economic inequalities. Inequalities are argued to be functional for the society because they supply a spur to ambition and an incentive to produce more, which in turn can be used to benefit the entire society.[36] These incentives should influence artistic as well as economic production. Thus, to critics of Rawls's philosophy, the tendency toward equality may be inappropriate on ethical grounds because it would deny individuals something they have received through either genetics or education, and it may be wrong on utilitarian grounds because it reduces the total production of the society along several dimensions.

Finally, the Rawlsian framework is discussed primarily within the context of a single society, or a single institution in which cooperative principles would at least be considered, if not always followed. Can these principles be applied to a broader context; in particular, should they be applied to a global community? In other words, should the riches accumulated in the industrialized countries be used to benefit the citizens of the most impoverished countries of the world? Such a policy would, of course, be politically difficult to implement, even if it could be shown to be morally desirable. Nevertheless, the ethical underpinnings of foreign aid may be important, especially as the world moves into an era of increased scarcity as well as increased interdependence.

Although we have been discussing issues of fairness primarily in economic terms, increasingly these issues are conceptualized in terms of race, ethnicity, and gender. The same logic of analysis may well be applicable, and fairness could be maximized by assuming the same veil of ignorance for making decisions about these social differences as is used for decisions about economic differences. For these social categories, however, issues of compensation for past injustices also arise, along with the perceived need to create structures and programs that will encourage future achievement by members of the previously disadvantaged groups.

This remedy for past ills, in turn, creates resentments by those who feel that their natural endowments of skills and abilities are being devalued. This resentment arises in reference to scholarships granted on the basis of race or gender, hiring quotas, and a variety of other "affirmative action" policies intended to change existing social and economic patterns.[37] In addition, economic inequalities may be justified as providing incentives for individuals to do more for themselves and to change their own conditions, while it is generally not feasible for individuals to change gender or race. No question of equality and fairness is easy to resolve, but these issues of race and gender have proved to be among the most difficult to cope with in the political system.

While opinions may differ as to the applicability of Rawls's ideas in the real world of policymaking, and the desirability of such application if it is indeed possible, his work does raise interesting and important ethical questions for those attempting to design public policies. Many industrialized democracies have been making redistributive economic policy decisions for years. These decisions often have been justified on pragmatic or political grounds rather than on ethical principles.[38] The work of Rawls provides intellectual underpinnings for these policies, even though no government has gone as far in redistributing income and wealth as Rawls's difference principle would demand. These governments are now facing more decisions about race and gender inequalities, and they too require some guidance beyond simple political expediency.

The Concept of Desert

The above discussion of the values of the welfare state raises the question of desert. What does a citizen deserve as a member of the society, and what does the individual deserve as an individual with particular needs and virtues? As discussed earlier, there are some rights that the American people enjoy by virtue of the Constitution and the Bill of Rights. The existence of these rights is largely incontestable, although there certainly are multiple interpretations of their meaning. The more interesting cases, however, are benefits coming from government that have come to be considered rights but that are much less clearly grounded in the basic law of the land.

The concept of *entitlement* is the most important case of desert being constructed by policy and then being accepted by the population. Social insurance programs are the clearest example of entitlements, with the citizen having paid for the program over his or her working lifetime and government making a commitment to provide the benefits when the citizen needs them (e.g., when retired, unemployed, or disabled). These programs were designed so that citizens would not consider them charity or a government "handout"; they would be a right. Further, entitlement programs were designed to make it difficult for subsequent generations of politicians to dismantle them.[39]

When we move away from social insurance and other contributory programs, the concept of desert becomes more difficult to sustain within the public sector of the United States. It is clear that young people have a right to a free public education but only through high school.[40] Why is it not available through college, or even through graduate school? Likewise, the debate over health care in 1994 raised the question whether citizens have a right to health care, and if so, to what level of health care. If there is a right to basic health care, is there also a right to the most advanced and expensive treatments available? If the rights are restricted to basic services, where does the entitlement stop, and why? Certain public goods (e.g., clean air and water) also are often conceptualized as the entitlements of citizens. Why?

Can there be a "negative desert"? Do some citizens deserve certain punishments and sanctions? It is sometimes argued that the perpetrators of certain crimes "deserve" the death penalty.[41] It is also argued that those responsible for economic or environmental crimes "deserve" certain severe (but not death) penalties. On what basis can it be said that people deserve a particular form of punishment, particularly one as severe and final as the death penalty? At a less extreme level, do people who have other perceived failings (e.g., having to accept public assistance) deserve to be punished or controlled in other ways?[42] Chapter 10 discussed an increasing number of restrictions and regulations being imposed on AFDC clients; do those people "deserve" that treatment, and if so, why?

Ethics and Public Policy: Alternatives to Utilitarianism

The ethical system most often applied to public policy analysis is utilitarianism, with actions being justified as producing the greatest net benefit for the society as a whole. As noted in chapter 14, this principle underlies the dominant analytic approaches in the field, such as cost-benefit analysis. In this chapter we have discussed several ethical questions that arise in making and implementing public policies, as well as some possible answers to these questions. Most of the answers presented here for these questions come from a nonutilitarian basis. Ultimately, no one can provide definitive answers to these questions. Likewise, public officials may face policy questions that have no readily acceptable answers, politically or ethically. Values and ethical principles are frequently in conflict, and the policymaker must frequently violate one firmly held ethical position in order to protect another.

Despite these practical difficulties, it is important for citizens and policymakers to think about policy in ethical terms. Perhaps too much policymaking has been conducted without attention to anything but the political and economic consequences. Of course, those economic consequences are important as criteria on which to base an evaluation of a program, but they may not be the only criteria. Both the policymaker and the citizen must be concerned also with the criteria of justice and trust in society. It may be that justice and trust ultimately make the best policies—and even the best politics.

Notes

1. Russell Hardin, *Morality within the Limit of Reason* (Chicago: University of Chicago Press, 1988).

2. Victor Grassian, *Moral Reasoning* (Englewood Cliffs, N.J.: Prentice Hall, 1981).

3. Arnold Meltner, *Policy Analysts in the Bureaucracy* (Berkeley: University of California Press, 1976), 3–25.

4. Abraham Kaplan, "Social Ethics and the Sanctity of Life," in *Life or Death: Ethics and Options,* ed. D.H. Labby (London: Macmillan, 1968), 58–71.

5. Guido Calabresi and Phillip Bobbitt, *Tragic Choices* (New York: Norton, 1978), 21. See also B. Guy Peters, "Tragic Choices: Administrative Rulemaking and Policy Choice," in *Ethics in Public Service,* ed. Richard A. Chapman (Edinburgh: University of Edinburgh Press, 1993).

6. As a part of its rationing program, Oregon (see pp. 244–45) made this determination. The justification was primarily utilitarian, assuming that the treatments would be less beneficial for people with substance-abuse problems.

7. Bonnie Steinbock, *Life Before Birth: The Moral and Legal Status of Embryos and Fetuses* (New York: Oxford University Press, 1992).

8. Ronald Dworkin, *Life's Dominion: An Argument about Abortion, Euthanasia and Individual Freedom* (New York: Knopf, 1993).

9. Steven H. Miles, "Doctors and Their Patients' Suicides," *Journal of the American Medical Association* 271 (8 June 1994): 1786–88; Daniel Avila, "Medical Treatment Rights of Older Persons and Persons with Disabilities," *Issues in Law and Medicine* 9 (1994): 345–60.

10. Jonathan Glover, *Causing Deaths and Saving Lives* (Harmondsworth, England: Penguin, 1977).

11. Robert Nozick, *Anarchy, the State and Utopia* (New York: Basic Books, 1974).

12. This individualistic and conservative interpretation of the law was common during the late nineteenth and early twentieth centuries. See, for example, *Lochner v. New York* (1905).

13. Robert E. Goodin, *Reasons for Welfare* (Princeton: Princeton University Press, 1988), 312–31; Christian Bay, *The Structure of Freedom* (New York: Atheneum, 1965).

14. John Kultgen, *Autonomy and Intervention: Paternalism in the Caring Life* (New York: Oxford University Press, 1994).

15. Jerome S. Legge, *Traffic Safety Reform in the United States and Great Britain* (Pittsburgh: University of Pittsburgh Press, 1991); Kenneth E. Warner, "Bags, Buckles and Belts: The Debate over Mandatory Passive Restraints in Automobiles," *Journal of Health Politics, Policy and Law* 8 (1983): 44–75.

16. Howard M. Leichter, *Free to be Foolish* (Princeton: Princeton University Press, 1991).

17. The FDA has to some extent relaxed its usual guidelines for drugs that may help victims of AIDS and a few other extremely deadly diseases (e.g., "Lou Gehrig's disease"). See Harold Edgar and David J. Rothman, "New Rules for New Drugs: The Challenge of AIDS to the Regulatory Process," in *A Disease of Society,* ed. Dorothy Nelkin, David P. Willis, and Scott V. Parris (Cambridge, England: Cambridge University Press, 1991).

18. Sissela Bok, *Lying: Moral Choice in Public and Private Life* (New York: Vintage, 1979).

19. See Raymond L. Goldstein and John K. Schoor, *Demanding Democracy after Three Mile Island* (Gainesville: University of Florida Press, 1991).

20. James C. Petersen, *Whistleblowing: Ethical and Legal Issues in Expressing Dissent* (Dubuque, Iowa: Kendall/Hunt, 1986); Daniel P. Westman, *Whistleblowing: The Law of Retaliatory Discharge* (Washington, D.C.: Bureau of National Affairs, 1991); Myron Peretz Glaser and Penina Migdal Glazer, *The Whistle-Blowers* (New York: Basic Books, 1989).

21. See, respectively, Edward Weisband and Thomas M. Franck, *Resignation in Protest* (New York: Penguin, 1975); David Burnham, "Paper Chase of a Whistleblower," *New York Times,* 16 October 1982.

22. William T. Gormley, Jr., *Taming the Bureaucracy: Muscles, Prayers and Other Strategies* (Princeton: Princeton University Press, 1989). In addition to the academic literature on the freedom of information, the novel *So Now You Know* by Michael Frayn (London: Penguin, 1992) provides interesting insights into the question.

23. Michael Walzer, "Political Action: The Problem of Dirty Hands," *Philosophy and Public Affairs* (1973): 160–80; Thomas Nagel, "Ruthlessness in Public Life," in *Public and Private Life,* ed. Stuart Hampshire (Cambridge, England: Cambridge University Press, 1978).

24. Jan-Erik Lane, *The Public Sector: Concepts, Models and Approaches* (Newbury Park, Calif.: Sage, 1993).

25. See Robert E. Goodin, *Protecting the Vulnerable: A Re-Analysis of Our Social Responsibilities* (Chicago: University of Chicago Press, 1985). Even a committed conservative like Charles Murray could argue that "there is no such thing as an undeserving five year old." See Charles Murray, *Losing Ground* (New York: Basic Books, 1984).

26. Richard Allen Epstein, *Takings: Private Property and the Power of Emi-*

nent Domain (Cambridge, Mass.: Harvard University Press, 1985).

27. Karl Marx, *Criticism of the Gotha Program* (New York: International Universities Press, 1938), 29.

28. For an important attempt to provide such a justification, see Goodin, *Reasons for Welfare,* 287–305.

29. Edith Brown Weiss, *In Fairness to Future Generations: International Law, Common Patrimony, and Intergenerational Equity* (Tokyo: United Nations University, 1988).

30. Peter S. Burton, "Intertemporal Preferences and Intergenerational Equity Considerations in Optimal Resource Harvesting," *Journal of Environmental Economics and Management* 24 (1993): 119–32.

31. John Rawls, "Justice as Fairness," *Philosophical Review* (1958): 164–94, esp. 166.

32. John Rawls, *A Theory of Justice* (Cambridge, Mass.: Harvard University Press, 1971).

33. Ibid., 19.

34. For an earlier literary treatment of this view of fairness, see L.P. Hartley, *Facial Justice* (London: Hamish Hamilton, 1960). On desert, see George Bernard Shaw's *Doctor's Dilemma* (New York: Brentanos, 1911).

35. Epstein, *Takings.*

36. This is obviously related to the utilitarian logic that undergirds cost-benefit analysis. See pp. 426–28.

37. Richard A. Epstein, *Forbidden Grounds: The Case Against Employment Discrimination Laws* (Cambridge, Mass.: Harvard University Press, 1992); Russell Nieli, ed., *Racial Preference and Racial Justice: The New Affirmative Action Controversy* (Washington, D.C.: Ethics and Public Policy Center, 1991).

38. Douglas E. Ashford, *The Emergence of the Welfare State* (Oxford: Basil Blackwell, 1986). But see T.H. Marshall, *Class, Citizenship and Social Development* (New York: Doubleday, 1965).

39. W.E. Leuchtenberg, *Franklin D. Roosevelt and the New Deal, 1932–1940* (New York: Harper & Row, 1963), 133.

40. In a few places (e.g., City University of New York) there was once free higher education as well, but budget restraints have forced the imposition of fees in those institutions.

41. See pp. 411–12.

42. Frances Fox Piven and Richard A. Cloward, *Regulating the Poor,* 2d ed. (New York: Vintage, 1993).

Photoillustration Credits

The author and publisher acknowledge with thanks the institutions, firms, and individuals that supplied the photoillustrations for this book.

Index